BE:
The Humanity Blueprint

─── ❦ ───

Volume I

One in Soul

Unlocking the Power of Your Soul

IANA LAHI

BE: The Humanity Blueprint - Volume I
One in Soul

Published through Spirit Gateways® Publishing
All rights reserved
Copyright © 2019 by IANA LAHI
BELIGHT MEDITATION™
Cover art copyright © 2019 by Autumn Skye Morrison

Interior Book Design and Layout by
www.integrativeink.com

ISBN: 978-0-9862384-3-7 (Paperback Edition)
ISBN: 978-0-9862384-5-1 (Hardcover Edition)
ISBN: 978-0-9862384-4-4 (Ebook Edition)

Library of Congress Control Number: 2018910451

No part of this publication may be reproduced, stored in a retrieval system, or transmitted in any form or by any means electronic, mechanical, photocopying, recording, or otherwise, without the written permission of the author or publisher.

All information, content, and material in *One in Soul* is not intended to serve as a substitute for the consultation, diagnosis, and/or treatment of a qualified healthcare provider, practitioner, or physician.

CONTENTS

PREFACE...ix

CHAPTER 1: SUSPENDING DISBELIEF ON THE PATHWAY
TO BEING ONE 1

CHAPTER 2: TAKE THE CALL OF YOUR LIFE 13

CHAPTER 3: WHO ARE YOU? 29

CHAPTER 4: THE LIGHT OF YOUR SOUL & RECONNECTION 39

CHAPTER 5: YOUR SOUL 101 49

CHAPTER 6: YOUR SOUL 201: UNDERSTANDING YOUR
SOUL JOURNEY 59

CHAPTER 7: PORTALS TO YOUR TRUE SELF 77

CHAPTER 8: THE SOUL INTEGRATION CENTERS 99

CHAPTER 9: THE INFINITE POSSIBILITIES OF
YOUR POWER POINT CENTERS 111

CHAPTER 10: AWAKENING TO THE VOICE AND
THEMES OF THE SOUL 155

CHAPTER 11: FRAGMENTING OF THE SOUL 183

CHAPTER 12: THE COMPONENTS OF THE SOUL:
            YOUR DIVINE FEMININE & MASCULINE 213

CHAPTER 13: PRACTICAL CONSIDERATIONS WHEN
            CONNECTING YOUR SOUL ENERGIES 263

CHAPTER 14: SOUL RECONNECTION: WHAT TO EXPECT 283

CHAPTER 15: THE WHOLE SOUL:
            ONE IN SOUL RECONNECTION 307

CHAPTER 16: SOUL INTEGRATION ACTIONS 335

CHAPTER 17: SOUL CHALLENGES AND SOLUTIONS 363

CHAPTER 18: LIGHT AWAKENS YOUR WHOLE SELF 395

CHAPTER 19: LIVING IN THE LOVE AND POWER OF
            YOUR WHOLE SELF 437

CHAPTER 20: THE SONG OF YOUR SOUL 475

CHAPTER 21: THE END IS JUST THE BEGINNING 485

CHAPTER 22: THE ONE IN SOUL PRACTICE ROADMAP 495

CHAPTER 23: EXPANDED BELIGHT PRACTICES 565

DEDICATION

To all who choose Love and are willing to BE One,
To all who are willing to make what
appears impossible possible,
To all Beings on All Dimensions Holding
the Torch of Light and Truth,
To my team on earth; my daughters,
dear friends, students & clients
Whom I adore
Thank You

With special gratitude and love to:
Beloved Meher Baba
Issa (Yeshua)
Mahavatar Babaji

To my daughters Sharina Stubbs and Satia Stevens
Thank you for your unconditional love, support, and friendship

With loving thanks and gratitude to artists extraordinaire:
Autumn Skye Morrison
Thank you for your beautiful illustrations
of light throughout the book, and for giving
permission to share your painting *Day One*
To experience Autumn Skye Morrison's work go to:
www.autumnskyemorrison.com

and

Mia Bosna
For your exquisite *Power Point Center* Illustration
To experience Mia Bosna's work go to:
www.miabosna.com

With deep appreciation to:
Stephanee Killen of **Integrative Ink** for your
patience with editing, layout and design

**With deep thanks & heart-felt gratitude for
your unwaivering love & presence:**

Ginette Fertel, David Goldschmidt, Bill Bauman, Ganga Nath & Tara Leela, Jodie Jaimes, Tina Campbell, Stephanie Pieczenik Marango, Jessica Roberts, Argena Marie, Laura Vida, Angelika Almirall Torrel Fürstler, Ceslie Rossi, Shakti Jivan Kaur, Alessandra Carey-Gardner, Eileen Shuchat, Priti Robyn Ross, Jennifer Milligan & Pascal Fouquet, Barbara Haney Alag & Sartaj Alag,

Richard Hews, Michael & Fruzsina Perlin,
Arjan Deva Kaur & Sachraj Singh,
Dhee Koenig & Cheryl Reed, Akal Simran
Kaur & Justin Beau LeBlanc,
Vivienne Lorien, Gabrielle Young, Therese
Russo, Molly Jarchow, Marika DuRietz,
John Wozencraft, CJ Gedeon, Susan Catherine
Collyer, Tahisha Mayfield, Nancy Cragin,
Morrisa Rose & Briella Luna, Daniel Stone,
O'Shana Kosarev, Laurent Weichberger,
Meibao Nee, Marsha Nieman, Rick Pathman,
Christian Germain, Seva Narayan,
Emily Nussdorfer, Nathan Drew, Travis Brown,
Mark Riesenberg, Joseph McConnell,
Elizabeth Smith, Patrick Stewart, Karen &
Mike Stewart, Robert Abrahamson,
The Meherana Community, Sangeet Kaur
Khalsa, Amma, Sat Siri Kaur Khalsa,
Umashankar Chandrasekharan, Swami
Vidyadhishananda, Qingsong Xiao,
The Chocolatree, Sedona, AZ

With loving acknowledgement to:
Nicole Carey

It shall come to pass, that as a global culture, the soul within every individual regardless of the outer classification of nationality, race, sex, religion, or creed will be honored and supported to BE all that they are meant to BE.

It is time to end the inner battles.

A new way of BEing is upon us.

I invite you to take the call.

Iana Lahi

PREFACE

Some might say, especially my family, that I was not an ordinary child; perhaps I was even a little unique. I first became aware of my soul when I was four. I had a more conscious awareness and experience of my Self as a separate being that was vastly different from those around me. I seemed to be able to see and feel things that others around me were blind to. While most two-to-four-year-olds attempt to engage and connect with the people and world around them by talking up a storm and asking questions, I was silent. I didn't speak a word, and my parents feared that I was stunted in some way.

    I was brought to see a doctor after I turned four to find out what was wrong with me. I felt connected to myself and couldn't understand what everyone's concerns were. It's not that I couldn't speak. I just simply chose not to speak. The world in which I lived was filled with exquisite color, inner music, and light. I lived in a zone of pure love and wonder. At that tender age, I longed for a level of authenticity and connection that I wasn't experiencing in my family of origin. I had a deeper inner knowing of who I was and what I longed to BE and express. And yet, I was unsure what it all really meant given what I experienced around me. The external world seemed to have no connection to Source and lacked feeling. It was black and white, and my inner world was alive in energy and movement. My silence created the space for me to be in spirit. Sitting in front of the psychiatrist on a cold, metal chair was the last day I chose to be in silence.

No one in my family knew how to really connect to themselves or to anyone else. Connection for them was related to sharing family preoccupations with suffering, challenges, and the dramas of life. They had come from severe survival crisis as immigrants and I grew up in a home of worries, stress and anxiety. I remember sitting and watching my family members speak German discussing their problems, gossiping about others and the hardships of their life, and their various aches and pains that came with arthritis and eating too many sweets, bread, roasted or boiled meats, and potatoes. They didn't see me, but I *saw* them. I wanted to live from a more centered place of knowing inside of myself. I wanted to live and know a lightness and joy that was totally foreign to all around me. That was just the first of thousands of moments in my life that awakened me to my own soul and how to reconnect and live from it.

Like many people who feel that they are born "different," the early years of my childhood were marked by ongoing deep questioning, which would later manifest as direct rebellion against the traditions of my family.

I struggled to understand why I felt so different, and at the same time, I was unwilling to submit to their rules, roles, and restrictions. I just couldn't fit into their version of "normal."

When I was 14 years old, I began reading the works of Krishnamurti, much to the dismay of more than one family member. If I could sum up their collective comments it would be something like, "Why are you reading such nonsense? Why can't you just be normal like us? Don't believe a word that you read." Nevertheless, this great teacher awakened within me the question, *"Who am I?"* I was electrified and ignited by the idea of being awake and conscious to *who I am* as a soul and whole being. It unlocked a gateway into the inner realms of my soul consciousness that I had longed to experience.

At the age of 16, I was the second person in New York to receive the Transcendental Meditation initiation on Long Island. I remember bringing my fruit and flower offering and practiced faithfully twice a day. Love and peace were my mantra.

My growing self-awareness and exploration of this uncharted consciousness path was further reinforced at the age of 17 when I asked one of my modern dance teachers, the late Thelma Hill of the Alvin Ailey American Dance Theater in NYC, whether I should go to college or not. After being on scholarship for a few years with the company, she stared me directly in the eyes and said, "Get to know who you are." Her words hit me hard and became the inspiration and confirmation that I had to stay on track with my search for discovering and knowing my True Self and the greater truth within my heart and soul. The great existential question of *"who am I?"* would guide the adventures of my life for many years to come through travel, meditation, spiritual awakening, professional dance training and performance, holistic healing trainings, mentorships with shamans, seers and healers, and stepping into working as a visionary and energy healer, and then beginning to raise a family.

At the age of 18, I had no idea how to find myself, but I decided to try to fit in academically and chose to go to college as a dance major instead of staying in the dance world in Manhattan. I explored life and myself in all of the wonderfully freeing ways that were possible when no longer under the judgmental eyes of my family. I soaked up the joys, sorrows, and growing pains of life and love. I explored my own physical, emotional, and spiritual expression through dance, music, art, and eastern religion. I was at times brilliantly self-expressed and at others, monumentally misguided and confused. Mercifully, I did not grow up under the microscope of modern social media where a person's highs and lows can be plastered for eternity across an electronic superhighway. I gave myself the freedom to fully explore who I was. I absorbed and took in all of the subtle nuances that life all around me had to give. I was a cosmic barometer trying to experience and interpret all aspects of life and my place in it. I was a definite "work in progress," continually trying to feel and express my deepest soul Self.

My hours alone in the dance studios at California Institute of the Arts, in southern California, in the early 70's, late at night became my "holy time." I began to channel in divine energies of blissful connection with Infinite Source through movements directed by my Higher Self. Sometimes, as I would open into the energies of light moving through my body, I would begin to sob as I was opened to a whole new dimension of dance and movement by feeling my soul light my path. It was a profound time of awakening as I struggled with the opinions and judgments from my peers, and the dance faculty who had no idea what I was doing. I began to improvise with musicians who could travel into the depths of the movement in music with me, and it was through becoming One with music, that I began to express and experience the power of the dance.

From college I went on to study Polarity Therapy at the Polarity Health Institute near Mt. Shasta, California. I had a thirst to understand how energy moved in the body, its purpose, and how it connected to the soul. I began to integrate movement, and how energy works in the body with the power of the sound current through music.

I took my choreography on the road and performed with some incredible musicians who helped me take my craft to the next level. Through improvisation we were able to unite our passion for sound and light into uplifting experiences for our audiences.

I gravitated into the healing arts because I wanted to help people feel greater joy and connection to their soul. My curiosity about how the soul worked in relationship to the body, mind and spirit led me on a profound journey touching into many spiritual ancient traditions.

Years later, while I was serving as a dance therapist in a clinic for psychotic, schizophrenic, and bipolar teenagers and young adults in San Diego, California, that I began to realize my true gifts. While I had been working as a healer for over a decade, I hadn't fully embraced my uncanny ability to really see, read, and feel people. I was initially hired for dance therapy at the clinic, but I was eventually promoted to be a primary therapist because of my abilities to see who the patients were on a soul level.

While working at the clinic, I realized that I could be with a person and see their interior soul blueprint. I could see what happened to them in their childhood and past lives. I could see them on all time frames from all lifetimes, in the present, and in the future. A few years later, after I left the clinic, I applied my gifts to working with people from all backgrounds and walks of life. I could see the cause and internal workings of their psychological, emotional, and physical issues. I could see what their body, heart and soul needed to heal. I realized that I was clairvoyant, clairaudient, claircognizant, and clairsentient. I knew if people should be in relationship or in partnership with someone, whether for business or love, and if the connections were likely to result in success or failure. I knew what people were likely to face if they didn't heal the soul separations inside of themselves. I could see their past lives and what their soul lessons were in this lifetime. I could see what blocked their relationship with the divine and why they turned away from God. I could clear their energy field, see the cause of their health, psychological and emotional issues, and help them to find their Higher Self. I began to hear the guidance of their inner Masters as I worked with them. I was given direct messages for my clients and instructions of what I needed to clear and align to help them heal. I realized how deeply I wanted to help people find and live their higher destiny path.

By this point, I had spent years pursuing dance, meditation, and certification in over twenty holistic healing therapies to enhance my healing skills, creativity, and abilities to work with others and to do my own inner work. Despite all that work, I still found myself yearning for greater happiness and connection to life. Even with all that I experienced and learned, none of the healing modalities helped me beyond a certain point. I longed for my next step. I knew I had not yet "arrived."

A series of life changing transitions—including the end of my 12-year marriage and moving back to the East Coast from San Diego—left me feeling drained, unsure of myself, alone, and longing for something more. Little did I realize that, by walking through the unknown, I would be catapulted into a whole new realm of awakening and transformation.

While living in the woods of Westchester County, New York in 1993 with my two teenage daughters, I prayed to God and asked through my tears for a way to fully heal myself and to step into my Whole Self. It never ceases to amaze me how my prayers are answered. I began receiving divine guidance and instruction from Sananda—also known as Issa, Yeshua, or Jesus—who would appear in his radiant white and gold form to visit and teach me. He would show up every evening for the next two years after I spent time with my daughters and they were in bed. I would meditate and prepare for his visit where he would speak through my heart and share, step by step, a process for reconnecting a person's soul into Oneness. His radiant body of pure white and gold light would be with me as he communicated the basic principles of what has now become the *One in Soul* work. His presence became a daily gift that helped me to step through a veil into providing others with profound healing work and movement/dance work.

PREFACE

I was told inwardly that this process was crucial at this time because over the millenniums, people had experienced so much soul fragmentation that they were now unable to successfully find and walk their true path to God. A few months later, I was then graced by the daily visitation and Over Soul presence of Mother Mary, Meryamana, who shared a parallel process to clear the cords, chakras, and energies in a person's subtle and physical bodies to liberate their consciousness, heal health conditions and to restore their body, heart and soul connection. Their combined wisdom truly was a revelation—an awareness of the greater divine truth of the universe.

Issa taught me how to teach people to see from the light of their higher awareness and to reconnect the power and essence of their soul fragmentations into their heart. When a person's psyche and soul energies fragment, they search for a place of safety and security within their body. The soul fragments take up residence in the body's base *Power Point Centers* (expanded chakra center system). The base centers, the feminine and sexual God *Power Point Centers*, provide a secure container for soul aspects given their grounding with the earth and life force energies. Our souls naturally align to life force energies, and they will naturally gravitate to the base centers to find comfort and safety. The base centers allow soul aspects to survive amidst the chaos, control, and fear that may be occurring within and around a person.

When a person reconnects their spiritual power and life force energies in their body through mending their karmic fragments and splits, a surge of consciousness is released in the body and mind that brings deep joy, peace, exaltation, and contentment. As newly found soul aspects are invited into a person's heart center, an awakening into Oneness is set into motion. Once their soul begins to integrate through their heart center, they can begin to experience Oneness with the divine.

Mahavatar Babaji began showing up in my daily meditations thirty years before a friend brought me a picture of him, and I recognized him as the master who was teaching me on the inner planes about the new light paradigm that is shared through the BELight Meditations™ taught in the Spirit Gateways® BE System work. Mahavatar Babaji known as the "deathless saint," initiated many Perfect Masters who went on to teach the hidden secrets of attaining God Realization such as Kabir, Lahiri Mahasaya, Issa (Jesus), Krishna, and Buddha.

Another one of my inner plane teachers, Paramahansa Yogananda, told me that after becoming *One in Soul*, it would then "be possible to climb step by step through the chakras into Infinite Light and consciousness." After lifetimes of living in body, mind, and soul separation, a process to reunite a person into their Whole Self would be needed to help accomplish the further shifts that are needed to be made during these radical times of change on earth.

When I was called to Avatar Meher Baba, I was deeply moved beyond words how his message and the work that I had been slowly putting together for 40 years fit like a hand in a glove. In Avatar Meher Baba's messages to the world, even though silent for 44 years, shared that all humanity are one soul, and to think of separating individuals by nationality, religion, race, and gender as being impossible. *One in Soul* is the first step needed to realize that we are all connected to the Infinite Source of creation as one soul. Avatar Meher Baba, the incarnation of God in human form, lived from 1894 to 1969 and continues to be an awakener of divine love and truth for millions of individuals.

One in Soul is the compilation of direct experience with the divine, my own past and present life healing modalities, and the tools that Issa and Meryamana (Mother Mary) taught me so many years ago that I have practiced with my clients, and in my own daily spiritual practice. As I maintained a steadfast connection to Infinite Source, I was able to help others reconnect to their Original Self. I witnessed miraculous healings for my clients. Breakthroughs exploded. My clients began to have rapid shifts in their lives like never before. I realized I had been given a profound gift and, I felt a new calling to share this breakthrough healing process. Now, many years later, I offer these *Original Way Teachings*™ in the Spirit Gateways® BE System Experience, and in all of the Spirit Gateways® Institute intensives, retreats and trainings.

When I first began doing the *One in Soul* work, I was stunned to experience how every person with whom I worked, regardless of religion, color, nationality, or gender, experienced the same universal separation from their spiritual power. Everyone had experienced the same kind of "splitting off" but through their own life circumstances. While their splits created different yet similar "issues," the desire to be whole and connected was universal and, once experienced, brought great joy.

The *One in Soul* practice outlined in this book is really a simple and loving way to meet yourself and learn how to show up for your own spiritual core truth. It helps you to develop your capacity to love yourself, others, and to experience what you are meant to be doing to evolve and fulfill your soul in this lifetime.

We are all on the same journey to be *One in Soul* and to BE One with Infinite Source. We all experience similar pain, love, loss, sorrow, fear, joy, successes, and challenges on our paths. Many of us share the same core beliefs about our Self. The only thing that separates us from Infinite Source is our lack of understanding of how we create and live in separation instead of our essential Wholeness. We identify from the separations in our mind and choose to call that state "living" and "being alive." The *One in Soul* experience begins to bridge your true aliveness and spiritual power into your body. You will begin to BE, feel, and live in connection with your authentic, real, and incredible Self.

Along the way, the experience of reconnecting into your light and the power of your soul may feel foreign and awkward at first. Yet, you are actually becoming whole. You may find yourself feeling out of sync with the way most people are "doing life" but I can guarantee you that this phase will pass. You will move forward and blossom from a new Oneness with yourself. You will have greater clarity, creative genius, new ideas, and more ENERGY to live your life.

I invite you to embrace your soul journey to become your best friend, discover your True Self, find joy, wholeness, and to fall in love with your spiritual power and expression in whatever delightful form it takes. Your journey begins by simply looking for the light beneath whatever "block" may exist within you. When you do this, you are following the simple spiritual technique of focusing upon the light.

For millennia, a basic exercise to develop spiritual power was to gaze upon the flame of a candle as a way to learn how to focus your mind with Spirit. Mantra from many traditions also serves to focus the mind with the frequency of the soul. Another basic exercise to develop spiritual attunement is to be in nature and to listen, see, and feel yourself become One with what shows up for you. The *One in Soul* work is exactly this. It teaches you how to show up for yourself and BE fully present with all that is in and around you, just as you would if a hawk landed on a tree right in front of you, or if a deer walked towards you without fear. As you gaze at the hawk or deer, you would still everything—your mind, body, and breath—and BE in the moment. You would BE One with what is. This is the exact same experience. You learn how to BE YOU and experience the shining, eternal soul light that is the foundation of who you are.

You will come to know and love not one but many unseen, hidden, or blocked aspects of your soul that hold the key for you to know and BE who you are. Once your "soul aspects" are reconnected, you will begin to feel something vibrant and new inside of yourself awaken. Most people are unable to describe it in words, but what it feels like is being aligned, in sync, and connected with the universe. Your heart, soul and God unite. The challenges of your life and your past circumstances take on a new meaning. You feel your feelings with greater ease. You have creative inspirations and solutions happen literally out of the blue. You feel less alone in your life. You will feel your heart open, feel closer to yourself and life, and begin to fully shine. You reconnect and reclaim the Whole You and the true destiny of your soul. Your life purpose becomes clear, and you feel a new relationship with your Self, others and the world. From here, life brings you what you need—whether it's the idea for a new business; a life partner; conceiving a child; creative and financial expansion and opportunities to support your needs and dreams; health and vitality; friends who stand by your side; and the immeasurable gift of spiritual guides, mentors, and masters revealing their presence and teachings to you on the inner and outer planes of life. You begin to discover the golden bridge of Oneness within you that paves the way to BEing ONE with Infinite Source.

This has been my journey, and I lovingly offer it to you,

With Infinite Love,
Iana Lahi

> *"The ground of God and the ground of
> the soul are one and the same."*
> *— Meister Eckhart*

CHAPTER ONE

Suspending Disbelief on the Pathway to BEing One

> *"They both listened silently to the water, which to them was not just water, but the voice of life, the voice of Being, the voice of perpetual Becoming."*
> *— Hermann Hesse, Siddhartha*

Suspending Disbelief & Opening to Possibility

Whether you are reading a book, watching a movie, or experiencing any activity for the first time, if you are exposed to something new, you inevitably come to that activity with a particular perspective. Your past experiences, education, family background, closely held beliefs, and even personal baggage shape how you will take in that new experience.

If you go to watch any science fiction or fantasy movie, one of the first things that you frequently have to do is suspend disbelief. To suspend disbelief means you are willing to accept as true or believable the premises, events, or characters of something that would ordinarily be seen as incredible. Typically, in the case of a movie, you do this in exchange for a benefit—the promise of entertainment. While it doesn't seem humanly possible for a character to narrowly escape another series of bullets or survive a plunge over a waterfall given all logic, reason, and physics that you know in life, you suspend disbelief. You accept that it is possible for him or her to survive and triumph. You might even utter the words "Hey, you never know," because perhaps anything really *is* possible.

The promise of *BE: The Humanity Blueprint*, and this volume in particular, is not just to inspire or engage your mind (although I hope it does both), but to truly begin to enlighten your whole body, beliefs, and practices as you live your everyday life. While this volume and the pathway that is shared may contain some points that seem familiar if you have read any form of human potential or spiritual texts, there is much that is different and new. How everything is linked together in all of the *BE: The Humanity Blueprint* volumes has not been shared for thousands of years.

The information and practices shared on these pages are not only meant to open you in profoundly new ways, but they may also turn many of your commonly accepted beliefs and practices on their head. Therefore, the first step to fully absorbing the contents and possibilities contained in this book is to try and put aside all of the "stuff" that you bring to the table when you approach something new. Let go and be willing to suspend disbelief when reading and absorbing this book. Come to this material without all of the drama, baggage, judgments, and past experiences that populate your mind. Breathe and find a neutral zone. Let go of all of your preconceived notions about what you know and who you are supposed to BE. Release your beliefs about change, the inevitability of life and death, enlightenment, religion, and new age spirituality. BE with the material

SUSPENDING DISBELIEF ON THE PATHWAY TO BEING ONE

and consider the possibility that what you are reading and the practical pathway outlined in these pages IS POSSIBLE.

The great poet and mystic Rumi wisely taught that as you ask the relevant questions to Infinite Source of how to walk your own life path with clarity, it is important to not be attached to understanding or knowing. Even if your mind does not understand, your soul does. Sometimes you don't have to intellectually understand every last thing or detail that you are reading or experiencing to get what you need. This is particularly true for the spiritual aspirant or person seeking to step into their whole soul and Self. As you read this book and absorb its content, you may not fully "get" everything you are reading the first time. That's okay and not unexpected. What you do need to do is BE WILLING to let go of your pictures, your rational thoughts and beliefs that you've held as "true and real," and open to feel the light within and all around you. This will set you free. Trust that the seeds will be planted within you to receive new levels of awareness as you read this book.

> *Even if your mind does not understand, your soul does.*

In this and the other volumes of *BE,* you are going to read about ideas related to your body, spirituality, energy, your mind, your brain, truth, cellular memory, integration, wholeness, sexuality, love, power, the light, fearlessness, and the action steps that you can take that will shift your life. Some of these things will seem like common sense. Some may make you roll your eyes or think, *I can't do that.* Suspend disbelief. Consider that what you are reading is right on, real, very possible, and exactly what you need to know at this very moment in your life. Consider that if you actively follow through with the tools, practices, and techniques contained in these pages, you can shift your life and reconnect with who you authentically are.

For thousands of years, people have been searching for a path to enlightenment or a state of being where pure joy, bliss, and love exist. They've searched for a way to permanently end the darkness that exists within their lives and in the deepest recesses of the soul and psyche. They want total peace with "who they are" and to feel connected to others and the universe. Somehow we *just know* there is a mind-body-Spirit connection that must be tapped into to get to this "place," feeling, or state of consciousness. The BE work helps the brain to receive greater light and consciousness and teaches how to go beyond the limitations created by the mind. Beyond the state of limited perception exists unlimited infinite consciousness.

Some may feel that to achieve touching into and embodying higher consciousness, one has to practice mantras and recite prayers to reach a heightened state of spiritual connection. Yes, this is absolutely a beautiful and important part of training the mind to experience connection with the divine. In the BE work, you will first learn how to directly access the light within you to reconnect the lost and forgotten love and power of your soul. Once your soul is unified within your psyche and body, you are able to embark upon your true spiritual path, which already lives within you.

For over 5,000 years, the soul has experienced severe separation from the divine. Religion and history as we know it has been based upon the separation of love and power. Once the soul is realigned, one's life path and purpose become clear. You can successfully clear and let go of what no longer supports you living your highest destiny path. The BE work aligns you directly with your individual energetic matrix and supports you to connect to all of the levels of living in your divine Self while manifesting your message, work, vision, clarity, and presence in the world. The BE work can save you tremendous amounts of time, energy, and focus that can be spent actually living your life as an integrated practice. Always know that there is more than one way to arrive at your final destination of consciously being conscious. However, the *BE Pathway* supports you to stay fully present and connected in your daily life and provides an integrated direct route back to your True, Essential, Divine Self. You are shown how to reconnect to the divine essence within you. Surrounded by all of the impressions created by your emotional body and mind, it can feel overwhelming to think of yourself as a vital and integral spark of the One—Infinite Source. Yet, you are always connected to divine consciousness. Here, and in all of the BE Volumes, you are given the way to reconnect to the divine through your soul in your body. Your reunion with the divine within your body, mind, and soul has the power to bridge your whole Self into Oneness.

    The practices in this book and in the other volumes of *BE: The Humanity Blueprint* go directly to the core of all spiritual practices throughout time, space, and eternity. They get to the heart or center of spiritual actions that create the openings, connections, integration, and alignment that are necessary to BE who you really are and stop the endless cycle of leaving yourself.

    God—Infinite Source is fully alive and present in you, all of the time. It is our perceptions that must shift to help us crack the belief that we are separate and alone. We need to learn how to let go into the greater reality within ourselves that is the gateway into integrating our divine and human heart.

    To rediscover your true inner Self and connection with all that is, you will learn what will help you to open to your infinite potential, why you should do it, and how you can do it most effectively. This is a book that is meant to move you mentally, emotionally, spiritually, and physically. What you are learning is more than just adding new items to your shopping cart of spiritual tools and techniques to attain peace. These teachings are the *Original Way* to directly connect with yourself and all that exists in the universe. The *Original Way Teachings* align the essence of your soul to the heart of Oneness. It becomes possible to live in clear presence and inner awareness.

As you move through all of the BE volumes, you are going to be guided through all of the connections in your body on a spiritual and energetic level, enabling you to experience what most meditators awaken to after ten to fifteen years of practice. You will enter the moment where Spirit and the body meet and where your soul and Spirit meet. These are the signposts along the way that "light" the road to your full illumination and integration.

You will access portals of energy in your body that are ready to be awakened and connected into the full light grid within you. When you reconnect them, you will be zapped into your own power super highway. Your mind wants to BE connected and is most likely ready to make this shift into a cosmic connection with your soul. In this day and age, our minds work so quickly from one moment to the next, that by learning to redirect its attention, you will begin to walk the path of spiritual empowerment.

Most of us believe that only other people have spiritual powers. The truth is that most of your power centers have not yet been opened. When they do open, you will feel more connected and aligned with your True Self and authenticity. You will find your spiritual power and love, which are the foundation of your BEing. The spiritual gifts that are available to you will open just through your commitment to connect with your soul and know who you are. You will learn to hear, see, feel, and BE in new ways. But first you must suspend your disbelief.

Be willing to let go of the beliefs taught by your family, traditions, role models, culture, school, and religion. Be willing to

SUSPENDING DISBELIEF ON THE PATHWAY TO BEING ONE

shift how your body relates to energies within and around you. Your beliefs have the dual function of guiding or shutting down your life and all of its possibility. When you become willing to let go of what you "know" and are open to the possibility of new ideas, beliefs, experiences, and realities, you create an opening for your higher senses and inner bodies to connect in new ways and levels. When you go past your beliefs, you will find yourself open and receptive in a new way to the possibility of your divine magnificence as a human and spiritual being.

To suspend your beliefs *and* suspend disbelief, you must be ready to receive. To receive requires being willing to open. It is only your belief that blocks your life. It alienates you from life itself and keeps you feeding off of the same situations day in and day out that keep you separated, numb, and disconnected. Suspend your belief and suspend disbelief as you absorb this new approach and enter a world full of fresh possibility.

> *To suspend your beliefs and suspend disbelief, you must be ready to receive.*

When you suspend disbelief and really begin to absorb the words and practices within these pages through your heart and soul, you will begin the process of opening and connecting with your higher senses and inner bodies in new ways and levels. When your higher senses and body become acquainted, you will find a new relationship with yourself.

If you hold onto an old belief that says, "I know everything or I know enough and there is nothing new that I can really learn," try a new belief that pronounces, "I am open to the possibility that there are new things for me to learn and new ways that I can BE that can transform my life." Let go of your mental and emotional shackles and suspend disbelief as you read and absorb the ideas and practices of this book. BE OPEN to its possibility.

The One in Soul Experience

The BE *One in Soul* experience fills the needs within you to move beyond your pain, suffering, limitations, and patterns in your body and mind that block full access to the abundance of light and love within you. You can then discover and integrate your ultimate spiritual and physical life. All of the ways that you see, feel, and think about yourself and others will change once you make use of the key that you are being given in *One in Soul*. I promise that the key works. It will fit the door before you, which will give you direct connection to the core truth, creative brilliance, love, power, and light that brings about your healing and awakening. Once you open and walk through that first doorway, you will be given the next series of keys and doorways so that you can unlock and walk through all of the entryways into the heart and light of your Whole Self.

If you face this work uncertain or questioning what is really possible, know that the BE work is not a band-aid; it is a permanent solution to heal what most ails you. Throughout all four volumes of *BE,* you will be accessing and recovering your internal "logic board" that, once restructured, gives you total connection to all of the emotional, spiritual, energetic, mental, physical, and etheric aspects of yourself. The work spirals you into a parallel reality of all aspects and levels of yourself so that you co-exist with the truth within each and every moment. Once wired together in this way, you will be given back the amazing and beyond belief YOU.

Instead of compartmentalizing your life, you are removing the road blocks so you can access and drive down your personal spiritual highway in your "new" car—it is an updated model structured on your integrated Bodymind, wholeness, and connection. Your soul aspects are calling out to be reconnected and healed in this way. It's time to Go Big and Go Deep and fully embody the strength, humor, compassion, wisdom, and love within you. If you are reading this, there is a good chance that you are ready to live and BE in this new way so you can break free and finally BE the YOU that you are yearning to BE.

The *One in Soul* Roadmap brings you into a new relationship with yourself that begins with finding a lost part of yourself. Metaphorically, when parts of yourself are lost in the woods, cast out to sea, unable to sprout, stuck in the birth canal, or left behind in your childhood treasure chest under your bed, it becomes impossible to leap through the doorways of your life that the universe is trying to give you. Once you reconnect to the divine intelligence found within your soul aspects, and integrate them into your body, you get the new and improved model of you. *One in Soul* gives you a spiritual tune-up and helps you to function on levels from which you may have been disconnected for hundreds and sometimes thousands of years.

You will learn how to bring in the light, which is the strongest energy in the universe and focus it into the areas of your being that have been living in a restful slumber waiting for your return. You will learn how to work with energy to open the portals within your body to receive higher awareness and to ignite the hidden gems of love and power within yourself. You will rediscover your soul and awaken your capacity to BE big and create a new internal home for the Real You to live in. The BE work brings you home into your integrated state through time tested practices that connect you into living and BEing One with Infinite Source. Your Infinite Source is my Infinite Source; it is *the* Source. It is beyond a creator being, it is beyond your imagination, it is the essence that connects all of life. It is unlimited light, love, and power—beyond the concepts of separation and duality. Once you are consciously realigned into Infinite Source, your life will shift from living out the disconnections of your body, mind, and soul into experiencing a tangible and wonderful reunion of your Whole Self. You will be living as you are meant to BE, fully participating and manifesting in this lifetime.

> *Your Infinite Source is my Infinite Source; it is the Source.*

One in Soul will help you live in your daily existence as a whole human being who has integrated their divinely lit inspiration into life. You will be able to step through the veils of limited thinking and fear and BE integrated and aligned with the core resources within yourself that assist you in accomplishing what you came here to BE.

One in Soul helps you to establish the relationship needed to awaken your True Self and to serve humanity from BEing whole. By learning how to hear, listen, and BE with your needs, your true and false desires, and in the pure truth of your BEing, you can create an unbreakable bond with the love that is You.

Trust in the experiences that the *One in Soul* practice gives to you. It is the foundation for BEing whole. Know that in each *BE Volume I-IV*, you will be advancing through progressively light-filled gateways that awaken, clear, activate, ignite, and align all of the components of your body, mind, soul, and Spirit to bridge you into a new power of BEing Love in action.

REMEMBER:

- The promise of *BE: The Humanity Blueprint — One in Soul* is to begin to enlighten your whole body, beliefs, and practices as you live your everyday life.

- Come to this material without the drama, baggage, judgments, and past experiences that populate your mind. Let go of all of your preconceived notions about what you know and who you are supposed to BE.

- BE WILLING to let go of your pictures, thoughts, and beliefs that you've held as "true and real" and open to feel the light within and all around you. This will set you free.

- The ideas and practices in this book support you to know yourself and to open into the truth, light, and power that already reside within you.

- The BE Pathway supports you to stay fully alive and connected in your daily life and provides the shortest and most direct route back to your True, Essential, Divine Self.

- Your spiritual power and love are the foundation of your BEing. The spiritual gifts that are available to you will open just through your commitment to connect with your soul and know who you are.

- You are accessing and recovering your internal "logic board" that, once restructured, gives you total connection to all of the emotional, spiritual, energetic, mental, physical, and etheric aspects of yourself.

- You are being given the steps through the veils of limited thinking and fear so you can BE integrated and aligned with the core resources within yourself that assist you to accomplish what you came here to BE.

BELIGHT MEDITATION™

Relaxing

Create a space and a time to open and read this book when you have few distractions. Take a deep, full breath from your diaphragm, through your nose, and when you exhale, let go of all of the stresses and dramas of your day and the mental backlog that remains stuck in your head out of your mouth. Breathe long and deep four times.

Now, as you inhale through your nose, send the breath into your lower belly; and as you exhale, pull the breath up through your spine and out of your mouth. Repeat four times.

Place your hands with palms facing up on your thighs or above your knees while either sitting in a chair or cross-legged in an easy, relaxed position sitting on a pillow or mat on the ground. Take a few moments to follow your breath and to allow your mind to rest into the rhythm of your breathing. Sit for as long as you can. Just BE.

CHAPTER TWO

Take the Call of Your Life

> *"Faith is taking the first step even when you don't see the whole staircase."*
> — Martin Luther King, Jr.

Take the Call

You're sitting at your kitchen table, and there's that call again; the ringing that seems to appear at the worst and strangest moments. Inevitably you're busy with dinner, taking care of your kids, creating plans for the weekend, paying bills, putting in extra work hours, doing laundry, working out at the gym, fixated on an electronic device, or watching TV. It's not the telemarketers, your family, or that friend you've been avoiding. The call is coming from inside of you. It might be saying, "What are you doing?" "Is this what you really want?" It is a voice of longing, questioning, and hope. You've been avoiding or just plain not listening to this call for too long. Turn off your internal answering machine, stop caller ID, and answer this call. It is the first step to changing your life.

If you read, watch, or listen and pay attention to the wide range of political, social, and natural events occurring across the globe, you might "get" that we are living in a time of profound spiritual and physical change that is unlike any other moment within the last 2,500 years. The dimensional planes of our existence are altering. The earth's polarity is shifting; it's getting warmer everywhere, and weather patterns are becoming more extreme.

The world is being thrust into greater social unrest and turmoil. We are witnessing increasing instances of seemingly inexplicable violence, "dis-ease," and disconnection at global and individual scales. "Undeclared" war, civil conflicts, acts of hatred and greed, suicide bombings, terrorism, ethnic cleansing, mass murder, drug-related violence and death, governmental controls, ego-driven politics, and global pandemics are becoming all too expected aspects of life on Earth. More and more people are tuning out with the assistance of drugs and alcohol, food, sex, video games, electronic media, or other addictions of the day. Disconnection to human truth and higher values are being accepted as the norm.

On a spiritual level, there are some people who are turning away from God and any notion of religion. There is a focus on the material reality of life and surviving and accumulating as much as one can. And yet, there are also more people turning to religion or some form of spirituality as a way to make sense of the craziness of life and of their own hearts. Even people who are not religious are searching for ways to be grounded and connected to the earth and people around them. They are searching for greater connection and meaning among humanity and within themselves. You may not be sure what all of this means, but somehow you **know** that things are shifting, and you wonder what the future will bring.

On an internal level, something instinctive is stirring inside. You might have an unsettled, restless feeling, as if somehow the way you've been thinking and living your life doesn't work anymore. It is no longer enough. After years of living in survival-mode, or even pursuing your dreams, there is something inside of you saying "it's time to change." It may come out in your thoughts and feelings as fear, uncertainty, passion, or even longing for something new or different. You're starting to wonder about the greater desires and aspirations that you've held. You are questioning what you are doing with your life. You are wondering whether you can break through your obstacles to BEing who you are and succeed. There has to be more to the meaning of life, *your* life, than what you've experienced to date, but what? What is your purpose, and why are you really here? Why do you feel so utterly disconnected from so much of what is happening in your life? Why do you feel that no matter how much work you have done, you are still spinning the same wheels? You are feeling and hearing a calling deep within your mind and soul.

To acknowledge that your life doesn't work anymore, that you definitely need to honor your life dreams and goals and shift direction, that you can't keep on doing the same ol' same ol' and expect different results, or question everything you've done and been up to this point in your existence, creates a whole host of potentially scary, life changing uncertainties and possibilities. It would be so much easier to ignore this feeling, this calling inside of you. Why not just have a big piece of chocolate cake, kick back, and have a few drinks with your friends, or just move on to the next task on your mile-long to-do list and forget about it? You can't. Deep down inside of you, you know there is something more that you are supposed to do and BE. There is greater meaning and purpose to your life. You must find it and act upon it.

This inner voice is asking you to embark upon a hero's journey[1]. It includes a path into the unknown and hidden aspects of yourself and the universe. But what exactly is this journey, and is it something you are equipped to handle? It is a journey worthy of Moses, Buddha, Christ, Muhammad, Luke Skywalker, Mary Magdalene, and even Harry Potter. But how many of us think we are actually capable of following in their footsteps?

The journey that you are being called to take is not a random event that is happening to you alone or that is reserved for a select few superhuman individuals or fictional characters. There are millions of other people like yourself who hear an inner voice of truth, knowingness, and guidance that is calling for a shift. You may feel alone and completely different from most people in your life, but rest assured, you are not alone. Your destiny is knocking at your door. Open the door and open yourself to the possibility of profound transformation.

Know that you can stop all of that searching for something outside of yourself to fill the void, to make you happy, or to soothe the discomfort and disconnection you feel inside. There is no secret, universal law, guru, healer, spiritual channeler, nor material possession that can give you what you're looking for. *However, there is an answer.* It lies within you, and only you can discover it. It has always been there, although all too often it has been covered, blocked, and even encased in the reinforced steel of your illusions, beliefs, wounds, and ego. You can find and reconnect with it. But first, you have to take the call.

The call is the gift of your lifetime—the gift to become WHO YOU TRULY ARE. You may not know exactly who you are at this moment, or what that really means, but this is a journey into the Real You. You are more than the conditioning you were raised in, more than your position in life, your job or lack of job, more than the roles that you play as a husband, wife, mother, father, son, daughter, or child, more than your material things, more than your mind, your body, and your ego. You have an authentic Self that you left so long ago that you're not even sure if it ever existed. The authentic you IS *magnificent*. It is whole, complete, grounded, connected, and filled with an unfathomable love and power. It is truly human and divine.

Most of us have no problem recognizing our own humanity. We are often too quick to see our flaws, imperfections, and shortcomings. We are all *too* human. Yet, few of us embrace our own divinity and see God or the source of all creation within ourselves. You are a human being with a body, mind, and heart. Yet, you also have a heart center, Spirit, and soul. Within your heart and soul, you carry and are a part of the divine flame of creation. This is where your call is coming from.

> ***Within your heart and soul, you carry and are a part of the divine flame of creation.***

Whether you consider yourself religious, spiritual, agnostic, or atheist, the energy that allows all things to exist and grow is part of your fundamental essence. When you rediscover your authentic Self, you are tapping into and connecting with the source energy of your life and *all* life. You begin to feel and know that you are a spark in the flame of universal creation energy. You realize that you have a soul and a Spirit that is uniquely yours and yet interwoven with the fabric of *all that is*.

Your soul is your consciousness, the embodiment of creation, and the strength of your existence. The more you become One in soul, the more you can accomplish. When the magnificence of your True Self opens to give and receive, you get more life, abundance, joy, freedom, and light. When you listen to and embrace the calling of your soul, there is a spark of recognition that you are more than the thoughts you have, the emotions that run you, or your physical challenges. You begin to realize your limitless possibility, and the fears and dramas of your life dissolve. But first you have to take the call.

You are being called to find the naked, fully enlightened you that has always existed. The "you" that was brought into this world the moment you were born. The you that has an eternal Spirit and a soul purpose in this lifetime. The you that has been abandoned, rejected, and betrayed and that longs to be loved, to be seen and heard, and to complete its purpose and destiny. You are more than what you have been for all of these years, and what you are feeling inside is a longing to truly know yourself. It is time to go home and feel the light, the spark, and the "groundedness" of your authentic Self. It is your essence, your core truth, and your purpose. Your soul and spirit ache to go back to the center of your creation. They long to feel connected to the original you.

Listen and open to the voice of your authentic Self, for it holds the promise of an extraordinary life. You no longer have to settle for anything less or for a life that is merely okay, safe, secure, or acceptable. You can stop pretending. You can stop holding in your frustrations, fears, and lost hopes and dreams.

You may harbor an old belief that says, "There's no such thing as an authentic Self. I am who I am, that's it. There's not much I can do to change things. I just have to deal with how things are." Yet consider adopting a new belief that unequivocally states, "I have an authentic Self and a purpose, and I have the power to change my life to live that purpose."

This is about being BIG, living BIG, and creating and completing the life and the purpose you were always meant to have in this lifetime. When you listen and embrace what is inside of you, you can truly manifest full abundant joy in all aspects of your life. You really can be yourself in the truest sense and have a life that you love. It is possible, if you take the call.

TAKE THE CALL. Listen to what is inside of you.

Listening

When you are willing to listen to the call inside of yourself, you are beginning your journey, your personal road to BE the fully Enlightened YOU. What does it mean to listen? Truth be told, it isn't just about listening with your ears. You must also listen, focus, and feel with your whole body.

Most of us were raised in families that were afraid of silence. Television and chatter about unimportant issues that you didn't care about or couldn't relate to probably filled your home life. You most likely experienced being talked at, instead of spoken with. When you were told to listen, there was always an agenda, and rarely was it your agenda. And when there was something important to you, more often than not you didn't feel like you were being heard. Can you remember feeling how your heart ached when that happened? Unfortunately, most of us have terrible listening skills because we have never been taught to listen, to one another or to what is inside of us.

The act of listening requires that you open your entire body, not just your head. What's the difference? If you're asked to listen to the wind and you do it from your head, you hear a sound, the whistling of the wind, and it does not affect you. When you listen to the wind from your body, you feel it through your entire body, and eventually the wind speaks to you. Imagine the wind as a strong nor'easter that can bring a shiver through your entire body through its strength and the wetness that it holds as it touches your skin. It enlivens all of your senses. When you really "listen"—or more specifically, listen, feel, and focus on the wind—it says many things, including *you and I are One,* and we come from the same Source. You hear and begin to experience its true force and power.

Our ears can register pitch and frequency, but our hearts register feeling and resonance. Sound can awaken you, but it has to be taken inside. To listen is to take in. The pores of our skin must open; the emotional armor around our body must dissolve. To listen is to get out of your head, breathe, and re-direct where you place your focus and attention in your body. Think of it as hearing through the center of your body where you are grounded into the earth, into who you really are.

The ability to listen opens in your body as you contact your lower belly with your breath. Feel your whole body move and expand as it takes in the sounds, vibrations, and energy that may come from another person or your immediate surroundings. BE PRESENT and aware to what you are taking in, and let yourself absorb its full content.

> *The ability to listen opens in your body as you contact your lower belly with your breath.*

Take a moment and place your hand on your lower belly. Inhale into your hand and into your lower belly at the same time. Feel your belly. On the exhale, pull your navel in. Allow your attention to drop into your lower belly as you repeat this circular breath in and out of your nose. Rest. Now, gently and simply breathe in and out of your mouth and "move" your mind into your lower belly. Feel your lower tailbone come alive. On your next breath, connect into your heart center while staying rooted in your lower belly. The next time that you speak with someone, practice staying in your lower belly and heart at the same time.

If you are really listening to another person, you are "hearing" more than their words. You are also soaking in the range of meaning, emotions, and energy that exist within the words. If you are listening to yourself, you are beginning to connect with the gut-level, raw truth of your soul. Its expression is conveyed through your thoughts, emotions, and the physical responses you feel in your full body. This may seem abstract, but you can actually practice listening in this new way. Like any skill, it is something that you can learn how to do and then, like riding a bike, it will become second nature. The exercises in this book will teach you how.

As you practice listening in this way, you will find a spiritual connection that begins to communicate with your heart, and you will hear the voice of your True Self. The most important key to listening is to focus in your lower belly (your *Second Power Point Center, which will be explained in greater detail in chapter 7*) and in between your ears (in the center of your head) at the same time. You will be listening from a place of power and acceptance while you learn to hold space for yourself and another person.

The bottom line is that until you learn to listen to yourself and the truth that is inside of you, it is almost impossible to truly listen and open to another. To hear others, you must first hear yourself. Instead of ignoring or hanging up on the parts of you that are sad, depressed, fearful, and angry, listen to their call. You will then be able to hear yourself. The emotions that you hear are the expressions covering up your True Self. Those emotions may not be ultimate truth, but they are road signs directing you to find and listen to your real Self. Your heart is calling out to you, and it wants you to open to your True Self. When you really listen, you are hearing from the integration of your *Power Point*

Centers, what you may know as your chakras—it gives you the ability to hear, feel, and see in a new way, but it can only be felt when you are moving into the body in a new way.

Once you can hear yourself, you can hear another person and will be able to show up in ways you never thought imaginable. Your presence with yourself and another is life changing. You will begin to hear a voice that is connected to a person's soul and heart, not just their head. You can truthfully open to them.

Learning to listen is the first step to finding your power. When you sit in nature and just listen, your mind can become very still, and you can begin to hear the voice of your true nature. You will find that you want to be listened to and you are no longer willing to be ignored. When you begin to listen and hear what you need, you are taking the first step to being able to reconnect into your authentic and empowered Self. You will learn that there is a difference between what you really need and how you want to control to get your needs met. Your true needs exist within your heart, not in your head. When you tap into the needs that help your soul grow and evolve, all of a sudden the universe supports you in miraculous ways. You will no longer be just in survival mode; you will be living in union with your soul and creation directly.

To listen authentically, you must slow everything down inside your mind by listening for the *space between* sounds, words, thoughts, and your breath in your body.

> **The 7 Actions to BEing**
>
> **Expand and Contract into the *space between*.**
>
> **Focus and Connect into your body.**
>
> **Recognize and Receive that which is waiting.**
>
> **Surrender and Release into the energy.**
>
> **Open and Feel what is present.**
>
> **Align and Integrate the feeling.**
>
> **Merge and Enlighten into your heart.**

When you enter the listening space within yourself, you enter through a gateway that links your body and Spirit. You feel lifted up, unveiled, and present to a power stronger than your mind. When you listen and are true to yourself, a vibrant power will open in your body. Ground that power by sending it down into the center of the earth and anchor your power to its core. Grounded power supports you to listen, take action, and commit to your inner truth. Ungrounded power is having your power take hold of you, and then it runs you. Grounded power is connected all the way through your body, and ungrounded power is centered in your head.

Your old way of being may typically involve listening through your head, not really paying attention, or hearing just enough to position yourself to look or appear a certain way or to get something you want. Now choose to listen with your full body to feel the greater truth in yourself and others. Enlighten into the *space between* in your Bodymind and spirit, and discover your power.

REMEMBER:

- If you really want to know yourself, your purpose, or change your life in any way, shape, or form, the first thing you must do is **TAKE THE CALL**. Take the call coming from inside you, and listen to what is being communicated.

- When you develop the courage to answer your internal phone, you have taken the first step on a pathway to discovering your authentic Self, your soul purpose, and what enlightenment can actually look and feel like in your everyday life.

- We all have an authentic Self that longs to be loved, seen, and heard. It is now your time to find and embrace it.

- You are more than the conditioning you were raised in; more than your position; your job or lack of job; more than the roles that you play as a husband, wife, mother, father, daughter, son, or child; more than your material things; more than your mind, your body, and your ego.

- Within your heart and soul, you carry and are a part of the divine flame of creation. This is where your call is coming from.

- Your soul is your consciousness, the embodiment of creation, and the strength of your existence.

- Learning to listen with your whole body is the first step to finding your power. The key to listening is to focus into your lower belly (your *Second Power Point Center*) and in between your ears (in the center of your head) at the same time.

- There is a difference between what you really need and how you want to control to get your needs met. Your true needs exist within your soul, not in your head.

- Grounded power is connected through your entire body and supports you to listen, take action, and commit to your inner truth. Ungrounded power is centered in your head and runs you, disconnected from your Whole Self.

BELIGHT MEDITATION

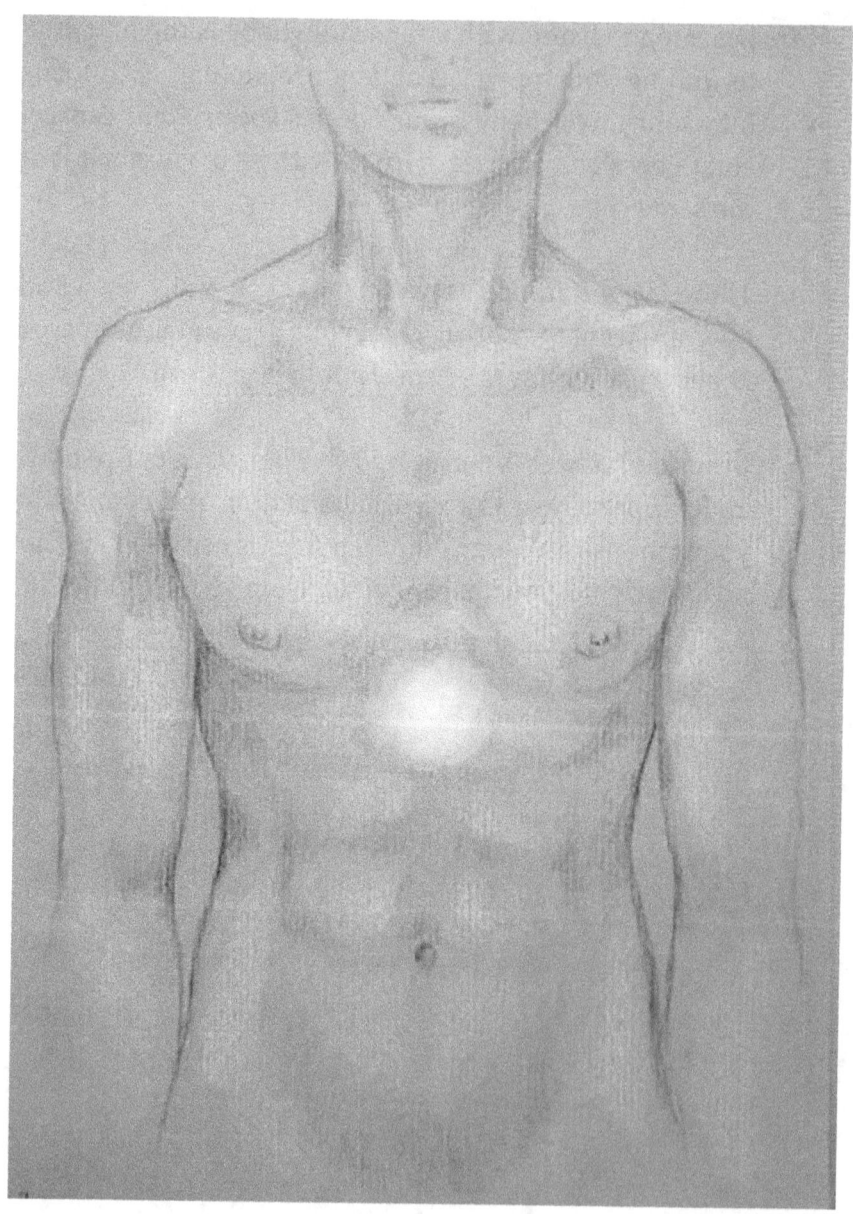

Solar Plexus

STEP 1: TAKE THE CALL

To prepare to take the call of your soul, you must shift how you LISTEN. Instead of engaging in the limited listening through your head that most of us do, practice listening from your whole body, focus into the space beneath your rib cage, into your solar plexus. This is the central switchboard in your body where Spirit, emotions, and your mind meet. The goal is to LISTEN, FEEL, and FOCUS your attention in a new way. This will allow you to connect with the deeper truth within yourself and to hear the truths that others are giving you. Listening creates an opening and a space for you to realize and begin to embrace the true force and power of your soul.

Inhale through your nose and exhale out of your mouth. Become aware of being in your head. Then, slide down a waterslide from the inside of your head into a pool of warm, golden water in your solar plexus. Immerse yourself into the pool and sit in your solar plexus in the golden white light.

STEP 2: LISTEN IN A NEW WAY TO WHAT IS INSIDE YOU

Have a journal or notebook and pen by your side.

Instead of ignoring the thoughts, feelings, and emotions inside of yourself that may be giving you a sense of discomfort with your life, open to them. Find a few minutes (10 minutes) in your day, possibly first thing in the morning or at the end of the day, to focus on yourself. Tune out all of the mindless noise around yourself, and **turn up** the volume on the feelings inside your entire body. Be present with whatever is inside of you. Breathe deeply from your gut. Don't try to stop it, clear it, or ignore it. What is it saying? How does it make your body feel? What is it telling you that you may want or need? Acknowledge what you are feeling.

Pick up your journal and pen and, with your writing hand, direct a question to the feeling. Ask one question, then switch your pen into your non-dominant hand and allow this aspect of you to respond. Begin by writing with your dominant hand: "I am here for you. What do you need me to know about you?" Switch your pen into your non-dominant hand, close your eyes for a moment, and allow this soul aspect of yourself to respond as you open your eyes and write. Next ask, "How can I be here for you?" Receive and BE with the energetic feelings from within you.

STEP 3: OPENING THE INNER CIRCUITS

While lying down, place your left hand approximately 2 inches below your collarbone, in the center of your upper chest. Here you will find your heart center. Breathe into your upper chest, into your heart center. Listen, Focus, and Feel. Now, place your right hand on your lower belly, in between your navel and your pubic bone, and breathe, allowing the breath to fill your belly and move into your lower spine. Focus your attention into your lower belly and heart center at the same time, and bring your breath into both locations. Allow the sensation of energy to move from one hand to the other hand and through your body. Listen, focus, and feel what is inside you.

CHAPTER THREE

Who Are You?

*"Wherever you go, east, west, north or south,
think of it as a journey into yourself!
The one who travels into itself travels the world."*
— Shams-i-Tabrizi

Who You Are

Imagine you have just stepped onto an elevator. As you walk through the doors, you notice an usual person who is uniquely dressed. It could be a man or a woman, but he or she has piercingly clear eyes and a smile on their face that penetrates somewhere deep inside of you. As you look at this being, you think to yourself, *Who is this person? Do I know her or him?* Before you can think of what to say, you hear in your mind the question: *WHO ARE YOU?*

What would be your response?

Do you have an elevator speech that you can recite in less than 60 seconds? Do you have a response that is less than 140 characters and retweet worthy?

I am an accountant, an administrative assistant, or a student. I am unemployed. I am a CEO. I am a daughter or son. I am a parent. I am a Christian, Jew, Buddhist, Muslim, Hindu, Sikh, or agnostic. I am African American, Italian, Chinese, German, Canadian, Japanese, Dutch, Native American, French, or Latino. I am a woman or man. I am a frustrated artist. I am a wounded warrior. I am a healer, leader, or entrepreneur. I am a work-in-progress. I am so freaking exhausted, sick, and tired.

Perhaps your response is, Do I really have to answer this? *I don't know. I have no idea.*

Perhaps what you really want to say is that you are uncertain, but so much more than you might seem. You might be afraid or longing for something more—to BE something more than you have been up until this point in your life.

Who you are is a unique, divinely inspired spark of light. As shared in the last chapter, you are more than your job, more than your roles or identities, more than your thoughts, and more than your emotions or physical being. It seems like such a cliché to assert that you are a completely unique individual, BUT YOU ARE. The way that you give and perceive life, the ideas that you have, how you care about people, the foods you prepare or things you do around your home, your kindness, how you always choose to love but do not know how to consistently love yourself—these are all things that make you who you are.

There will never be anyone exactly like you. While you may be one of billions, you are truly an authentic, shimmering, multifaceted, one-of-a-kind perfect expression of creation. Your unique design adds to the evolution of all humanity. YOU MATTER. WE ALL DO. As a soul you are born, dissolved, expanded, and reborn over and over again, connecting you into the Source and continuum of life, whether you know it or not. You and your life have a magical interconnection that, once realized, creates unending joy and possibilities.

Alas, we are raised in cultures that, from birth, separate us from being our Whole Self. We are taught to split off from ourselves to meet the needs and expectations of others. Most of us have become so caught up in roles, identities, attachments, and just surviving that we have lost touch with our fundamental essence and truth. We have gaps, holes, and longings inside that no material object can ever fulfill, no matter how hard we try and how much we buy or consume.

> **We have forgotten who we are.**

What is missing inside of you is your connection to your soul. Deep down inside, you know. You know that there is something intrinsic inside of you that is calling out to be heard. It is calling out to be seen. It is calling out to be received and embraced.

Without knowing why or how, you have stopped your own energies from naturally flowing in your body, living in a state of separation and fragmentation. You have been managing the energy of *"who you are"* your whole life. A split between your mind and Infinite Source occurred, and this began the journey of mismanaging your body and soul. Perhaps you are at a place where you know that you want everything to be different. You want everything to work together, to flow smoother, and to be more joyful and free. You realize that how you have been doing your life doesn't seem to work anymore. You have issues with your health, job, kids, career, or marriage, and you ask yourself, *Why me? Why now? Why this?*

> **The answers to your questions can be found in your soul.**

Your soul is like the pilot light in your gas oven. It is the fuel for your existence. When its energy is released and allowed to flow, it explodes from ignition and then grows into a brilliant flame of white and blue source-connected light. It provides the foundation that makes everything possible. You are a spark of light, and all of your daily actions either enliven or diminish the inner fire of your soul. Your soul is your consciousness and the strength of your existence. It is the embodiment of creation.

To embody creation means that you are embracing the energies of Infinite Source. When it comes to your innate soul-Source connection, the universe plays no favorites. It doesn't matter what religion, spiritual belief, or secular idea with which you connect or identify. We all possess a soul. We are all connected to the heart of creation through our souls. The more expansive and expressed that your soul becomes, then the more the magnificence of your True Self shines through and is revealed. You are able to give and receive more life, abundance, joy, freedom, and light. You can take on greater work and accomplish more than you ever thought possible.

> **You are a spark of light, and all of your daily actions either enliven or diminish the inner fire of your soul.**

Regrettably, we live our lives as though our souls do not exist. This lack of meaning and soul-connection manifests around us as thriving and unchecked greed, poverty, brutality, scarcity, fear, and control. We live in survival mode going from activity to activity. We try to shut out the chaos and drama of the planet and just "live our life." We only think about the tasks that we have to do each day so that nothing falls apart and everyone likes us. We do what we have to do to meet all of the expectations that have been placed upon us. We try hard to be perfect while fearing we are not good enough. We cover up being seen to avoid being judged. We fear failure and life, feeling out of control. We cannot even find the person inside who yearns to be loved. We have separated ourselves from the truth that lives as a still, small flame within. We fear igniting the flame. There is no time for self-reflection, let alone self-actualization. We focus more on "doing" than feeling what is really going on inside of our bodies and lives.

The truth of the matter is that you cannot fully live life if you are separated from your soul. You also have to recognize that you have a soul, and it is speaking to you, perhaps even shouting, at you to listen and wake up. No matter how altruistic your life intentions may be, you cannot stop the screaming and crying hungry children around the globe until you can hear and face the screaming child within yourself. Your soul is aching for you to recognize, receive, and reconnect with its whole essence. It longs for you to complete the circle of your life—to thrive more than merely survive.

The only way to break the karmic circle, in which we are all collectively caught at this momentous point and time, is to listen and become realized as the souls that we are. In the listening, you will find the answers to all of your big life questions and the solutions to what ails you. Your soul knows why you have come here to live; you just may not know it yet.

Your soul is fed by the currents of energy emanating from your connection with Infinite Source. The currents can be weak or strong, providing a trickle or waterfall for your soul's full expression. Your challenge as a human and divine being is to learn how to access those currents and stabilize them in your daily life. The more access you have, then the more your soul can ground you and open you to deeper, more profound levels of joy. All of your daily successes, your dreams and goals, and your inspiration and visions with money, love, and happiness come from knowing and learning how to trust your own soul. Every enlightening BEing, no matter what their status is in life, hears the voice of his or her own soul. It says sit, walk, fly, and leap forward into limitless possibility. It teaches you how to move through your life with a flow and ease that feels like water running through your hands.

> *Your challenge as a human and divine being is to learn how to access those currents and stabilize them in your daily life so that your soul grounds you and brings limitless joy.*

Your life journey is a profound adventure created by being open or closed to the expression of your soul. Your soul is a unique blueprint that reveals the secrets of your Original Self. As unique in design as a freshly fallen snowflake, your soul is an iridescent, geometric pattern of light and beauty.

The true work of your life is the magnificent awakening of your soul so that you can experience who you authentically are and fulfill your destiny. As you experience reconnecting the inherent God energies of your soul, your blueprint will be revealed. If you follow your Humanity Blueprint full circle, you are destined to become whole and ONE inside.

Your soul is the most precious part of yourself. When contacted and listened to, what you find is a treasure map to your complete liberation and freedom. It is your powerhouse of wisdom, creativity, and knowledge. By walking through the door of your soul, you have the opportunity to break through the obstacles, barriers, baggage, and fears of your life to finally know the True You. You can take the fast track to the core of who you are, what you need to heal, and move directly into living the roadmap to the ENLIGHTENED AND IMPASSIONED YOU. As you follow this roadmap to your Whole Self, you will experience how all of the powers of Infinite Source live within you. The separations between you and Infinite Source will eventually no longer exist. You will understand a new kind of relationship—one that becomes vital to your happiness.

> *Your life journey is a profound adventure created by being open or closed to the expression of your soul.*

This book is about re-finding a long, lost friend. In fact, it is about reconnecting with your *best* friend. But to reconnect with your soul, you have to be willing to clear your mind, open your heart, and let go of your controls. Your soul reconnection process is your own unique experience. You might initially find your inner best friend and partner to be immersed in sadness, hurt, loneliness, or despair. Alternately, right from the beginning, you may discover a soul explosion into love and so much joy in your reunion that any pain that was there will instantly dissolve.

If negative emotions arise, know that they come from your original separation from your True Self. Keep in mind not to identify yourself with those emotions. They, too, shall pass. Through opening and touching into your soul, you will learn how to heal any pain or upset that may exist, but you won't have to "go into the pain" to dissolve it. As you begin to end your separations with your core power, you will immediately begin to feel lighter and clearer. You will feel a new level of love and power emerge within you, along with the vitality to more fully participate in the dance of your life.

Before you are able to trust your new power completely, you may wonder what you can hold onto. Everything may seem to change around you. Ways of being and even your relationships may shift before your eyes, leaving a feeling of uncertainty. By following the voice of your soul, you will be gifted with the courage to live amidst the uncertainty of outcomes. Letting go of knowing and controlling everything somehow becomes okay. If you stay connected in your heart, then no matter what happens you will experience an equal feeling of renewed vitality and presence that will give your life inner support. Eventually, you will realize that there is no "thing" or person that you need to hold onto to BE whole because *you are becoming the pillar of your own soul.*

Your soul is the strongest structure in your ancient temple. Through the challenges of growing through life, surviving loss, letting go, personal drama and tragedy, economic fallout, conflicts and system collapse, the pillar of your soul will remain standing. Your soul has served you for lifetimes. Even when you feel weak, it gives you courage to find and be your authentic Self. To reach that place, you have to come from more than a belief about who you are. There must be a knowingness that only comes from reconnecting to the love and power of your soul.

As you walk, waltz, tango, or moonwalk the path to your soul, what you will discover is life energy, clarity, creativity, and the power to succeed in every aspect of your life. You will end up with love, joy, trust, and extended moments of authentic bliss. And even if you don't know how to get to where you want to go, you can trust your growing connection with your soul. It is your direct connect into Infinite Source that will always guide you toward your highest good and connect you into the true values, heart, and meaning of your life.

REMEMBER:

- As a soul you are born, dissolved, expanded, and reborn over and over again, connecting you into the Source and continuum of life whether you know it or not.

- You are a unique, divinely inspired spark of light. You are more than your roles, more than your thoughts, more than your emotions or physical being.

- We are raised in cultures that, from birth, separate us from being our Whole Self. We have forgotten who we are.

- You are a spark of light. All of your daily actions—your choices, thoughts, and behaviors—can ignite, diminish, or extinguish the spark of your soul.

- We live our lives as though our souls do not exist. The only way to break the karmic cycle, in which we are all collectively caught, is to listen and become the souls that we are.

- Your soul is fed by currents of energy emanating from your connection to Infinite Source, and your challenge is to learn how to access those currents and stabilize them in your daily life.

- Your success in achieving your dreams and goals, and your inspiration and visions with money, love, and happiness, come from knowing and learning how to trust your own soul.

- To reconnect your soul, you have to be willing to clear your mind, open your heart, and let go of your controls.

- Your soul is the strongest structure in your ancient temple. Your soul reconnection path helps you to become the pillar of your own soul.

BELIGHT MEDITATION

Your Right to Exist

Take a moment and contemplate an experience in your life where you felt or perceived that you "did not exist." This could be a time when you felt who you really are was not seen or honored. Feel how this impacted you. Call up from within yourself what decision you made in that moment of feeling that you did not and "could not" exist. With your intention, dive into the truth and hear the voice within your heart that exists and just sense it. Whether it has a mighty roar, a song to sing, a tearful plea, a peaceful presence, or an impatient request, invite the "you" that wants to emerge to step up and be with you in this moment.

CHAPTER FOUR

The Light of Your Soul & Reconnection

"You have to grow from the inside out. None can teach you, none can make you spiritual. There is no other teacher, but your own soul."
— Swami Vivekananda

Your Light

The light that lives within your soul is your ultimate teacher and healer. She is an all-embracing mother and a compassionate father who will meet all that is weak, ill, fearful, hesitant, doubtful, and in pain within you. Your divine presence, your ultimate Self, your I AM presence loves to BE ITSELF, and it will trudge through the barriers and blockages within you to unlock its full expression and connection. We all have light within us. Its full expression—*your* full expression as a divine light being—will just vary depending on what you hold onto and ultimately what you are willing to let go of.

Any defensiveness, anger, control, denial, "shut down," or disconnection that may exist in small or large measure in your life all stem from how your ego Self and your individuated human Self battle to exist. Yet, there is more to you than your ego and "survival mode." Ironically, when you feel most hopeless, or like it is just too hard to face life's challenges or make it through another day, then you can begin to recognize that your current ego structures and modus operandi are ineffective and worn out. The way out of your own limitation is to access the greater wisdom and connection waiting within the gifts of light of your whole soul.

The *One in Soul* pathway helps you turn to your true and authentic Self for guidance. The light that lives in your heart awakens by reconnecting, rebuilding, and restructuring your soul's truth and essence. As the light increases, your heart center expands and merges with the cellular presence of your Whole Self. Your light becomes powerful enough to find your precious soul aspects that have been hiding in the dark. We are all divine, enlightened, and highly evolved beings who have a built-in capacity to live in alignment with light rather than the darkness. Many of us have simply failed to recognize the light within ourselves and how we have lived in fear and separation rather than in the light.

> *The light that lives in your heart awakens by reconnecting, rebuilding, and restructuring your soul's truth and essence.*

Darkness exists and grows from living in separation with the Infinite Source of all healing, creation, and life. The dark serves as a comfort and safety zone for the aspects of yourself that have lost a direct conscious relationship with Infinite Source. By restoring your connection with your soul aspects, you set the groundwork for experiencing direct access with the light of God—Infinite Source. This is your birthright.

The soul path that you are entering is intended to rebuild and expand your light, love, power, trust, and grace to help you return to the complete and whole you. You will travel through the terrain of your soul and transform your fear of vulnerability into love and connection with joy. You are renewing your vows to finally and fully love and cherish yourself. This path is about creating a divine love affair with the Source of who you are. You are the hero and heroine of your own life. It is time for you to take charge and *BE all that you are meant to BE*. Your soul is the one thing that will help you make it through the brambles and thorns of your life to step into your full light. Here together, you are being guided through to the richness, magnificence, and abundance of your True Self.

The Soul Reconnection Process

One in Soul, simply put, is a straightforward "how to" roadmap that teaches you about your soul and how to reconnect it into wholeness. This book is about actually living an empowered life, in every single breath you take, and being exactly who you are meant to BE. The reasons why you may engage in this process are deeply personal, but if you have a desire to tap into your unique, full human and spiritual potential, then soul reconnection will help you on your path.

Soul Reconnection is an experience that heals the deepest primal and spiritual energies within you. Your primal energies are the raw, pure, undiluted experience of how you are in relationship to life in your body. Your primal energies always exist in your first and second chakras, or what you will come to know as *Power Point Centers* in your body. They are the root energies of this planet and are connected to the earth, fire, air, and water elements. They define your relationship to and perceptions of survival. How you respond to your primal energies creates how you relate to the most important things in your life, including family, home, commitment, relationships, sex, money, food, and your health. When you are clearing your soul energies in your body, you are reconstructing your primal archetypal energies and spiritual power together.

Your soul or life force energies are currents of light and vitality that maintain your original connection to life. When your life force energies flow smoothly in your body, you feel One with the most subtle levels of Spirit and can differentiate between living in your head or being in your body. Your soul parts carry life force energies, and when fully embraced and integrated in your body, they connect you to living and being sourced into divine connection. The purpose of this powerful and indeed life changing work gives you back your complete and Whole Self. Instead of going through your life living in separation from Infinite Source and constantly seeking it through outer experiences alone, you are being given a simple and efficient way to reconnect your original and pure life force energies that make you distinctively who you are.

For most of us, we are a soul essence trying to survive beneath or behind a wall that is of our own making. Through the practices in this book and the *One in Soul* Process, you can make friends with, accept, and meet the *Real You* and eliminate the separations that you have with your core light and HOLY WHOLE SELF. You can reconnect with the spiritual power and light within, beneath, and behind the illness, sadness, anger, hurt, depression, fear, or despondency that you may feel.

The *"real you,"* your spiritual essence and soul, already exists within you. Thousands of individuals have done this work and have stepped into who they really are. The joy of this work is that you do not have to unduly suffer or be broken or go broke in any way to come back to you. You can mend the gap within you, and you already have the tools within you to do it.

Most of us do not even know we have a gap. For some of us, there might be one gap to mend, and for others there may be 5, 10, or 20. Everyone who takes the *One in Soul* Process deep enough will experience the aspects within their heart and soul that were not allowed or given permission to exist. These aspects are the expression and living presence of God living in you, and they are attempting to live and thrive as you. It is amazing but true that we live in a world culture that teaches us to abandon, betray, and reject the most important and crucial energies within us. If allowed to exist, they give us total freedom, harmony, abundance, and the ability to create a whole life. Amazing, isn't it?

To begin to experience living fully embodied as your divine and empowered Self, you must create a foundation of wholeness. Your foundation is created by accepting the light within all of you—one step at a time. The idea is so simple, but we often make the practice so hard. Within these pages you will receive the tools, meditations, and practices to help you along your path of acceptance. However, one thing you should know about this pathway is that it is not about taking on a belief system or particular approach to become more spiritual or evolved. It is simply and truly about recognizing and embracing what exists within you and letting go of all of the ways you hold back, cover up, block and limit you BEing YOU.

In the *One in Soul* experience, you are also *not* being asked to go into the raw, unhealed emotions within you and process them to attain healing. Instead, you are being guided to fully embrace yourself with absolute love and accept all that is within you—even the parts that feel like the darkest, most unlovable aspects of who you are—within the intention of transmuting them into the light. As you live *One in Soul*, you will be able to transform and release the expressions and beliefs of your body, mind, and soul that no longer serve your evolution into Oneness. On this adventure, your role is to be the "acceptor." Accept, embrace, and radiate light to whatever presents itself within you. As you shine your greatest light onto the parts of yourself that long to be uplifted and transformed, an expression of greater peace and love will wash over you, like the rays of the sun on a cool, autumn day. The pain and drama that exists within your unhealed emotions will organically begin to dissolve through light and love's embrace. Being *One in Soul* will give you back your *I AM Self,* and you will be able to release all that you are "not."

> *As you shine your greatest light onto the parts of yourself that long to be uplifted and transformed, an expression of greater peace and love will wash over you, like the rays of the sun on a cool, autumn day.*

Unlock the Door

This work is an adventure that tests your desire to LOVE. You must be willing to move and live beyond your attachment and identity with the beliefs and behaviors that enslave you. You must be willing to step through the initial discomfort and fear that may rise up, which serves as a barrier to your inner breakthrough. Your desire will take you home. Practice being in the light and in your heart as often as you can. The light in your heart will become your sanctuary, your temple of love. It is the place that you can call home. Allow the homeless, confused, disorientated energies from your mind and body to be touched and embraced by the light within your heart. If you do nothing more than meditate into the light within your heart and ask Source Light to fill you with more light, more love, and the ability to surrender to the call of your soul, you will begin to break through the deepest resistances and challenges of your soul to find your Whole Self. Please know that the most important key to unlocking the power of your soul is to unlock the door guarding your deepest essence and soul Self. *All that is needed is a willingness to LOVE.*

REMEMBER:

- The light that lives within your soul is your ultimate teacher and healer. The way out of your own limitation is to access the greater wisdom and connection waiting within your soul aspects.

- When you feel most hopeless, or like it is just too hard to face life's challenges, then you can begin to recognize that your current ego structures and modus operandi are ineffective and worn out.

- You are a divine, enlightened, and highly evolved being who has a built-in capacity to live in alignment with light rather than the darkness.

- The currents of energy that emanate from the strength or weakness of your connection to Infinite Source feed your soul. Your challenge is to access, stabilize, and reconnect your energies so that your soul blueprint can be fully revealed and expressed.

- Your primal energies are the raw, pure, undiluted experience of how you are in relationship to life in your body. Your primal energies always exist in your *First* and *Second Power Point Centers.*

- Soul reconnection is an experience that heals the deepest primal and spiritual energies within you. When you are clearing your soul energies in your body, you are reconstructing your primal archetypal energies and spiritual power together.

- When you reconnect your mind, body and heart, you will experience the aspects within your soul that were not allowed or given permission to exist. These aspects are the expression and living presence of God living in you, and attempting to live and thrive as you.

- Your foundation for wholeness begins by accepting and embracing all aspects of yourself—those you perceive to be both good and bad—one step at a time.

- To unlock the power of your soul, you must unlock the door guarding your deepest essence and soul Self. *All that is needed is a willingness to LOVE.*

- If you do nothing more than meditate into the light within your heart and ask Source Light to fill you with more light, more love, and the ability to surrender to the call of your soul, you will break through the deepest resistances and challenges of your soul to begin to find your Whole Self.

BELIGHT MEDITATION

Opening

Find one moment in the past 24 hours that you chose to judge something about yourself or someone else.

Choose unconditional love and forgiveness for yourself for falling into judgment. Breathe into your heart center.

CHAPTER FIVE

Your Soul 101

"Feelings and emotions are only the creation of mind and energy. Love is the creation of the soul."
— Meher Baba

Soul Questions & Answers

To assist you on your journey into the complexities of your soul, it is helpful to make sure you know what is meant by "the soul." When someone throws around a concept like "the soul," most people have at least some general sense of what it is, even if they cannot always put it into words. In the initial chapters, you received at least some understanding of how the soul is being defined. If you were to Google it or look it up in an encyclopedia or Wikipedia, it might be defined as "the immortal essence of a person, living thing, or object; the immaterial part of a person, the sum total of one's thoughts and personality;" or something that is "synonymous with the Spirit, mind or Self."[1]

---
1 Soul. (2013, August 21). In Wikipedia, The Free Encyclopedia. Retrieved 01:36, August 28, 2013, from http://en.wikipedia.org/w/index.

All of those possible variations might still leave you a bit unclear about what, in fact, it *IS*. You might still ask if the soul is really just what is in your mind. Is your soul something that exists because you make it exist, or can it truly be something completely separate from the mind that transcends your body and even this lifetime?

To help you in your own soul discovery process, consider these commonly asked questions about the soul that have come up over decades of working with clients. Think of this is as your SOUL 101 "fast pass" that gets at *the heart and soul* of the soul.

What Is A Soul?

While there are numerous definitions of what a soul is, it is fundamentally a light body. The soul is a form or expression of light and energy made manifest in the physical world that comes from Infinite Source. If you could see your soul, it would appear as a charged ball of white and gold light. The soul is a core or seed of consciousness that exists in all human beings and animals. It carries the essence of all life and *your* eternal essence. It is who you really are. Your soul and every soul is unique and eternal. Each soul has its own needs, purpose, and soul-journey to experience in this and over many lifetimes.

Your soul is not something that appears visible to the average person or naked eye given the way that most people see the world. To see the soul, you must live and function at a multidimensional level that taps into your higher spiritual centers. Most of us don't see from our spiritual centers. However, as you learn to open up your spiritual faculties, you will begin to see and perceive the way things really are and actually see a person's soul. You will see the light body within a person and the

php?title=Soul&oldid=569521997.

deeper reality that we are all containers of light. We all express varying degrees of energy in motion or stagnation, depending on the state of our mind, body, and soul connection. Through opening the spiritual centers in your body and shifting how you see, feel, and experience everyday life, your soul and the soul of others will be revealed.

Imagine an egg. The outer shell of the egg is your body, and the yolk inside is your soul. It is the primary "content" of your egg. Your yolk, or soul, is meant to remain intact. While the ideal is to maintain a pure yolk and a whole shell, various circumstances or things we do to ourselves tend to scramble, fry, or just plain break our yolk and outer shell in more ways than can be imagined. More often than not, we are like humpty dumpty who has fallen off the wall, and then we spend this and possibly many more lifetimes trying to put ourselves back together again. We are all just trying to become whole again and reconnect with the source of all life and light. At some point on our soul journey, we want to be "who we really are," freed up from the pain and baggage that we've carried for many lifetimes.

Your soul is really so much bigger than your current body, and bigger than this lifetime. As you may recall, one of its core functions is to help you remember who you truly are. As the repository of your higher essence and truth, it moves you forward and pushes you to experience life in ways that open up the possibility for greater wholeness or completion. When a soul is whole, you are in effect reconnecting with your essential Self, your truth, and the deeper reality of your Oneness with all of Creation. For most of us, this reconnection process occurs over many lifetimes and through living in different human and animal forms.

As strange as this may sound, the essential you never really dies. Your soul, which is light, lives on forever. Why? Light cannot be destroyed. It is only transformed into a different creation. Given that you and your soul are light, you are always connected to Infinite Source. This is true even at the moment when you inevitably leave your current body. When you leave your present-day physical manifestation, your soul is then freed to transform and take on another form.

Where Does A Soul Come From?

The soul originates from the creation energy contained within God—Infinite Source. Creation energy is the spark of life. It is the original light that created the universe. It ignites pure consciousness into formlessness and form. You might think of it as raw, formless power that, like an atom, contains positive and negative energetic charge. It feels like a combination of hot fire and an open sea, holding the possibility of all of creation. Souls are created directly from Infinite Source through the feminine expression of raw power. When a soul is created, it is the birthing of light into pure energy and matter. Imagine a female deity, creating and birthing new souls into the world. This being has a full time job. We are all connected to the same source of power. *Souls are created through the union of divine energetic forces, which are expressed in the body as positive and negative energy, masculine and feminine force, and love and power.*

Infinite Source itself has an internal capacity and desire to discover and express itself in every possible way. The creation energy of Infinite Source expresses itself through the creation of souls, which are fundamentally an extension of its core light. It sends itself as light into the universe to explore and experience existence in all forms. Infinite Source experiences itself through all of our personal journeys of expansion and contraction—what we know as the human condition—through being conscious and unconscious.

When Infinite Source creates souls and sends them out into the universe to experience life in a multitude of ways, it is then able to experience itself more fully and completely as we learn to fully embrace and experience the light and dark that is within us. As we consciously awaken to our relationship with Infinite Source, there exists a continual process of creation, expansion of light, and reconnection back into original light. This exploration of the universe and the human condition never stops. As we move with the power of its guidance in our life, we are able to expand in our soul awareness and in the world with others simultaneously.

Why Do Souls Exist?

Souls are created by Infinite Source and are given the opportunity to awaken, individuate, and explore their full connection and full BEing. Each soul is an expression of Infinite Source itself. A soul is always connected to Infinite Source, but when it chooses to become individualized, it is given the choice to remain consciously connected to Infinite Source as pure light or to begin its journey of awakening by creating separation and disconnection from Infinite Source in order to explore, discover, and become self-actualized until it rediscovers that it is love and has always been the love that God Is. It expands itself into different expressions like an atom or molecule would in order to discover, create, or experience new aspects of itself. Your soul has a drive and a desire to find itself and express and discover itself in different ways. It goes through the gateways of exploring human will or free will and ultimately surrenders into divine will. Built within your soul is the longing to be whole and to remember its full connection and relationship with Infinite Source and to return home to BEing its true essence once again.

If you take the time to be present and connect with a child, he or she provides a window into how the soul works and what it is. Children are pure expressions of soul and use the faculty of imagination to discover themselves and explore what and who they are. Through creative exploration and the trying on of roles, emotions, and experiences, they, like the soul, come to understand and find their essential Self. The purpose of each soul is to become and experience all aspects of itself, which ultimately ends in its complete or "whole" expression. Once each soul does this, they are then ready to begin the journey home to Infinite Source.

This process is really what the 13th century fable of the Holy Grail was all about. Your soul longs to return back to Infinite Source, light, and to know creation energy. To discover the way or path into the Source within yourself, you must move through the vast terrain of your heart and soul. As in any good fable, each soul goes through all of the experiences that life can bring in order to ultimately know itself. For example, everyone goes through lifetimes or stages of finding their power, and even identifying and feeling their power to the point where they believe that their ego Self is God. It takes courage and perseverance to choose to reconnect to Infinite Source and to dissolve our old ties with the ego. We are all here to explore all facets of Infinite Source, and the love and power associated with it. People often use, misuse, and abuse their power. When guided by their Whole Self, they can do "good" with it. Our journey to find the Holy Grail is in actuality a state of unified consciousness that is discovered within the center of you where Spirit, your body, and soul interconnect. This portal—your inner Holy Grail—is the gateway into infinite consciousness. Here you will have a glimpse into your God Self and have the opportunity to become One with its omnipresent state of love. Here you will find the eternal treasure of life that brings long life, happiness, and spiritual fulfillment. Finding Oneness with Infinite Source is to drink from the Holy Grail.

We each have to find the voice and presence of our soul so we can consciously experience BEing awakened. We are all here to get clear and in touch with our pure selves in order to be able to live as One with Infinite Source. *We must all learn to find our inner light and learn how to use our power and love appropriately.* This is what the journey of the soul is about. We learn through the various circumstances and experiences of life, including, but not limited to, parenting, being a subordinate, being born discriminated against, running a company, choosing a family that challenges our core truths, an addiction, being in a dead end job, passionately following our dreams, dealing with a chronic illness, losing someone we love, finding a real spiritual teacher, mastering an artistic expression, travelling, etc. Whatever we face offers the potential for us to become even more expansive than when we first entered this world.

We are here as humans to successfully navigate through this maze and to go past the limitations of our minds and belief systems to find our real light. The more we become an authentic expression of our true light, the more whole we become, and the more connected we are with Infinite Source. It is an enormous gift and opportunity to explore and become one with God through human form. We make it more difficult because we fail to understand that we are already actually ONE with God. Infinite Source offers us the opportunity to remember that we are One with life by helping us to remember and embrace the truths of birth and death. Each time we are birthed, we can then bring in more experience, understanding, light and love to expand—to become a bigger, fuller version of ourselves. God is constantly expanding, helping us to be conscious participants in the process of life so that we all become bigger. Then, we have more to give to the universe. Each time that we die we can learn from our choices, make new choices, experience the power of the light, recreate our relationship with life and Infinite Source, and evolve to the next level of being a conscious co-creator.

Why Does the Soul Matter?

Your soul is your fundamental Self and the pure essential image of God—Infinite Source. It encompasses all of the characteristics of life and creation. The soul is filled with your purpose, and the expressions of your authentic and True Self over eons of time. Your soul knows truth and will relentlessly create circumstances in your life to awaken you to its existence. Your soul matters because it is the part of you that reincarnates from lifetime to lifetime, and most importantly has the ability to touch, know, receive, and integrate all of the life forces and powers of Infinite Source.

Ultimately, the soul has a need to dissolve into Infinite Source and reunite with its original creator. It will do this any way that it can until you choose the path of least resistance and self-created pain. Your soul will seek its reconnection or disconnection to the creator through career challenges, relationships, artistic endeavors, drugs, alcohol, sex, positions of power, health challenges, religion, meditation, and love. Your goal is to find the path within you that will give you the ability to consistently stay connected to Infinite Source while your consciousness is integrating all aspects of your soul.

Some people move through life numb and asleep. Some people possess a certain degree of awareness about life and who they are. Some people have a higher consciousness and understanding about their place and role in the universe. Your challenge is to listen to your soul and be fully present, aware, and engaged with all of the feelings and hidden parts of your

Self. You are on a treasure hunt for the divine aspects of you, and you always have a choice as to what path you will take. Your mind makes choices every single moment, whether you know it or not. If you think of yourself as a car, when your soul is awakened you have to choose if you are going to give the steering wheel of your car to your soul or let your mind and preconceived belief systems continue to run you. Who will drive? When you decide to let the soul drive, you can then move on a path of freedom.

REMEMBER:

- Your heart and soul are the core of your human and spiritual essence.

- The soul is fundamentally a light body. It is an expression of light and energy made manifest in the physical world that comes from Infinite Source. It feels like a combination of hot fire and an open sea, holding the possibility of all of creation.

- Souls are created by Infinite Source and are given the opportunity to awaken, individuate, and explore their full connection and full BEing. Ultimately your soul desires to be whole and to remember its full connection and relationship with God—Infinite Source.

- Your soul reconnection process is really your own Holy Grail path. Your soul longs to return back to the light of Infinite Source.

- The journey of the soul is about learning to find your inner light and learning how to use the power and love within you appropriately. We are all here to explore all facets of God, and to embody the light that we each are.

- The soul is filled with your purpose, and the expressions of your authentic and True Self over eons of time. Your challenge is to listen to your soul and be fully present, aware, and engaged with all of the feelings and hidden parts of your Self and bring them into the light within your heart.

- You are on a treasure hunt to discover the gateways to the divine presence and truth of your BEing. How you get here is always your choice.

CHAPTER SIX

Your Soul 201: Understanding Your Soul Journey

*"Your truth lives in the light of your soul.
Trust the wisdom that you find there and live it fully."*
— Mahama Iana

You have a soul, and it matters. It is the eternal part of you that lives on lifetime-to-lifetime and carries the DNA of your essential True Self, which is part of the tapestry of Infinite Source. Each of our souls has its own unique threading and connection to the universal whole. The interlaced colors and facets of your BEing bring meaning and shape to the textile of existence. The purpose of your life is to know, express, and complete your soul and experience its connection with Infinite Source. We are all on a great soul journey back to the ONE, and your life is a hero's journey to rediscover the whole you. Your soul journey is uniquely designed and directed by you, and only you can walk, jog, or run it. You have the power to choose and know your own soul, regardless of the people and circumstances of your life. What are you going to do?

Accepting the call of your soul often means going on a journey into the unknown terrain and depths of your integrated human and Divine Self and your intimate connection to unseen dimensions. You may wonder what you will face as you follow your path to your soul. What will it be like? What experiences can you expect? How will you know you are on it? These and other questions that have been asked by fellow soul travelers will be answered here. The journey of your soul often initially feels like an uncertain, unpredictable mystery, but it holds the wondrous possibility of your complete fulfillment.

Soul Journey Questions

Can You Describe How Souls Change Or Evolve? How Do Souls Begin?

It is helpful to think of the soul as going through seven progressive evolutionary levels of development as it expresses itself on this physical, earthly plane. Avatar Meher Baba shared a very helpful understanding of these evolutionary levels in his book *God Speaks*. He identified that the soul passes through seven kingdoms: from stone to metal, from metal to vegetable, from vegetable to worm, from worm to fish, from fish to bird, from bird to animal, and from animal to human being. The soul in human form is a collective of all of these states of being. It is level seven along the evolutionary path. Each level that we have passed through leaves energetic imprints within us. Your existence and expression as a human being means you are an expression or composite of that entire soul collective and all of the experiences you had while living and moving through the seven levels. It also explains why human beings are such creative, expressive, multi-dimensional beings.

YOUR SOUL 201: UNDERSTANDING YOUR SOUL JOURNEY

As wonderful as human beings are, making it to level seven doesn't mean your spiritual work is done. In many ways it has just begun. As the soul evolves through the various levels, it collects sanskaras (impressions), which are imprints left on the subconscious by past and present life experiences, which determine and condition one's desires and actions. Upon stepping onto the path back to God—Infinite Source, the sanskaras imprinted in your soul must be unraveled and dissolved. Your soul carries these impressions from previous lifetimes into your next physical body incarnation through the subtle and mental bodies.

All human beings must clear their sanskaras (projections, attachments, perceptions, and illusions) as part of the evolution of their souls into higher states of consciousness and being.

Being a human being is a great gift. After eons of time, we are given the opportunity to master the traits of being a conscious human being. We must learn the basic lessons of taking responsibility for our own thoughts and actions, discover how we separate from Infinite Source, and become aligned in every aspect of our life to the divine nature of our True Self. The truth of who we are in the center of our soul once ignited, honored, and implemented shifts our existence from living in a narrow and confined mental perspective that causes suffering and pain, into the expansive, unlimited, and full potential of our humanity.

> *"Learn the art of taking your stand on the Truth within. When you live in this Truth, the result is the fusion of mind and heart and the end of all fears and sorrow. It is not a dry attainment of mere power or intellectual knowledge. A love which is illumined by the intuitive wisdom of spirit will bless your life with ever-renewing fulfillment and never-ending sweetness."*
> —*Avatar Meher Baba*

As your soul becomes whole, the natural power and love of your soul will guide your life. You are able to slow down or stop collecting more sanskaras because you are following the guidance found by your soul and Infinite Source being in divine union. When you make "errors," "false judgments," or "mistakes," you are aware of them faster than you might have been in the past. As you move forward along your path, you begin to experience your original infinite state of consciousness and will eventually come to know yourself as pure bliss and divine expression.

What Is The Soul Journey? What Is Its Purpose? Does It End In This Lifetime?

The soul journey begins with the awakening of the part of your heart that yearns for greater happiness and the feeling of "there has got to be more than this." Your soul desires to be at peace with, in love with, and most fully expressed as itself. Your Soul comes to touch and to be touched by Spirit's grace. Spirit comprises all of the energies of life and holds together the matrix of life. It is the eternal intelligence of Infinite Source. When connected to Spirit, you possess "knowingness" about life and your relationship with everything around you. Through your soul becoming whole and integrating with Spirit, you fulfill the purpose to connect into the love that is in everything.

The soul needs to experience itself in relationship to light, love, expansion, and fulfillment while on its earth journey. It seeks to awaken itself through expressing both its individual nature and by merging with all universal energies. It is constantly exploring its relationship to itself and all things. The soul exists beyond time and space and is a multidimensional consciousness. It discovers greater expressions of its light and love throughout eternity. It explores itself through different life forms in other solar systems and galaxies. Through the soul's powerful expressions and explorations, it is in a constant process of evolution. It evolves through becoming aware of its true nature and the bliss, peace, and expansion experienced merging consciously with Infinite Source.

When The Soul Leaves The Body Does It Always Come Back As A More Evolved Form Of Itself, Or Can It Come Back As A Different Life Form, Such As A Mouse Or A Bird?

One's afterlife depends upon one's spiritual advancement when in the body. Once a soul develops into human form, it must go through many incarnations over lifetimes to realize its True Self.

One's True Self is the essence of one's God Self that eventually merges into Oneness with deeper levels of Infinite Source as it evolves.

If a person *severely* misuses the powers they have gained on their spiritual path during his or her life, it is possible to fall back to the lowest phase of evolution, which is the stone state. He or she will then have to begin their soul journey again. If the powers gained through the life path are used correctly, the individual soul will continue to reincarnate as a human until they have reached full enlightenment. Most souls continue to evolve through taking on different statuses in each lifetime. Most reincarnate and balance themselves by taking on female and male lifetimes or coming back with different religious beliefs and practices, or by being born into different races and creeds. Having a different status in each lifetime does not catapult you backwards into past life forms of consciousness.

People continue to go through the world of human duality until they have had an awakening that beckons them to look deeper and to seek Infinite Source, which is their true "home." In some rare cases, some souls choose to incarnate as an animal to be able to experience being and serving in total surrender, such as coming back as a horse, dog, elephant, dolphin, etc. Your soul will continue to come back in numerous incarnations to fully express and know itself in all ways. This is part of your soul journey back to Infinite Source.

The purpose of being a soul in human form is to experience conscious reconnection with Infinite Source. The soul journey consists of becoming aware of how it believes that it left or "separated" from Infinite Source, or that "it was left, abandoned, and separated from." In truth, the soul is always One with Infinite Source. Being in a human form, because of its highly developed DNA, offers the opportunity to become realized of its true identity as a divine being and as a "molecule of Infinite Source" who is constantly shifting, changing, and merging into higher states of existence.

If A Soul Does Something Bad, What Happens To The Soul?

If a soul does something truly bad or evil in a lifetime—for example, if they are a mass murderer—then the soul has to compensate for its bad actions. It will have to repeat rounds of lifetimes to learn the lessons from the mind-thread and actions that caused pain, hardship, grief, and loss in another or others. The soul will also have to go through the same kind of situation again, but it will be on the receiving end in a lifetime in order to complete its karma. For example, a soul that has acted as "a perpetrator" will quickly experience being "a victim" in order to complete the full circle of its actions. Everything we experience and do has an impact on our soul, even if the results of those actions may not be fully felt until future lifetimes.

It is also possible to come into complete transparency and truth with one's actions. A person can release the patterns that created an offense or act of violence through BEing One with

Infinite Source through the process of self-forgiveness, atonement, honesty, and transcendence of their ego nature. They must "come clean" regarding their violations of spiritual law through complete forgiveness of one's self and returning to Oneness with Infinite Source. Everyone has a different balance of positive and negative karma, which is built up over lifetimes and creates different outcomes. One's positive and negative karma must be balanced to return to God.

What Are The Specific Things People Go Through For Their Souls To Move Forward?

We all begin to question who we are at some point. Most of us begin as a child to question and explore who we are. Our soul yearns to belong and to feel a part of something bigger than itself. Our soul wants to be seen, heard, and received because when these three qualities are fulfilled, the soul feels like it exists.

The soul has the choice at birth to derive its identity from its parents or from its connection to something greater—its divine essence. Most of us choose to leave our Self in order to be loved by the people in our lives. It is what "we know" and the model within which we are raised. We are taught that if we look, act, and can be a certain way that mirrors our own parent's needs and desires, then we are lovable. Unbeknownst to most of us, our choice to connect with the more external, conditional love from family and friends means that we end up letting go of parts of our Self and the bigger love that has always existed inside of us. We lose touch with the reservoir of internal love within us as we reach for the external love of others. What we all really want to experience in our soul is unconditional and infinite love. What we frequently get is something less.

As much as some parents may dislike hearing this, there are not enough parents who know how to love their child on the level of complete unconditional and infinite love. Love is given if a child is good, behaves, or fulfills what parents want, need, or expect. When a child is loved with the devotion and intensity of God—Infinite Source itself, the child knows that it is worthy of life just for being itself. It does not matter if the child fails to fit the parents' own needs, expectations, or desires. Every child deserves to be exactly who it is on a soul level and loved for BEing who they are. The greatest gift that a parent can give a child is to support him/her to fully develop in their true essence. This gift allows the child to stay true to itself, develop its authentic identity through union with Infinite Source, find her/his full inner light, and learn to BE ONE with their divine Self rather than solely identifying with his or her external environment as the mirror to who they should be. The child grows up knowing who she or he is.

Most of us spend our lives trying to find, receive, or give the love we have longed for since birth. The soul's journey is fundamentally about doing whatever it takes to find that love within us. Only when people can love themselves will a greater love then manifest in their external relationships and environment. Therefore, what all souls must go through to move forward is to find and become unified through **LOVE**.

To embrace and explore your soul:

- Put aside your fears for even just a moment to find love. The soul loves love and will sacrifice everything just to taste love's sweetness.

- Move towards living in full connection with your heart. Your soul wants to live through your heart but needs you to say "YES" to opening up your heart. Only you can make the choice to allow your soul to take up space and enter into your heart. When this happens, you can truly be "in love" in yourself.

- Embrace grief, sadness, or depression. Be with it and meet it with all of your heart. When you open to your soul and all of its fragmented parts, your soul begins to express how it has felt being separate from your Whole Self and the full light of Infinite Source. Yet, if you can be with its expression and begin to reconnect your separated parts, the negative emotions will fade. Underneath the emotions exist your kernels of wisdom, truth, and light.

- See through the dark into the awaiting light.

- Allow the awakening light within your consciousness to begin to reconnect your body, mind, and soul with Source Energy.

- Move towards being ONE with life and with others around you. When you feel ONE with your soul, you will automatically begin to feel ONE with life and with the world around you. You may feel drawn to helping others and shifting your career or your perspective to help you live a more integrated and empowering lifestyle.

Along with this desire for love exists an equally compelling push for **FREEDOM**. Your soul will:

- Seek to know itself beyond limitations, projections, and identifications from your mind and the external world. Your soul wants you to expand and know yourself in relationship to the universe. This means that you must be willing to move beyond the typical mind chatter that runs you to find your deeper truth, which comes from the true expressions and feelings emanating from your soul.

- Explore and find all of itself through adventure, energy awareness, service, expression, creativity, love, fulfillment, and awareness.

In order for the soul to feel ONE with life and the universe, it must be connected and aligned to all of itself. These "selves" or aspects of your soul are always ready to be found. You just need to know what to look for. When you find an aspect of your soul that hasn't been fully allowed to exist, your job is to acknowledge and love it and let it be expressed. As previously stated, your soul will try to complete itself through and with another person if it has abandoned its conscious connection with Infinite Source as its identity. Yet, as the soul awakens, it will come to realize that the only way to *BE complete* is through itself. When you love another, it will come from an overflowing wellspring created by being sourced from within yourself. Your relationships will be created and sustained through sharing the joy that you are rather than trying to be filled up by another. You will feel One unto yourself.

Your soul will always move toward the light. It may meditate, emote, create, love, or explore itself through the arts, love, God, or nature. It may choose to seek what it has lost through new life experiences that touch into forgotten parts of itself that are waiting to be found. Your light is deep inside your soul, and it is the wayshower or guide leading back to Source energy. The light is what illuminates the parts of your soul that have been sleeping in the dark. As your soul awakens, it is common to feel some amount of sadness and grief. This occurs as the soul realizes all of the moments that it has been disconnected, or became foreign or separate from itself. It may also feel like it is impossible to live the life that you are born to live. Yet once you are reconnected and "in the love" within yourself, you can trust your feelings completely and move forward on your soul path.

Until that time, your soul will feel disorientated and disempowered when it is living in separation. To compensate, your personality Ego Self will try to exert its influence through acquiring material objects, staying in control, sabotaging your ultimate freedom, living in denial, or focusing on distractions. Your ego will take over to become the predominant communicator or lens by which you perceive, feel, and interact with yourself and with the world. While living in separation, the soul has no direct "in" or way to communicate with itself or with others, so the ego becomes the mediator. Your ego filters your feelings and perceptions until your True Self fills your heart. When your soul unites with your heart, there is a moment of realizing that you can choose the wholeness of your soul over your ego.

Fundamentally, your soul is bigger than your ego, mind, or body alone. It knows that it is the source and power for moving your life forward. As your soul aspects are reunited in your heart, you feel ONE with life. When your key soul aspects are separated and disconnected in your body, you will most likely feel that your life is not yet yours and that it belongs to someone or something else. There is a sense of a giant hole within you that you want filled. Once you have reconnected the love and power aspects of your soul, and have found your Whole Self, you can open to and embody the spiritual forces of life. You can access the profound vastness of the universe and embark upon finding your True Self, the essence of your divine Oneness. When you are one with your soul, you can release your mind from its duty of being in control. It will attempt to hang on to control until your awakened power is restored. Your fully awakened power is restored once your soul knows that it is ONE with Source, living in its full light, and can trust the love within itself.

How Do You Know Your Soul Is Complete and Whole?

You will know your soul is whole when it is reconnected into its authentic and original love and power, and is happy just being itself. The need to possess and accumulate ends. The need to be right ends. The need to live through others ends. The ability to handle major life challenges with grace, surrender, and trust inspires you to be responsible in every area of your life. You understand that practicing your ability to respond to life with integrity is being responsible. You will be able to handle the ups and downs and unexpected turns of life with a greater peaceful ease and serenity. You feel stable and empowered, even when things may be rough. Life is filled in perfect synchronicity.

This process, where your full, internal love and power co-exist, cannot be realized until you let go of control. No matter how enlightened you may think you are, how much you meditate, or how many vegetables you eat, your soul's completion will not happen until your mind lets go of its need to run or control your life. You must lead your life from the integrated center of your heart, Spirit, and soul rather than solely from your mind.

You may naturally resist this process. The reason you may resist is because the creative energies and life forces that come from your awakening soul threaten your egoic mind. Your ego attempts to maintain control over everything in your life. It has worked hard to compensate for what it perceives as your weaknesses. It wants to see you survive but from its own interpretations of Maya, illusion. For the soul to be whole and fully expressed in its truth, the ego mind must release and let go.

YOUR SOUL 201: UNDERSTANDING YOUR SOUL JOURNEY

Your Whole Self, led by your heart and soul, is the true leader of your life, not your mind. Your mind is the servant of your soul.

When the soul is whole, it will naturally move your life forward in the right direction for your life. You, and more specifically your mind, have a choice to make. Your mind can surrender to the unknown that awaits, which may feel a bit like you are a little out of control, but feels freer and happier. It can also choose to stay in battle with your soul. In the latter instance, it may lead to disease, or repetition of negative patterns, relationships, or events over and over until you get that you need to shift. Eventually your mind will release its hold on you, even if it means the death of your body. Yet, you do not have to wait until a life or death situation arises before you let go and allow your heart and soul to take the lead by reconnecting the power of your light in your body. Beyond all resistance lives your God Self.

You can be complete and whole and live your life from joy. As you live from your heart and no longer fear or separate from the aspects of yourself that have been alone and isolated, you will grow stronger. You will experience saying from your heart to your ego mind, "I no longer give you my power to keep me in fear. It is time to serve the light that I am." Then, the fears that hold your ego mind in place can begin to let go. As you choose actions that free you up, rather than constrict you to the dictates of your ego mind, you will open with lightning speed.

It is important to get that it does not matter what you are presently dealing with or how you have lived your life last year, yesterday, or two seconds ago. You can change your focus, perspective, and initiative for your life in a moment. You can maximize your effort and learn what you need to practice in your mind, heart, soul, and Spirit to live as a fully expressed human and divine BEing right now.

What Happens To The Soul When It Feels Whole?

When the soul is whole, it is able to perform its highest service from a state of total detachment, love, and divine intelligence. The whole soul at first has moments of knowing that it is intimately connected to the divine and moves in and out of being conscious of BEing One in Source. Reality between the inner and outer worlds feels harmonious, and while there may still be difficulties that arise on the physical plane, there is trust and faith that permeates every situation. A sense of limitation and despair disappear, and in their place resides an ongoing infinite bliss and communication with Infinite Source.

Each of us has different challenges to master to become one in our soul. For example, discovering the qualities of compassion, humility, selfless giving, unconditional love, kindness, etc. need to be awakened to become our Whole Self. These are a by-product of reconnecting and BEing One. We have to develop the awareness of how we shut down or push away the truth living within our soul and remain stuck in false thinking. We need to become aware of the energetic polarities of our personality Self in order to become balanced between our mind and heart. For example, if there is a need for outer approval, we would need to practice loving ourselves and accepting the power within our soul. If we tend to be extreme in one direction, we must balance it from another direction.

The whole soul has faced itself and has illuminated both the shining and dull aspects of itself. To become whole, we must let go of contracting into judgment, projection, and fear-based thinking. This practice also assists in ending further sanskaras or impressions from forming. By also practicing non-reaction, we give ourselves the opportunity to be in Infinite Source rather than spin out into false thinking. This is all part of becoming *One in Soul*.

REMEMBER:

- Your existence and expression as a human being means you are an expression or composite of an entire soul collective and all of the experiences you had while living and moving through the seven levels of existence.

- All human beings must clear their sanskaras as part of the evolution of their souls into higher states of consciousness and BEing. Your soul carries sanskaras or impressions from previous lifetimes into your next physical body incarnation through the subtle and mental bodies.

- The purpose of your soul journey is to connect into the love that is in everything and especially in you.

- It does not matter how you have lived your life last year, yesterday, or two seconds ago. You can change your focus, perspective, and initiative for your life in a moment. You can maximize your effort and learn what you need to practice in your mind, heart, soul, and spirit to live as a fully expressed human and divine being.

- When you reconnect the aspects of your soul that comprise your Whole Self, you find your core energy. Your work is to stay tuned and connected to knowing and BEing true to yourself through embracing all of the aspects of yourself from your heart and using them to feel and BE full and whole on the inside.

- What all souls must go through to move forward is to find and become unified through LOVE. In order for the soul to feel that love, BE One with life and the universe, it must be connected and aligned to all aspects or fragments of itself and be willing to let go of its old patterns.

- Your soul is bigger than your ego mind or body alone. Until your soul is whole and its full power is restored, your ego mind won't give up sole control of you.

- You will know your soul is whole when it is reconnected into its authentic and original love and power. This will show up in your life as being able to handle the ups and downs and unexpected turns of life with a greater peaceful ease and serenity. You feel stable and empowered, even when things may be rough.

- You don't have to wait until your life is in crisis to finally complete your soul.

BELIGHT MEDITATION

Select the ones that "speak to you" most. Be mindful and practice them on a daily basis as you live your everyday life.

Here are *Twelve Practices* to help you clear and release sanskaras to evolve your soul:

- Practice forgiveness

YOUR SOUL 201: UNDERSTANDING YOUR SOUL JOURNEY

- Chant and vibrate these sounds of God long and deep into your heart center or third eye—or both. Allow the tongue to touch the roof of the mouth when natural. Place your hands on your thighs, palms up, with your thumb and second finger (index finger) touching. Experience which of the following vibratory sounds of God work the best for you:

    AH HUM (ah-hoom)
    OM HUM (oh-mm-huu-mm)
    ELOHIM (ee-lo-heem)
    EE-AH-OO-AY
    OM-AY-AH
    OM (AUM)
    SAT NAM
    HU (huuuu)
    ONG SO HUNG (ang so hung)
    EEE (eeee)
    EEE VAH (ccee-vah)
    ELAH-HA (eeee-la-ha)
    AH (ahhh)
    SO HUNG (so-hunngggg)
    ONG SAU (ong sa)
    OM KAUR
    HAM SA (ha-mmm-sa)
    SO HUM (sew-hummm)
    AESHAMAY (ay-ee-sha-may)
    EASHOA (ee-ay-show-ah)
    LA ILAHA ILLALLAH (la-ee-la-ha-il-lal-lah)

- End cyclical patterns of giving away your power, repressing your creativity, personally loving the wrong people, empowering your ego, separating from your divine feminine or divine masculine, or both, living in your head, etc.

- Refuse to act out of greed, ignorance, attachment, anger, vanity, and pride—Avoiding these can prevent the creation of new sanskaras

- Practice non-attachment to outcomes

- Realize the beliefs you created during a past experience, trauma, or situation and let them go

- Do your *One in Soul* reconnection work to initiate the truth of your soul

- Live fearlessly, and find the light in your heart

- Be self-less and giving to others

- Meditate, develop breath awareness

- Live in your Whole Self by connecting your mind, body, and soul as One in the light and wisdom of Infinite Source within you

- Pay attention to what the universe is trying to teach you

CHAPTER SEVEN

Portals to Your True Self

*"What a wonderful lotus it is,
That blooms at the heart of the spinning wheel of the universe!
Only a few pure souls know of its true delight."*
— Rabindranath Tagore

Seeing, Feeling, and Being in a New Way

Within you are powerful entry portals into the unlimited realms of Infinite Source in your body—a safe haven for your True Self to be able to experience its God-inspired aliveness and love. You possess wondrous portals of light and meeting zones within your body known as *Power Point Centers*[2] where your Bodymind and Spirit can become ONE.

This multidimensional cosmically connected matrix of light and energy within you automatically connects you into your whole soul and True Self.

If you have had any exposure to yoga or meditation, you may be familiar with the concept of chakras. Chakras are energy

---
[2] *Spirit Gateways® Power Point Centers*

points or spinning wheels of energy within your subtle (non-physical) body that connect the spiritual and physical energies in your body and regulate their functions. Understanding that you embody *Power Points Centers* provides an expanded understanding of how energy and Source light flow and interact to open, align, and unify you with Infinite Source. *Power Point Centers* join together the essence of your soul selves with the distinctive ray of Spirit that flows through your body. By reconnecting into your centers, you can reunite the light of your consciousness with the physicality of your soul blueprint.

You are embarking upon a journey of exploration and integration of the light within your inner bodies. The power and love from the light of Infinite Source and Spirit will guide and teach you how to touch into these powerful energy portals to align your inner super highway. Through accessing the *Power Point Centers* in your body, you will gain "fastpass" entry into the energy grid of your True Self and a whole new level of integrated being.

> *Power Point Centers are light portals and meeting zones within your body where your Bodymind and Spirit can become ONE.*

The light that lives within you is the generator behind all of your spiritual growth, decision-making abilities, career and leadership successes, relationship fulfillment, creative gifts, and healing outcomes. The circuitry of light intelligence is always moving through you. When the light of Infinite Source is aligned within you, your higher mind can tap into new ways of seeing life, birth new ideas, live authentically, easily access creative solutions, and access a power of creation that is based in love. Your heart can feel the truth of love, and your soul can be restored and heal its splits. The *Power Point Centers* in your body are a 24/7 portal into the new light consciousness grid within you. As the light strengthens your Bodymind, pain and suffering lose their hold on you. If you connect into the light within your body, you can respond, act upon, and be empowered to change your life. You can learn how to align and connect into the Source of your life and know you are ONE with the divine. By listening and connecting into your body, you can feel, know, and see the truth for yourself. You can end all of the ways that you remain deaf and blind to the spiritual higher powers living within your body and soul.

Moving Through Blocks, Fear & Control

For most of us, the gifts of our soul hide below the surface. We live our lives unable to touch the real creative fuel of our inner Self. We each have our own inner reservoir filled with unresolved despair, loss, pain, anger, grief, sorrow, or fear. For many of us, we have tried many healing modalities to resolve our soul level issues, without total success. When you reconnect your soul energies into your physical and emotional bodies, and spiritual light grid, you rediscover the joy and divine connection that can guide you through your deepest challenges. The truth and essence of your BEing will miraculously manifest in your everyday existence.

The light of God, your divine truth, lives within you as your soul. Yet, through life circumstances, and ancestral, cultural, and past life issues that are brought forward, you create blockages that prevent you from accessing your light body. Your light body is the awakened consciousness of love that receives, transforms, and transmutes the direct energies of Infinite Source into a pure state of integrated physical and spiritual awareness. Your light body is awakened through activating your light grid, which is connected to your soul. It is an electro-magnetic system of light channels that connect you to universal light consciousness.

The journey to freedom begins by awakening the consciousness of God light in your light grid, Bodymind and soul. Through reconnecting your soul and clearing, healing, and integrating your *Power Point Centers*, you will feel the grounded presence of your heart come alive in your whole body. Through adopting a simple way of shifting your attention into your *Power Point Centers*, you will tap into being with yourself in a new way. When you activate the light within your *Power Point Centers* with the light of your soul, you will experience a divine and tangible connection into the light of Oneness.

To find the light that is your sanctuary within your mind, body, and soul, you have to access a new matrix of awareness. The fears and pain that you have held onto, through no fault of your own, can be released as you root yourself in the sanctuary of light within you. As you integrate your *Power Point Centers*, the sanctuary of light within you becomes accessible. Your inner center point of Oneness with God becomes tangible. A new way of thinking and being awakens within you that is a pure and direct connection to infinite intelligence, light, and brilliance.

After months of exploring the soul choices that I made as an infant and young toddler in this lifetime, I realized that I had chosen to close the door to the light that I AM. As a newborn, and within the first months of my life, my eyes sparkled like diamonds of light. By the age of one and then by the age of two, my energy field and my eyes were duller and filled with sadness. I thought about why I shut down to the light that I came in with. No one around me responded to the expressions of my light. I felt invisible and literally was invisible to my family of origin. I wasn't related to as a beautiful and unique new life. I was something that had to be taken care of and fed, which caused stress to my mother. I made the decision to be in the light that I AM in my inner world. I chose to be invisible and to not want or expect anything from anyone around me. I became self sufficient with the light in my inner world. Yet, I was also in conflict because the light that I felt within me gave me a deep need to express myself and to feel greater expansion.

I realized as an adult that we all have the choice to leave the light that we each are to seek love and acceptance from an external source, or to receive the light that is our connection to all of life in every moment and live in fulfillment. Some people will reincarnate just to learn the lesson of choosing to BE in the light of their True Self no matter what. Leaving the light that I AM caused me so much pain and suffering as a child that it pushed me into becoming a seeker of truth and spiritual light at the tender age of fourteen. This choice steered all of my life decisions for years to come.

> *To find the light that is your sanctuary within your mind, body, and soul you have to access a new matrix of awareness.*

The old matrix of established values and systems has taught you to separate and compartmentalize your mind, body, soul, and feelings. You are not taught how to know, listen to, see, or respond to your soul. Instead, you are taught to numb down your body and control it from your mind. The old matrix system teaches you to develop an ego mind that you use full time to evaluate your existence by staying disconnected and separate from life and living in the belief system that you can live your everyday life from being disconnected to the truth of your soul.

You are taught how to be a fake, live in your ego projections of others and towards your self, and block out the true meaning and reason for your existence.

The control and fear of your ego mind, when allowed to direct your life decisions, reactions, and responses, take you on a long, indirect path to your goals. Through choosing to come into the integration of your body, mind, and soul, you can enter a new matrix that opens the inner doorways beyond fear and control to your core strength and empowerment and realize that love is more powerful than fear. The purpose for igniting and reconnecting your *Power Point Centers* is to create a strong light body that can support your soul growth, implement your life purpose, and be a bridge to the new earth paradigm of Oneness. The *Power Point Centers*, once awakened into the light matrix within you, will connect you to your spiritual guides, universal consciousness, fearlessness, and love and help you trust in your own ability to walk forward on your highest destiny path.

> *The gateway through fear is accomplished by first sourcing the light within you.*

Finding Your Inner Light

History is the story of how light and dark are in relationship to one another. Their relationship is always evolving. The times of battle between light and dark, creating peace and breaking through light and dark conflict, embracing light and rejecting darkness, embracing darkness and rejecting light, all point to cracking the wall of illusions and resistance within our minds that sustain separation thinking. We are at a pinnacle in human history of beginning to recognize the patterns of how light and dark work. Our present matrix supports the values and beliefs of the systems set in place to govern people and use them for purposes that deny their humanity. Control, creating confusion, being careless, reckless, and self-serving to promote greed, arrogance, fear, violence, and separation has become a model that is beginning to be challenged and proven ineffective. The old matrix was developed to control the masses and establish fear on Earth instead of valuing the higher values of love that initiate freedom, expansion, and prosperity.

In order to move out of the traps of the old matrix, which usually require that you deny or repress your own power, heart, connection to infinite intelligence and knowingness, you need a new place within your body to reside from. The old matrix is an energetic grid constructed from the separation of the body, mind, soul, the universe, and light and when you allow it to define your life and who you are, you can feel yourself falling into ruts and repeating dead end patterns. The new matrix expands your focus from fear of the unknown into embracing the unknown. It works as an inner connection of Oneness that is found through reconnecting the body, mind, and soul into the light. The new matrix aligns the light consciousness of heaven and earth, and the divine intelligence of Infinite Source within each human being on a cellular level. The new matrix exists beyond the illusions of separation and initiates new response patterns to your Self and life. It takes you out of any of the careless or destructive patterns that you live out towards your self or others.

To find your inner light, you must connect into an expanded space of love and awareness that exists within you. For most of us, our frustrations with the world, our programmed emotional responses, our self-rejection of our body, and the denied truths living beneath our feelings make it almost impossible to discover and fulfill the destiny of our soul. The light existing in your *Power Point Centers*, when focused, cleared, and aligned with the Infinite Source of your soul, can help to dissolve the ancestral, cultural, and genetic patterns that create suffering in your life and block living in full expression of who you came here to BE. Your *Power Point Centers* are gateways into the pure, unchanging truth of your True Self.

The Light Within Your Body

Your body is a remarkable biological wonder. Within the cells and structures of your body live reservoirs of light. Your body chemistry, organs, muscles, ligaments, joints, skin tissue, and nervous and circulatory systems are all infused with the light of Infinite Source to create a highly intricate web of love. When you learn to open to the light within you, you are able to uplift your whole being into a profound reunion with Infinite Source and have the capacity to heal and BE a creator in ways you have not yet known. Through accessing your *Power Point Centers*, you will learn a new form of communication that will activate and communicate with your inner light system. It will translate and transform how you feel, see, and experience your body, mind, heart, and soul; your relationships; the world around you; and your place in it.

Vortexes of Power

Your *Power Point Centers* are portals of energy and consciousness that connect your soul, Spirit, Bodymind, and heart into Infinite Source. Within your *Power Point Centers* live the qualities of movement and stillness, positive and negative, light and dark. Your *Power Point Centers* touch into the transformative forces of love and power found within the divine masculine and divine feminine energies of your soul. They fuel your energies with infinite grace, divine guidance, and faith in the unseen forces of LIFE that take you out of despondency, pride, and fear into exuberant aliveness, clarity, and self-confidence. They resonate to truth, infinite intelligence, color, and sound. They are direct portals into God consciousness. Each *Power Point Center* is linked into the grid work of your physical and spiritual consciousness. When connected, they look like a geometric design of sheer beauty that is unique to you.

Your *Power Point Centers* directly connect into your nervous, digestive, endocrine, and circulatory systems. They awaken and connect life force in your body, integrate your sexuality and Spirit, balance your hormones, and allow for healing to occur in your body. They infuse your consciousness with your inborn wisdom, ground you, and make possible the full realization of your ideas and true soul mission. They open the gateways to your Original Self, bridge your conscious connection with Infinite Source, and assist you to release and let go of your old patterns and beliefs that no longer serve you. As you open and align to your *Power Point Centers*, you will feel more alive, integrated, and confident to transform and support the unfolding of love within yourself and BE YOU in the world. Directing the power of your light into greater action, focus, and creativity in all aspects of your life will feel natural.

> *Your Power Point Centers open the gateways to your Original Self, bridge your conscious connection with Infinite Source, and assist you to release and let go of your old patterns and beliefs that no longer serve you.*

As vortexes of spiritual light and power, your *Power Point Centers* connect you into multi-dimensional levels of divine consciousness. The deeper you go into them, the greater the depth of awareness you can tap into. However, rather than thinking of each *Power Point Center* as separate functioning generators of power, imagine them as linked power plants tied directly into Infinite Source. They are connected and synced up together to light up an inner city of light and power within you.

These generators of light heighten your connection into an inner space of stillness and Oneness that encompasses a vast, untapped void of spiritually charged energy. It is a space of untapped divine creation energy that opens and allows you to become one huge, self-generating portal in the universe. From the integrated light network of your *Power Points*, you are able to access and become One with the highest possibilities of your soul and live in the center of yourself. Your *Power Points* are a gateway into the sacred Holy Grail within you—a wellspring of your divine power, grace, light, and eternal God connection.

Your Power Point Centers In-depth

Many of you are already familiar with the seven major chakras that are aligned in an ascending column from the base of the spine to the top of the head within one's body. Expanding on what is currently known about chakras, there are actually 28 *Power Points Centers* in and around your body that are portals to the new paradigm of light within you. There are seven unique *Soul Integration Centers* that have the specific function of integrating your emotional, causal memory body with your soul body. Two of the *Soul Integration Centers* also serve "double duty" as specialized energy *Power Point Centers*. They, along with your five other *Soul Integration Centers* and your 21 other *Power Point Centers*, create a network of energy healers built into your body. These 28 *Power Point Centers* collectively work to integrate and strengthen all of the life forces within your body.

The 23 *Power Point Centers* that you will come to know and access are made up of the traditional chakra centers and also include added energy centers that are important to work with to make the needed shifts in consciousness during these times of spiritual expansion and integration. These energetic points of power are the portals of pure light that connect all facets of our divine and earthly Self in the body. The five additional *Soul Integration Centers* deepen your connection to the Source of Life and God within you and create the 28 *Power Point Centers* in total.

When you activate your 23 *Power Point Centers*, you create a bridge for your Bodymind to merge with pure consciousness. Your 23 *Power Point Centers* begin in the earth and move up into your root center, the space between your pubic bone and tailbone, through the inside core shaft of light in your body, and go all the way up into your crown center, through the top of your head and up 10-20 feet above your head. When your *Power Point Centers* are aligned through the light, they move you into unlimited love, higher planes of awareness, and assist you to come home to your loving, integrated, and innovative Self. Your 7 *Soul Integration Centers* begin directly below your solar plexus and move up to your heart center.

The *Power Point Centers* simultaneously ground and connect your Higher Self into your body. The *Power Point Centers* in the upper region of your body align higher frequencies of consciousness and light. The lower *Power Point Centers* in the base centers of your body create a foundation and grounding for your memory and energetic bodies to find a new level of security from within your Whole Self, align with Spirit and the earth and to unify your spirituality with your divine sexuality. Heaven and earth meet through your *Power Point Centers* and create balance, wellness, a quiet joy, and inner and outer abundance. As the light of your soul and the light of the universe merge in your body through the *Power Points*, you can experience a permanent merging of your mind, heart, soul, and body. Once fully illuminated and awakened, you are able to anchor yourself and live in the full light and power of Infinite Source.

> *As the light of your soul and the light of the universe merge in your body through the Power Point Centers, you can experience a permanent merging of your mind, heart, soul, and body.*

Each of the *Power Point Centers* within your body has a specific location and purpose. As you learn how to touch into them through focused actions and intention, you can achieve specific outcomes that further open and enlighten you. All of the *Power Point Centers* see, feel, and hear at very subtle levels. When you place your attention inside the center of a *Power Point*, your light power and higher consciousness open. The focused intention of your mind meeting the light energies within your *Power Points* activates your spiritual power.

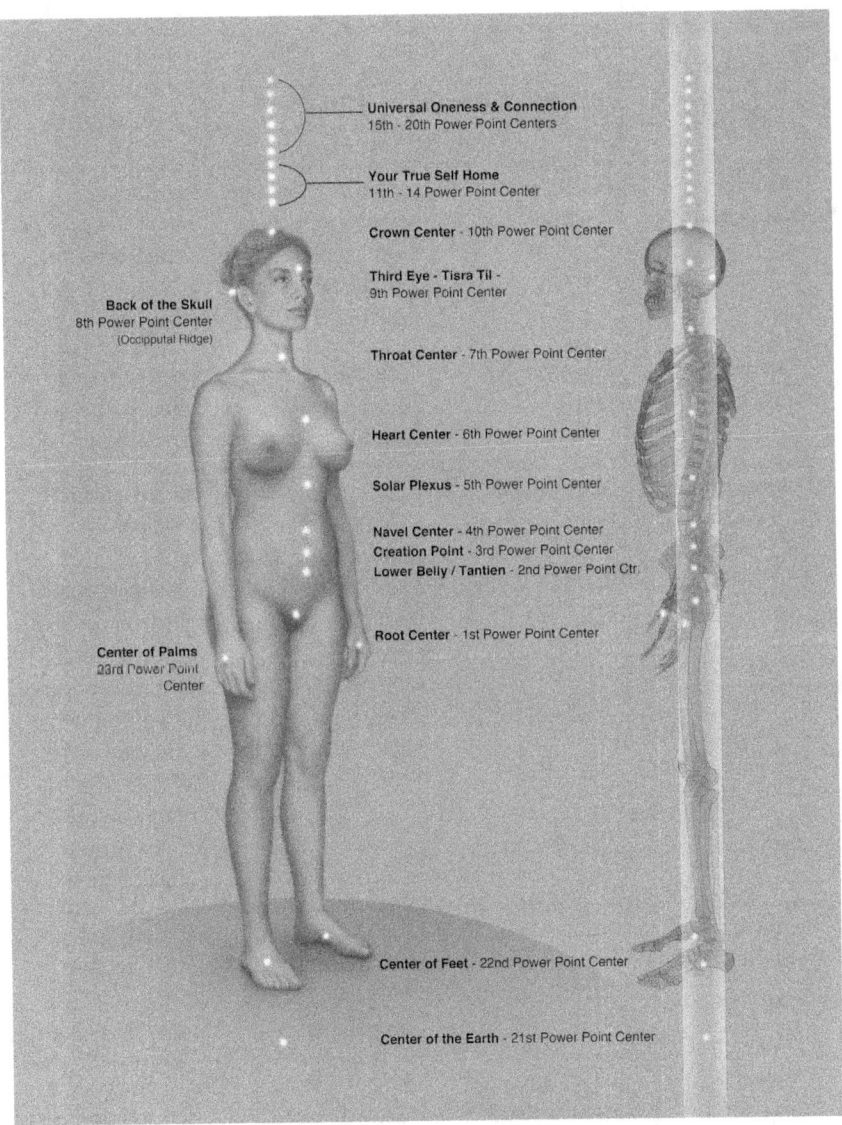

The Power Point Centers

POWER POINT CENTER OVERVIEW

Power Point Center	Location	Purpose	Action & Outcome
1st Power Point Center	Pubic bone/tailbone	Receives feminine power energies and stabilizes all life forces in the body	Spiritual union and Oneness with sexual, creative, and life-giving energies
2nd Power Point Center	Lower Belly/tantien	Sustains creative, sexual, and expressive power	Healthy expression, vitality, and joyful abundance
3rd Power Point Center - The Creation Point	2.5 inches below navel	Strengthens connection to Spirit, body, and mind; center point for creating health, balance, longevity, courage, clarity, protection, spiritual purpose, and manifestation	Humble awareness, unified follow through, universal trust, vitality, expression, understanding, compassion, integrated leadership, emotional integration, conscious communication, heart and soul connectedness
4th Power Point Center	Navel	Builds strong Self and universal relationships and connections	Self-sufficiency, autonomy, and clarity with Self and other beings
5th Power Point Center	Solar Plexus – also a soul integration Power Point	Supports feeling One with one's divine nature and living in union spiritually, emotionally, and physically	Love of life, the True Self, and feeling One with God Source

Power Point Center	Location	Purpose	Action & Outcome
6th Power Point Center	Heart center – also a soul integration Power Point	Opens one's true soul nature; brings experiential happiness to be alive, and fulfills each moment with love	A knowingness that one is aligned with one's true purpose and living one's soul truth
7th Power Point Center	Throat center	Gives the gift to speak and live the truth that blossom when the soul can be itself	Centeredness, empowerment, fearlessness, and creative success
8th Power Point Center	Back of the skull	The mystic "secret third eye" that opens the doorways to the divine; Opens and clears divine masculine energies	Integrates mind and body, clears misconceptions of one's existence
9th Power Point Center	Third eye	The gateway into seeing and being directly connected with all expressions and dimensions of Infinite Source	Clairvoyant, clairaudient, clairsentient awakenings, direct knowingness, and presence with Infinite Source
10th Power Point Center	Crown	Serves as the portal to the omnipotent powers of light in the universe	Ease of movement and BEingness with higher realms

Power Point Center	Location	Purpose	Action & Outcome
11th-14th Power Point Centers	Soul Sphere Dimension- 5-10 feet above your head	The gateways that integrate your life energies with Infinite Source and uplift the deepest nature of your being	Interconnected consciousness and realizations within the light that lead to living in divine love
15th-20th Power Point Centers	God Sphere Dimension- 10-20 feet above your head	The connection points to higher beings and Masters of Light; Help find one's ultimate spiritual connection and perfection	Complete union with the bliss and enlightenment of All That Is
21th Power Point Center	Center of the Earth	Awakens your core connection with creation energy and makes possible integrating higher plane realizations and awareness into your Bodymind	Groundedness, healing, spiritual alignment, and body-soul Oneness
22nd Power Point Center	Center of Both Feet	Receives the life-giving energies from within the light core of the earth	To know one's human Self with love and compassion
23rd Power Point Center	Center of Palms	Helps you absorb and remember the light that flows through your body and the universe into you	Awakened healing energies and receptivity to the divine

Spirit Gateways®/Iana Lahi All Rights Reserved ©

Within the center of every *Power Point* exists the vibration of Oneness—*beyond-the-beyond* love. As soon as you activate this love within you, the flow of your life energies ignite, motivate, stimulate, and fulfill the meeting of divine truth and power in your consciousness. True love begins by accepting the parts of your consciousness that were not allowed to exist earlier in this lifetime and in past lifetimes. This energetic explosion of light and love ignites the truth of your BEing. As your body opens to receive the greater Truth of *who you are*, the new energetic paradigm that is within your universal Self is activated. Your consciousness is an active expression of Infinite Source *consciously* meeting your Bodymind and soul.

An immense gift of consciousness and light is opened in you when you experience connecting two, three, or more *Power Point Centers* at the same time. *Power Point Centers* are your inner network of multi-dimensional activators that integrate the light and consciousness in your body and give you access to the power of Oneness in your everyday life. They are intended to be your Bodymind systems generator for a new level of living and BEing in spiritual attunement and realization.

As you begin to understand, feel, and connect into your electro-magnetic light system, know that your *Power Point Centers* are like flowers sensitive to the sun and to the moon. They respond to your thoughts and the energies in you and around you. *Power Point Centers* can be shut down or opened with the expanding or contracting energies from your mind and emotional body. How your mind responds to them is what makes you healthy or unhealthy, creative or blocked, loving or resentful, and depressed or content. The *Power Points*, whether semi-open or fully open, create how "at peace" you feel inside and your capacity to love and be loved. Experiences from your past that were emotionally difficult can be held and stuck in the cellular memory contained within your *Power Points*, making it more challenging to connect with Infinite Source. Until you release any negative energies, memories, or emotions into the light of Infinite Source, you may feel as though you are hitting a wall of repetitive emotional and spiritual roadblocks.

The negative energies that you hold onto need to be given into the light. As you reconnect into your *Power Points,* the light of Infinite Source will be awakened and strengthened. Learning to let go happens by moving energy and light into your Bodymind and by opening your heart to the truth of your soul. Letting go is a choice that, once mastered, stabilizes you emotionally, mentally, and spiritually in any given moment. Negative energies created from your perceptions of being separate from Source will be healed as you reunite with the Infinite in your body. The light will clear your pain and restore peace from within.

> *Letting go is a choice that, once mastered, stabilizes you emotionally, mentally, and spiritually in any given moment.*

The light removes and clears the walls that create separations between your body, soul, heart, and Spirit. It reunites the life force energies that are hidden beneath the pain created by your inner separations. The light ignites, revitalizes, and heals your body. By clearing your *Power Point Centers* with the vibration of light, you shift out of being tied and attached to your past responses and feelings of separation, pain, and discomfort. As your mind merges with their layers of frequency and dimensionality, and the portals of your heart open and clear, you can access wisdom, knowledge, and intelligence directly from Infinite Source. Your *Power Point Centers* help open the doorways into feeling and knowing from your deepest truth. When depressed, alienated, aloof, disconnected, sad, or experiencing other life stresses, by connecting into just one *Power Point Center*, it becomes possible to completely shift out of heaviness and burdens into the fluidity and ease of the moment. The *Power Point Centers* enable the powers of your soul to integrate into your light grid matrix. Through awakening your light body, you can live in the full truth of who you really are.

REMEMBER:
....

- *Power Point Centers* are portals and meeting zones within your body where your Bodymind and Spirit can become ONE. They are a 24/7 portal into the light and a new consciousness, where pain and suffering can dissolve and presence and vitality can take their place.

- Each of the 28 *Power Point Centers* within your body has a specific purpose. As you learn how to touch into your *Power Point Centers* through focused actions and intention, you can achieve specific outcomes that further open and enlighten you.

- Your *Power Point Centers* directly connect into your nervous, digestive, endocrine, and circulatory systems. They connect life force into your body, integrate your sexuality and Spirit, balance your hormones, and allow for healing to occur in your body.

- By reconnecting into your *Power Point Centers*, you can reunite the light of your consciousness with your soul blueprint.

- The control and fear in your ego mind directs your life decisions and responses. Control creates fear, and we are all moving through its grip. The gateway through fear is accomplished by sourcing the light that you are. When you align with the light created by the union of your *Power Point Centers*, you set into motion a force of power much greater than your ego mind.

- The light removes and clears the walls that create separations between your body, soul, heart, and Spirit. Your cleared *Power Point Centers* enable the powers of your soul to fully live through your Bodymind.

BELIGHT MEDITATION

Accessing Your Power Point Centers

Think of your mind as a strong and gentle beam of light that has the power to merge with any *Power Point Center* inside of your body. To access a *Power Point Center*, begin by placing your attention into the chosen *Power Point*. Similar to how you would gaze into the flame of a candle, place your focus into your root center, your *First Power Point Center*. As you focus into the *Power Point Center*, look for the light within it. Then, breathe into the *Power Point Center* to expand your connection with it.

Begin your practice time at 11 minutes and work up to 22 minutes.

Each day, begin with your *First Power Point Center* and then add the next *Power Point Center* into your practice. When you connect to the spheres of light above your head, invite the light to show itself to you. Allow yourself to open and connect to the light around you while you are holding a connection to your solar plexus, navel, and *Second Power Point Center.*

CHAPTER EIGHT

The Soul Integration Centers

*"Awareness is like the sun.
When it shines on things
They are transformed."
— Thich Nhat Hanh*

Your Soul Integration Centers

As you begin to touch into the *Power Point Centers* within your body, you can also connect with the more specific *Power Point Centers* that I call the *Soul Integration Centers*. Your *Power Point Centers* and *Soul Integration Centers* are stars of light that connect the inter-dimensional physical, etheric, and spiritual energies within your body. Each star is an integrated matrix of earth and heavenly energies that open you to living in the divine. Each divine design connects you into greater light and energy. Imagine a bright galaxy of stars and planets on a clear night, and bring that majestic sky into your body. As you are lit up, you go beyond your present limitations and fears and can reach into the vastness of the Infinite Source within yourself.

When you align and activate your *Soul Integration Centers*, you open to the full potential and expression of your integrated soul because your *Soul Integration Centers* are portals into the presence and power of your soul. They are connection points that integrate and unify the light and power of Infinite Source in your body and soul.

Integrating your body and mind with your *Soul Integration Centers* awakens your core truth and light. Seeing and bringing in light, embracing your soul parts, and integrating your inner bodies through your *Soul Integration Centers* initiates your path back to the whole you.

THE SOUL INTEGRATION CENTER CHART

Soul Integration Center	Location	Purpose	Action & Outcome
1st Soul Integration Center	In between navel and solar plexus	Clears the core of static and old energies; brings you into the now, and grounds self-awareness	Surrendered openness to what is most valuable and real about who you are
2nd Soul Integration Center	Directly beneath the rib cage, in your solar plexus, your 5th Power Point Center	Maintains balance and the integrity of your emotional, physical, and mental bodies	Calm, clear, integrated thinking and action
3rd Soul Integration Center	Pointy tip at the bottom of the rib cage, in the center	Supports self-acceptance	Promotes expansion and integration of your feelings and soul energies
4th Soul Integration Center	1st indentation in rib cage up from the bottom	Grounds you in your body, creates centeredness, inner connection, and self-trust	Helps the soul take up space and feel at home in your body, creates confidence and inner strength
5th Soul Integration Center	2nd indentation in rib cage up from the bottom	Releases fear and transforms it into truth	Gives you the clarity to BE your True Self with ease

Soul Integration Center	Location	Purpose	Action & Outcome
6th Soul Integration Center	3rd indentation in rib cage up from the bottom	Connects you to BEing and living your truth	Confidence, conviction to BE You, clear expression, heals self-existence issues, strengthens immune system
7th Soul Integration Center	In the center point between your nipples, 4th indentation up from the base of your rib cage	Takes you through the energy blocks to BE, receive, and give love	Bridges you into the light and joy of Infinite Source living within your BEing

Spirit Gateways®/Iana Lahi All Rights Reserved ©

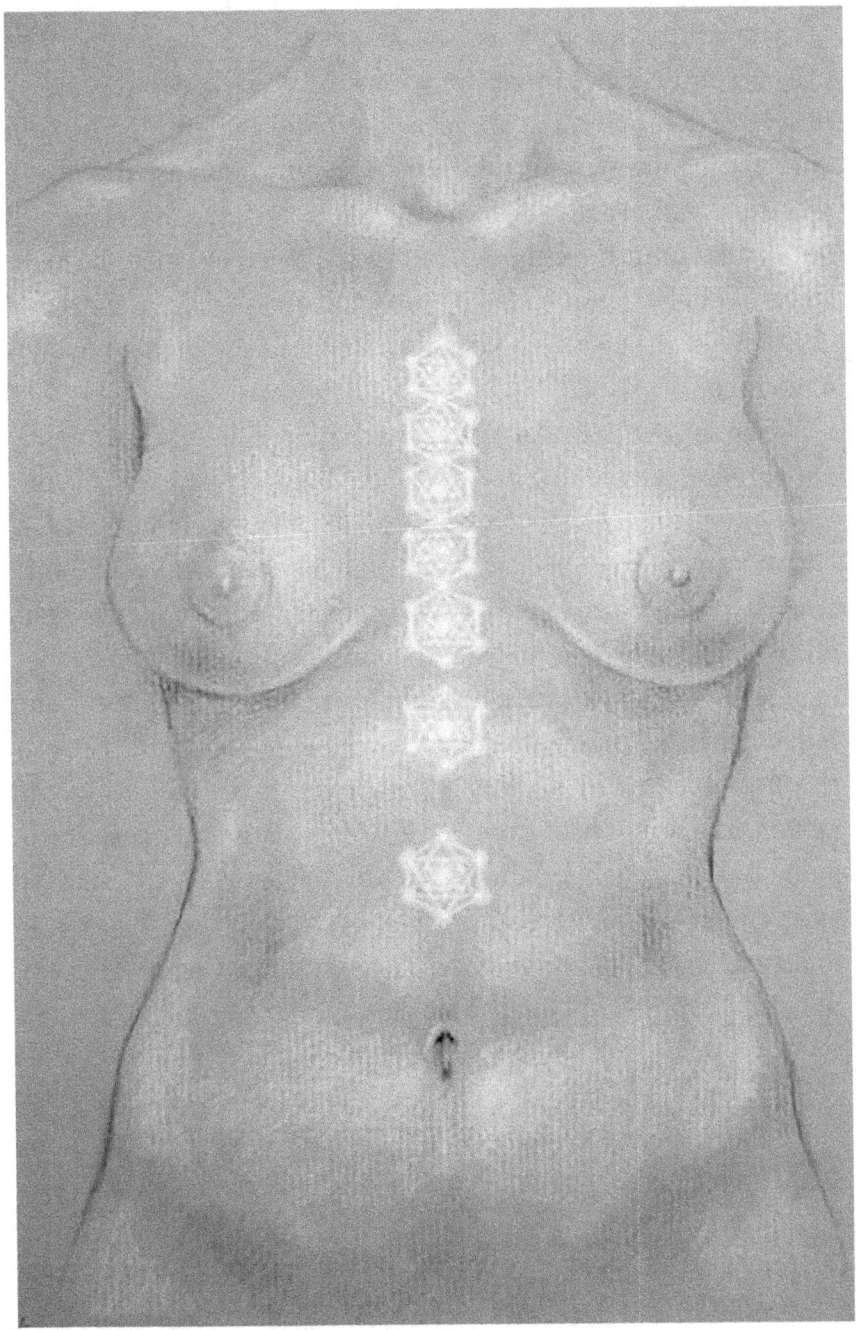

Soul Integration Centers

The ability to feel all of your *Power Point Centers* and make use of their energies increases when you access your seven *Soul Integration Centers* that directly align and integrate your soul energies in your body. When you shift your mind into them, one at a time, and breathe into them, they open your awareness to BEing One with Infinite Source. They can crack open and dissolve old beliefs and codes of consciousness—on an energetic DNA level—that prevent you from living in the divine wisdom of your soul.

Your soul energies are always creative in nature, restoring, enlightening, insightful, and connected to the whole. Once your *Soul Integration Centers* are awakened, your mind and body have a way to reconnect with your soul energies in your body. Your *Soul Integration Centers* connect the wisdom of your soul, universal intelligence, and the wholeness of the total you. They begin in the space between your navel and solar plexus and move up your torso into your *Heart Center—your 6th Power Point Center*. Just by shifting your focus into a *Soul Integration Center*, you are able to connect into the truth and presence of your soul in every moment. As the white light of God is engaged as an integrator and grounding rod of your whole Self, you can make rapid breakthroughs and shifts into creating a new relationship with Infinite Source and life.

How to Find and Connect with Your Soul Integration Centers:

Lie comfortably flat on a blanket, mat, or towel on the floor. You can be naked or wearing a long shirt, tunic, sarong, robe, or dress that is light weight to assist you in easily finding your *Soul Integration Centers*.

THE SOUL INTEGRATION CENTERS

Practice this simple 1-time-a-day exercise for one month to open access to your feeling body and soul.

Preparation:

Place the middle finger of your right hand into your navel. Place the middle finger of your left hand into the soft indentation below your rib cage, into the soft hollow of your solar plexus. Breathe into these two points at the same time, inhaling and exhaling deeply with focus into the present moment.

First Soul Integration Center

To find your *First Soul Integration Center*, place your pinky, the little finger of your right hand, into your navel and your right thumb into your solar plexus. Drop your middle finger down into your torso and press into your body. This first *Soul Integration Center* is the clearing & self-empowerment point. It may feel tender. This point can hold a lot of past unprocessed or un-dealt with emotion. Tenderly breathe into it, for it contains the spiritual power to help shift willfulness into alignment with Infinite Source. Your first *Soul Power Integration Center* is a portal into the vast silence of the universe and the inner expansion of your soul and its power.

Allow your mind to drop down into your first *Soul Integration Center*. Breathe until you can maintain the connection. Give yourself the message to breathe, let go, release, and relax into this *Soul Integration Center*. Release your mind and let go into the point. Trust your connection into your body.

Second Soul Integration Center

To find your *Second Soul Integration Center*, place your middle finger into the deep hollow space at the base of your rib cage. This is your solar plexus. Your *Second Soul Integration*

Center is the center where your emotional, soul, etheric, and physical body meet. Ignite your *Second Soul Integration Center* by pressing it gently in a clockwise circular motion with your third finger. Relax, breathe, and focus your attention into your solar plexus. Open to the unlimited light dwelling within this inner sun. When your solar plexus *Soul Integration Center* is balanced, you feel energetically and emotionally secure within yourself. You know what are your energies and what are other people's energies. You can be who you are.

Third Soul Integration Center

To find your *Third Soul Integration Center*, gently slide your third finger up from your solar plexus until it touches where the bones of your ribcage meet. It will feel like a pointy ridge. This is your *Third Soul Integration Center*, the self-acceptance point. Press your finger into the point and move it in a clockwise circular motion while continuing to breathe into your *Third Soul Integration Center*. Continue breathing and deepening your focus into the tip of your ribcage for at least two minutes, until you feel a mental and energetic connection into the point.

Fourth Soul Integration Center

To find your *Fourth Soul Integration Center*, slightly inch up your finger, approximately 1/8 of an inch. Feel for a slight indentation, a valley, a concave slight softness. This is your *Fourth Soul Integration Center* the grounding point for body and soul integration. You are in the "first indentation." Bring your mental focus fully into this point through shifting your attention down into the solar plexus. Breathe and be in yourself. You will feel a sense of being centered and coming into your body. The *Fourth Soul Integration Center* helps you to let go, feel connected, and trust yourself.

Fifth Soul Integration Center

To find your *Fifth Soul Integration Center*, inch up another 1/8-inch, and press into the next hollow indentation. Sense an opening and widening of your soul as you enter into the center of your breastplate. You are now in the "second indentation." Continue the process of gently moving your *Fifth Soul Integration Center* in a circular motion. Breathe into your breastplate and focus into what you feel. This *Fifth Soul Integration Center* helps you release fear and transform it into positive self-expression.

Sixth Soul Integration Center

To find your *Sixth Soul Integration Center*, slide your middle finger up another 1/8 of an inch into the next hollow indentation. Gently press your finger into this spot and just feel the energy within the point. Breathe—keep your mind focused into the indentation. You are now in the "third indentation." Feel your breath expand deeper and allow your body to connect into your breath and become "larger." The *Sixth Soul Integration Center* connects you into your truth. It brings you into the reality of being one with what is true for you in that moment.

Seventh Soul Integration Center

To find your *Seventh Soul Integration Center*, slide your finger up into the next and final *Soul Integration Center*. This final point is located in the center point between your nipples if you were to draw an imaginary line. You are now "in the fourth indentation." Allow your breath to expand into the space in the center of the valley of your upper chest and simultaneously into your upper back. The *Seventh Soul Integration Center* opens you into love and takes you through the blocks to receiving, giving, and being in love. It prepares you to move into your heart center, which is directly above the *Seventh Soul Integration Center*. Your heart center is the meeting point where your soul and spirit meet. It is the gateway into the light and joy of Infinite Source.

The *Soul Integration Centers* help to clear your core wounds and help you to live "present" and in the moment of your life. The *Soul Integration Centers* ground, calm you, and bring an inner peace. They help you to find and BE who you are. When they are blocked, you will feel disoriented and separated from your truth. When they are clear and open, your energies will flow, your mind will be clear, and you will feel One with your Self and life.

Recap of The *Soul Integration Centers*

Soul Integration Center #1: Clears and supports self-empowerment. Contains the spiritual power to help shift willfulness into alignment with Infinite Source.

Soul Integration Center #2: Creates stabilization in the physical and emotional bodies. It is the meeting point of your soul, etheric, emotional, and physical bodies.

Soul Integration Center #3: Promotes self-acceptance.

Soul Integration Center #4: Grounds you.

Soul Integration Center #5: Releases fear and transforms it into positive self-expression.

Soul Integration Center # 6: Connects you to your truth.

Soul Integration Center #7: Opens you to infinite love and prepares you to enter into your heart center.

THE SOUL INTEGRATION CENTERS

Your *Soul Integration Centers* are focus points for you to place your attention while you integrate your soul with your heart center. If you are feeling anxious or overwhelmed, you can focus light just by your intention into the *Soul Integration Centers* two **"notches"** above the tip of bone that protrudes at the base of your rib cage. When breathed into, this *Soul Integration Center* will immediately recalibrate your emotional, soul, and energy field. Whether you focus and meditate into one *Soul Integration Center*, or two, or more at a time, you will experience the multi-dimensional awareness and presence of your whole soul in your body. Similar to enjoying a long and sensual dinner with many tastes and nuances that bring relaxation and fulfillment, when letting go and deeply surrendering into your *Soul Integration Centers*, you will experience greater balance and increased clarity and happiness.

REMEMBER:

- There are 28 *Power Point Centers* in and around your body. There are seven that function as *Soul Integration Centers*. Two of the *Power Point Centers* are *Soul Integration Centers*. Collectively, they work to integrate and strengthen all of the life forces within your body.

- The ability to feel your *Power Point Centers* and make use of their energies is increased when you access your seven specific *Soul Integration Centers*, which directly align and integrate your soul energies in your body.

- Your *Soul Integration Centers* provide a fast track to integrate and align your emotional, physical, and spiritual bodies.

- Ground your soul aspects in your body through connecting into the seven key *Soul Integration Centers*.

BELIGHT MEDITATION

Uniting With Your Soul Integration Centers

Practice connecting with your *Soul Integration Centers* once a day, for at least one month to open access to the love and power of your soul. Focus and meditate into your *Soul Integration Centers* to directly align and integrate your soul energies in your body and further open your inner connections to the light of Infinite Source.

CHAPTER NINE

The Infinite Possibilities of Your Power Point Centers

Activating the Infinite Possibilities of Your Power Point Centers
"Embrace your Self."
— Mahama Iana

All of the gateways to your True Self live within you. The light contained within each *Power Point Center* is a portal into the matrix of divine intelligence beyond your limited Self. Your *Power Point Centers* serve as a treasury of energy light that generate vitality, clear thinking, and empowerment by linking you to higher understanding. Reconnecting your mind into the matrix of light within you awakens your infinite Self.

As you make moment-to-moment choices to step forward into a new way of BEing One with your soul, you will find a new direction that goes beyond living in the separation of your mind and body. As enlightening human beings, we are being given the opportunity to shift toward a radically new way of soul-centered living and being on the planet. You are being called to awaken, open, let go, and leap into your own transformation to meet a new matrix of consciousness that can take you from being trapped in the fear and limitations of your lower self into a heightened state of light and awareness.

By beginning with integrating your physical and spiritual bodies, your transformation can be accelerated. You may have begun to feel in sync with a greater calling. You may have begun to know things before they happen, or to realize an energy within you that, once focused, is unstoppable. Everything is changing in our personal lives as the energies within our physical, emotional, energetic, and mental bodies are being spiritually directed to merge with a new higher frequency coming into the planet.

In this chapter, we will explore more deeply the possibilities and functions of your *Power Point Centers* and how you can connect, open, clear, heal, and expand them to take you into new states of integration and connection with Infinite Source. Understanding the full nature of your *Power Point Centers* and how to BE with them is essential for your soul reconnection, expansion, and integration path.

Your *Power Point Centers* began to develop while you were in utero, before birth. The development of your *Power Point Centers* is shaped by your past life spiritual experiences, perceptions, and attunement; the energies within your mother's womb; and the energies that you were born into within your family and surrounding environment. How you relate to yourself, Infinite Source, and your environment creates imbalance or balance within your *Power Points* and your Bodymind circuitry.

Whether you find yourself presently feeling and living in a state of balance or imbalance, you have the potential and inner power to open and activate your *Power Point Centers* to heal old issues; recreate your health; restore and heal your mind, body, and soul; and activate a new alignment to catapult your Whole Self into BEing One with Infinite Source. When you learn how to drop your focus from being in your head into the light within your *Power Point Centers*, your true healing can begin. Then,

THE INFINITE POSSIBILITIES OF YOUR POWER POINT CENTERS

by clearing and aligning your *Power Point Centers* to become One with them, you are able to jump-start and advance your spiritual progress.

As you focus and connect into your *Power Point Centers*, you enter the gateways that integrate your divine energy matrix, soul, and Higher Self. Within your *Power Point Centers* exist both the old and new matrix of universal evolution. They are windows into a finely attuned latticework of the divine that give access to the human blueprint. When your *Power Point Centers* are open, you can access their universal intelligence to en"light"en yourself. Your *Power Point Centers* give you access to your inner network of light awareness and assist you to BE connected to Infinite Source through your Bodymind. To access your light, you must first face and clear what blocks it.

Fear blocks our light and prevents our greater truth, vitality, and clarity from emanating. It hides in anger, grief, mistrust, insecurity, doubt, shame, guilt, and illusion and prevents you from feeling and BEing in the love that is within you and that you are. When you clear your *Power Point Centers,* it allows for their positive and strengthening life force energies to shift your consciousness. When you receive streams of light into your centers, love will begin to dissolve stuck beliefs, old fears, and blockages. This is all part of a new paradigm that the planet is moving into, which is grounded in BEing the essence of love. By aligning with the light frequency of love in your *Power Point Centers*, you can experience BEing in the nucleus of your own power.

> ***When you clear your Power Point Centers, it allows for their positive and strengthening life force energies to shift your consciousness.***

The following meditation exercise will begin to help you clear and awaken the light within your *Power Point Centers*.

Power Point Center Clearing Meditation:

Sit comfortably in either a chair or on a comfortable cushion on the floor. Create a stream of pure white light to pour down from above your head, through the center of your head, and down through a wide column of light that extends through your torso, legs, and feet into the earth. Bring the light from above your head down into your heart center, your *Sixth Power Point Center*. Gaze into your heart center and look for its light. Look for a glimmer or a blaze of light in the center of your heart center, which is in the center of your chest. As you gaze into your heart center, focus with a steady connection into seeing a wide-open space of light, then look for a flicker of light, then a blaze of light. Gently draw the light up into your third eye, your *Ninth Power Point Center*. Feel your third eye by entering into it through the center of your head and fully immerse yourself into it. Your third eye is located about one-half to three-fourths of an inch above the area in between your eyebrows. Stay in your third eye until you sense its light. BE in your third eye until you feel yourself enter its "expansive zone," then once again shift your focus into your heart center and, when fully in its light, reconnect into your third eye and be in both centers at the same time—unite your heart center and third eye.

Each time that you do this meditation, go into your heart center a little more. Feel the vibrational quality of your authentic Self and open into the presence of light.

Each of your *Power Point Centers* has a specific function to access and translate the vibrational frequencies of Infinite Source. Your spiritual "work" is to feel when your *Power Point*

THE INFINITE POSSIBILITIES OF YOUR POWER POINT CENTERS

Centers are open or closed and to learn how to shift them into a state of openness and expansion. The blocking of a *Power Point Center* occurs when you are cut off from, numb to, or in denial of the inner battle within two or more energy centers. Within your energy centers, you will find an aspect of your soul Self that was not allowed to exist as well as parts of you that agreed on some level to perpetuate your disempowerment and false beliefs.

An inner battle develops when parts of your Self, at some moment in time, split off from your God Self or Oneness Self. The unresolved separation creates inner conflict. Your mind must then decide, assess, and objectify life from separation and illusion. You may have created an energetic belief to turn against your own wisdom or creativity. You may block love from coming into your life or are in battle with money and your ability to receive what the universe wants to give to you. You may believe from past life memories or present life experiences that you do not deserve, are not worthy of, or are not "enough" to BE ONE with the divine Source of Infinite Intelligence, bliss, abundance, love and power within you.

The *Power Point Centers* hold the cellular memory of your separation from Infinite Source. As your centers are cleared and filled with the light and love of Spirit, you will experience deeper and more integrated levels of connection with Infinite Source. Unlimited possibilities and expanded creative power open in unexpected ways. As you let go into the light, and release your agreement and contracts to creating separation, disempowerment, and fear, the inner battle between your mind and soul will come to an end. Just by bringing light up from the center of the earth and down from the divine centers above your head into your body, you will begin to heal and unify yourself. These spinning vortexes of shining light will increase in God energy just by your attentiveness of love. As the God energies within each *Power Point Center* merge into your Bodymind and soul, the difficult and negative blocks within you are given a new foundation to dissolve. The return to wholeness and peace within yourself will be your new reality.

> *Your spiritual "work" is to feel when your Power Point Centers are open or closed and to learn how to shift them into a state of openness and expansion.*

THE POWER POINT CENTER FUNCTIONS

Power Point Center	When Open & Clear You Will Feel	When Blocked or Closed You Will
First Power Point Center - Root Center - Space within Pubic Bone-Tailbone	Energetically and emotionally grounded; secure in the world and in your body; financially, mentally, and physically strong; creatively vibrant and flowing; happy; connected to your passion and spark for living authentically; fearless; sexually rooted; clarity in expression and communication; a willingness to try new things; the need for order, cleanliness, and comfort in your home; and a willingness to step out of your limiting thoughts and beliefs	Control others and yourself; become overly analytical, and judgmental; react to fear; tend towards empty and impoverished thinking; be overly swayed by family beliefs; be stuck in a limited box of reality; experience nervous system disorders, psychological issues, and chronic health issues such as heart conditions, constipation, anemia, immune system function breakdowns, and hormone imbalances

Power Point Center	When Open & Clear You Will Feel	When Blocked or Closed You Will
Second Power Point Center - **Lower Belly/Tantien**	Confident; able to maintain clear boundaries; healthy bonding abilities; able to let go of emotions and situations that no longer serve you; joy from giving and receiving; desirous to go beyond Self-constructed limitations; joy and love in the body; sexual and creative joy and fulfillment; physical and emotional abundance; capable of creating trust with another and oneself; your voice of truth; self- nurturance; happiness and contentment; self-empowerment; fearless expression of one's Self and feelings	Control and manipulate others; misuse sex; abuse anger; act greedy; hold back from living fully or go the opposite extreme; be sarcastic; experience a lack of purpose; feel jealousy, blame and guilt; feel lacking and stuck around financial prosperity; spiral down into disgust with your self and others; feel separate from Source, hopeless, depressed, and sad; develop food issues; feel incapable of speaking your real feelings; feel overwhelmed with your emotions yet unable to process them; create health issues in the ovaries, uterus, breasts, testicles, prostate, genitals, spleen, pancreas, stomach, digestion, intestines, liver, gallbladder, kidneys, and spine

THE INFINITE POSSIBILITIES OF YOUR POWER POINT CENTERS

Power Point Center	When Open & Clear You Will Feel	When Blocked or Closed You Will
Third Power Point Center - Creation Point- 2.5 inches below navel	A calm, gentle and strong connection into your core energy, soul, and inner guidance; grounded and in touch with universal reality; a deep security and strength within your body; the strength to come through any challenge; your kundalini energies coiled within the 4th lumbar are more accessible; a natural connection to all of your *Power Point Centers*; deeper and more focused creative & life force energies; greater ease & grace for your mind and body to integrate; greater clarity; a strengthening of the nervous system and brain; increased physical energy, emotional stability & balance; sexual connectedness; spiritual alignment; strengthening of your auric field	Fear speaking your truth; have difficulties manifesting your life dreams and desires; feel overwhelmed by tasks; feel challenged to complete and finish projects; live from your head; lose energy; lack vitality; avoid your own creativity, power, and gifts; sabotage your own actions; give away your power; have difficulties having an orgasm; feel alone in the world and isolated; live in fear of rejection and abandonment; be challenged with poor digestion and elimination; doubt, reject, and judge your Self; lack the power and positive will to stand up to your own ego; feel sexually insecure; afraid to let go of the past; hold on to unhealthy relationships

Power Point Center	When Open & Clear You Will Feel	When Blocked or Closed You Will
Fourth Power Point Center - **Navel**	Connected and One with your higher nature and to life; secure with being and expressing your feelings; able to self-nurture; create healthy individualization with family and loved ones; allow others and yourself to be real, honest, genuine, and whole; step into self-empowerment; be able to create healthy bonds and commitments, live through your True Self and Source; honor and respect others; be determined to use your will appropriately to accomplish your soul purpose	Overly need others to validate you and make you feel good about yourself; experience excessive worry; feel separate from God Source; feel inadequate and disconnected to others and life; stuck in your life; overreact to others who do not "get you"; hide your feelings; stay in incompatible relationships for too long; become impatient; deny anger; misuse sexuality; be unable to love without attachment and obsessiveness; have a need to always be right; be attached to an imbalanced parent; be unable to accept someone for who they are; blame rather than source how you disempower yourself; develop digestive, circulation, and psychological issues

THE INFINITE POSSIBILITIES OF YOUR POWER POINT CENTERS

Power Point Center	When Open & Clear You Will Feel	When Blocked or Closed You Will
Fifth Power Point Center – **Solar Plexus**	In your body with loving and defined boundaries; personal strength; your truth; heightened clarity; sourced energetically; protected with a strong sheath; a unified physical and emotional body; grounded; the love and power of your soul; a healthy self-image and a sense of wholeness, joy, and individual expression	Absorb others' energies; feel a loss of Self; experience an Ego Self taking over; experience anxiety attacks and depression created from abandoning your solar plexus; feel a lack of self-esteem; have fear of rejection; have an absence of will power; experience depression; have learning disabilities; be stubborn; have an inability to make decisions or trust your intuition and gut instincts; create stomach, small and large intestines, pancreas, spleen, nerves, lymph, and ulcer issues

Power Point Center	When Open & Clear You Will Feel	When Blocked or Closed You Will
Sixth Power Point Center - Heart Center	One with the love within your own BEingness; centered in light; accepting of what is; receptive to nature and its lessons; open to others' true intentions; living your passion; fearless to take risks; forgiving, compassionate, tolerant, and patient; trusting with Infinite Source; willing to release your ego; passionate about truth; connected to Masters of Light on other planes; a desire to give to life and to be totally who you really are	Create drama that hurts yourself or others; feel like a victim and unable to love or be loved; feel inauthentic; act out the unheard and unseen issues of your wounded inner child; feel split in your divine masculine-feminine energies; live in mistrust and fear; create ongoing suffering and pain; disguise your intentions; create illusions, intolerances, and blocks in your soul development; feel disconnected to being ONE with life, passion, and soul-centered relationships; feel judgmental and self-repressed; experience allergies, lungs, heart, blood pressure, insomnia, procrastination, psychological, sexuality, and control issues

THE INFINITE POSSIBILITIES OF YOUR POWER POINT CENTERS

Power Point Center	When Open & Clear You Will Feel	When Blocked or Closed You Will
Seventh Power Point Center – **Throat Center**	A creative impulse to express your truth and purpose; a desire to be direct, self-responsible, fearless, live with integrity, and create financial success; self-love; personal and divine strength; the right use and practice of your will; enhancement of your senses; improved bone strength, B Vitamin utilization, endocrine system functioning, and enzyme production	Disrespect and dishonor yourself and others; repress your vital life force, creativity, and sexuality; control and manipulate; judge and blame; become passive-aggressive; feel stuck in familial patterns of disempowerment, humiliation, and shame; experience a lack of spontaneity and forgetfulness; be unable to hear Spirit, speak up, or hold one's own; feel unable to let go of negative situations; be unable to forgive others and yourself; have flus, colds, viral infections, back pain, scoliosis, kidney problems, hearing issues, arthritis, and periodontal disease

Power Point Center	When Open & Clear You Will Feel	When Blocked or Closed You Will
Eighth Power Point Center - **Back of the Skull**	A deeper connection with your heart center; acceptance of what is; non-judgmental and natural curiosity; spiritual clarity; ease; able to surrender; more loving; happier; closer to God; live in the moment; directed by Infinite Source; creatively unblocked; open to change; a willingness to express fully; rooted to ancient and divine wisdom and trusting in your intuition	Feel stressed, angry, pushy, and opinionated; feel a lack of compassion; fearful and quick to blame and judge others; develop headaches, eye problems, brain chemistry imbalances, ADD, emotional problems and insecurities, tension, lower back issues, security and financial issues

THE INFINITE POSSIBILITIES OF YOUR POWER POINT CENTERS

Power Point Center	When Open & Clear You Will Feel	When Blocked or Closed You Will
Ninth Power Point Center – Third Eye/ Tisra Til Center	Connected into your body and to all dimensions and planes; energy moving through your body; able to see life with clarity from a 360-perspective; integrated and whole; loving; a healthy emotional detachment; enhanced thinking; Bodymind unity; connection with Infinite Source; your natural clairvoyant, clairsentient, and clairaudient gifts; enhanced focus and concentration; awakened creativity and imagination; sexual heights; a connection to all physical and etheric senses, your nervous, respiratory, circulatory, and hormonal systems; overall health increase; able to utilize minerals and vitamins better; deepened sleep; able to see, feel, and hear your spiritual guides	Be drawn down into anger, rage, torment, and fear; feel the lack of desire to live; take things too seriously; get stuck in spiritual pride and arrogance; live in avoidance; choose to be in denial and sarcasm; become controlling and humiliating to others; experience headaches, digestion issues, depression, indecision, apathy, panic, and other psychological issues, strokes and nervous system disorders

Power Point Center	When Open & Clear You Will Feel	When Blocked or Closed You Will
Tenth Power Point Center - **Crown Center- Portal beyond Duality**	A new unified thinking between the third eye, spirit, and the heart; integrated spiritual power in the body; access to your Higher Self, spiritual guides, and wayshowers; universal consciousness flowing through you; the ability to go beyond human limitations; a connection to absolute love; a direct knowingness to wisdom beyond the mind; higher states of enlightenment; brain health and stability; a strong muscular and skeletal system, and a balanced endocrine system	Live in fear of the unknown; remain in your comfort zone; see life from lack and limitation; feel isolated, closed, judged, separate from God; afraid to love and be loved; be unaware of personal needs, and unable to process your feelings; experience delusional thinking, exhaustion, immune dysfunction, guilt, and an inability to focus; experience sleeping disorders, circulatory, nervous, digestive, and endocrine issues

THE INFINITE POSSIBILITIES OF YOUR POWER POINT CENTERS

Power Point Center	When Open & Clear You Will Feel	When Blocked or Closed You Will
Eleventh-Fourteenth Power Point Centers – Your True Soul Home	Enhanced spiritual powers; trust; faith; insight; wisdom; patience; brilliance; enlightenment; living on purpose; true detachment; genius; direct connection to Source; Oneness with all life and dimensions; healing powers and miracles; inter-dimensional communication; healthy assimilation of nutrients; connection to animal kingdoms; extraterrestrial life; excellent heart, blood, immune, hormonal, and respiratory functioning	Feel despair, doubt, judgment, blame, hatred, lack of love, the inability to love, sorrow, trapped in the body, disconnected from Source; be unable to hear others and yourself; be antagonistic; experience unexplainable events that knock you in a new life direction; health conditions that become severe very rapidly; draw to you negative experiences and other people's fears
Fifteenth-Twentieth Power Point Centers - Universal Oneness and Connection	A deep connection in your heart; in touch with the angels, the Elohim, Council Of Light, and profound spiritual dimensions; ONE with Source; in love with the divine; inner stillness and peace; awakened to Mother Father God; bliss; Oneness; limitlessness; cellular remembrance of your original creation and soul's essence	Forget why you are here; fall into suffering and pain; disregard sacred messages; identify with your ego; create stories in your mind that you project on to life; feel separate from your heart, humanity, and Infinite Source

Power Point Center	When Open & Clear You Will Feel	When Blocked or Closed You Will
Twenty-first Power Point Center - Center of the Earth	Emotionally balanced; in tune; light filled; clear; relaxed; accepting of what life brings; able to give and receive love; access the incoming spiritual light from above your head and from the earth; empowered to make clear decisions; enlivened with life force energies; exuberant contentment and joy	Feel trapped in your body and in your life; feel unloved and untrusting; experience low energy; feel stuck and imbalanced and unable to shift; feel easily reactive; feel disconnected from your soul and its purpose
Twenty-second Power Point Center – Center of both Feet	Grounded and connected to your heart and the earth at the same time; feel present, receptive, and integrated	Forget who you are; stumble your way through situations; analyze and withdraw to feel safe; see from a limited mind set; be impulsive, ungrounded
Twenty-third Power Point Center – Center of Palms	Creates connection between heaven, earth, and Spirit through the heart; able to feel and receive light	Feel the need to control life and others; judge others; withdraw from life; have difficulty nurturing Self and others

Spirit Gateways®/Iana Lahi All Rights Reserved ©

THE INFINITE POSSIBILITIES OF YOUR POWER POINT CENTERS

Opening, Healing & Expanding Your Power Point Centers

Light abundantly flows from the creative center of the universe. Once you begin to allow the light from higher dimensions to move through you, an initiation of unlimited love, creative abundance, and inter-dimensional intelligence aligns your consciousness in a new way. To feel fully awakened and in tune with the source of life, you have to be willing to release all the ways that you stay in control, practice avoidance, and create stress. Just by becoming still and sitting in the light each day, you awaken grace.

The light essence of Infinite Source will move through your *Power Point Centers* and fill your physical and emotional nature with vitality, clarity, and health. Opening, clearing, and aligning your *Power Points* will clear many psychological issues and physical diseases that seem untreatable. As you activate your *Power Points*, they will receive life force energies directly from Infinite Source and enable you to shift into a state of ongoing healing and wholeness. By removing the blocks and obstacles that prevent the *Power Point Center* life force energies from flowing freely, you can heal the separations of the body, mind, and psyche.

Karmic health challenges are often healed when deeper, repressed energies within the *Power Point Centers* are seen, felt, opened, and released. Since the *Power Point Centers* are connected to all of the bodies—mental, physical, emotional, etheric, and spiritual—when you learn to live in the center point where Spirit and the body meet, you can experience living and being fully integrated and One in your Self. When unified, the *Power Point Centers* serve as a wellspring of energy that integrates your spiritual and physical energies. You will feel connected into the source of love in your heart and be able to access ancient and progressive wisdom, visionary clarity, health, wealth, and happiness.

> *Just by becoming still and sitting in the light each day, you awaken grace.*

Healing

Your mind and body have typically been on a lifelong path of developing separately. Through the force of your mind, ego, and personality, you have created a "False Self," which you use to navigate and project into the world. The deeper, dormant "True Self" of your existence is buried somewhere in the deep recesses of where your Bodymind and the light meet. The energetic gridwork of your "False Self" and "True Self" tend to collide and create subtle or sometimes massive mental, physical, and emotional chaos within you. Your mind and body can come back together again through the opening and awakening of your *Power Point Centers* with Infinite Source. As you realize that your emotional reactions are not your true reality, you can begin to access the truth of who you are through building a relationship with the source of who you are. Your *Power Point Centers* are gateways into your essence and authentic spiritualized vibration. They help to reconnect the light energy generator within your body to make possible opening into the essence of who you are. Once you are aligned into the universal stream of cosmic life energy, it is possible to create and BE the miracle of your own life.

When you reconnect your mind into your energetic *Power Point Centers*, your thinking body is able to make major shifts.

THE INFINITE POSSIBILITIES OF YOUR POWER POINT CENTERS

Your mind may fight "shifting downward" from its "lofty" position, but if you can surrender into the energetic openings that your *Power Point Centers* provide, you will begin to significantly bust through your health, financial, relationship, life purpose, emotional, and spiritual issues.

Your *Power Point Centers* are incredibly important to your overall health and well being because they can close down, open up, align with Infinite Source, or release fear and whatever is foreign to their true state of being. When you focus your mind into your *Power Points*, you open a gateway into the energetic healing force that constantly lives within you. As you disengage from the chatter in your mind and focus into the light within your *Power Points*, you awaken permanent states of surrender, peace, and acceptance. All it takes is the willingness to come into your body and acknowledge the power of Infinite Source coursing through your body.

> *Your Power Point Centers are gateways into your essence and authentic spiritualized vibration.*

As a reminder, when you also engage your specific *Soul Integration Centers*, they bridge your soul into your physical and etheric bodies, which set into motion manifesting the clarity, gifts, and pure God energies that are uniquely yours to develop. Your *Soul Integration Centers* are bridges of truth between your soul and your higher Self and Spirit. You will experience feeling your true and authentic nature ground itself through opening into your *Soul Integration Centers*.

The Power of Being You — A Daily Practice

Place your right hand on your lower belly and begin to breathe in long and deep breaths filled with light and love into your entire body. When relaxed, bring your breath into your chest. Now, bring the middle finger of your right hand into the hollow space in between the nipples on your chest. Breathe in light into this portal of light. It is your *Seventh Soul Integration Center*. Bring your middle finger down a notch, into a hollow space directly below your *Seventh Soul Integration Center* into the *Sixth Soul Integration Center*. Press your finger into the hollow space a little deeper and bring light and your breath into this *Soul Integration Point*. Bring your shoulder blades together just a bit. Allow yourself to BE and experience what you feel. Your *Sixth Soul Integration Center* strengthens you to BE YOU and activates the confidence within your Bodymind to express who you are.

Expansion

The *Power Point Centers* expand into higher frequencies as your soul aspects are integrated. Your *Power Point Centers* become "holding tanks" of energy for the recovered parts of your soul that are actually expressions of your most enlightened Self. As you purify your relationship with your soul and Spirit, your *Power Point Centers* become ripe with vibrancy and sustaining power. By first harnessing the sustainable energy within our own bodies, we develop the insight and "know how" to heal our planet and mend our hearts with one another. As we develop a sustainable relationship with our own inner universe, we are able to create a sustainable relationship with our "outer" universe and life.

THE INFINITE POSSIBILITIES OF YOUR POWER POINT CENTERS

As your *Power Point Centers* open and receive the energies of your cleared psyche and soul, you not only feel whole within yourself but you can feel One and whole with others who also hold the space of light. It is an incredible feeling that will continue to grow as your expansion continues. As the aspects of your soul are remembered and reconnected into your *Power Point Centers*, they will continue to bring life experiences and inner teachings to further awaken you. As you open and expand in your mind and body to the truth that lives within, you will find yourself needing to let go and get out of the way so the simple and higher truths of Infinite Source can come in. It may happen in the moment or down the road, but it is all a natural part of your awakening.

> ***The Power Point Centers expand into higher frequencies as your soul aspects are integrated.***

Expansion is an innate part of the universe. When you expand, you are opening to truth, light, and love. Energy expands and contracts. Through every breath and every thought you can create a state of expansion and receive the wisdom the expansion is giving you through the contraction. As your Bodymind receives the essence of your soul, the expansion and contraction gifts you with greater light. Through expansion, your wisdom and intuition can grow. When you contract, you are absorbing the energies created by your creative and spiritual expansions. By BEing in the center of the contraction, you are in receiving mode. Rather than thinking that contraction is negative, compare it to an ocean wave moving and ebbing back into the tide. Each time that you have an awakening and realization, allow yourself and your *Power Points* to absorb and receive heightened awareness and consciousness. It is through receiving that you will make all of your breakthroughs. The contraction is the force of nature that pulls Infinite Source energy into you. Both processes of expansion and contraction create a momentum to fill you. Every moment, sound, action and movement are created by expansion and contraction. You must expand to encounter and be with the life shifting powers of the light and you must contract to receive and take in the light to the center of your cells. By opening and receiving through your *Power Point Centers*, you are creating an anchor to the creative Source of your Bodymind and soul. As the light in your *Power Point Centers* open, your body is able to embrace your spiritual essence—your complete and True Self.

The Creation Point —Your 3rd Power Point Center

Each *Power Point Center* has a significant purpose. Similar to your *Fifth Power Point Center*, your solar plexus, the Creation Point, once activated, can dramatically shift your connection with your Bodymind and your ability to BE a vibrant expression of your True Self. The Creation Point, your *Third Power Point Center*, has the power to rebalance your mind and help you to conquer your greatest fears, apprehensions, self-doubts, heal stored issues of self-sabotage and self-rejection, and build your life force sustaining energies for optimum health and well being.

What Is Your Creation Point?

Your Creation Point is the seat of the life force current called kundalini energy, which can be activated through the 4th lumbar vertebrae in your spine. Once switched on and awakened, your Creation Point activates life force energies to move up through the spine to heal and restore your Bodymind and awaken the currents of God light that connect your consciousness to infinite sweetness, bliss, power, and Oneness.

Your Creation Point is a generator of energy and, when tapped into, has the power to rejuvenate your body, restructure your light body and energy grid, and help you to put your creative ideas into action.

What Does Your Creation Point Do?

When your awareness is One with your Creation Point, you will be able to feel greater balance and less fear controlling your thinking processes. The power of light that exists within your Creation Point supports you in shifting out of fear into love. The Creation Point is a portal into grounded spiritual power and intuition. It awakens a deep and true security and strength within your body. It awakens the secret gateway into your kundalini energy, which is your life force energy that has been depicted over thousands of years as a coiled serpent. The Creation Point is a significant connection point to your whole brain. When you are anchored energetically and focused in your Creation Point, along with other higher *Power Point Centers,* you can feel empowering conscious energies click on in your brain. Your Creation Point is a meeting point for all of your *Power Point Centers* to communicate through to your entire nervous system.

An awakened Creation Point can relieve lower back pain by realigning your sacrum. It can help to open the energies in your sacrum, womb, pelvic floor, middle, and lower back. Stress and long-held mental limitations can be worked through by connecting your awareness into the Creation Point and letting go of old anxieties and fears that have been grabbing your attention. When you connect your speaking or singing voice to your Creation Point, you begin to step into BEing embodied as the presence that you are.

Your Creation Point is a portal into the multi-dimensional consciousness within your physical and energy bodies. It bridges and connects what needs to be awakened in your consciousness with the light of your True Self.

Your Creation Point also has the ability to expand your field of energy as a sphere of power and protection around you.

Activating your Creation Point awakens your life force energies and opens your creative powers to create from your soul. When you are simultaneously connected into your Creation Point, root center, heart center, the back of your skull, and third eye, you will feel a flow of power that integrates your body and mind with the light. You feel the strength to come through any challenge and learn how to manifest your highest ideals into your life.

How To Find Your Creation Point

Your Creation Point is located approximately 2.5 inches below your navel. An easy way to locate it is to place your thumb in your navel, your pinky on the top of your pubic bone, and then drop your index finger down on to your lower belly with your right hand. This point is your second *Power Point Center*, also known as your tantien or second chakra. Now, bring your index finger from your left hand down on to your belly in between your index finger and your thumb. This is your Creation Point.

How To BE in Your Creation Point

Bring your focus from your mind down into the Creation Point. Close your eyes, lift your eyelids up just a bit, so only a slight amount of light can come through. Your eyelids are 1/10 open. Raise your inner gaze into the third eye. Sit and breathe, inhaling through the nose and out of the nose.

Once you are in your Creation Point, you will feel a calm, gentle, and strong connection into your core energy. It may feel new, or like an old forgotten friend, but in time, women will feel a deep connection into their divine feminine power within their womb and comfortable with moving their kundalini serpent energy. Men will feel a body-level connection to their truth and an enduring strength to support feeling connected into their body and into their feelings. Both women and men will be able to be in their feeling self, while also being able to stay grounded, rooted, and in touch with universal reality rather than just the thinking mind reality.

What Happens When Your Creation Point is Open and Clear?

When your Creation Point is open and clear, you are able to access your feelings, power, clarity, positive energies, inner strength, and compassion. You are able to embody your True Self, go deeper into your soul, live from your heart center, and experience greater confidence and self-love.

You will also:

- Increase your physical well-being and health by strengthening your digestion and life force energies

- Be able to articulate your thoughts and feelings

- Complete projects that are important to you

- Find it easier to let go of past hurts, compulsive behaviors, resentments, and fears

- Feel more connection to the earth and life

- Increase your ability to meditate

- Enjoy whole body sensuality

- Have better results with yoga, working out, and sports

- Find the power within your speaking and singing voice

- Maintain your frequency of light

- Embody the presence of your Whole Self

What Happens When Your Creation Point is Blocked or Shut Down?

You will:

- Fear speaking your truth

- Have difficulties manifesting your life dreams and desires

- Feel overwhelmed by tasks

- Feel challenged to complete and finish projects

- Live from your head

- Lose energy

- Lack vitality

- Avoid your own creativity, power, and gifts

- Sabotage your own actions

- Give away your power

- Have difficulties having an orgasm

- Feel alone in the world and isolated

- Live in fear of rejection and abandonment

How to Create a Sphere of Protection Using Your Creation Point

Your Creation Point is a powerful meeting place of highly attuned energies that, when activated, can supercharge your energy field and amp up your focus to fulfill your life tasks and goals. The Creation Point, being a generator of pure energy, has the ability to be a source of energetic protection for you. We all need to know how to create a sphere of light protection to protect our energy field. One effective tool to put into practice is to create a sphere of light from your Creation Point.

To begin, bring your focus into your Creation Point and look for sparks of light that are moving and shooting upwards from deep within its center. Bring your awareness into the core of light within you and merge with them. As you keep your eyes closed, send the sparks of light out around your body and create a strong crystalline sphere that completely encompasses you. Your Creation Point Sphere is a full 360-degree circle that can help you hold the frequencies of your light and support being in full awareness. As you create your Creation Point Sphere, step into the center of your Self and breathe into your Self with a long inhalation and exhalation. Keep your focus in your heart center and then create a layer of gold light around your sphere to add to its strength. Feel free to add a layer of platinum, bronze, or silver for added protection. Your Creation Point Sphere will be sufficient to protect you from negativity, low vibrations, and other people's projections.

3 Steps to Awakening Your Creation Point

As you begin the following three-step process, bring your awareness into your heart and into the present moment.

Step 1

Sit in easy pose, a simple cross-legged position, spine upright. If sitting on a chair is more comfortable for you, please do. Reach your chest forward, reach your shoulder blades together, and extend your tailbone towards the earth.

Raise your chest upwards a bit, slightly bring chin down towards the chest.

Begin to breathe into the Creation Point.

Allow your breath to fill the space within your Creation Point.

See the light within your Creation Point.

Feel the light.

Bring your focus into the Creation Point.

Merge your focus into your Creation Point.

BE One in the Creation Point. See flames of pure white fire in the Creation Point.

Feel them begin to move.

See, Feel, BE. Allow them to expand into the spine and to take up more space.

Very slowly, very, very slowly, like a butterfly emerging out of a cocoon, begin to allow the breath and prana (life force energies) to move up through the spine. Focus into each vertebrae, filling them with light.

Feel warmth rise up the spine. Visualize the energy moving through the spine into the center of your skull. Expand your attention and energy into the back of your skull. Allow the energy to expand into the center of the head and then into the third eye, which is the pineal gland, about two inches inside of the forehead.

Once again, move the energy slowly up the spine, through each vertebrae, into the back of the skull, and then into the third eye. Relax. Remember, it is subtle.

Allow the energy and light to move down inside of the central core channel of the body as you allow your breath to gently inhale and exhale into your Creation Point.

Step 2

Sit in easy pose, a simple cross-legged position, spine upright. Raise the chest upwards a bit, slightly bring chin down towards the chest.

Inhale through your nose and fill the lower belly as you gently pull the Creation Point into the lower spine. With as little effort as you can, exhale your breath through your nose in a continual rhythmical breath. Gently pump the Creation Point through the action of your breath. Focus on the exhalation through your nostrils, and the inhalation will happen naturally. This is the breath of fire. See the light in your Creation Point as flames of pure white fire. Feel the energy gently massaging your spine. BE One with the breath.

Let it BE.
Subtle.
Gentle.
Relaxed.

As you gently pull the Creation Point into the spine, expand the breath into your sacrum and tailbone area. Fill your lower back with breath. As you gently draw the light energies up your spine, let them kiss your third eye with butterfly wings.

Stay with the Breath of Fire for as long as you want and is comfortable. Feel the prana gently move up the spine, touching the third eye. Rest and BE in the stillness within your third eye. Rest and BE in stillness in your heart. Rest and BE in stillness in your third eye and in your heart at the same time.

Step 3

Place your right palm on your lower belly and your left palm on your forehead.

Feel the connection of the energy as you gently inhale and exhale.

Begin a very gentle Breath of Fire. Make sure that you focus on the exhalation of the breath through your nostrils, pulling the Creation Point into the spine.

Now, shift the positioning of your palms on your lower belly and forehead to placing your left thumb on your third eye and your right thumb on your Creation Point. Feel the connection of energies between the two points. Continue Breath of Fire until you feel a deep connection. Take a deep inhalation in through your nose. Hold the breath. Suspend the breath. To suspend your breath, you will pull up your spine out of your navel, pull up the muscles around your genitals, pull up your diaphragm, and lower your chin a bit. Maintain your thumb positions. Exhale. Rest. Relax.

Activating Your Power Point Centers

Spend 5-15 minutes each day activating your *Power Point Centers* with the following practice:

Begin by bringing light into your heart center from above your head. Fill your heart with light. Then, bring your focus

THE INFINITE POSSIBILITIES OF YOUR POWER POINT CENTERS

into the light within your heart by dropping your focus into the larger space between your heart center and solar plexus. Allow the energetic pull into your solar plexus to center you. BE in your heart.

Next, bring light down from above your head into your root center, your *First Power Point Center*. Fill your root center with light. Then, bring your focus into the light within your root center.

Continue the exact same process, bringing and focusing light into each *Center*:

- *Second Power Point Center*, your lower belly

- *Third Power Point Center*, your creation point center

- *Fourth Power Point Center*, your navel

- *Fifth Power Point Center*, your solar plexus

- *Sixth Power Point Center*, your heart center

- *Seventh Power Point Center*, your throat center

- *Eighth Power Point Center*, back of the skull

- *Ninth Power Point Center*, your third eye

- *Tenth Power Point Center,* your crown center

Remember to:

- Focus light into each *Power Point Center* for as long as you can.

- Keep your focus into each center of light up against the inside of your spine.

- Accept however the experience happens for you. All that is important is practicing shifting into the light and BEing in the light.

- Just stay with the intention and focus to increase being in the light in each *Power Point Center*. By doing this exercise every day you will experience rapid results.

Enlightening Yourself

Power Point Center Integration

When your *Power Point Centers* are connected, they create a holding tank of vitality, light, and power that, unless experienced, is sometimes difficult to comprehend. The key to integration occurs when the circuits of energy and consciousness between the *Power Point Centers* interconnect smoothly and easily. If you allow your breath to be slow and deep and move into the core shaft of light within your body, you will be able to feel your *Power Point Center* energies connecting. Your core shaft is a wide-open elevator shaft corridor, which is a super highway of light that connects all of your organs and nervous system. Since the light is always moving in you, the more that

THE INFINITE POSSIBILITIES OF YOUR POWER POINT CENTERS

you can relax and allow the love to fill you, the more you will enjoy the journey.

As your *Power Point Centers* integrate, the essence of your True Self creates a harmonic network of energy in your consciousness. At times your mind will resist, but each time that you choose to feel the expansion of your energy field expanding, your integration will deepen. Without a doubt, you can trust that all of the unresolved parts of your Self from this and all previous lifetimes and dimensional time frames will be able to be unified.

Your *Power Point Centers* integrate the essence of your soul aspects and release the dissonance and disharmony of the energies in your subconscious created by living in separation from your spiritual core. Your whole energetic and soul matrix is reconfigured in the light of Infinite Source. You will be able to access and integrate the forgotten aspects of yourself with your Whole Self. Your *Power Point Centers* are your stability through this process. They will hold the power and the light for any and all transformational shifts that you, as a unique being, must make to evolve. They help you find and become the miracle of who you truly are.

To begin to interconnect and integrate your spiritual light and power in your body, start with your solar plexus, the gateway to spiritual and emotional freedom. Whenever you feel a bit out of balance and tired, or seek to become connected to your Self in the moment, breathe into your solar plexus. It is the entry point into your energetic, spiritual, and soul matrix. Breathe in gold light and fill your solar plexus with its radiance. Mentally release any energies that you might have taken on that are not "yours."

INTEGRATING YOUR *POWER POINT CENTERS*

You can step into mastery levels of integration by working daily with your *Power Point Centers*. First, practice holding your focused attention into one *Power Point Center*, then two or more *Power Point Centers* simultaneously. Each time that you hold the light in one of your *Power Point Centers*, you establish an anchor into your core strength. A profound synergy that resembles the interconnection within a molecule opens in your body as you reconnect the energy grid of light that is found within your *Power Point* network.

Here are some outcomes when you focus, integrate, and unify two or more of these *Power Point Centers* at the same time:

POWER POINT CENTER INTEGRATION CHART

Integrating Your Power Points	*Outcome*
6th, 3rd, 1st **Power Points** Heart Center, Creation Point, Root	Energy Field Protection & Whole Self Empowerment
9th, 5th and 1st **Power Points** Third Eye, Solar Plexus, Root	Integrated Thinking
9th, 5th, 2nd **Power Points** Third Eye, Solar Plexus, Tantien	Integrated Emotions
6th and 2nd **Power Points** Heart Center and Tantien	Aligned Intuition
6th, 3rd and 2nd **Power Points** Heart Center, Creation Point, Tantien	Personal Power Integration
8th, 6th and 1st **Power Points** Back of Skull, Heart Center, Root	Grounding of the Heart
10th, 5th, 2nd and 1st **Power Points** Crown, Solar Plexus, Tantien, Root	Clear Decision Making
22nd, 21st, 11-14th, 6th **Power Points** Center of both feet, center of earth, 4-dimensional levels of soul above the head, Heart Center	Energetic Healing and Awakening
9th, 6th, 3rd, 2nd **Power Points** Third eye, Heart, Creation Point, Tantien	Being Present

Integrating Your Power Points	Outcome
21st, 20th, 8th, 6th, 5th, $1st$ Power Points Center of earth, God dimension above head, Back of Skull, Heart, Solar Plexus, Root	Sexually Connected
10th, 9th and 6th Power Points Crown, Third Eye, Heart	God Focused
7th, 6th, 3rd, 2nd, 1st Power Points Throat, Heart Center, Creation Point, Tantien, and Root	Standing in and Speaking Your Truth

Spirit Gateways®/Iana Lahi All Rights Reserved ©

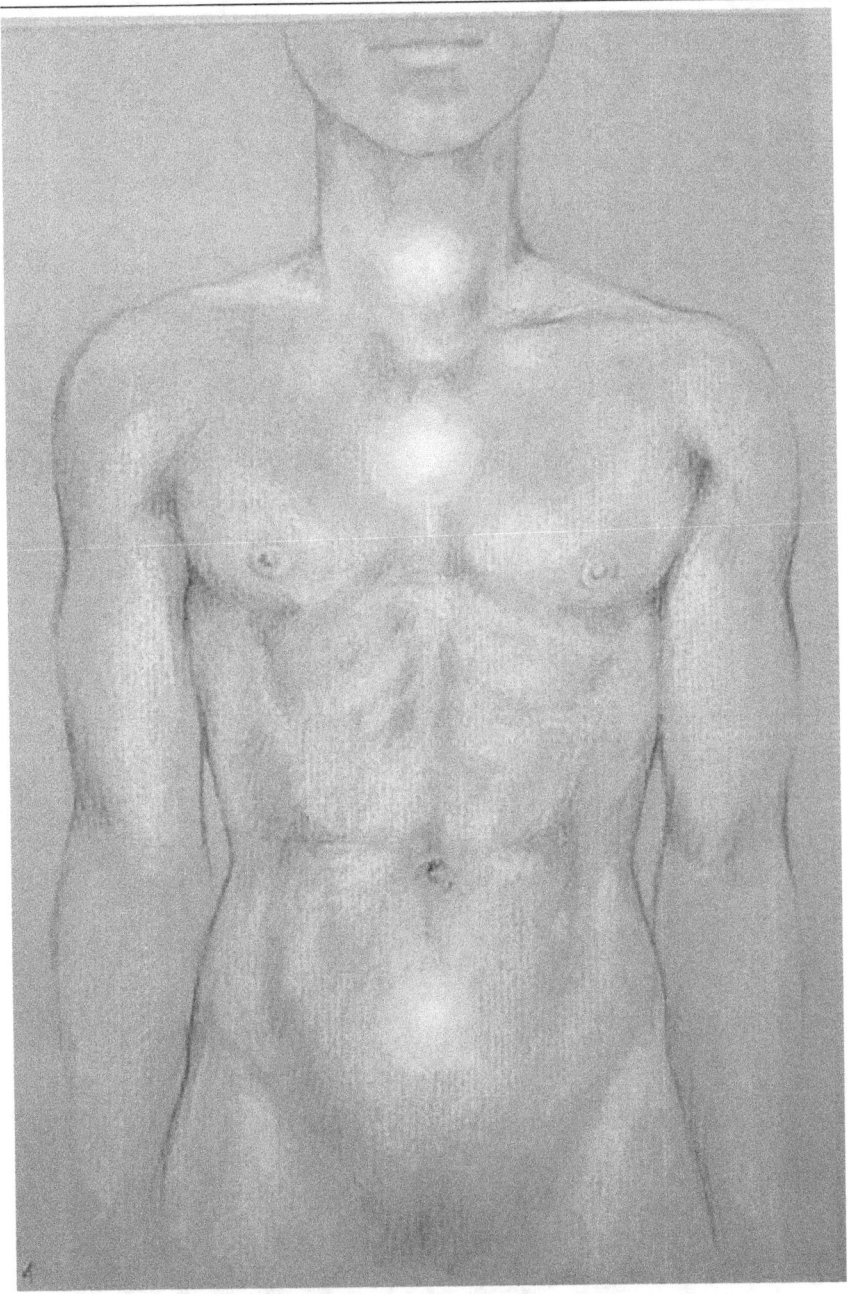

*Power Point Integration Centers -
Creation Point, Heart, Throat*

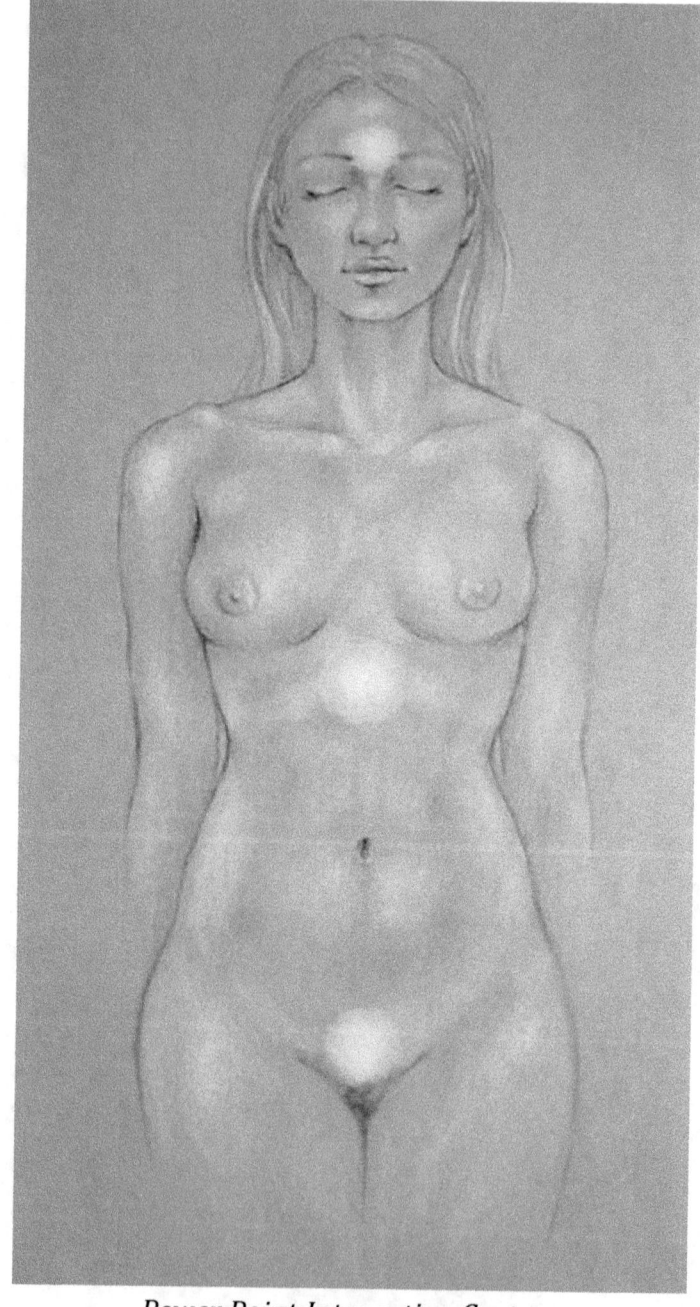

Power Point Integration Centers
Root, Solar Plexus, Third Eye

THE INFINITE POSSIBILITIES OF YOUR POWER POINT CENTERS

Your integrated *Power Point Centers* give you back your original energetic connection to BE One with Infinite Source. Through the unity of your *Power Point Centers* and your Bodymind and soul, you can experience direct communication and messages from your Higher Self, your spiritual guides, the universe, and Infinite Source—God directly. As you access your connection with Infinite Source, you will feel in your body when you are "plugged in" and when you are not. You will find yourself trusting your responses more and the actions that come to you to create and bring unified consciousness and clarity into every situation around you.

- You will know that you and Infinite Source are one force of love.

- You will discover that Infinite Source is the crystalline power of light living within you as YOU.

- You will behold the reunion with your authentic Self as possible within each moment of your life.

- Your soul will know that it has a safe, nurturing, and loving internal home to live within.

- You will be able to build a foundation from within yourself that enables you to be in tune to your higher needs and the calling of your wisdom into action and sets into motion your enlightening.

The possibilities to stand within the light of your God-inspired Self become endless. As you light up your inner network of truth, you will naturally light up the world around you with the gifts of your soul.

REMEMBER:

- Your *Power Point Centers* are gateways into your authentic vibration. They help to reconnect the light energy generator within your body to make possible rising into the essence of who you are.

- Fear blocks our light and prevents our greater truth, vitality, and clarity from emanating. It hides in anger, grief, mistrust, insecurity, doubt, shame, guilt, and illusion and prevents you from feeling and BEing in the love that is within you and that you are.

- Each of your *Power Point Centers* has a specific function to access and translate the vibrational frequencies of Infinite Source. Your spiritual "work" consists of being connected into the light energies within your body through your *Power Point Centers*. You want to stay present in a state of openness, connection, and expansion.

- Your inner conflicts begin when your core spiritual Self separates its consciousness from Infinite Source and creates an ego expression of itself to manage living life from fear and separation. These unresolved separations create inner conflict—where your mind chooses, assesses, and objectifies life from separation and illusion.

- By clearing and reconnecting your *Power Point Centers* with the vibration of light, you shift out of being tied and attached to your past responses and feelings of separation, pain, and discomfort.

- Each of the *Power Point Centers* within your body has a specific location and purpose. As you learn how to touch into your *Power Point Centers* through focused actions and intention, you can achieve specific outcomes that further open and enlighten you.

- You can heal the separations of your body, mind, and psyche by releasing the old beliefs and fears that prevent your *Power Point* life force energies from flowing freely.

- Your *Power Point Centers* are the most direct highway into your original energetic connection to Infinite Source and you can step into mastery levels of integration by working with them daily.

- Just by becoming still and sitting in the light each day you allow the limitless light of grace to enter and shift your life.

BELIGHT MEDITATION

Revisit the *Power Point Center* and Creation Point exercises in this chapter and follow the practice recommendations:

- *Power Point Center* Clearing Meditation

- The Power of Being You – A Daily Practice

- How to Create a Sphere of Protection Using Your Creation Point

- 3 Steps to Awakening Your Creation Point

- Activating Your *Power Point Centers*

- Integrating Your *Power Point Centers*

CHAPTER TEN

Awakening to the Voice and Themes of the Soul

"The infinite Soul sits within the center of consciousness. If you can feel its breath upon you, you will know intrinsically the purpose of your life."
— Chris Griscom

Awakening to Your Soul

Take in for a moment that you have had thousands of different experiences from the day you were born. Every breath, feeling, and interaction with people and the world around you fuels, enhances, challenges, or diminishes the bright, energetic light that you are. The soft touch of someone you love can make your inner light crackle like a sparkler on the Fourth of July. The feelings of not being heard or of being rejected can dim your inner light even for a moment and stir up old, unresolved experiences that can be held on to or quickly released.

Your journeying soul seeks resolution from the incomplete and negative moments in your past. It also desires to find and feel a permanent, steady, and expansive expression of love and union, and to complete whatever it is that you came in this lifetime to fulfill. You have a mission in this life. Even if you are initially unaware of your soul or its mission, your soul knows. If you listen, it will speak to you in the language and frequency that is uniquely its own, and show you what is true and false and most important for your life.

Think of your soul as the artistic, creative, healing, intuitive, insightful, and knowing part of your Self. When you quiet your mind, you are making it safe for your soul to emerge and "talk." Your soul will guide you to expand, to trust, and to listen through its ears and see through its eyes.

To hear your soul, you need to grow quiet inside and listen. At first you can sense the pulse, flow, and energy of its unique language. The doorway to divine intelligence is opened, and you feel more alive and in tune with your Self and what life is trying to teach you. Once your soul opens and you listen, feel and trust in its guidance. Your inner visual and feeling levels will also open and soar. You will just "know that you know" things. You will trust your feelings and be able to listen to what you need to express, manifest, expand, and heal. You will begin to see through the eyes of light and be able to differentiate what supports your life and what works against you walking the path of your soul.

Your soul will communicate with you through color, sound, imagery, symbols, and words. You will discover that your soul has a language that is distinctively its own. Your soul functions and communicates to help you understand how your life purpose and the world co-exist and co-create together. Your soul is a bridge between your mind and your emotions, your mind and your body, and your mind and Spirit. It is an interpreter, guide, healer, lover and innovator. Your soul wants you to WAKE UP to what has always been right inside of you, and in front of you. At times you will be amazed at the contrast between how your mind interprets life and how your soul will guide and awaken you to the life that you are meant to be living. Moment by moment, the old sanskaras and deeply embedded beliefs about your Self are chiseled away, making space for the light of your soul to emerge.

Alas, most of us spend far too much of our lives lost, numb, or too afraid to see or listen to what the soul is trying to reveal. Yet rest assured, your soul will do whatever it takes to awaken you. Its internal drive for wholeness requires it. Your soul is not just the spark of your life; it is also the catalyst and gateway that make it possible to BE ONE in yourself and with all of life. There is no escaping the soul or its call. There is also no faster way to enlightened living than through your soul.

> *Your soul will do whatever it takes to awaken you to your True Self.*

Soul Themes

Directly before you came into this present life, you existed as the whole light of your soul—your eternal and Original Self. As you seek to connect with your Original Self—the expansive light that you are—you will begin to recognize certain core themes that are part of your soul's expression. All of the life experiences that you choose are meant to help you to pay attention to the messages and guidance of your soul.

There are four basic soul themes that play a role in how we experience the surrounding world and ourselves. The themes are LOVE, TRUTH, UNION, and JOY. While we are all unique expressions of human and divine energy, these four basic themes manifest in varying degrees within each of us. The degree to which these themes drive aspects of your life impacts the challenges and joys you may experience along your soul journey. Your soul themes touch into the core of your existence and shape the story of your life. As you begin to reconnect into the greater aspects of your soul and light, having an awareness of your soul themes will help "make sense" of the deeper stirrings and impulses emanating from within you.

You have all of these soul themes within you, and you will move through each of them in your lifetime. As each theme is activated and deepened throughout your life, they will move you closer to knowing who you are. You will be guided to find truth in your life and love within your soul. You will feel a longing for the exhilaration of joy or union with something bigger than your mind and into the unlimited realms of Spirit as a way to come closer to Infinite Source and be touched by its light. Yet, you will also come to know that you have a primary soul theme that rises above all others and seems to direct the trajectory of your life. By paying attention and being attentive to what is yearning to be seen, felt, or heard within your heart, you will gravitate to your soul theme.

When you know and recognize a predominant soul theme, you can trust your thoughts and feelings associated with its wisdom and guidance. You can make use of what each soul theme brings into your life as a way to align your life to your inner power. When you begin to recognize your soul themes and their composition within you, it becomes easier to trust how you want to express BEing You. "Why you are here" and how to access your higher consciousness to fulfill your destiny become clearer. As you come to "know" your soul themes while you integrate the parts of your soul that have been forgotten, suppressed, or hidden, you discover the power to be both the director and leading character in the story of your life. Each experience in your life provides the opportunity to help you know yourself. By knowing the themes of your soul, you will be able to make the most use of what life brings to you to help you become all that you are. You will begin to consciously heal humanity's core wound and how it plays out in you. You will come to the realization that who you are on a soul level has the right to exist. Who you are truly matters. The light that you are, the love that yearns to be expressed, guides your way home.

The Theme of LOVE

The ultimate theme of every soul that exists is love. It may come as no surprise given that so much of our lives seems to revolve around love—wanting it, not wanting it, figuring out how to get it, maintain it, or find a better, deeper version of it. Love is the soul's theme. If lived deeply, it moves us out of the cycle of mental and emotional repetition and pain and opens us to profound peace and fulfillment. To see and live from love shifts you out of living in a paradigm of separation and pain into wholeness and remembrance of your true nature.

The love that you are is a higher and deeper expression of the original, pure love that flows from within the center of creation. You were born connected to this pure love. The love within your soul is unconditional, expansive, and freeing. It guides your path back to the Source of life. You have the power and capacity to open into original love when you reclaim your soul and trust in the direction of its knowingness instead of the workings of your mind. To enter into unconditional, original love as a first step, you are called to participate in ending all judgment towards yourself.

> *The original, unconditional love you seek lives within you.*

To unconditionally love yourself, you must first accept yourself and release the unconscious patterns of judgment and fear passed to you from your ancestors and our culture. Within your ancestral lineage are patterns that you are given as part of your birth experience into your body. These patterns hold the key to your transformation. Upon arrival as a soul in a new body, you assess your family and living environment and make the decision from infancy into your younger childhood years whether to remain ONE with your spiritual light and power or to leave it. As you recognize the original decisions that you made in your earlier years to leave your inner light and begin to vibrantly reclaim it, you can begin to step into and live in the union of love, power, and compassion that has always been within you.

By changing your loyalty from old alignments of separation and control into alignments of compassion and acceptance, you can make a shift and permanently change your life. Old alignments may include deciding that you cannot live for yourself unless everyone around you is functioning and happy first. You may hold onto the belief that it is your responsibility to have everything together and to be perfect. You may believe that you will be rejected, or even worse, left to die emotionally because your light is too intense and strong. You may believe that you do not have the right to exist. You may believe that unless you prove your worthiness, you have no right to succeed in life, be loved, or to be honored.

You have been taught to leave yourself and maintain certain belief patterns and ways of living that further diminish your connection to Infinite Source. Each time that you leave yourself, it creates a false feeling state of being separate from life and others and deepens the illusion of not being good enough or worthy enough of love. You must refuse to leave yourself, even if others taught you as a child that you had to relinquish BEing your True Self to be loved. As you reclaim the love and essence of your True Self now, you will empower yourself and find the meaning of your life. When you end the cycle of abandoning your True Self, you will stay planted in living your truth and vision. You will be able to remain steady living within the center of your Self, while the rest of the world and the people around you act out their fears and the emptiness of their hearts and souls.

As the soul theme of love manifests in your life and challenges you to be true to your Self—BE anchored in your love. You can be busy from sunrise until sunset with life responsibilities yet remain united and One in your love. Be willing to stop being what others expect and want you to be, and instead be the love that you truly are. If you are judged, bless and forgive the person. They have served to help expedite the clearing of your karma and their own, and to help you to realize that you have the power to stop judging yourself and others. If you are rejected, look to see what you might still be rejecting in your Self. If you feel alone, explore how you are abandoning your Self.

When you abandon yourself because of the expectations or needs of others, it becomes more difficult to hear what your heart's intuition is telling you. You might change yourself in order to get what you think is love because you are not sure you are truly worthy of love. It is easy to feel imperfect and unworthy.

> **BE willing to stop being what others expect
> and want you to BE.
> BE the love that you truly are.**

Remember to be present and to listen to the inner voice of your soul. The more that you stay with yourself, the more you will be able to feel and receive the unconditional love that lives within you. Unconditional love lives in every cell of your body and drives your soul forward to meet and merge with the divine. The light of Spirit unlocks a deep knowingness within your cells. Discover and embrace the love within you by bringing together your soul parts with unconditional acceptance.

As you let go of your fears, judgments, and attachments to fixed ways of being, unlimited possibilities will open within you and pour to you from life. Your heart will burst open, and you will begin to trust being open and connected. It may feel painful at first, given that coming out of separation can reveal the hurt that has accumulated for years and over lifetimes from living in separation. The habitual relapse of seeing life through pain can be recognized and released so you can let go of who you think you need to be in order to be accepted by others, and of your expectations of how your life is "supposed to be." Through surrendering your old identity and simply feeling the love that you have always carried in your heart, unconditional love will bloom within you.

You will find yourself choosing to be "in love" with yourself, with love, and with all of life over and over again because it just feels right. This original love from Infinite Source is the flame of Oneness in your heart. The realization that you are love is felt as you continue to bond with the love within you. The more you agree to surrender into love and Infinite Source and become One with its divine essence, the more unconditional love for yourself and others becomes grounded in your body. This is a doorway into the core vitality of life. Love is truly the backbone for all transformation. For whatever you look upon with the eyes of love has the possibility of completion, renewal, and healing. All of the painful qualities of separation that we all suffer through can heal by seeing them with love and releasing our attachment to having external circumstances fix them.

> *Unconditional love lives in every cell of your body and drives your soul forward to meet and merge with the divine.*

The Theme of UNION

Union is a desire that originates in the soul to become one with God—Infinite Source. Your desire for union is natural. It is an innate part of your soul DNA. It began the moment that you were conceived.

A sperm and an egg come together and unify to create new life. In effect, this is the same urge or drive of the soul. We all strive for union or connection with others and all things in life to experience the bliss of creation and love. The parent connects with the child, a lover with his lover's lips, the writer with the written word, an artist with her canvas, the dancer with the vibrancy of energy within the body, or a hummingbird seeking the nectar of a flower. All seek union in some form that can replicate the ultimate divine union with love. Our hearts and souls seek to find completion, fulfillment, and peace in the union of love.

From the first moment of your life, you vibrate and resonate to love. Whether or not you are given love or your love is received, you will naturally seek to replicate how this feels for the rest of your life. If your initial experience with love was a healthy connection, then your soul will remain more intact. Love that you receive early in life allows your soul to be recognized, seen, and to know that it exists. It gives you a greater capacity to create strong and long-lasting relationships.

In contrast, if you had a difficult beginning that lacked love, you are likely to experience a feeling of being lost, confused, and depressed because your soul develops an even greater need to be received and to know and express itself. Each day open to life, nature's beauty and simplicity, new hobbies, new friendships, the joy of serving and giving to others, and the love that waits inside of you—waiting to be received by You.

While your soul resonates to BEing unified and directly connected with the source of all life, the state of your life may often feel more separate than unified. That feeling of separation comes from having separated your heart and soul with Infinite Source, and it is often intensified by the world around you. Ironically, your fragmentation and separation from the love within you can attract individuals and situations that only intensify your feelings of separation until you are willing to face it.

At this time in history, we have to reunite our soul aspects to walk our life path with full awareness. The pain of feeling separate from others, your Self and from your life purpose is exasperated every time you choose to leave, deny, suppress, or hide who you really are. When you leave yourself to survive, fit in, or receive love from another, you split apart the love and power of your soul and fragment from Infinite Source. Aspects of your power will look for places to hide, feel safe, or just hang out in the recesses of your body until you are ready to fully accept and BE who you are.

The good news is that no matter what your experience is, your soul always has an opportunity to expand and go past its present separation, limitations, and fears. Life itself is the experience of your mind and soul expanding and contracting to learn and BE. We are all given opportunities to grow through the smallest and most difficult challenges of our lives with mastery. The union that is possible within your mind, heart, body, and soul creates the opportunity to experience your original, divine love and Oneness with Infinite Source. Your soul remembers the experience of BEing One in Infinite Source. Whether or not you know it consciously, deep within the essence of your being dwells the divine memory of BEing One and living in the heart of Infinite God Source. This remembrance is the barometer of all of your experiences and helps you to know and live your truth.

Experiencing direct connection with the divine comes from union with your light, truth, inner love, and creativity. As you trust, surrender, open, and receive the nourishment from BEing in union, a new level of conscious awakening is ignited. Union with love is the whole point or drive of your soul. It is the very specific task that defines why you are alive and here on this earth.

> *Union with your inner love, light, truth, and creativity give you direct experience with the divine.*

The Theme of Truth

The desire to be truly happy will guide you to find the truth of your soul. There is an "isness" to truth that exists beyond external circumstances, material possessions, wealth, superficial roles, and the need to control. Truth exists independently of everything, but when synchronized into your daily life has the ability to create miracles. The truth of who you are blazes within your soul. It is a silent partner, an ally guiding you home to where God and your soul are One.

By relying upon your truth, "who you are" is revealed. Your truth is a loyal friend, sometimes difficult to follow because it means you must change your relationship to specific situations, people, and behaviors. Your truth is found through silence. It speaks to you through the infinite and limitless intelligence that is found in Spirit—the essence of your BEing. Through nature, through being open and empty, your ability to connect with your truth quota grows. You can find your truth through all aspects of your life. Everyday searches for truth might include choosing which social cause you may want to support, saying what you feel to a friend or partner, building a heart-centered business, beginning a relationship that forces you to move through old fears, moving away from your home town, or something as simple as what music you listen to. You may need to choose a mentor, a new doctor or healer, which online blog or newspaper to follow, face healing a health issue, contemplate whether someone would make a good business partner or not, whether a particular spiritual teaching is right for you or not, whether to continue dating someone, whether to follow a certain career path or not, stay or leave your marriage, go to your high school reunion, or decide whether juicing and organic foods really do make a difference in your life. The moments that you are able to laugh at yourself, or feel and hear God speaking through your heart, are all everyday honest connections with truth.

Until you know the truth of who you are, it is more than likely that you will pretend to be who you want to be. It takes a lot of courage to find your truth. To find your truth moment-to-moment, you must be flexible and willing to surrender your lower will to your higher will. Your lower will exists out of its need to survive. When abandoned and left alone to survive on its own, your lower will loses faith and trust in others. Once your lower will is acknowledged and supported by your higher will, it will begin to let go of controlling you through fear, withholding, scarcity, poverty, and resentment. Your higher will is driven to unite with super consciousness, the power of your light that will set you free and lift you up out of suffering. Most of us create suffering to find the truth that we have continued to push aside time and time again.

The modern world matrix makes it easy to go along with the latest thoughts and theories and to reject our True Self. Socially, most of us at some point create a False Self to hide behind being the truth of who we are. As we take the plunge to be fully authentic, we find that others want to be around us more and open up. The gift of this work is to support you to BE fully embodied as your authentic and whole Self in everything that you do. Your life is art—creative and empowered interaction with all of life in every moment. Living your truth becomes the ultimate creative play and fulfillment for yourself and others.

When you live in the light of the truth within you, the controls and fears of others have less impact on you and will not be able to control you. Many think they are aligned to their truth, but in reality, they have separated from Infinite Source within themselves, created a False Self, and set themselves apart from others as being "special." They align with the beliefs of their False Self and call that "truth." When we are honest enough to admit how we really feel about ourselves, even in our darkest moments, the light of truth, no matter how painful it may feel, *is* ignited. When faced, pain can push us to the light. To use the cliché, "the truth will set you free."

> **The truth of who you are drives your soul whether you know it or not.**

Remember that your truth is discovered through expanding beyond belief, dogma, judgment, attachment, and fear. The battles that you create within your mind, between one part of yourself and another part, struggle to keep you wondering and doubting whether your actualized truth is of value or not. Sometimes, following the truth of who you are would set you apart from the comfort zones of family, society, and money and feels too risky. So, you choose to dance around your truth and still try to manipulate and control how you are in relationship to a situation until you can't move forward in your life. Then, you are brought to a crossroads of having to choose between what is truth for you and what is false for you. You have to choose between your projections and fears or surrender and acceptance of what really is.

If you follow the truth that lives within you, you will be guided to live the life that evolves your soul for your greatest good. If you live your life copying others, playing a role suited for others, or remain attached to a role you have created for yourself, you are avoiding your truth, and deep down you will know it.

Each time that you open to Spirit by listening and feeling into your body and allow it to touch your soul, it activates and awakens your truth. As you clear your own attachments and beliefs regarding how you think things should be in your life, you make it possible for truth to live through you. The more you can understand, feel, and define who you are separate from your cultural, familial, and religious beliefs, the greater access you will have to your truth. You will begin to see through the illusions of life that are created by cultural standards and familial expectations. They will no longer run you or have what feels like inescapable power over you.

AWAKENING TO THE VOICE AND THEMES OF THE SOUL

> *Your truth is a living power that is found only by expanding beyond belief, dogma, judgment, attachment, and fear.*

When your soul truth is activated by a relationship, a circumstance, your own efforts to surrender and open, or by your higher guidance, you will face all of the ways that you keep yourself from living your truth. You might have to confront anger, fear, and resentment because your truth will demand that you let go of what keeps you living a false reality. The truth of your soul will communicate to you however it can to get through to you. You might experience a loss of a relationship, a health crisis, an intense financial struggle, or an emotional issue. All are ways that your soul is trying to communicate its desire to become consciously One with Infinite Source through your life and teach you to let go of control.

> *Your truth demands that you let go of what keeps you separate.*

To hear your soul truth, meditate in the stillness of your BEing. Imagine driving a manual stick shift car and every time you move from one gear to the next, from first to second, second to third, or from third to fourth, you go through neutral. Within the space between your body and mind resides this same kind of neutral zone that links you to truth. When you reside in this neutral zone, it allows the universe to merge the truth of cosmic consciousness with your soul. Within your neutral zone resides the stillness that you can meditate and focus into to receive unlimited presence, light, and expansion.

When you live each moment from your soul's truth, you will manifest everything for your highest good. As your truth becomes aligned with the greater universal truth, everything that you need to grow into who you are will be given.

The more aligned you are to your truth, the greater the light and love in your life. The more you clear the beliefs of who you thought you "had to be" to be given some version of unconditional or conditional love just to survive, the more love can integrate your heart and soul. As you drop the illusions that you created to separate yourself from Infinite Source, the greater love, power, and presence can fill the core matrix of your BEing. A new relationship based upon deep internal acceptance, release, and surrender help you to BE One with Infinite Source and the joys that this can bring.

> *As your truth becomes aligned with the greater universal truth, everything that you need to grow into who you are will be given.*

The Theme of Joy

Joy is the experience of liberation from any level of suffering. In the moment of realizing that you have come through a difficult or challenging experience and have released resistance, fear, pain, or shame—joy floods your body.

Experiencing joy requires presence. A joyful child is fully aware and present in the moment with all of their senses because they are one in their Whole Self.

To discover joy, we must let go of our barriers to love in all of its forms and welcome in the on pouring of bliss from the divine.

AWAKENING TO THE VOICE AND THEMES OF THE SOUL

To discover joy, we must choose authenticity and connection to the flow of life through our body. Joy is experienced when the mind is not attached to struggle and control. The body, soul, and Spirit united as ONE experiences itself as joy.

Joy is distinctly different from happiness. Joy can be defined as your mind being empty and elated and a feeling of contentment and bliss fill you. While happiness creates pleasure, gratification, and comfort, joy will give you a feeling of exuberance and connectedness to the universe. To feel joy, your heart needs to be connected and open to the divine moment. Living in wonder and gratitude creates a divine relationship with Infinite Source for joy to be released within you.

Joy is a state of being where you are able to soak in and be with the perfection of what is. There is a feeling of lightness and playfulness. It is an abundant and overflowing expression created when you feel united and in synch with all that is around you and in you. Time and space disappear as the heart, body, and soul unite in a zone of bliss. When joy takes you over, your body, breath, Spirit, and life force merge. Joy has no limits, no boundaries. It reaches out into the universe and beyond the confines of your mind into soul. Joy cannot be put into a box. It is as big as the sky. Once you experience joy, it opens your soul to what exists beyond the normal reality of everyday life.

> *To discover joy, we must choose authenticity and connection to the flow of life through our body.*

When the universe calls you to be in joy, follow it. Whether an hour, a day, a month, or a lifetime, let the lightness of your soul open to itself and life. Follow the callings from within your soul. Swim with dolphins, dance in the moonlight, write a poem, decide to start your own business, pay off a credit card, move to a new place, buy yourself or someone that you love roses, take a solo adventure to a place you have never been to before, learn a new language, study something that intrigues you, support a cause, say what you feel, donate what you do not need or use, be kind to a stranger. When you look for joy, it will come into your life sometimes in expected ways. Sometimes you have to switch gears and look for the joy. Run through a field of flowers on a spring day, walk in the rain on a hot summer day, allow yourself to feel seen by someone who means a lot to you, complete a project, watch the full moon rise on a crystal clear night, see a shower of shooting stars, receive being really kissed by your lover, have a baby, be loved by a daughter or a son, BE in God, dance or play music—ask the universe for what you need and open to receive it—with joy.

> *Joy is a healer and has the power to remind us of what is really important in our life. Joy teaches compassion, honor, respect, sacred connection, loving kindness, and acceptance.*

Many of us have experienced emotional pain for being the joy of our Original Self. We felt shamed as a child or young adult for "being joy." Judgment projected at us for being happy and self-expressed, not being seen for who we are, ridiculed, abused, rejected, controlled, feeling like who we are is not enough, all create shame.

Shame is the experience of feeling that who we are does not matter. We feel unsupported to be who we are and doubt our right to exist.

When we are shamed, the inner gateways to our heart shut down, and we experience feeling separate and alone. Like a grey cloud on a foggy morning, shame rolls in taking the place of where joy would usually reside.

When past pain, suffering, and attachments are embraced by the joy within our heart, the courage to release the past can blossom. Within even the most wounded heart exists joy, and its light has the power to illuminate even the most painful past experiences.

To experience joy, you must be willing to go beyond how your mind controls and holds on. Letting go of how you block joy from emerging in you can only happen when you let go and release your beliefs that you do not deserve joy and all that it brings. Joy teaches you to let go of what you think you need to be and do, and all the ways that you block love from coming into your life. Joy teaches you to get out of the way and to just BE. Joy teaches how to receive support from the universe. Once you open to receive help and support from the universe, joy can flow in through the door you have opened. The more you yearn for joy, the more you must release and let go of your own identity, any attachments to the role that you have in the world, and what you believe you need to be to get what you want. From a place of being empty and receptive, life can begin to fill the goblet of your heart.

> *Throw away your false perceptions, judgments, and expectations and fully experience a moment in its most simple and divine truth.*

When you experience joy in your life, it opens you to love. The greater the joy that you choose to be in, the deeper the love you can find within yourself and others. If you find it difficult to find joy in your life, first seek the peace that comes from being real with what hurts inside yourself. Peace will bring you joy because joy is a state of being where conflict does not exist. Once inner pain is recognized, acknowledged, and accepted, the joy of your soul will guide you through any conflict. Joy stabilizes both the integrity of love and truth within your soul and ultimately pulls you into union with the divine. By trusting your joy, you will come through even the most challenging moments and circumstances of your life.

The Human Theme of Abandonment, Betrayal, and Rejection (ABR)

As you begin to become more aware of how your soul themes manifest and shape your everyday experiences, you will come to realize that the four core themes of love, union, truth, and joy are mediated by what might seem like a fifth soul theme—the tri-fecta theme of Abandonment, Betrayal, and Rejection (ABR).

Abandonment, Betrayal, and Rejection are not only the themes of some of the greatest dramas ever written or viewed on screen, they are also an essential theme of human existence and the experience of our souls.

From our earliest years, we all seem to live in fear of being abandoned, betrayed, or rejected. All too often when it occurs, it sends us reeling into a spiral of fear, self-doubt, self-loathing, and anger at the people and world around us. While there is no doubt that at some point in our lives we all experience some degree of ABR (abandonment, betrayal, and rejection) from others, the broader truth of the matter is that we also spend our lives doing it to ourselves, which fuels and reinforces our inner separation. Most of us live our lives denying the truth within our soul, heart, mind, and body and who we really are. However, the more you can heal your relationship to how you abandon, betray, or reject yourself, the more you can benefit from the power and strength of your true soul themes to transform your life.

> *Most of us spend our lives abandoning, rejecting, and betraying ourselves.*

Our agreement to self-abandon, betray, and reject ourselves is bred into us. We are taught to shove aside our body rhythms, inner voice, melodies, intuition, power, creativity, truth, light, and our knowingness. This counterproductive behavior is fueled by the social conformism and cultural norms of society, expectations, and controls from family and our own illusions and ideas about who we think we should be. At first blush, everything we do seems to work to create comfort or safety. You follow a certain behavior, action, or belief because "that is the way things work." It is how you will get what you need or want most in this world.

You ABR yourself when you live in the safety net of someone or something else even if it does not make you happy. You ABR yourself when you shift out and judge yourself based upon how one or more individuals in your life respond to you. Losing yourself, giving over yourself, shutting down yourself, living in a facade, hiding in yourself, doubting yourself, manipulating yourself, and rejecting yourself are acts of ABR (abandonment, betrayal, and rejection). Most of us create psychological and physical conditions that break down our vital energies because of ABR. We abandon, betray, and reject ourselves because we think if we do not, we will be alone. This fear of aloneness creates terror in the body. It is so deep that we have no way of accessing it except through pushing it away. This terror is really the fear that who you are is not enough to BE loved.

Living in ABR keeps the lie of being separate from God—our Infinite Source, and from love alive. Within Infinite Source, ABR does not exist. It only exists in the matrix of separation. By allowing your heart to open to the higher purpose and themes of your soul, you can surrender to the genuine expression of who you are. Underneath all of the inner sorrow, pain, or fear that you hide behind or use as a barrier to living fully lives the essence of your True Self.

We all abandon, betray, and reject ourselves to differing degrees. Most of us at some moment in our lives feel undeserving of joy or happiness. We may have felt that we let ourselves or someone else down. Perhaps we could not make everyone else happy or our way of thinking and acting was so different from everyone else that we decided we were the cause for the discomfort all around us. We may remain wired to fulfill our family of origin's belief systems and needs and never feel in touch with being the source of our own fulfillment. We value ourselves based upon how we are "there" for others. We secretly believe that we are unlovable, and no one will ever truly love us. To continue these beliefs, we continue "ABRing" ourselves for our entire lives. Our core beliefs become bigger than our inner truths.

For example, a woman might possess a core belief that she is responsible for her parent's divorce. She unconsciously wishes that she could have succeeded in helping them to stay together. Therefore, she spends her whole life betraying herself, wishing she could have been better, bigger, more powerful—just to make a difference. She lives a life trying to make up for supposed inadequacies in her job, as a mother, and as a marriage partner. She is always trying to be what she thinks other people want and need, failing to listen to what she really needs.

Another example could be when a man or woman is asked by their mother or father to give up their own dreams and career choices, which later creates a relationship, career, or health break down. Or, a woman abandons her own creative power because as a child and teenager it threatened her parents and siblings, and she always felt like the rejected outcast.

You can end your cycles of abandoning, betraying, and rejecting yourself by looking for the parts of yourself that have been pushed away or denied. See what or where you were not acknowledged or seen. You have to show up for yourself completely. You have to pay attention on a daily basis to what is really calling from your soul. You must begin to choose to love all aspects of yourself, whatever you find inside. The voices of your abandoned, betrayed, and rejected selves may sound sad, fearful, judgmental, or negative, or they are bouncing in happy anticipation to be rediscovered and received into your life.

As soon as you listen and receive who is beneath the voice of painful emotions, you can begin to heal and receive the voice of your divine power. There is pain because you have shut the door to the truth of your divine power. Your emotions will always be the gateway to your deeper truth. No matter how sad, hurt, angry, lost, or confused an emotion may feel, beneath it exists the authentic presence and voice of your True Self. This is about choosing to fully meet, embrace, accept, and love your entire being to become your Whole Self. Through embracing and accepting yourself, you end ABR. When you meet yourself, you free yourself.

> *This is about choosing to fully meet, embrace, accept, and love your entire being to become your Whole Self.*

When you stop ABR, then greater energy exists to move you into your truth, love, joy, and union. The more you heal ABR, the greater the ability to live in the union of love inside of yourself and with others. You are then able to live in the core of your true BEingness, fulfill your soul destiny, and do what you came here to do.

When you practice showing up for yourself by responding to yourself with honor and loving-kindness, you are developing the ability to respond—authentic responsibility. You are strengthening an inner muscle as you feel, listen, see, and become One with the love within you. This is taking true responsibility. Your soul gifts can begin to flourish, grow, and seek to find their deeper and more enlightened integration with life. Your ability to respond to your self with tenderness, courage, and vulnerability is the ultimate exercise in taking responsibility for being on your spiritual path.

REMEMBER:

- You have a soul mission in this life. Your journeying soul seeks to find and feel a permanent, steady, and expansive expression of love and union.

- Until your soul theme voice is liberated and supported to BE expressed, you will feel as though something is missing in your life.

- Remember that the soul themes of love, union, truth, and joy are within each of us. Their greater or lesser expression depends upon the degree and amount of abandonment, rejection, and betrayal (ABR) within you.

- While you possess all of the soul themes within you, you have a primary soul theme that rises above all others and will direct the trajectory of your life.

- You have a choice to open or close to your own inner love, truth, joy, and union. Choosing these powerful soul expressions means letting go of your hurt. You must stop hurting yourself and letting others hurt you, whether intentionally or not.

- Living with ABR keeps the lie of living in separation from God—Infinite Source alive.

- You can end your cycles of abandoning, betraying, and rejecting yourself by looking for the aspects of yourself that have felt pushed away or denied and then choosing to love and accept them.

- The more you can heal your relationship to how you abandon, betray, or reject yourself, the more you can benefit from the power and strength of your true soul themes to transform your life.

- Your soul work is about choosing to fully meet, embrace, accept, and love your Whole Self. The more you open and expand into the love within you, the greater will be the fruits of Oneness and wholeness.

- Ask yourself the question what are you willing to let go of or embrace in order to become fully who you are?

Your soul knows what it needs, but are you willing to pay attention and do what it takes?

BELIGHT MEDITATION

Opening to Your Soul Theme

Take some time to sit quietly and gently begin to look for the light within you. Prepare to practice a meditation to open your senses. Bring an image of a rose into your mind and inhale its scent. Receive the feeling that it arouses into your body. Open all of your cells to the bliss of the rose. Fill your body with this feeling. Receive the light from within the feeling. See the light glow within you. Now, listen for a sound emanating from the light inside of your body and in between your ears. Focus upon the rose opening within you.

Allow yourself to:

Smell what you are seeing. Hear what you are seeing. Feel what you are hearing. Invite your inner knowing to emerge and be present with yourself.

Be open to align your senses to one of four soul themes: joy, truth, love, or union. Which one of the following four soul themes do you relate to the most? Are you most aware of joy, truth, love, or with union in the present moment? Be with what is real for you. Breathe in the feeling and presence of one of these soul themes into your body. Next, be with a present life challenge from the perspective of one of the soul themes. Align

AWAKENING TO THE VOICE AND THEMES OF THE SOUL

a challenge in your life to this soul theme. Each day, consciously align your thoughts and perceptions to your chosen soul theme. Allow it to help you make decisions and to shift your priorities. Make use of being in your soul theme as a grounding exercise to help you stay true to yourself and to not abandon, betray, or reject your Self.

CHAPTER ELEVEN

Fragmenting of the Soul

"So come, return to the root of the root of your own Self."
—*Rumi*

Listening to Your Fragments

For the briefest of moments, stop, BE, and breathe. Focus in on the space between your thoughts. Focus into the center of your chest. BE in the stillness of your soul. What do you hear?

Longing and desire?

Pain?

Crickets?

Listen. Your soul wants to speak, and it has a message for you. Trust your soul, for it wants you to BE whole and complete. It wants all of your spiritual power to be unified and to be expressed as the love that you are. Your soul won't let you down or steer you in the wrong direction. BE still. Listen.

A crucial step of your personal soul journey will involve identifying and reconnecting your soul aspects—energetic fragments of your soul that contain your most precious spiritual power. What tends to happen to most of us is that even if we are relatively whole at birth, the numerous circumstances and experiences of being human have a way of splitting us apart inside. How we respond to life in crisis moments can inevitably push us to choose to split off from our Original Self. We doubt who we are. We either identify with fear of our fragments or the love of our wholeness. If we chose the fear fragment that has a belief about its essential light essence and fears being consumed or judged by others, we lose the ability to be compassionate with ourselves and others. We separate from the God light that we are because we forget that we are One in Source. We think that our identity is created by how others respond to us. Our choice to separate aligns us to the paradigm that has created and continues to create all of humanity's suffering.

The paradigm of living in separation from who we really are is the core pattern of humanity's belief system for 3,500–4,000 years. To become aware of how and why we initially split off from the God light that emanates from our Whole and True Self awakens us to walk our individual path of awakening. We have all been through this, and most of us are coming out of a long dream of thinking that the power that we need to survive exists outside of ourselves.

Out of self-protection, we have fragmented our self to protect our highest and most awakened Self. As you begin to listen to yourself, the parts of your soul that have fragmented will reveal themselves. Some may come from those "wonderful" years of child and teen angst. Some may have existed for far longer than this lifetime. Your soul lives on lifetime-to-lifetime, and your journey may span thousands of years and often carries the same belief patterns that were created at the moment of separation from your Original and Divine Self. You may be carrying past life "baggage" or unfinished business that begins to be cleared as your soul comes into conscious wholeness. Each soul aspect

FRAGMENTING OF THE SOUL

brings with it the healing needed to live more complete in the now and to reclaim wholeness, physically and spiritually.

Every moment, your soul gently—or perhaps intensely—prods you open to feel, see, and be with life in a bigger way. It will do this so that it can heal your separations and be unified within the divine. Your soul wants you on the dance floor participating in your own life-giving and receiving dance. Maybe you're unsure or wondering if you even have the ability to "dance." What if you only know how to slow dance, and your soul wants you to do a tango or hip-hop? Relax. We all know the dance and music of our own soul. You just need to listen, open, let go, and move to your inner song. The secret is to let go of what you are holding on to in order to maintain your separation from living and BEing One with your divine Self.

When you begin to follow your soul's guidance and embody your Whole Self, joy is awakened in your body that alters your moment-to-moment perspective of reality. Angst, sadness, and fear begin to dissolve. It can seem like those feelings are just part of what it means to be human and alive. However, when you begin to connect with your soul, you will be surprised at how a 1,000-pound weight has been lifted off your shoulders and heart. You gain a momentum of light that begins to reveal the battles that you have created within you. It offers you the opportunity to choose moving higher into greater Oneness or to stay in your comfort zones and controls. From the clarity of your soul consciousness, you can tell your ego Self—the voice of fear and false power—to lessen its grip. Your body will feel lighter, and your inner light will actually expand and shine more brightly.

When I first contacted one of my soul aspects, I discovered my inner four-year-old girl who hadn't yet begun to speak. I asked her if she knew who I was, and she said yes that indeed she did. When I asked her why she hadn't yet spoken, she expressed that her feelings, perceptions, and the loving kindness she had to give would not be understood or received. She also hadn't figured out how to express herself, and she wasn't willing to be further ignored or rejected by her family. Her hesitancy to trust and to open up was how she survived, and she wasn't willing quite yet to take the risk of leaving her comfort zone.

When I asked her what she was here for, she implied that she had forgotten. This is when, for the first time, I made contact with my infant self, who was shining as a blaze of light. Even now, when I focus into this unbounded light within myself, I smile, for she is brilliant, radiant love and supported me to hold our connection until we would eventually become One. When I asked her what she was here for, she said, "I am here to love and to BE love." From that moment on, I brought her into every moment in my life. I enjoyed my work more and my interactions with all of life. She has held the torch for me as I have reintegrated the rest of me with her infinite love. As my four-year-old self received the love of my infant self, whom I would later realize was my Original Self, "we" grew through many stages of becoming more self-aware and self-expressed. I had to also face how I had grown a significant ego Self to repress the powerful love and voice of my pure self. Choosing to take off the locks to the love that I AM and to trust myself happened over many years. My journey through my fragmentations helped me to find and live in the center of the light that I AM.

Our Fragmented Reality

When your soul is whole and complete, it allows for a limitless expression and manifestation of your True Self. Yet, while we may come into this world as whole souls, our souls become split or fragmented from various experiences within our lives and from how we abandon, reject, and betray ourselves. We leave and lose ourselves until what remains is often just a faint expression of who we really are and what we are meant to BE. We may appear outwardly together. Yet, truthfully, we can become caught up in illusion and projections of our personality or ego Self, all the while really living from a "walking wounded" space.

The fragmented you that lives and functions in everyday life often has no idea or awareness of your circumstances. It may seem that when stressful or horrible things happen, there is no rhyme or reason to life. However, what will become a seminal truth along your path back to yourself is the reality that the moment-to-moment experiences of your life, those that bring joy or sorrow, loss or gain, resistance or acceptance, serve as the building blocks and doorway to your deeper Self and truth.

The intensified times in which we are living are inevitably creating life challenges and "existential crises" that are pushing us beyond what we often feel our hearts can handle. As we see and feel people from all nationalities suffer, experience how corporate greed is harming the earth, how the rights of women and children are being violated, how hard working and caring people are suffering, how health care in many places of the world is non-existent or indulgently expensive, and how craving power through control, arrogance, and deceit with money just to uphold a distorted self-image is creating suffering, fear, and disempowerment in the lives of millions of people.

As pain and discomfort come up in you, open deeper into your heart, into your soul, and into the light within you. A greater purpose and mission for your life is being revealed through your hurt, sadness, anger, or rage. These emotions, if allowed to come up, can be made use of as a gateway into what you want to accomplish in this lifetime and will reconnect you to the hidden and lost aspects of your spiritual power. By opening to the love and new power within you, a new integrated place of wholeness is revealed. As you integrate the light of your True Self and release the ways that you energetically stuff down and control your powerful and creative energies, you will be able to step out of the old matrix of suffering, illusion, pain, and separation and be able to take the actions that support your gifts and desired life experiences.

New ideas, new ways of expressing your talents and past experiences, life purpose, and work in the world will evolve. New ways of doing business in the 21st century are evolving as we become Whole. The old systems were created out of separation consciousness. The old matrix of creating disempowerment, lack, fear, and egoic values instead of soul values has created global unrest, hatred, and a growing desire to support peace and well-being rather than anger, religious extremism and distortion. Presently, everyone is facing having to move beyond the ways that we have individually kept ourselves in some way isolated and separate from our full potential and brilliance and come into the whole of life and existence.

Your soul fragmentations that develop over the course of your life need to be understood, and faced, if you want to find and experience BEing your authentic Self and living your soul purpose in this lifetime. Reconnection, acceptance, openness, and reunion to the joy, light and bliss within you help you to step out of the cycles of recreating disappointments, frustrations, and lack. The very idea of finding and facing your soul fragments may seem daunting at first glance, but this is really a path back to loving and embracing all that you are. Love and compassion are really the beginning, middle, and end tools that you will need to heal and reconnect. But, before diving into how your soul may fragment and what you can specifically do to heal and reconnect it, let's explore the deeper relationship of our souls and how they split from Infinite Source, which sets the stage for our journey into becoming ONE.

Why We Left Oneness

The journey of our existence has been a continual pathway created by leaving our conscious connection with Infinite Source and then re-finding our way back home. From formlessness to form and then through the gateways of transmutation into light, we leave our conscious connection to Source to bust through all of the illusions of separation that we make real. We originally left BEing One with Infinite Source to explore our own unique expression of *BEing Source* and to *consciously discover that we are the light of Source.* Once separated from BEing One with Infinite Source, a yearning ignited within us, creating a drive for having *conscious connection with Creation*. This decision began the process of our spiritual evolution as we now know it, leading us to experience conscious Oneness with Infinite Source in our Whole Self —the body, mind, psyche, and soul.

When we left our original state of Oneness, our souls split into the divine expressions of feminine and masculine energies in order to consciously become aware of how to BE in the state of love that is our True Self. Our divine feminine and masculine energies are the pure embodiment of the love and power and light and dark of all Creation emanating through our Whole Self. In our moment of separation from Infinite Source, these dual aspects of our soul fell out of alignment with one another. No longer One, they instinctively began a search to reunite, creating a new roadmap back toward their reunion. For eons of time we have lived in duality because of separating from divine union. How our world religions and nations have exasperated this separation is now at a peak. The pathway home ignites a journey to embody the divine feminine and masculine energies in our everyday lives and navigates through the multiple worlds of duality that we experience as human and divine beings.

The roadmap to return home to Infinite Source is a pathway to reunite the two facets of Creation within our soul, the light and the dark—divine masculine and feminine. The dark—the divine feminine—holds the consciousness of the unmanifested raw creation of Infinite Source and the light—the divine masculine—holds the consciousness of all life.

> *In our desire to discover our unique expression of Creation, we chose to separate from Infinite Source.*

Our divine feminine and masculine energies are experienced as the consciousness of love and power. The love and power that we express as human beings is a manifestation of the light of God. Through learning how to be in the positive and negative expressions of our love and power, we are given the opportunity to find the path back to the true reality of Oneness with Infinite Source. To do this, we must become aware of how we use and misuse love and power.

We lost the ability to BE One with the love and power of Infinite Source when we left our original light and joy-filled home, the consciousness of union that we can call the Garden of Eden. Leaving the light and entering into duality pushed us into learning how to create in a new way. We tried to regain Oneness by seeking it outside of ourselves through an external search for connection, fulfillment, and completion. Our lives became a hunt for what we could physically get or emotionally connect with outside of ourselves to fill our gaps; e.g., love from others or power from or over others, rather than looking within ourselves. Some might call this the original sin, but there is no sin, only a need to end judgment of ourselves and others, live in integrity, be open to taking down the barriers we have to others, rediscover innocence, curiosity, adventure, and learn to honor love over fear and hatred.

Our drive for survival took us on a journey through duality, and the human race became caught in scarcity. The patterns within our mind grew more fearful as we doubted our abilities to have what we needed to survive and to feel powerful. We were no longer receiving divine power and so became hungry for false power. Over time, we lost connection with the true power of our divine Self. The external search began to erase the memories of living in Oneness. We forgot how to live in the fully awakened state of our divine nature. Over time, we began seeing, feeling, aligning, and identifying with illusion. The light of God manifesting as the love and power within our soul, split apart, creating struggle, darkness, and internal battle. For eons of time, we've been on a constant search for forms of love and power outside of ourselves, which has only served to reinforce our separation from Infinite Source. We've lost connection with this original state of Oneness and the ability to feel, see, and touch the truth of our light-sourced, Whole Self.

> *The light of God manifesting as the love and power within our soul, split apart, creating struggle, darkness, and internal battle.*

The further away your conscious connection to Infinite Source becomes, the more your heart closes and the more you disconnect from the fundamental essence of who you are. It becomes harder to feel loving kindness, truth, courage, fearlessness, and grace. God becomes something outside, rather than inside of you. You lose access to your full, integrated, divine, and human potential and the "knowingness" that everything you need is already inside of you and that who you are is enough. This reality has been a core experience of the human condition since ancient times.

For the last ten thousand years, humanity has experienced separation and has been struggling to re-find the gateways into Oneness. We are all at different places in our journey, yet we are all connected and share the experience of splitting off from our ultimate Self and yearn to go beyond the pitfalls of our own mind. There are many ways to return to wholeness. However you begin, once your soul energies consciously align into the light, the blueprint of your soul is revealed. Each time that we separate from our spiritual power, we create inner pain and anger. As we come back to our spiritual power and rework our relationship with our ego, we can end the cycles of how we create pain and suffering. Each time that we leave our Self, the wounding created from living in separation, once filled in light, can heal. As we mend the tears and gaps in our energy bodies, we are able to recreate how we live in the moment and can collectively begin to shift into a new embodied planetary consciousness.

To evolve, we must be willing to surrender everything that is not real, but that we have assumed is "real." We must move beyond the fear and controls created through aligning with the dark within ourselves and shutting out the light. We must end disconnecting from the source of Oneness within ourselves.

Despite the fragmentation of human beings throughout time, there has always been a part within each of us that remembers the light that we are. It pushes us to ask the important questions that we all ask at some point. Who am I? Why am I here? How can I make the changes needed to be happy? What is my role here while I am alive in this body? What do I need to heal to fulfill my destiny path?

The spark of our soul consciousness that pushes us to remember who we are seeks to re-awaken us to the deeper reality and connection of our lives and to the divine. There are many souls who have harnessed that spark and spent lifetimes reconnecting to Infinite Source through BEing in service to others, creating loving families, building sacred relationships, implementing visionary ideas, bringing peace and prosperity to others, or exploring a connection through the arts. Some have focused on creating new social structures and positions of power and being in relationship to the earth and her resources in more aligned ways. Still other souls have gone further and dedicated themselves to finding connection in every aspect of life. They step forth as gateways of truth, freedom, and light and live in accordance with forgiveness, compassion, love, and giving. We ALL have this opportunity during these times of great shifting to become One and whole.

Those who are fortunate enough to come into this lifetime more whole, are not necessarily different from you or me. They may have lived many conscious lifetimes and done so much soul work that they come into the world further along on their paths; hence the idea that some people are more "advanced souls." Generally, one might think of certain spiritual healers, performers, or artists as being in this group. Yet, there are also typically "average" people who you might meet that have this sense of inner peace, calm, and radiance. They make you pause for a moment and wonder, "Who are they?" Who they are is more fully themselves. They embody a greater degree of soul connection and integrated awareness of their human and divine essence. They have made decisions over past lifetimes and in this lifetime not to split off from their Original Self—their pure expression and Oneness with Infinite Source. They trust their relationship with Infinite Source—God. They strive to BE the best that they can BE.

In contrast, many souls have operated in a perpetual state of denial and in turn have misused their love and abused their position of power. They've identified themselves with their external need for getting "more" from others and life itself, and live in a cycle of "taking and getting." They've stolen the energies of other people, places, and things as a way to fill the gap or holes within themselves. A person can live an entire lifetime in an unhealed and unawakened state, despite the calling of their soul for reconnection and expansion.

We are all traveling home to Infinite Source in our own way and on our own timing. We all long to consciously remember that we are One with God—Infinite Source. To become conscious co-creators with God and feel who we "really" are is one of the greatest gifts that life has to give. The new humanity is here to serve and to create new ways of working together to save our planet, increase prosperity for all, to learn how to live in peace and to end the battles between the ego Self and the True Self.

If you are reading this book, then you have heard the calling of your soul or yearn to hear its call. You feel or sense your soul's desire for awakening, recognition, or enlightenment. Within your heart exists the power to consciously choose the rediscovery and reconnection of your soul with Infinite Source. Finding and integrating the soul aspects that give you direct connection to Infinite Source will help you step through the veils of your consciousness leading to your True Self—the eternal and vibrationally aligned YOU. As you become integrated and whole, you will be guided through the gateways of duality and your ego's state of separation and illusion into a new state of BEing, filled with light, love, and conscious attunement to all within and around you. You will realize that you have always been One with the light and that your True Self is a blazing fountain of God Itself. By becoming conscious of how you have created separation from the light that you are, your True Self is given the opportunity to guide you out of your self-created pain and suffering. To find your True Self, you must surrender your beliefs about yourself and others, and follow your inner path to peace.

Lifetime-to-Lifetime Fragmentation

People often live and die carrying forward soul fragmentations into their next lifetimes until they are able to reconnect and let go of what they take on from others and blossom into their deepest truth and Self. Every soul has a path and a plan to awaken to its Self. As it is said, there is a timing, season, and reason for everything in life.

Every time a soul is born into a physical body, the unresolved issues of light and dark, love and power, and pain and suffering experienced from past lifetimes are brought in at birth, creating a matrix of energy that is either consciously worked with, transformed, and released or coded into the Bodymind to deal with at a future time. Before coming into a lifetime, most souls choose whether they will work with their soul truths and lessons or not. A soul chooses a new family that will assist it to heal whatever fragmentary baggage it is carrying. Whether through positive or negative experiences, a soul will face the belief structures and emotional and spiritual patterns that must be addressed in order to return to Oneness with Infinite Source. No matter how challenging the Bodymind grid of oneself or one's family ancestry is, they will test and assist a person to reach their full potential or, if they choose, to stay in a comfort zone of denial and illusion.

When a soul chooses to come back in human form, at birth it either stays consciously connected to its Original Self or leaves the conscious connection by creating a set of beliefs about its own existence. It diverts from its conscious connection of its

True Self, and instead attaches or holds onto beliefs it carries in from past incarnations and from its family of origin in the hope of receiving the love that it needs to survive. Losing oneself and leaving oneself can happen at any point from utero, at birth, right after birth, a few weeks or months after birth, to the next 4–10 years of childhood and into adolescence. From the initial separations of one's formative years, it sets the stage for continued fragmentation until such time that you awaken to the deeper truth within and take the call of your soul.

How Your Soul Fragments

So how does a soul actually "fragment?" Your Bodymind energetically separates its conscious awareness of its soul when your heart holds the burden of being deeply abandoned, betrayed, or rejected (ABR) by yourself or by another person and you feel that you are not being received, seen, or heard. Your soul is connected to your mental and causal bodies, and they create the sanskaras, the impressions that set into motion your survival Self overriding your soul. A loss of soul energy is experienced that lessens the ability to directly connect with God—Infinite Source on one's own. The aspects of your soul that feel like they are "too much" or "not enough" find solace in a safe space in your body, which is usually in the comfort of a space within your lower *Power Point Centers*—your base centers.

The fragmentation happens as we slip out of Oneness with Infinite Source and self-judge. As just mentioned, fragmentation can begin from the moment you are born, as an infant, or as a child. It happens in any moment when you feel unsafe, unloved, or unseen and you deny the power of the light that is within you and go into the darkness, or "remote hide out," within your *First and Second Power Point Centers* (the space between your tailbone and pubic bone, your genitals and lower belly) for comfort and security.

Throughout your life, this may occur at various times when you are not allowed to BE who you are or are judged for who you are by others and you haven't yet chosen to BE who you are. This typically occurs through relationships with someone close in your life, such as your parents, siblings, lovers, a mate, or a friend. What happens when you are not received, seen, or heard? You respond by going into survival mode. Often in order to receive love and acceptance, we let go of who we are to "fit" with those around us. You choose to fragment in order to get what you may think is "love," to meet others' expectations, or to give another person what they "need." You create a projection of love based upon a false perception, which is created from your separation with your Infinite Source of light.

A classic example of how you may leave yourself might be deciding to go to school, entering a job, or taking on a profession that meets the ideals and expectations of your parents, cultural, or religious background rather than your true desire. Have you ever heard anyone say, *"I always wanted to be a painter, musician, or teacher, but I went into business instead because that's what my parents wanted"*? Another common refrain is *"I've always been the good son or daughter because I never wanted to disappoint my parents. They had so many other things to contend with—their jobs, health, money issues, etc. I didn't want to add to their problems."*

We also all know someone, perhaps it is even you, who has been in a relationship with someone and he or she suddenly changes their personality and typical way of being within the first 18–36 months of the relationship. You hear friends say, *"After dating so and so, he or she stopped being genuine or doing all of the things that he or she seemed to like so much. Something changed, and they are not the person that I originally began to love so deeply. I don't know what happened."*

Perhaps you are someone who has discovered your true life's calling, and you desire to have a new career or want to leave an old situation that blocks your soul energies. Yet, you don't seem to be able to move forward and through unknown barriers that you know are there, but that seem untouchable, and manifest your dream. All of these experiences are a part of the fragmenting of your soul.

What happens to your divine essence—your soul—when you are confronted with such situations? Your divine essence, your spiritual power, retreats into your base centers in your body as you simultaneously create a functioning Self to fulfill the challenges that your divine essence—the light that you are—were willing to do, but your developmental human Self had no idea "how to." Your divine nature chooses to hide out in the dark cavern deep in your base centers waiting for the day when you return to invite it into your heart center. It needed a positive and life supporting Self to support it—the light that you are—to BE fully expressed.

These divine parts of you that are unseen, unheard, or unreceived react and follow one of several different paths.

1. Retreat into a dark zone inside of you to sleep, wait, or create emotional upset, which creates inner shut down and disconnection from your soul truth.

2. Fight for recognition and expression where you become a warrior for your own truth, which results in your greater soul expression but possible separation from your family of origin or people closest to you because you refuse to conform.

3. Seek support through the expansion of your ego Self to keep you from being and feeling hurt, which keeps you in a perpetual state of fear and control.

This ***first soul fragmentation path*** is the most common outcome of your soul separations. Parts of your soul split off and find the safety of a dark comfort zone in your base energy centers, creating a separation between your heart center, Bodymind, and Infinite Source. The dark can be in the deep recesses of your mind and body and even in an "abandoned dead zone" inside of you. Your fragments will stay there and wait to be rediscovered until you are ready to reconnect with your Whole Self. As people's source-connected soul parts fragment, they go into hiding in the root and base *Power Point Centers* to seek protection from being judged, controlled, betrayed, exiled, and even the fear of being killed. They seek refuge there until such time as they feel safe to re-emerge. The safety needed to emerge comes from creating both a sacred inner and outer space.

Soul separations can create anxiety, fear, physical and mental illness, addiction, sexual and intimacy problems, financial and career challenges, spiritual crisis, trust issues, parenting, and self-worth issues. When your soul essence is fragmented into parts and your connection to Infinite Source is not connected through your body, your emotional Self repeats patterns, addictions, and difficulties in relationships over and over again. Your mind sees people and situations from illusion and misperceptions, and your body struggles with health, relationship, and career issues. All of these struggles are experiences to help you learn and awaken to the fragmentations inside of you and discover the profound light and spiritual power that exists within you.

Following the ***second soul fragmentation path,*** your soul aspects fight to guide your life and personal growth into creative and action-oriented directions. You develop independence and a strong personality, refusing to fit into cultural or familial controls. Rather than bending to the control and manipulation around you, you become a warrior for your own truth and way of being. This could look like a young girl standing up to her family's expectations and values to live her life as she believes, even if it means she must separate from them for the rest of her life. If you have the experience of being the "black or white sheep" of your family, this could be you. In this path, you make your own soul mission more important than the expectations and egos of others around you. Yet, you may still experience a sense of loss on this path because sometimes taking this road means that you have to let go of people that you love, and inadvertently lose relationships with people who choose not to grow with you. You eventually need to heal your heart and come into greater spiritual union with the divine to feel whole. Finding others who have stepped into being and living in connection with their Higher Self, becomes key to feeling happy.

While you are more authentically living your truth, at first you can still feel abandoned by the family or friends you care about most. Thus, your emotional heart may still feel rejected, unseen, or unheard until you birth and accept your True Self, and then from here, you can receive and give love to others, and BE fully connected. You must give yourself the time needed to fully open to the love within yourself, heal your wounds, embody your essence, and to surrender into the light and wisdom of your God Self.

Following the **third soul fragmentation path**, your soul fragments struggle for recognition but fail to be adequately received, and your ego Self will expand to compensate for the vulnerability of your soul. Following this pathway, if your soul is not received, your ego develops to protect you from the experience and feeling of not existing. Your ego is really a false Self created by the soul aspect, which goes into hiding in your base centers to handle the pain from not being received, seen, or heard as your True Self. Rather than staying in your light, you shift into fear, and in a split second your ego is developed from the depths of your survival nature. The growth and expansion of your ego Self is often expressed through your need to be right and to feel in control. If you have ever met someone like this, they might talk about themselves or the dilemmas of their life and their worries, all of the time. In their most extreme moments, they are unable to really listen to anyone but themselves.

The need to be right and remain in control comes from the false Self's desire to exist. At some point earlier in your life, the fear of feeling insignificant and unworthy of being loved was strong enough that your ego was created by you to make sure that you could go on existing. When you feel like you don't or can't exist, being "right" covers up your fear of not being connected and gives you the illusion that you are "okay" even if you are in fact separate.

You bypass the truth of your True Self by creating controls that build walls of separation from the terror and fear living within yourself. Your True Self lives in the light, and until you choose living and being in the light, you will habitually feed your ego fear-based thoughts and projections and make it extremely difficult to know your True Self. Your ego Self will continue to rule you until you refuse to feed its insatiable need to be in control, repress your wounds, and remain disguised as "concern and care" for your survival.

We all want to feel that our existence counts and matters. When we feel that who we are is insignificant and not valued, we believe we cannot BE who we really are. Yet, the irony is that existing through our false Self or ego only perpetuates our separation and suffering. It keeps you in a state of illusion and despair and leaves you unable to truly fulfill your soul's deepest desire. It prevents you from receiving the love you truly desire because you are living in relationship to your fear, rather than love. The fear that you really do not exist as a "real Self" and are not okay colors every action, thought, and belief. The only way that you can really know your Self is through experiencing being whole and integrated in your body through union with the divine nature of your soul.

> *Your ego Self will continue to rule you until you refuse to feed its insatiable need to be in control, repress your wounds, and remain disguised as "concern and care" for your survival.*

Healing Your Splits

One of the greatest lessons received by healing your soul fragmentations is that the soul aspects that you leave behind or shut off from always contain your spiritual power. Your spiritual power is made up of your inner divine masculine and feminine energies, which are the basis for the love and power that fuel your existence as a human and divine being. To be separate from the full expanse of your inner love and power can create a perpetual state of disempowered living and being. Your spiritual power is also found when you make contact with the soul aspect of your self that is most connected to Infinite Source. For each person, the essence of your soul is found within the aspect that you split off from the most difficult time of your earlier years.

The separations of your soul can disempower you to the point where you cannot see, feel, or even imagine being anything different from what you currently are. You cannot find anything resembling unconditional love for yourself or others.

The power that you might feel is spent on trying to be in control and "keeping it together." Your spiritual power is your healing, sexual, and creative power, and it also manifests in your life as intelligence, brilliance, love, perseverance, integrity, and ingenuity. The loss of your spiritual power ends up translating into a loss of your personal power and human potential.

> ***The soul aspects you leave behind always contain your spiritual power.***

Our soul separations leave many of us in a disempowered, unhealed state, which is expressed through our emotions and way of thinking as feeling incomplete, unsettled, separate, or alone. It may become difficult to reach your career or financial goals, heal your body and mind, sustain a significant relationship, find peace, fulfill your soul's purpose, or let go of the past. When you feel this way, your soul is really trying to express its longing for union and wholeness, and it will do whatever it takes to wake you up to the true direction of your life.

How might this look in your life? All of a sudden, you begin to feel things that you have never felt before, and you wonder what is wrong with you or with life. Your mind moves in one direction, your common sense in another direction, or perhaps your heart feels stuck. Something may happen that shakes up your world. A partner breaks up with you, your mother dies, your dog dies, you fail important college classes, you lose your job, you are fired, your lose your house, you leave your laptop on a train, you end up in the hospital because you have chest pains, have an anxiety attack at work, or find out you have cancer. You find yourself irritable, afraid, creatively stuck, ill, exhausted, needing excess attention from others, ending relationships out of anger, running from the truth, feeling devastated, alone, feeling fear about manifesting your life dreams, or unable to communicate to those around you.

It is no wonder that when such things happen people often seek out new ways to heal themselves or to deny the pain or fear being activated. You might choose to leave the religious practices you were raised with; or increase your devotion to them, take more vitamins; drink more superfood smoothies; eat organic food; go out with friends more; get high or drink more alcohol; or shut down, and spend more time on the computer and away from others; or go on a trip, go to a concert, take up meditation, become an activist, give up meat, write a memoir, or find a new sport or hobby. You might seek out and begin to listen to the wisdom of a spiritual teacher, mentor, or healer. The bottom line is that you will look at anything and everything to help deal with what is going on within you or to run. We live in a world of duality and can leave the light that we are or walk towards it. The most important wisdom to consider is whether what you are choosing will keep you in denial or take you out of denial of BEing friends with your divine Self.

The more you take responsibility for coming back to your Self, by increasing your ability to respond to all of You, the more you will grow and learn. We're not always willing to do the soul work to heal ourselves and find the love within. Some of us don't know that this is what we have to do. Some of us are afraid of taking responsibility because we have to be willing to discover and face the true source of our pain and fear and give up our positioning and stories. The stories so many of us hold onto include our fear of not being good enough, that who we are is unlovable, and that life cannot give us what we want. We also have fear of not living up to our full potential and that we won't be able to BE or do what we are meant to do in this lifetime. We doubt our value and our inherent worth. Most of our fears are subconscious and are out of the everyday functioning zone of how we think.

To move through our fears, we have to trust that there is something more within ourselves than the beliefs that take us on a downward spiral. When we activate the positive spiral of infinite life energy within ourselves, we can begin to live the truth within ourselves.

It takes true dedication to listen and follow the truth within ourselves once it is revealed. If we take up a spiritual practice, we have to take it all the way and go through the karmic bumps along the way. Our emotional, mental, and spiritual truths must become more important than doing the practice alone. Many people think they are doing "their work" because they are mastering various spiritual techniques or practices. They embody "good spiritual practice" and can even tap into temporary states of spiritual highs, peace, or bliss. Yet, if you don't take responsibility for healing the gap that exists between your mind-body-Spirit-soul, where your "stuff" is, and become aware of the stories that you repeat over and over again in different situations, then no amount of spiritual practice or healing work will be able to fundamentally change your life. You will still have relationship problems or money issues or whatever your "thing" is because you keep avoiding the centerpiece or the thread that controls and runs your life. Feeling whole and complete will remain elusive until you address how you abandon, betray, or reject (ABR), the light of your True Self. As you embrace the aspects of your Self that yearn to be embodied so you can evolve as a Whole Self; the walls of protection that you have built around your heart can dissolve. The gateways to your spiritual truth and power are opened and the light needed to heal your life is released. You no longer feel under the control of your core wounds and belief systems that have had the sole purpose of helping you cope, survive and deal with the splits, dogma, pain, and disconnection around you and within you.

The light and presence of your True Self awaits you within a new operating system of Oneness that begins with the union of your soul. To begin, you must see how you have blocked yourself from full embodiment of your truth and light and make the decision to open.

> ***No amount of spiritual practice or healing will permanently change your life until you take responsibility for healing your soul's fragmentation and core wounds.***

The reality of your life and experiences, and even for the most spiritual among us, is that no matter how "high" you go spiritually, and no matter how many spiritual techniques you master, unless you recognize, acknowledge, and heal the wounds created by your emotional, mental, and soul splits, your physical and spiritual life will always feel separate. The abandoned, betrayed, and rejected parts of your soul remain entrenched in duality and will use your ego to stay in fear and control. Your ego will still be the ultimate driver of your life, keeping you separate. However, if you reconnect your soul fragments and bring them out of hiding, you can then create a core internal foundation that can successfully handle releasing your ego.

Your soul reconnection will serve as a catalyst for the energetic death process from living in ego identity to BEing free of a controlling, resistant, judgmental, or repressive ego. Unless your deep karmic wounds are addressed, you will continue to live out your fears and separations in your daily existence. You will feel like you are in a version of the movie *Groundhog Day*,

FRAGMENTING OF THE SOUL

where you will constantly revisit and relive the same wounds, baggage, and emotions over and over.

Remember that your emotions are just a reflection of your relationship between your heart and soul. To heal the feelings and emotions housed within your emotional body, you have to go deeper through your heart center to connect into the truth within your soul; otherwise, you are just opening into your emotions with no direction. When you allow your soul to BE Whole and One with your Bodymind, you are simultaneously healing your emotional body. What truly heals you is the light and consciousness that is being awakened by reconnecting your awareness with the love and power within your soul—which has always been who you are.

When your soul awakens and remembers its Self as Infinite Source, you experience that you are vibration, awareness, light, love, and power. Your emotional, etheric, mental, spiritual, and physical bodies are *all* vibration. They resonate to love, and as you unconditionally love what may feel or look unapproachable within you, real love is born. To really heal, you must take responsibility and go into the foundation and construction of your internal house or container, which looks like diving into an inner universe of light and dark. Here you will find love. Here you will find the doorway through the dualities of love and hatred, pain and acceptance, sorrow and joy. Through the doorway is an open space in your heart ready to be filled with your love—the light of your soul. It is your temple, where you can free your mind and come to with an open heart. Here, without the hindrances of your mind, you can expand inside the infinite space of light and power within yourself, leaving ego behind.

In the core center of your Whole Self resides a knowingness of who you are that has always been in existence. Beyond the clustered positive and negative belief systems that you have created to maintain a false identity resides the joy and truth of your True Self.

> *The light and consciousness that comes from your soul's reconnection with your Bodymind and spirit has the power to heal you and transform your life.*

REMEMBER:

- We all face a certain amount of separation in ourselves. It is part of the human condition and part of why we are here.

- Our souls become split or fragmented from various experiences and from how we abandon, betray, and reject ourselves. While we may appear outwardly whole, we are often caught up in illusion and projections of our personality or ego Self, and living from a "walking wounded" space.

- The moment-to-moment experiences of your life, those that both make and break you, serve as the building blocks and doorway to your deeper Self and truth.

- Love and compassion are really the beginning, middle, and end tools that you will need to heal and reconnect.

- You are not just an expression of the light of Source; *you are the light of Source.*

- Through knowing and learning how to be in our love and power, we can find the path back to the true reality of BEing One in Source.

- We began to forget who we are when we sought to re-find our "missing parts" through looking externally for connection, fulfillment, and completion.

- The further away one's soul becomes from Infinite Source, the more the heart closes, and you lose connection with the fundamental essence of who you are.

- Finding and integrating the soul aspects that give you direct connection to Infinite Source will help you step through the veils of your consciousness, leading to your True Self—the eternal and vibrationally aligned YOU.

- Every soul has a path and a plan to eventually face and heal all aspects of itself. Whether through positive or negative experiences, a soul will face the belief structures and emotional and spiritual patterns that must be addressed in order to return to Infinite Source in the body, in this lifetime.

- Your Bodymind and soul separate each time that you are not received, seen, or heard in your life until you are clear of who you are and can stand strong in your presence.

- Existing through your False Self or ego only perpetuates your separation. It keeps you in a state of illusion and leaves you unable to truly fulfill your soul's deepest desire. It prevents you from receiving the love you truly desire because you are living in relationship to your fear, rather than love.

- The soul parts that you leave behind always contain your spiritual power. The loss of your spiritual power ends up translating into a loss of your personal power and human potential.

- Our soul separations leave many of us in a disempowered, unhealed state, which is expressed through our emotions and way of thinking as feeling incomplete, unsettled, separate, or alone. It becomes difficult to live an integrated life.

- If you don't take responsibility for healing the gap that exists between your mind-body-Spirit-soul, then no amount of spiritual practice will be able to fundamentally change your life.

- No matter how "high" you go spiritually, and no matter how many spiritual techniques you master, unless you integrate and heal the wound created by your emotional and mental body splits, and come into the core matrix of your True Self, your physical and spiritual life will always feel separate.

BELIGHT MEDITATION

Reconnecting Your Soul Fragments with Light

Breathe into your heart center. Feel into your heart and allow any feeling of hurt, the realization of something important not coming to fruition, sadness, emptiness, aloneness, longing, grief, or sorrow, etc. to BE present.

Focus so deeply into your heart that you can feel the feeling, *yet do not become the feeling.* Have compassion for the feeling. BE with the feeling as a friend and partner.

Go so deeply into your heart that you find light. Keep going inside as you enter into a wide space, or cave of safe space. Now, bring light into your heart using just your intention. Focus light from about 10–20 feet above your head directly into your heart. Fill your heart with light. The light that you send into your heart is going to loosen up the feelings that have been blocking you, holding you back, or creating angst. Invite the light to clear the feelings that have been holding on. Then, fix your attention into the space of love underneath the old feeling. BE in the love, in the light, in your heart center.

Remember the soul is accessed through the heart. So, anytime that you move light into the heart, you will awaken, open, clear, transform, and have the opportunity to heal a soul fragment into the light of acceptance, grace, and love. Your soul fragments can be directly accessed through your heart. The light can and will bring you into a state of aligned focus, healing, and renewed vitality.

Each time that your mind plays out an old tape loop from fear, come back into your heart. Each time that your ego Self works to separate you from the love that is your True Self, and divides you from life through being judgmental, resistant, defensive, manipulating or controlling, align your heart, love, and power to the light.

CHAPTER TWELVE

The Components of the Soul: Your Divine Feminine & Masculine

"Light, being the strongest force on this planet, exists independently of passion. But when unified with the human and divine experience of BEing, light unified with passion becomes a power of transcendence."
— Mahama Iana

The Divine Currents of Light Consciousness

We all have a soul journey to follow that is encoded within our BEing. As an energetic light body that holds the divine and human essence of who you are, your soul is really a beautiful and multi-dimensional expression of the divine. The sacred sanctuary of your body is a container for its infinite love and power. As you reconnect the parts of your soul that hold your spiritual power, you are introduced to the divine energetic expressions and grounding creative light of your divine feminine and the unifying compassionate light of your divine masculine.

Infinite Source creates a direct connection into our bodies through the polarity of divine feminine and masculine energies. The divine feminine and divine masculine energies are always flowing, weaving, and integrating our true nature into our lives. They move synchronistically from the spheres of light above the head and from within the earth to connect us into the multidimensional realities of our body and the universe. These two energetic flows are direct currents of light intelligence and consciousness. They hold the power to activate, awaken, and ignite the soul.

The union of your divine masculine and feminine energies manifest as the consciousness of light in your body, mind, and soul. The light heals, unifies, and evolves your soul into its full potential. It reconnects the parts of your soul that have been stranded in the sea of darkness of humanity's pain. It awakens the cellular consciousness of your DNA that evolves your heart center. It strengthens your ability to expand past contraction, fear, and suffering and clears the pain created by your mind, which overrides the joy, beauty, bliss, and love of Oneness.

When the divine masculine and feminine energies are opened and integrated in the body, a powerful channel into Infinite Source is created. These soul forces of God support one another, interact, and upgrade your health, mental state, emotions, creativity, and your ability to solve problems and engage in relationships.

> *The sacred sanctuary of your body is filled with infinite love and power.*

The divine masculine and feminine live as One within each cell of your body. Their light has the ability to ignite and balance all of your *Power Point Centers*. When your *Power Point Centers* are spinning in a clockwise orbital spin, your divine feminine and masculine energies are in a high cosmic relationship of receptivity and activation. How you treat your body, go beyond limiting thoughts, honor your soul, and accept personal spiritual guidance from Infinite Source is what allows the light of your divine masculine and feminine energies to nourish, transform, and enlighten you.

When your masculine and feminine divine forces are balanced and in union, you feel in love with love and it is easier to *live in love*. Life feels sweeter, and the goblet of your life is no longer half empty but completely full of profound joy, happiness, and contentment. You feel a power that flows through you that is refined and uniquely yours, ready to be channeled into your soul purpose. When your passion is united in light, new miracles in consciousness can occur because light will always enlighten the truth within you. The light will point the way to living your truth and help you to move beyond your ego into love. The light of your divine masculine and feminine energies can transmute your fear-based Self into infinite love and move you through the gateways of awareness that lead to full enlightenment.

> *When the divine masculine and feminine energies are opened and integrated in the body, a powerful channel into Infinite Source is created.*

As we explore our divine feminine-masculine aspects, we are gifted with meeting the core values and motivating forces within our soul that empower our evolutionary process of becoming whole and One.

Present within the light of our soul dwells the truth of our True Self. Often caught in the fear and darkness of our ego, our divine masculine-feminine energies are the compass to help us move through the possible pitfalls of our soul journey. Their wisdom is the lantern shining the light to guide our way. Once revealed and activated, we can create our life to be a chalice for our soul's highest destiny expressions.

When I first saw my wounded inner masculine sitting on a couch staring off into space many decades ago, appearing completely unmotivated, I wondered how is this possible? I was raised to be a child who would take up as little space and attention as possible. I was raised to not have any needs and to remain silent unless spoken to. Any form of expression, whether physical or emotional, had to be contained. If I went outside of the tight box that I was put into each moment, I would somehow upset my parents.

My inner masculine loved competing and wanted to excel at school in all areas. I loved science and entered science competitions, where I would win blue ribbons. But, when my father ridiculed my brilliance, I shrank and began to hide my love for academics. Stage left, my inner feminine stepped in and, through pursuing movement and meditation as a teenager, I was able to not get stuck on the couch with my inner masculine. My feminine was awakened to be the conduit for the divine and to live from her heart. The gap between my unhealed feminine and masculine energies had to be healed to fulfill my dreams and begin a career as a visionary healer, mentor, teacher, and movement artist.

I ended up marrying a man who did nothing around the house, could not fulfill his dreams, and had difficulties providing for his family financially, emotionally, and spiritually. My original moment of finding my own inner male inept helped me to understand and accept how I had chosen a man in my life, now many years ago, that was addicted to blocking and controlling the feminine light and love that was erupting within me. Unable to receive and honor his own feminine, he lived through me, while hiding within his inner delusion, seclusion, and intimidation.

I was so shut down inside that I didn't even know I was being controlled by my ex-husband. My mother's control was so extreme when I was a child and teenager that she would become enraged when I spoke my truth. My mother had zero tolerance for her daughter, who was curious about life and spoke her heart and insights. At the age of eight, she would hit the left side of my face, which I would later discover is the feminine side of the body, until grief-stricken tears flowed down my cheeks, to make sure that I would never say what I felt or question anything.

My ex-husband, while we were married, would begin to argue with me and make everything that he couldn't succeed at or understand my fault. He believed that his uncomfortable feelings were always caused by someone else's doing and were never caused by his own inner disconnection or unwillingness to face himself. The more I spoke my truth, the greater his rage and control grew. I had to come through the trial of speaking my truth even in the face of emotional control and abuse.

I was expected to abandon my inner masculine as a young child. I was only allowed to wear pretty little dresses, which I had to keep from becoming soiled. Yes, I was raised to be the perfect, well-behaved girl, which forced me to repress my masculine intellectual brilliance and feminine creative fire for decades.

The first time that I met my inner masculine hanging out on the couch, I asked him if he knew who I was, and he said no. He didn't know that there was life outside of his world of being a couch potato. I was already in the super woman stage of my life. I was devoted and successful as a single mom and as a soul-energy healer and mentor for many clients. I told my inner boy masculine that I needed him. I asked him what he had come into this life to do. To my surprise, he said that he was a composer and a musician. I had a sudden flash of my father's love for music and how he had given up his passions to work for his father in the family business.

I bought myself a used baby grand piano and began to resurrect my inner masculine from the dead. I would close my eyes and feel the music within myself soar. One day, as I was sitting at the keyboard on a cold, snowy day in New York, I saw a hawk sitting on a tree branch outside the window of my house. A melody moved through me, and my fingers played the piece that I have called "Hawk Ascending."

My inner masculine loved being loved by me—by my inner feminine presence—and as he opened to the music, he opened to me. In time, as he grew from a wounded boy to a man, he merged with my divine masculine, who is a builder of dreams. It is my masculine energies in consort with my feminine seer, which fuels and inspires my clients with ingenious ideas and practical steps to create powerful businesses. As I feel and receive my divine masculine, I know that I am blessed and loved. His true and divine nature gave me the support and comfort to find my way home to God. Now, years later, he and I are One, and we are in service to one another's heart and to humanity.

Once your natural connection to Infinite Source is restored through becoming One in your divine masculine and feminine energies, you can be in touch with the divine at all times. The needs that you usually have that are more survival based shift into yearning for greater fulfillment in your relationships, work, and self-expression. Your soul will seek new experiences, people, and situations until it finds, experiences, and embodies what it is looking for—and what it is looking for is to live fully in the divine union of your love and power, your masculine and feminine as the real, Source-connected YOU.

As you begin to step through the doorway into your own light and higher consciousness, your next step on your journey is to open and reconnect your divine masculine and feminine energies. This will fuel the opening of your heart and soul to the next stages of your whole evolution.

Duality and Divine Energies

In the physical world that most human beings perceive, everything is experienced through the lens of duality. We perceive and understand the world through polarities, or opposites. We move through the world framed by concepts like black and white, light and dark, yin and yang, happy and sad, good and bad, motion and stillness, male and female, and positive and negative. Duality is presently the accepted matrix of how life is lived—how we, as human beings, learn and experience life in the physical world. This mental framework helps us to understand how objects, life, space, and time work in relationship to our own objective thinking and need for order.

Duality is the maze through which we move to discover that who we really are, are beings who live in a state of Oneness. When we live from the state of Oneness, we do not care what a person's skin color is, what religion they follow, what nationality they are born into, or how much money they make a year. We do not separate from love in our subconscious through judgment. We have learned to embrace what we hate about our self, choose to change it, and nurture what we love about our self. When we embrace both sides of duality and accept their oppositional nature, we find a point of neutrality. This point of neutrality is a gateway through duality and into the union of our divine and human natures. If we accept both good and bad, fear and love, and gain or loss without judgment, we can find a release into real freedom. As we end the drama coming from the pull of duality and expand our awareness into the multi-dimensional nature of reality, we can find union and the center pointe where all life forces meet.

When understood, dualism can help us connect into the often unknown, indescribable and invisible realms of Spirit and the soul. It plays itself out in the invisible, energetic flow of your body. Always remember that your soul, and in fact your entire being, is one big, highly charged consciousness of light. To borrow from Walt Whitman and the classic movie Fame—you *are* the body electric. You are a body of vibrating photons of charged light connecting in every moment. If you could see your true energetic Self, you would see yourself as waves of light flowing, like the ocean expanding and contracting in the universe. This is both a physical and spiritual truth.

Within each one of those photons of light exist positive and negative electrical charges, or energies that fuel the movement of light and life force. That positive and negative energy within the smallest structures of your body is expressed on this physical plane as masculine and feminine energies, forces, or characteristics within you.

> *Duality is the maze through which we move to find that we are really beings of Oneness.*

You may question how light energy can possibly have masculine or feminine characteristics. The short answer here is that they really don't. However, when energies exist within a physical body that live, breathe, grow, and interact in social environments on earth, they *appear or can be understood* as masculine or feminine qualities. The divine feminine and masculine energies that lead you through divine union into your True Self are different from the cultural, familial, societal roles and personas that typically define masculinity and femininity. Once we can recognize and define how we have sculpted our thinking and actions by our unconscious masculine and feminine tendencies, the easier it is to find our divine masculine and feminine energies. Many current ideas and expressions of masculinity and femininity are taken on by aligning to cultural and external values and beliefs passed to us through society and our family lineage. They are often a corruption and mutation of your true divine energies.

> *We need to become our true divine feminine and masculine energies verses what we have known and adopted as our masculine and feminine selves through our cultural, religious and social beliefs.*

When describing many of the energetic qualities of our divine masculine and feminine energies, they often align with many gender definitions about what it means to be "a man" or "a woman." Although important, certain stereotypical energies are actually "flipped," as you will come to learn and experience. The specific characteristics of your feminine and masculine energies contain your capacities for love, compassion, forgiveness, empowerment, true power, creativity, focus, opening, receiving, manifestation, vision, abundance, surrender, trust, commitment, and connection to life.

Understanding Your Divine Energies

Each of us has a unique expression of both masculine and feminine energies. When they are cleared and integrated, your masculine and feminine energies hold your unlimited power and capacity for love and connection with yourself and with all of life. They are the soul forces that integrate your spiritual and physical bodies so that you can literally feel how Infinite Source energy moves through your physical body. They set your energetic grid into place and align you to the universal forces of light that govern your soul's development and progression. Their union and expression create higher integrity, ethics and values, which support you to walk your life path with honor and love for all beings. The decisions that you make from a conscious state of divine masculine and feminine integration are usually not only for your highest good, but for the highest good of others.

> *Your masculine and feminine energies hold your unlimited power and capacity for love and connection.*

The Divine Feminine

Your divine feminine is the creation power of the universe that lives within your soul. She is an eternal, life-giving force that awakens the universal truth within your psyche, mind, and soul. Your divine feminine opens the inner gateways to knowing yourself as an energy that is both human and divine. The divine feminine is the essence of your soul and will do whatever it has to do to evolve you forward on your universal journey. It naturally births and creates the highest values and expressions of your soul. Before you can move into universal consciousness, you must find your personal divine feminine life forces, whether you are male or female. Her energies give you a direct connection to your wisdom, truth, and power. She is the initiator of your full potential, dreams, and desires.

The divine feminine is raw power. **IT IS YOUR POWER.** It is creation centered, knowing, certain, bold, fearless, expansive, receptive, trailblazing, ferocious, directive, empowering, perceptive, passionate, nurturing, intuitive, life-giving, unlimitedly creative, visionary, assertive, allowing, wise, telepathic, and receiving. As you open to your divine feminine, all of these qualities will emerge from within you. They will help you feel and experience the deeper truth that life is a gift meant to be fully lived.

Your divine feminine knows herself from the beginning of time and patiently awaits your return. Your divine feminine is One with all of life and continually gives birth to multifaceted expressions of raw creation energy that continue to birth and expand the universe. The divine feminine has no attachment to her creations. She creates because she loves to create. Her energies flow through your body, whether you are in a male or female form. When you block off from her energies, you experience illness, insecurity, confusion, loss, fear, and pain on all levels: mentally, physically, emotionally, and spiritually. On a soul level, you feel it the most, because you will long for something, but may not know what it is, until you find "her."

Opening and becoming One with the life force of your divine feminine is crucial to your awakening process. Without the divine feminine flowing through you, you feel stagnant, disconnected, fearful, and isolated. When you reconnect with her creative life-giving power, your self-doubt, fear, and pain can begin to dissolve. Your personal creativity opens, your spiritual gifts can flourish, your heart can remain open, your brain clicks into healing and enlightenment mode, and the fear of BEing You dissolves.

For over twenty-five hundred years, your divine feminine has been severely judged and condemned. There have been windows in time where she has been honored and given the respect and love that she deserves. However, those times have been too few and far between. Both men and women have suffered because their divine feminine power has been rejected and feared. Yet, once connected with her, you have unlimited access to the profound joy and revelations of your eternal True Self.

The divine feminine opens your direct access to Infinite Source and provides instantaneous direct knowledge and understanding of your true purpose. You become tapped into a power that never fails you and helps you to heal yourself and others just by shifting your focus. The divine feminine is the healer of the body. She has courage and clarity that, once integrated, directs life to recreate circuits and channels of power that are destined to heal our world. The divine feminine initiates your soul into action.

> *The divine feminine is raw power.*

The Divine Masculine

Within the soul of both men and women lives a divine masculine presence and essence. Your divine masculine contains essential life-sustaining and supporting qualities that enable you to flourish and accomplish your goals, soul mission, and life's purpose. Your divine masculine supports, sustains, and grows the creative spark of its divine feminine. It grows out of the feminine and has the built-in natural tendencies of loyalty, steadfastness, and unifying love.

Your divine masculine expresses as love. ***IT IS YOUR LOVE.*** More specifically, your divine masculine is unconditional love. It is embracing, compassionate, dynamic, gentle, patient, building, sustaining, and steadfast.

Your divine masculine is also your "follow-through." An awakened and pure divine masculine love is so great that it wants to make sure that everything and everyone works together to smoothly reach a designated goal and that all needs are being met. He is the shaping, accepting, and consistent presence that completes projects and explores the possibilities of success with an embracing and compassionate nature. Your divine masculine embraces all actions that build and support family both at home and in the world. Your divine masculine is the part of you that is action-oriented, goal-centered, structuring, shaping, propelling, accepting, unifying, consistent, discerning, exploring, determined, designing, and accountable.

The divine masculine is also the space holder. He holds space for the divine feminine both personally and universally to emerge. It is this ability that is crucially needed during these times. Both men and women need to learn how to hold space for their own divine feminine to enter into their bodies. Men are being spiritually asked by the divine not only to hold space for their own divine feminine to emerge, but also to hold space for the birthing process of each woman's divine feminine, pure, integrated power.

Over time, the pure divine masculine has been manipulated and mutated into what so many of us know as "masculinity," which is all too often tied to an overbearing, cut off, and imbalanced power. Your divine masculine *is your love, not your power*. And yet, the mutation of the divine masculine has created a world of masculinity where we are socially expected to be fearless but never taught how to BE. We are taught to separate from the earth, Spirit, our heart, and each other's hearts in order to be perfect and to perform what is expected within the old paradigm structures. We are taught to split body, heart, and mind while severely repressing the pain created through our separation. As a culture, we are rarely taught how to connect into the feminine by accessing the love within our pure, divine, masculine source. We are taught subconsciously to use the false masculine energies to repress the feminine power within our body and each other. This suppression has created the disempowerment of humanity's voice in our political, economic, religious, and social systems. The joy of these times is to seize the opportunity for awakening our Whole Self in Oneness.

> *Your divine masculine expresses as LOVE.*

Your Divine Masculine-Feminine Relationship

Simply put, the relationship and purpose of your divine masculine and feminine is union. They are meant to engage in an open, expansive, life-generating, and unifying dance of the divine to connect you into the full light, love, and power that you are. Your integrated divine masculine and feminine energies are your spiritual power. The divine masculine intelligence naturally grows and supports life instead of destroying it. However, throughout history, the human masculine has been forced to withstand the corruption of cultural, religious, and political institutions and roles that have been created through living in separation and denial from divine masculine and feminine integration. Truthfully, the desecration of our divine masculine and feminine soul energies was the harbinger for all future spiritual and human violations to come.

There are some ancient cultures around the planet that still understand the divine relationship between the divine feminine and masculine, but they are considered backward and primitive. The most holy and evolved divine masculine energies in both men and women understand that their relationship to the divine feminine is one of reverence. Those who live in integration understand that without a consistent connection to their divine feminine power, that inevitably everyone becomes addicted to emptiness, arrogance, and suffering. It is understood that it is the divine feminine power within them and within life itself that evolves and enlightens the Whole Self.

Without the connection with the feminine, the societal masculine has become a slave to the external forces of greed and corruption. Without a connection to the divine feminine, a constant nagging to fill the body, mind, and spirit with more and more thoughts, "stuff," and fluff is creating a world culture of internal emptiness. Both men and women who have disconnected from their divine feminine have lost the ability to embody their healthy power and to fulfill the higher calling of their soul in this lifetime. The divine masculine is purified by living in direct connection with Infinite Source and embodying full awareness of its presence. The building of this connection through love, honor and compassion has the ability to destroy the false masculine Self. The divine feminine initiates total transformation of our deep-seated patterns that hold the false masculine within each of us in place by her nature of being the flame of creation. It is within the total integration of our divine masculine and feminine energies that our higher purpose is revealed, activated, and implemented.

The strength and clarity found within the integration of our divine masculine and feminine consciousness, gives us the drive and focus to live the lives we are born to live. Our divine and liberated masculine presence must teach and liberate the socialized and imprisoned inner masculine energies within us all so that we learn how to emulate a new way of BEing ONE. The old paradigm of socialized masculine energies has taught us how to close the heart for the sake of accomplishment, and neglect and abandon our creative forces. It teaches us to reject our spiritual truth and remain attached to family and societal values that use and abuse the clarity, wisdom, and new power found within the heart. The divine masculine must be valued as deeply as we honor and revere the divine feminine. Together they can and will shift our planet back into balance. It is up to each one of us to come into a new relationship with our internal and external divine masculine expression.

> *Your integrated divine masculine and feminine energies are your spiritual power.*

The Masculine-Feminine Split

To further help you to feel and connect with how your divine feminine and masculine energies exist within you, it is useful to consider how separations or splits have become a part of what it means to be a "normal human being." When you begin to recognize how separation has created your consciousness in your life and in our world culture, you can finally begin to see with greater clarity and purpose what you need to do to move forward on your path.

Our world culture is severely imbalanced in its relationship to pure feminine and masculine energy. It emphasizes the over-development of an imbalanced male energy as the model for both men and women to follow. You are taught to over develop your rational mind and fill it up with both useful and useless information and experiences. You are taught to armor your personality with techniques to appear confident, successful, and spiritual, yet you remain separate from true power and divine union.

The separation that is encoded within individuals and the world began when the divine feminine and masculine became disconnected within Itself. It lost its remembrance of BEing One with its Whole Self. The divine masculine started to seek being God itself through separation, rather than operating from the understanding that it was a spark of God whose function was to co-create from the heart level with Infinite Source. As this desire for power increased, the feminine principle was acknowledged less and less and was used to empower and serve false power. It was given less value and excluded within religious and political systems. As soon as power became focused on what you own or control verses how unified you are with Infinite Source, the cultural masculine and feminine split in two; political, economic, and cultural pain and suffering followed.

The consequences of this split for humanity included the following:

- The body was dishonored.

- The heart was no longer the center of feeling.

- There was a shift into a dominant mental body focus.

- We split off from a conscious connection with our heart and soul.

- Our souls fragmented.

- Love and power split.

- Abandonment, betrayal, and rejection began.

- The emotional body became imbalanced; and as an expression of the union or disconnection of the soul, it became ill with unworthiness, self-doubt, self-judgment, mistrust, and fear.

- We lost the knowingness that we are all love and that we are here to create a world from a state of being in our love.

- We started looking up to God instead of looking up and down into our individual connection within heaven and earth.

- The Ego and Personality Self wanted to become the power of God itself. It created a struggle to be God through separation.

- The definition, value, and expression of power shifted. Power became about dominion over things or others instead of about our ability to self-source and BE ONE with Creation.

- We created pain through our resistance to trusting the source of love. We split off from love and created fear. The fear and separation in which we live creates our suffering.

- We grew to fear our own power, which comes from love, because of feeling that our love is not enough.

- We lost intuition and turned against the skills of the feminine, including the power of trust, clairvoyance, knowingness, and telepathy.

- We left union in the divine and began to look externally to be fulfilled, "have more," and accumulate things.

Within you there is a SELF that is ONE in God. It is the light and truth of your Whole Self unified. It knows and remembers the promise of ONENESS and will guide you forward if you allow it to. It is your emotional body that feels the pain from your original separation, which is cleared as your heart, soul, and the light become ONE. We have all carried forward and expanded that initial pain through the ongoing separation from our divine masculine and feminine energies, from our inner bodies, and with one another.

We have spent hundreds, maybe thousands of moments ignoring our own pain because we haven't understood where it comes from. The light within your heart, as it becomes brighter and stronger, has the capacity to bypass the ache of feeling separate from BEing One with your God Self. When we surrender into the light of our soul and allow it to be greater than our fears, we learn the art of Oneness. Life challenges us to trust our connection and commitment to BEing One and to choose it over running, hiding, shutting down, or following the overwhelm that is created from living in separation from our Original Self.

> *Within you there is a SELF that is ONE in God. It is the light and truth of your Whole Self.*

It is essential to remember that you have the power to heal and transform your own pain. All of your soul aspects hold divine love, light, and power. As you reconnect the divine parts of yourself that have been separate from the love within your heart, you are able to heal the core root of your pain. The *One in Soul* experience helps you to heal the inner separations that create your karmic challenges; financial and relationship challenges; and emotional, spiritual, and mental pain, while simultaneously aligning your heart and soul with Infinite Source—God. You are empowered to reunite the most significant divine parts of yourself to illuminate your life, your purpose, your potential, and your power from love.

The separations within your thinking and feeling bodies have created all of your physical, emotional, psychological, and spiritual dilemmas and crises. All too often you have remained separate from your heart so you could manage and tolerate the ongoing ache and hurt inside of you. You have created your own spiritual and energetic version of self-medication to block yourself from cracking open. For those who are ready, healing your body-mind-heart-soul separations brings you to the gateway of reuniting and healing with God—Infinite Source.

> *As you reconnect the parts of yourself that have been separate from the love within your heart, you are able to heal the root cause of your pain.*

Feminine Healing For Men and Women

The essential first step in healing the masculine-feminine separations within your heart is to heal your feminine energies.

THE COMPONENTS OF THE SOUL: YOUR DIVINE FEMININE & MASCULINE

The suppression of the feminine over thousands of years has been a primary source of creating suffering and misery on this planet and within our individual lives. When the divine feminine powers in both men and women began to be attacked and destroyed thousands of years ago for threatening the hierarchy of political rule, the natural balances and alignment with God— Infinite Source completely shifted.

The mind is unable to lead as a co-creator with universal forces when the divine feminine-masculine energies are split apart. The human will separates from divine will, and the imbalances created in the mind slip out of alignment with the natural order of creation. The outcome of this separation are societies, religions, and systems that control and create further division amongst the masses, destroying the harmony and balance of everyday life. Restoring the existence of our individual divine feminine-masculine relationship is where we must begin. When we rediscover the divine feminine power within us, we come to know it as a flowing, surging, rippling, invigorating, initiating, transformational healing light that is a direct expression of BEing One with the unmanifested, raw creative power within the universe. It has the power to align the soul to its highest expression and create healing, prosperity, and empowerment in every act of creation. When our consciousness is divorced from our divine feminine energies, we are unable to walk as the truth of our soul. We become mirrors of a shattered mind, lost, and confused without a home.

As you reconnect with the source of your divine feminine, you are reconnected to your soul. From here, you can become the healer of your own life and remove the obstacles that block your divine masculine from stepping up and rising up into the union with his highest Self. The divine feminine ignites the divine masculine to open and leave behind the old programming of the false, patriarchal masculine. The divine feminine within you is a wellspring of power that connects you to the integration and evolution of your highest Self.

As you integrate your soul aspects into the light of your heart, you build a source of strength that can receive your divine feminine and masculine energies into your body, and support their presence in your everyday life. It takes an inner strength to rebuild your inner matrix after lifetimes of living in separation from masculine and feminine union. Your inner strength is found through becoming One—in and with the light.

> *The divine feminine ignites the divine masculine to open and step out of the old programming of the false, patriarchal masculine.*

Whether female or male, most of us at some point have experienced having our divine feminine rejected, judged, exiled, betrayed, and even hated whether in this lifetime or in a past lifetime. As we build the strength of the light within, we are able to remain open and hold the space for the truth and power of our divine feminine to shine through.

When your feminine energy is repressed and denied in your body, it is likely to revolt, strike back, or acquiesce to its own detriment. Your body and mind can become ill, and your addiction to fear and repression take over. Fear in the feminine energy field manifests as follows:

- Tumors, cancer, heart attacks, arthritis, asthma, obesity, etc.

- Depression, sorrow, creative blocks, and narcissism

- Poverty, money issues, and sexual imbalances

- Chaos, disorder, denial, and addiction

- Self-destruction and destruction to the environment and human lives

- Repression and discrimination

- Repetitive anger that blocks your happiness and success

- Intimacy issues

- Materialism, greed, attachment, vanity, and loss

- Hatred

- Narcissism

- Disempowerment and self-sabotage

To discover and reconnect to your divine feminine soul energies, you need to create an inner container of pure light and love to welcome her energies. Your inner container is a chalice that is the sacred Holy Grail of the union of your spiritual and soul energies in your body. By creating an inner temple to come to, you create a safe space that can hold your awakening Self.

First, the wounded karmic, ancestral, and cultural feminine energies that you have experienced in both this lifetime and past lifetimes need to be acknowledged, seen, and transformed.

Your inner container—your chalice of light is crucial for the evolution of your feminine energies. They may hold shame, fear, and anger and to cross the bridge into your full healing, you need to set up sacred space. The feminine needs a safe inner space and a safe external space that can support you to express, explore, and BE You.

Your external living space needs to be able to support the integration of your feminine-masculine energies to co-habitat. Whether you are a man or a woman, you must have a space that is totally your own, no matter how big or small. Within this space, you need colors, fabrics, pictures, and objects that create a sanctuary for your heart and soul. The physical space sets the intention to give your Whole Self a place to exist. You will know the space is "right" when you feel safe in your body. It is a feeling that gives you inner and outer stability. You will find yourself with more energy, focus, and the ability to BE present with the people in your life. You will meditate better, write more easily, assimilate and digest your food better, plan your time more efficiently, and enjoy being in the flow of life financially, spiritually and emotionally.

> *You must create sacred space inside and outside of yourself to give your divine energies full expression and space in your body.*

By honoring your Self through BEing One with your Self—you develop the trust needed to heal. As part of your BE process, trust must be established before healing can occur. Your feminine needs to feel safe to express and evolve as you create an inner and outer container. How to build your chalice, your inner container, will be discussed further in Chapter Eighteen.

THE COMPONENTS OF THE SOUL: YOUR DIVINE FEMININE & MASCULINE

Everyday ways to build trust with your feminine:

- Place money in all of its forms—paychecks, business and personal checks, and cash that you receive—on a sacred alter that is filled with meaningful pictures and objects of beauty, and give thanks for the abundance given to you. Watch monies and opportunities increase in your life. (You are giving thanks to divine mother.)

- Notice when you have a pain in your body, then track the pain to a feeling that needs to be expressed and received by you. Practice an active mode of opening, inner listening, and receiving with full intention and full presence with your Self.

- Feel the earth element through your skin. Skin brush, apply balancing oils to your body, and drink medicinal herb teas daily. The earth element creates prosperity, longevity, health, grounding, and nurturing for the self and others, and the ability to complete projects. Warm sesame oil is very soothing.

- Allow yourself to live within the space within your heart as you speak, feel, and envision your life and work. Expand yourself in your heart to connect with God—Infinite Source. Bring the focus from your mind into your heart and open to gold light in your heart as you think about the fulfillment and completion of your intended project, goal, or dream.

- Remain open to all of your feelings without judgment. If you do not know what you feel, find a way that helps you find your feelings. Some of these ways include gardening, jogging, writing, cooking, pranic breathing, yoga, dance, journaling, painting, pottery, laughing, singing, sailing, hiking, BEing, etc. Each time you do a chosen activity, feel your way into the space of clarity and neutrality with the full range of feelings within you.

- Be spontaneous. Do things in your day in a new way. Practice seeing the world around you in a new way.

- Listen to your heart and BE in it. Practice shifting your attention from your heart, through your feet, and into the center of the earth. To find the core light in the center of the earth, look for a large, clear white crystal or flames of pure white fire. Then, breathe into your heart from your connection with the earth.

- Pay attention to being in and with your Self first before you try to make something better for someone else.

- Learn to give yourself "space" in the moment. Before you speak, or do "anything," give yourself space to feel where you are and how you feel. Receive your own energies first, then speak or "do."

The feminine energy in your body yearns to break through its cocoon into freedom and self-realization. You can do this through allowing it to exist and following its lead. It will communicate through directing you to receive her creative impulses. Through silence, entering stillness, and expanding into the light, your feminine will rise up out of the darkness and show you a new pathway to walk.

How Fear Is Created In The Feminine

The mind and body energetically split when the soul aspects of the feminine experience a direct abusive confrontation. Many men and women unknowingly shut the door to their feminine power because of verbal, physical, sexual, psychological, or emotional abuse as a child or young adult by a family member, religious leader, a teacher, or peers. The abuse wound can be healed when the original wound from previous incarnations is resolved. The present life abuse needs to be tracked to the originating betrayal, which allows for the memory (causal) body to release its pain.

As previously mentioned, the past life experiences of being persecuted for being a torchbearer of light resides in the DNA cellular structure and will hide until you make it safe for "her" to emerge again. She is a vital component of your True Self and, once restored to her Original Self, will elevate your life on all levels. Healing deep feminine pain within our causal body can help the scars of abuse in both men and women.

The mind splits off from BEing One in soul when it perceives that its right to exist is in question. When the mind goes into doubt about whether God—Infinite Source is abandoning it or not, it will experience the separation of that thought as fear. Fear can only survive in the moment of separation. The mind will align to fear and split off from its infinite connection. The mind experiences its separation from Infinite Source as fear. Only through reunion with the light in our heart can we experience directly that we are One with God and in that Oneness, fear does not exist. We abandon living, breathing and BEing One in Infinite Source. God—Infinite Source does not abandon us. Only our mind creates separation.

When we are aligned to separation, we live in fear, anger and hatred. We leave ourselves out of fear. Yet, our true existence can only be found by staying One with the light and grace of our True Self. There are saints and great beings who have come through being persecuted and hold steady to their knowingness that they are One with God—Infinite Source and refuse to split off into the darkness of fear. Thousands of us are waking up to the realization that by living in an unbreakable connection with the light and truth within ourselves, we can build a new world. As the people of the world are tested whether to give up their power, stand up in their love, or become victims to fear and control, we are collectively being given the opportunities to recognize the controls of the old paradigm and how it works to shut down and repress the powerful expression of the feminine Spirit.

By clearing and opening your solar plexus and lower belly, your *Fifth and Second Power Point Center,* and connecting their power with your heart center, you are able to see through and feel your way through the fear, which we have collectively created and which keeps us living in a dream world of false realities and illusion.

It is time for each of us to become fully awakened to the power and love within our hearts. We need this precious connection to help us to see through people and situations who use and abuse their own lack of connection with Source and create extremely empty solutions that serve their own needs alone. We need to be able to recognize false energies and words so we can stop giving our power over to individuals and systems that have no concern for the people who depend upon those very systems. But, first we must find our true power through coming back to our Soul and BEing who we are.

Through committing to the truth found within our hearts, we can embrace the courage and clarity needed to shift our relationship to our ego Self—who is in the "profession" of creating fear and blocking our most important Self-truths—and instead access the power within our feminine energies.

Healing and clearing fear in the feminine energy field makes possible:

- The flourishing of creativity, abundance, love and health

- The end of agreements and beliefs that perpetuate dogma

- The release of emotions held in the body, making it possible to BE Awakened

- Thinking and feeling at the same time

- Awakening to life outside the societal straitjacket

- A new kind of thinking created from honoring life and one another

- Trusting the strength that evolves from Oneness

- Implementing powerful vision, integrity, and social action

- Stepping out of disempowerment and inaction

As you create a healing environment that supports your divine feminine to awaken, you can then be a torchbearer and carrier of the light that allows you to walk into the destiny of your life.

Masculine Healing For Men and Women

Your masculine energies, as your feminine energies do, carry the DNA imprint of your family and cultural imprint. The values of masculine energy for both men and women are woven into societal and familial expectations and become imbedded in the subconscious until consciously dealt with. Your masculine energies need external structures to provide a playground to explore and expand the infinite expressions and possibilities of their Whole Self. Your masculine energies need to define themselves authentically to become self-reliant and not molded by the needs of others, to feel accepted and loved. Your masculine energies need to know they can exist independently and become reliant upon Infinite Source from within, rather than having to fulfill the expectations of others. When the masculine energies cannot make a clear connection to their core Self, the ego Self works hard to create a false Self to be the bridge to a reality that becomes fixated in needing to be better than everyone else. The masculine energy will feel extreme fear when it does not have an inner connection to its True Self, but because of its nature will do whatever it takes to save face. Masculine energies are naturally One with the web of life, yet need to explore their relationship with the role that they have in the larger kaleidoscope of life. Without a strong and secure connection to their heart center, the masculine energies become tainted in fear.

Fear in the masculine energy field manifests as:

- Mistrust of others

- The need to control

- Inability to take the steps to fulfill one's purpose

- Lack and self-doubt

- Unexplainable anger and reactions

- Going along with status quo

- Shutting down to core feelings

- Saying one thing but feeling something else

- Blaming others rather than being "Self" responsible

- Anxiety

- Putting others down to feel superior

- Avoiding intimate communication

- Creating a false Self

- Hatred and violence

Everyday ways to build trust with your Masculine:

- Journal with your wounded Masculine Self and look through his pain and see his light with compassion and acceptance.

- Spend a day doing nothing but being with him in your heart.

- Throw yourself into a project that you haven't done in a long time, and do it without judgment.

- Observe how you go into your head during the course of your day and create logical denial. Choose to let go of the stories that you make up to confirm your thoughts and perceptions.

- Do a word cluster on paper. Write down one feeling that you are having and circle it. Then draw a line connecting to the next level of feeling and circle it. Go down 20 levels into your Self, each time finding another word that describes the feeling, all the way into your core.

- Find an object that interests you and observe it, such as a piece of fruit, a sculpture, a piece of pie, a plant, an animal, etc. Study it first from your head, then your heart, then through your senses: feel, smell, hear, see, taste, and experience its movement. Write your observations.

- Choose to have compassion for a total stranger every day for a week.

- Breathe into your heart center once a day and envision a part of your inner masculine joining with you. Surround him in gold and light white with love.

- Move from one side of a room to another walking backward, breathing into your spine and allowing your spine to guide you.

Healing and shifting fear in the masculine energy field makes possible:

- Seeing through the eyes of love
- Humility and humbleness
- The offering of unconditional love
- Completing projects
- Holding space for someone else's heart
- Giving without being attached to what you receive
- Tenderness and self-confidence
- Allowing others to be themselves
- The full presence and expression of the divine feminine
- Physical and spiritual endurance
- Flexibility
- Living with loving kindness for oneself and others
- Listening, surrendering, and BEing
- Sexual connectedness
- Creating solutions that serve the greater needs for humanity

- Releasing shame

- Walking one's talk

The divine masculine is first experienced in your body as pure love. The societal masculine is created upon repressing its emotions and compartmentalizing its thinking, and fulfilling the expectations of others at the expense of itself. Your divine masculine comes to serve, to BE a light holder of truth, and BE steadfast. Your societal masculine is taught and expected to deny, repress, and reject the feminine energies within its body and soul and to find feminine connection outside of itself. Your divine masculine cares for the well-being of all. It strives to create unity and support for others. It will hold open the door for you to find what is real. It will give you space to know yourself. It will invite you to BE a space for truth to flow in and out from.

The divine masculine energy emanates love and compassion. The shame and humiliation held in your body from being judged for being unconditionally loving and creatively uninhibited begin to melt as the divine masculine opens. Light awakens the divine masculine through the initiation and ignition of your divine inner feminine. As the light moves in your body, your divine masculine energies will fill your heart, fill your solar plexus, and then move into your genitals and root center—your *First Power Point Center*. You will feel connected to life in a new way.

> **The masculine expression of your Divine Real Self
> is first experienced in your body as pure love.**

Masculine & Feminine Integration

As you explore the relationship of how your divine masculine and feminine energies work together, the unique energetic signature of who you are will manifest in all areas of your life. As your soul becomes aware of itself through opening to its masculine and feminine aspects, you become more of who you are and have always wanted to be.

Your divine masculine and feminine energies will unite, ignite, and merge to create a connection that opens and expands you into an integrated, multi-dimensional feeling of contentment and power. The reconnection of your divine energies gives you access to the larger forces within the universe to further empower you. It enables you to tangibly experience spiritual power in your body, possibly for the first time. Your energy field widens, providing greater energy flow, your mind and body feel connected, and you shift from emotionalism, where you react from one emotion to the next, into a steady and balanced presence with your higher feelings. The electromagnetic charge from your empowered divine energies connects you into light and creativity, a deeper passion for life, while expanding your belief in unlimited possibilities and your sense of purpose.

> *Unified masculine & feminine energies help you tangibly experience spiritual power in your body.*

On a practical level, the opening and integration of your divine masculine and feminine forces will create an opportunity for you to leave behind your old limitations and beliefs. You stop repeating life-long patterns of loss and gain, disempowerment and control, and illness and self-hatred. Your inner battles and dramas will end.

Everything inside of your mind and heart will shift as your body receives the union of your divine masculine and feminine forces. Your heart will feel connected to life, opening up access to your greater truth and the greater truth in the universe. New dimensions of self-expression, prosperity, work, and love will open for you. You will feel directed, enlivened, and empowered. Your sexuality, creativity, and spirituality will feel united into a core hub of inspired expression and co-creation with the universe.

You will discover that you want to live life fully and be the expression of who you are without fear. Imagine wanting to do something that initially seems improbable, like climbing a mountain, starting a new career, or leaving a negative relationship. In place of your "I can't" mentality will be a grounded feeling of "I AM One with myself, and I choose to trust BEing in tune with my heart and the clarity it feels." You shift into a more expansive view of reality, where the confidence and fearlessness to take the steps needed to accomplish your dreams become possible. This is about coming into life and living in a new way that is beyond what your mind alone could create.

> *Divine Masculine-Feminine Integration ends your inner battles and dramas and allows you to BE who you are without fear.*

Your divine masculine and feminine energies guide you on your soul journey by helping you to open, receive, focus, and direct the power and love within your soul so that your life unfolds from who you truly are. They bring you home into yourself.

Their union takes you through the gateway into the ONENESS OF BEING. You could say that they provide you with a "direct express to enlightenment," because as the aspects of yourself are brought back together, you feel a natural connection with Infinite Source and can trust how God is guiding you on your road to BE.

In men and women, your divine feminine is:

- A ferocious, bold, and wise life force energy that cracks open illusion, denial, and control

- The power of focus

- The unbreakable strength that provides you with the courage to make it through the hardest of life-challenges

- The pure power of creativity and force, providing unlimited possibilities and perceptions

- What makes you feel safe in your body and helps you trust and come into you

- What provides security and protection

- What busts you through your fear; you will have the knowingness and innate capacity to tap into the greater love and power within you

- The awakener, initiator of truth

- The gateway to crystal clear clarity

In men and women, your divine masculine:

- Welcomes fearlessness

- Integrates and implements the bigger picture of your soul purpose and divine truth

- Provides the trust to express compassion, acceptance, and the ability to embrace people and situations

- Fuels your exploratory nature and desire for unity

- Supports you to be structured, action orientated, and accountable to build and create your vision and dreams

- Ignites the processes of alignment and integration within your body

- Enables you to surrender to your own divine feminine and make possible living and BEing ONE with Infinite Source

- Holds the space of unconditional love

- Initiates integrity

- Embraces divine truth into action

Your divine feminine and masculine aspects have spent eons of time already BEing One in Infinite Source, so when you meet them, and align to them, you will feel as though you have come home.

Masculine & Feminine Energies & Soul Consciousness

Consciousness in your body comes from your connection to Infinite Source. That connection to Infinite Source comes from the ignition of your masculine and feminine energies and the degree of openness and connectedness of your body's multiple *Power Point Centers*. When all of your energies and *Power Point Centers* are cleared and aligned into Spirit, then consciousness can open into your body and evolve. Remember, Spirit is the movement, awareness, energy, and consciousness of how we experience Infinite Source in this realm. Your masculine and feminine energies are really the expression of your light and bodily power in the physical world. The movement and opening of light created from your masculine and feminine energies and power centers helps create a space or opening for consciousness to come in. As your masculine and feminine powers are lit up in your body, your soul responds to feeling connected to something "bigger" than what your mind perceives as "your life." It gives you an opportunity to awaken your soul consciousness and tap into your Higher Self, which gives you access to living in direct connection with Infinite Source.

The alignment and integration of your masculine and feminine forces creates an enhanced spin or energetic charge that connects you into the multi-dimensional geometric design of consciousness within your body. This is beyond what your mind "knows" about your physical Self. You have a geometric design that is an energetic merging of your soul, Spirit, and body. It is your Original Self. Just like all molecules have a shape and design, your consciousness has a design that has the power to integrate and make you whole. Each person is a unique design of consciousness. Your soul frequency creates itself into a dimensional geometric form that expresses as your distinctive signature. Similar to a multi-faceted snowflake, the shape and design of your soul resonates to the essence of your True Self. When all of the aspects of your soul and divine masculine and feminine energies unite in your heart and body, they uplift you into your unified consciousness or Original Self. You are unified into the heart of Oneness, the essential core frequency of the universe.

> **Each person is a unique design of consciousness that resonates to his or her True Self.**

As your two forces of the soul come into balance and alignment, your body can also handle greater intensities of universal consciousness. What does that mean? It means you will have an improved ability to live an "awakened and enlightened" life and connect into the greater light matrix and new source codes entering into the global consciousness. When this happens, it fundamentally shifts the cellular and DNA coding in your nervous and energy systems, which enables you to feel BEing ONE with Creation Energy—the Source of life energy in your body and in the universe.

The integration of your masculine and feminine energies lays the foundation for heightening the core "receptors" of your DNA structure. Your DNA provides the genetic code and building blocks for your physical existence and builds energy within your body. When your DNA can send out and receive information and energy properly, it not only keeps you healthy but also enables you to tap into light. Clear, receptive DNA improves the flow of energy in your body and access to your higher consciousness because, as you recall, higher consciousness is really light energy.

Yet, most of us live with a split between our spiritual and physical energies. This creates an environment in our bodies where our DNA cannot function optimally. Beneath a thick layer of goo covering your DNA strands is a smooth flow of light, universal knowledge, and energy. This gunk is made up of emotional, psychological, and energetic residue from the cellular memories of pain and suffering that is created while feeling lost, confused, and separate from Infinite Source in this lifetime and from past lifetimes. It clouds your DNA and the flow of energetic charge and light within your body. This inevitably numbs down your consciousness, access to your Higher Self, and the greater light in the universe.

> *The integration of your masculine and feminine energies lays the foundation for heightening the core "receptors" of your DNA structure.*

As you open to your divine masculine and feminine energies you will experience increased wisdom, clarity and power to awaken from the pain and separation that have blocked your energy field. The deepened flow of light and energy from your integrated divine masculine and feminine will enable you to access other aspects of your soul energy field that need to be awakened to deepen your Whole Self enlightening and become more unified with the infinite you.

The soul aspects that carry your authentic spiritual power must be accepted and integrated before you can move forward in your life. When you end your attachments to how you have identified and addicted to what it means to be "you," you will go through an inner shamanic death and letting go experience.

The feeling of "death" can feel like you are entering into the void. You will experience an infinite space of expansion. As you allow yourself to move into it, focus on the light in your heart and you will move through the gap in your consciousness that had been created by perceiving yourself to be separate from your God Self — your True Self. In your past the gap would push you to become attached to what your ego Self had convinced you would make you feel safe and secure.

As previously shared, the moment of separation from our True Self occurs for each of us at different times in our infancy, childhood or young adulthood. The age that you see yourself in the *One in Soul* reconnection work is the age that you split off, either for the first time or multiple times, from your core, light-filled—God Self connection.

The disconnection's between your unconscious and conscious selves creates the emotional and energetic reactions that you go through in your daily life. The conscious part of you knows, "Wow, I am the light and I want to BE the light that I AM." The unconscious parts of you say, "No one else cares, why should I?." The unconscious parts of you are created when your Ego Self split off from the divine intelligence within you. Your unconscious "parts" create beliefs that manipulate your life through fear: "I do not matter to those around me. Maybe I don't really matter to my community, my family, or friends. How I am being cared for, even though I am told that I am loved, has nothing to do with my needs. *I am not being seen, heard, or received.* Thus, I conclude I do not matter—I am not worthy of being loved." These messages then retreat to the subconscious where they hide in the dark and work through our unconscious mind. As we awaken and integrate the light in our Bodymind and soul, we can heal the beliefs that hold us back from living and BEing happy.

THE COMPONENTS OF THE SOUL: YOUR DIVINE FEMININE & MASCULINE

Every human being, whether a young child, teenager, or adult, wants to make a difference and feel that who they are is "okay." We all want to know that who we are is received and seen. Perhaps your parents were too busy with their jobs, or had marriage problems, or the school you went to made you feel that you didn't have what it took to be a great student or successful human being. Perhaps you could not fix a relationship that was falling apart. Perhaps you have a business or creative dream that yearns to be manifested but doubt your ability to make them happen.

In the moment of feeling and believing that you were not enough to be given the positive support and unconditional love needed to trust and BE yourself, you experienced a death. You let go of one reality and entered into a new one. Within that death is a sorrow that can feel so big that you think that you "are sorrow" and are unable to feel joy. In these moments, your trust and willingness to love and have compassion for yourself is key. In your willingness to know the truth of who you are, embrace the love that you are, and BE the love that you are, a tender yet powerful uprising from within you can and will happen.

> *As we awaken and integrate the light in our Bodymind and soul, we can heal the beliefs that hold us back from living and BEing happy.*

As you master the *One in Soul* reconnection process, you will be able to quickly reestablish a relationship with your "awaiting soul presence" and identify and accept the joy and love that is being revealed—in your body. Your soul truths will give you physical, mental, and spiritual cues to take action to resolve the conflicts or crisis that you may come up against. When you look within yourself, and rebuild a relationship with the disowned or lost parts of your energetic soul-body field, you will experience a magnetic charge and long term bond that is both uplifting and unbreakable. All of the parts of your physical-spiritual existence will come together, and the orbital spin of the "molecule" of consciousness that you are will be activated.

When you walk through the portal of your heart, you activate a field of electromagnetic energies that also exist within the universe. Once you are activated as a unified light being, the divine spectrum of the universe has the ability to move you in perfect alignment with the greater evolutionary molecular spin of your soul. In the center point within your heart is the treasure chest of profound love that you have always been and always will be.

The fire created from your fully integrated masculine and feminine energy has the potential to synchronize and build your physical and spiritual power. When you experience this new power, you will have the following realization: You have always had this power within you. You just have not had full access to it.

The self-doubt or fear you may feel at times is created from your internal separations, clouded energy field, and trying to be someone other than your True Self. The free flow of power and love from your reconnected energies creates an unstoppable energetic charge that not only enlightens your entire being but also puts you in direct connection to Infinite Source. Your identity shifts from *trying* to be who you are, or a version of who you are, to actually *BEing who you are*. The more consciousness that is awakened within the connection between your Bodymind and soul, the greater capacity you have to receive and translate your spiritual power and love into your life and the world.

> *You have always had more physical and spiritual power than you can imagine. You just never had full access to it. Now you can.*

As you reconnect the spiritual power within your soul making use of your Bodymind connection in a new way, you can begin to fulfill your soul's destiny in this lifetime. This happens through aligning and identifying yourself with the truth of your soul instead of the personality of your ego. As your soul is activated and unified into Oneness, your *Power Point Centers*—opened, cleared, and aligned into light—create more room for your soul to BE in your body and take the steps to BEing whole.

When you become conscious of the love and wisdom within your soul, your relationship with yourself and everyone in your life is enhanced. You then have the opportunity to say "THE BIG YES" to who you really are and your spiritual purpose. You are saying YES to living in your truth, YES to being the love that you are, and YES to guiding others from your whole physical and spiritual power.

When you say YES to living your soul's destiny, you also realize that the original agreements you made with family, lovers, friends, and with life itself while living in separation to your Whole Self may no longer serve you, your highest good, or your purpose. In place of what you have known grows an inner courage that helps you to let go of what no longer serves you to BE in the highest relationship with life. You become a lion or lioness committed to your own spiritual well-being—roaring and standing up for yourself and your soul's truth. If you follow your soul when making new agreements, and are willing to let go of what no longer supports your wholeness, you will be able to live in harmony with your soul's destiny.

> *Say YES to your spiritual purpose and who you really are.*

REMEMBER:

- Your soul is really a beautiful and multi-dimensional expression of the divine. As you reconnect the aspects of your soul, you are introduced to the divine energetic expressions and grounding creative light of your divine feminine and the unifying compassionate light of your divine masculine.

- Infinite Source creates a direct connection into our bodies through the polarity of divine feminine and masculine energies. The divine masculine and feminine live as one within each cell of your body and entire energetic matrix. Their light has the ability to ignite and balance all of your *Power Point Centers*.

- The light of your integrated divine masculine and feminine energies can transmute the fear within your Bodymind and awaken your Whole Self into infinite love to move you through the gateways of awareness that lead to full enlightenment.

- Your divine energies are the soul forces that integrate your spiritual and physical bodies so that you can literally feel how Infinite Source energy moves through your physical body. They set your energetic grid into place and align you to the universal forces of light that govern your soul's development and progression.

- The divine feminine is raw power. IT IS YOUR POWER. The divine feminine opens your direct access to God—Infinite Source and provides instantaneous direct knowledge and understanding of your true purpose.

- Your divine masculine is love. IT IS YOUR UNCONDITIONAL LOVE. It contains essential life-sustaining and supporting qualities that enable you to flourish and accomplish your goals, soul mission, and life purpose.

- The relationship and purpose of your divine masculine and feminine is union. Your integrated divine masculine and feminine energies are your spiritual power meant to be used for your highest evolvement.

- Within the total integration of your divine masculine and feminine energies, your life purpose is revealed.

- You have *always been ONE with God*, but you have forgotten and blocked your direct connection.

- As you reconnect the soul aspects of yourself that have been separate from your Bodymind and heart, you are healing the root of your pain while simultaneously aligning yourself into God force.

- The depth of the split within your heart center is what fuels all of your physical, emotional, psychological, and spiritual dilemmas and crises.

- Your Feminine Self is carrying the major brunt and force of your pain; therefore, it must be healed first. Once you heal your feminine, it then creates the space and energy to allow your masculine to fully heal.

- To heal your inner feminine splits, you must create an internal inner container inside your body and an external sacred space that supports your full expression.

- The masculine expression of your Divine Real Self is first experienced in your body as pure love. It will hold open the door for you to find what is real. It will give you space to know and BE yourself.

- The opening and integration of your divine masculine and feminine forces will create an opportunity for you to leave behind your old limitations and beliefs. You stop repeating life-long patterns of loss and gain, disempowerment and control, illness and self-hatred.

- The integration of your masculine and feminine energies creates the foundation for heightening the core "receptors" of your DNA structure. As your DNA energy grid is filled with light, ingrained thought forms can be let go, allowing your higher consciousness to expand through your cellular structure.

- Enlightening into higher consciousness is really about how you are in relationship with yourself and with all of life. It is the 21st century relationship.

BELIGHT MEDITATION

Clearing Your DNA Strands in Your Emotional, Etheric, and Physical Bodies

Begin by breathing blue light into your lower belly. Fill your lower belly with blue light as you inhale and exhale. As you inhale, in your own timing, carry the blue light up to your upper chest and fill your collarbone area in this light. Repeat 4 times.

Drop your focus into the center of the earth where there are flames of pure white fire. Draw these flames of pure white fire up through your feet, legs, and into the space between your pubic bone and tailbone. Just BE with these flames of pure white fire and sense them or feel them.

Now, allow the flames of pure white fire to become two strands of white light that reach up from the space between your pubic bone and tailbone, your root center—your *First Power Point Center*. As you inhale, begin to *arc* the strands to either side. On your exhale, crisscross the light strands so that you are creating a double helix of light, like a DNA strand, through each *Power Point Center*, slowly and deliberately. Focus your attention into the space between your spine and the inside of a column of light. Go through each *Power Point Center* from the root center up through the second *Power Point Center*, and through your creation point, navel, solar plexus, heart, throat, back of the skull, third eye, and crown. Allow the energy to flow up through your crown chakra and flow down the sides of your body. Repeat 12 times.

Now, create three strands of color on either side of your starting point in your root center, inside the space of your tailbone and pubic bone. Repeat the crisscrossing pattern with the three strands of color this time through the central core shaft of each *Power Point Center*. As you arrive in the third eye, crisscross the strands several times through the third eye before moving into your crown center. To complete, sit and bathe in the light overflowing through your crown center.

For those of you who want to take the practice further:

Create 6 strands of gold light on either side of your root center, crisscrossing them and looping them through each *Power Point Center*. When you arrive at the third eye, loop the golden energy through the third eye, then bring the light upwards through the crown center, allowing it to spill over and back down to the tailbone-pubic bone area. Repeat the circuit until it is flowing like a swift river of light.

CHAPTER THIRTEEN

Practical Considerations When Connecting Your Soul Energies

> *"The external world is a canvas where you paint with the colors of your soul."*
> Michael Bernard Beckwith

Practical Considerations

As you begin to touch into the deeper light, love, and power within you, it is essential to remember that your whole body must be awakened and engaged as you move into and through your *One in Soul* reconnection process. While your mind is an essential component and doorway into the realms of light and Spirit, it alone cannot take you where you need to move. Your body is the temple, the container and vessel for higher levels of love and light to move into the physical realms. The more we, as a global culture, cut off from the light and live from the dark, unresolved thoughts, behaviors, and beliefs within us, the harder the light works to break through our barriers. Our evolution is tied into the planet's evolution. The planets, our sun, and other galaxies are all interwoven with planet Earth. We are not a separate entity. We are part of a large collective consciousness of other forms of life intelligence. Planet Earth is a living, breathing being. Your body is an extension of the Earth, our planetary system, and the consciousness of not only our universe but also many other universes. Awakening into the light that you are opens you to BE One with the Earth and to Oneness consciousness.

When the circuitry of your soul, body, mind, and higher dimensional energies are unified, you become One in your Whole Self. Many other galaxies already live in Oneness consciousness. The Earth knows this, and if we follow her consciousness as the teacher, we will be able to end creating and living in illusion and suffering. Many people still believe that what they think is real. When thoughts are created from the consciousness of separation between the Bodymind, soul, and God—Infinite Source, we remain lost and confused and grasp for anything that resembles power. When our thoughts are aligned with the Infinite Creator—Source—we can create miracles everyday of lives, for our Self and most importantly others. The heart center is the meeting point for the mind and the body to reconnect with your Soul and the Earth. The purpose of this journey is to raise our frequency up high enough to step into Christed Consciousness—also known and experienced as pure illumination. The awakening into the light of your heart and soul lifts you up and out of the gravitational pull of fear.

You are being called to engage your entire mind and body, as well as your senses and cellular structures, to open, heal, and connect with the light of Infinite Source. When opening and engaging your greater spiritual powers, you are then able to see, feel, and hear at a frequency that would normally be difficult or impossible. To support your unfoldment and reconnection, consider these practical tips and strategies.

Your Masculine & Feminine Energies & Color

Your masculine and feminine aspects resonate to different colors, imagery, sounds, and sensations, all of which help you to reconnect and integrate spiritual energy in your body. While your physical body exists on the energies of fire, water, earth, air, and ether, as well as the breath and vital food nutrients, your soul lives on Source energy. When Source energy reaches the physical world, it is seen as color and heard as sound. We are going to dive into color because, as you experience seeing color within you, your gifts of inner sight will open. Colors help you connect into your soul because they help you resonate to energy. Colors are a way that we see, feel, and experience Spirit, and they resonate to different frequencies or vibrations of Spirit. Color integrates your physical and soul bodies with your higher Self, which lives in pure Spirit.

> *Colors are a way that we see, feel, and experience Spirit*

Color connects your soul and Spirit by activating the energy currents and *Power Point Centers* within your body. Remember, your *Power Point Centers* are portals and gateways of Spirit in your body that receive and transmit light and energetic frequencies. These frequencies are sound and light currents that move in each person's body through different colors. As you open to the energy matrix of light that connects all of your subtle and physical energy levels, you will instinctively know what color you may need in a given moment to heal, integrate, or align your Self.

If you close your eyes and just imagine that you can actually see the colors in your body, you will then be able to see them. Practice flowing pure white light down through the top of your head into your body. Send the light through a wide elevator shaft corridor through the top of your head into your root center. As the light begins to flow, ask your body what color it needs to feel healthy and relaxed and for the color to be shown to you. Allow the light to move through every cell in your body.

Light is always flowing in your body. As you increase your receptivity to the colors of the light spectrum in your body and soul, you will also increase your vibrational rate and atuneness.

> *Color connects your soul and spirit by activating the energy currents and Power Point Centers within your body.*

As you begin to reconnect the aspects of your soul, ask your body what color it needs to integrate your aspect into your Whole Self. Trust the color that pops into your head. The color that pops into your head will support you to open to the energies within you ready to be integrated. Your body speaks an intuitive language, and by feeling into the full spectrum of light, colors will always guide you to receive your spiritual truth and power. Every color has a meaning. The following table shows a few of the most common colors to use to heal and align your body, mind, and soul.

The Color Rays of Spirit

Color	Capacity
Blue is spiritual truth.	The blue ray clears ancestral and karmic cording. Blue brings the peace that pours through the body after family attachments and relationship entanglements are lifted and dissolved. Blue is the direct connection to Infinite Source.
Yellow is illuminated consciousness.	Yellow activates your will to merge with your divine purpose. Yellow builds the etheric sheath of your soul, the expression of your will.
Green resonates with healing.	It vibrates with the ray of the heart that integrates body and soul. Health in the body is created and maintained by green. The color green helps the natural spin of your DNA and molecular flows in your body.
Red represents life force, vibrancy, and passion of living.	Red is the power of passion and aliveness. Your red blood is the river of life in your body. When the fire is strong in your belly, it can feed your heart and bring health, vitality, and clarity.
Purple is higher spiritual truth and power.	Purple awakens the presence of your True Self. It aligns your spiritual energies with your soul and connects you into inter-dimensionality realities.
Orange is the power of enlightenment.	The power of enlightenment is first experienced in the mind as orange. Orange integrates the physical and spiritual. When united in Spirit, the higher mind emanates orange.

Color	Capacity
Violet is the energetic and spiritual transformer.	Violet purifies the mind to assist it to shift into higher thought. It activates the mind to release old patterns and beliefs that prevent the mind and the body to harmonize and focus the light.
Turquoise is associated with certainty, trust, and energetic alignment.	It calms the heart center and activates the union of divine masculine and feminine energies.
Silver represents the transformational movement of spiritual energy in the body.	Silver connects the astral and soul body and is seen in the auric field as a silver cord that connects the physical body and Spirit. It is an etheric cleanser and balancer.
Light blue represents highest love, devotion, compassion, peace, contentment, and alignment in Infinite Source.	Light blue initiates God energy in the body on a cellular level to activate the heart.
Brown symbolizes earth, groundedness, and growth, being rock solid, true to one's word, ambitious, flowing, and awakened.	Brown strengthens the will to fulfill the soul's purpose and to support taking the necessary steps to bring dreams into fruition.

You need different colors at different times to create integration. They help the spiritual and physical aspects of you to integrate, which then allows for energetic healing of your Bodymind and soul matrix.

Moving Your Mind into Your Body

When you bring color into your body to awaken and heal the core separations between your body, mind, and soul, one of the surprising things that it is trying to awaken is the greater truth that your mind is not relegated solely in your head; it is connected and lives throughout your entire body. You have a whole mind that is intimately connected to every facet and fiber of your body and being. When your body, mind, and soul are energetically separate and split off from the light of your God Self, you are unable to stay connected to your life path and what is best for you because your decision making process is disconnected from your "whole intelligence." Your total or whole mind resides in your heart center; therefore, your heart, not your head, is the true driver of your existence. Your heart center is your true mind because the heart is the integrator of the mind in your entire body.

You might ask, how is this possible? On a physical level, your mind is connected to your body through your spine and nervous system. Nerve endings throughout your body send messages to your brain, which teach and program your mind. Your heart receives and transmits pure light from the universe, supporting intercellular communication and action. On a spiritual level, the *Power Point Centers* within your body are the connecting links between your mind and nervous system. These spiritual focus points harness light energy and send it to all parts of your body, including your brain, through energetic pathways. All of the *Power Point Centers* contain the higher and lower aspects of your mind. They each serve a particular function of integrating the body and the mind, thus creating the Bodymind.

Your *Power Point Centers* feed and balance energy in the body and create a web of connection, which keep your mind intimately linked with all of your physical and spiritual components. As your mind moves out of being predominately stationed in your head into the center of light in your body—your heart center—countless stimuli allow it to see, feel, and respond to the impulses transmitted from the universe to you. You begin to be wired to a new technology of multi-dimensional love and divine intelligence.

You are expanding or contracting energy every moment that you are alive, whether you realize it or not. When you clear your energy system, your mind no longer *feels* like a separate entity but one that is closely aligned and connected with the rest of your body. Through reconnecting your soul fragments, opening to the light within the gateways and portals in your body, working with your breath and color, and aligning your inner vision into Infinite Source, you create an environment for energetic expansion.

When you open and expand your energetic pathways, you open up energy centers in your brain, which enable you to perceive and feel the light connection with divine intelligence. This intelligence exposes the illusion of separation between how your mind perceives and seeing from the light of your soul. When your *Power Point Centers* are connected into the light, the artificial borders separating your human and divine consciousness dissolve, and your physical and spiritual worlds unite to expand who you really are and how you are connected in this world to serve and evolve.

While the contraction of energy is a vital process of the energetic process of BEing alive, excess contraction will create energetic blockages. You contract energy within your body through holding your breath, holding onto belief systems and fixed ways of being, clutching onto fear, judging yourself or others, repressing your feelings and truth, thinking only about your own needs, worrying, refusing to let go of the past, or repeating thoughts over and over again. Energetic blocks are created in your mind each time that you contract the energy in your body and use your will or imbalanced Ego to hold on to old ways of thinking and being.

> *You are expanding or contracting energy every moment that you are alive, whether you realize it or not.*

Most people have a hard time opening to their spiritual energies and power because they continue to remain stuck living in and through their heads and in a state of energetic contraction. Shift your focus from just being in your head, constantly spinning around and around with your thoughts, and begin to open your energetic channels and move down into your heart and root center. Let go and "ground into" your body through your *Power Point Centers*. This will allow you to experience what is going on in and around you more fully. It will bring together your spiritual and physical consciousness where they can work together. Your life can then move beyond separation to become an integration of the spiritual and the physical.

When you shift from living in your head to BEing fully connected in your Whole Self, you open a portal where your spiritual and physical energies can meet. You are now able to align your mind into the spiritual energies that connect you into universal consciousness and power. From this meeting point, you are able to view your life challenges and goals with new eyes.

As a first step in this process, you will be bringing your mind into your solar plexus. Without this connection, nothing can move forward. The solar plexus as the first portal and gateway in the body is the first way station for your mind to plant and root itself into your body. The mind and the solar plexus must merge and fuse to open up the needed pathways for your

Bodymind, soul, and Infinite Source to be connected, integrated, and unified.

Senses

Given that your soul seeks to connect into the physical world and into Spirit at the same time, it also uses your multiple senses including touch, smell, taste, sight, hearing, and imagery as activators in your body. Your senses open and allow you to connect into what is energetically happening inside and around you. Your senses, in concert with your divine masculine and feminine energies, help you reconnect your body and soul together so that you live in union and feel ONE in and with your soul. They are the way your soul experiences itself. Given that your senses open you, they are connected to your divine feminine because the quality of opening is aligned with feminine energy. The feminine energy is the energy of creation, which allows you to open and connect to all aspects of life. Your divine feminine energies connect you to Spirit, so your senses will naturally open you to spiritual dimensions.

If you hear a bird sing and really stop everything—every thought, judgment, perception, or preoccupation inside your head—and are completely still and silent, you can hear it with your full body. Such a simple sound and act can take you into a feeling of bliss. If you deeply breathe in the aroma of flowers, of newly blooming orange blossoms or roses in springtime, the scent will touch and reach your whole body and soul. Distractions slip away as you focus completely into your senses. You come into present time. As your senses open, your feminine energies are ignited. When your feminine energies are open, all aspects of you open up, and you become more sensitive to touch, sound, and sensations, which connect you to the greater vibrancy of your soul and all life. Your senses can create a spark of remembrance of your full soul and who you are truly meant to BE. Your third eye and heart center can open, giving you the gift of knowingness, higher intuition, and spiritual vision.

> *Your senses spark remembrance of your full soul and who you are truly meant to BE*

All of these mechanisms help open you to an abundant spiritual reality. When opening into your spiritual faculties, you are then able to see, feel, and hear at a frequency that would normally be difficult or impossible. Your attention is typically focused on the shapes and form of the physical world; e.g., if you can't see it in front of your eyes, then it does not exist. Yet, the light of your feminine and masculine energies will allow you to see what's inside the physical on a deeper level. They are the gateways into the divine, which are felt and seen as energy and light.

As you shift from a one-dimensional view of the world to a three, four, or five-dimensional perspective, you are able to see what your "stuff is" and what is another person's stuff. You get to be responsible for your own stuff and have the ability to respond to your Self more clearly without taking on other people's stuff and thinking it is yours. You make this shift by becoming aware of the energies inside of you and choose to merge with your own energies instead of the energies of other's. Your boundaries are strengthened as you take responsibility for your own thoughts, feelings and actions.

For example, instead of blaming your partner for something, you would know that you need to shift something in yourself to open the doorways of communication and intimacy. You would understand that much of what happens in your world is of your own creation, and you could choose to be more compassionate, focused, and responsible for your thoughts and actions. You might also realize that you don't want to use your own power and other people's energies recklessly or carelessly.

All of this happens because you no longer want to do things that create separation in your life. You become tuned into what it takes to be whole, and you do not want to fall back into old behaviors. The opening and integration of your masculine and feminine soul energies enable you to BE CLEAR and PRESENT with what needs to happen in your life more quickly. Your ability to make all kinds of decisions about work, family, and the future path of your life shifts.

The purpose of the feminine as it begins to open in your body is to teach you how to embody and express the power within you, reveal your spiritual gifts, and compassionately meet your deepest inner fears. It is like an all-embracing loving mother. The purpose of your divine masculine is to be a supportive, embracing divine-father that supports you to live the truth inside of you, believe in your Self, learn to let go, and to increase and heighten love in every situation, in any given moment. Masculine energy helps you focus and BE steadfast and committed to your highest path. When these two forces are reopened, they help you take on greater responsibility for yourself. There is a tremendous amount of joy and pleasure when the inner masculine is received by the inner feminine and vice versa. When your feminine and masculine receive one another, your inner battles end. You find peace, contentment, a release of expectation, and deeper acceptance of what is. Your body relaxes, supporting health and stress issues to heal. You will find that indescribable something that provides the love that you have been craving and seeking your entire life.

Again, the ultimate reason to discover and find your divine feminine and masculine energies is because they open you into your soul. They help you experience who you are in this lifetime and who you have always been that you may have been unable to touch. They bring you into the awakening of your body, heart, and soul more deeply. When you open, receive, and reconnect your masculine and feminine life-force energies, your soul can fully integrate into your body.

> *Your divine feminine and masculine selves are the awakener of your body, heart, and soul*

You will experience feeling whole as your divine masculine and feminine life-force energies meet in your heart center and come together in union. This happens because your heart is the entryway into the love and power that make up all of life. Your heart center, which is your true mind, is like a tuning fork that resonates to the thoughts and feelings of the universe. It is the entry way into unlimited consciousness and infinite awareness. You will experience spiritual realms that shift you out of your typically limited perspective of yourself and life into new possibilities. Your heart takes you into the healing realms where shamans and mystics go. You are able to "travel" beyond the flat and fixed perspective of fear and control.

When your divine energies become unified, you can think, feel, and BE from your heart and consciously connect into the DNA Source Code of spiritual light. From this expanded place, living your soul purpose becomes possible. Your DNA Source Code is the blueprint within your soul of how you have served and have been in relationship to Infinite Source. As your soul is reconnected into your heart and through your body, you recognize that all of you is sacred and always has been. You recognize the joy of your existence as the sparkling light that you have always been. Our first step together is to begin to uplift and rewire how you are in relationship to your Self and Infinite Source.

When your masculine and feminine energies merge and unite, there is a dance of positive and negative charge, light and dark, the known and the unknown, the conscious and the unconscious, and the human with the divine.

When your feminine and masculine energies are reconnected and in relationship to one another, they are able to keep the "spark of passion alive" within your body. You will experience vitality and vibrant health because the energetic charge within you is alive. This spark is ignited by your decision to BE the flame of truth that awakens your cellular memory of Oneness.

Your body is the container for your soul's energies. So, the more your inner divine masculine and feminine energies are interacting and "in love with one another," the greater the joy and empowerment you will experience. The more your energies interrelate, the more love flows through you. The more that love flows through you, the more you can be fully expressed with your life work and in all of your relationships. You will find yourself being able to listen to others more easily, find solutions to your own and other people's difficulties, have less anxiety and fear, and feel more at ease with your life. It allows you to be yourself and trust in the universe. BEing whole feels like a love affair with life. You will feel encompassing Oneness and the ability to just BE. You will see the wholeness within others and strive to create greater wholeness for others to enjoy greater peace, happiness, and kindness.

> **BE the flame of truth that awakens Oneness.**

REMEMBER:

- Your divine feminine and masculine energies resonate to color, imagery, and frequency, which help you connect spiritual energy in your physical body.

- Color activates your *Power Point Centers* to be able to integrate your higher dimensional energies in your physical body.

- You need different colors at different times to create integration. They help the spiritual and physical aspects of you integrate, which then allows a new relationship of Oneness to exist between your body, mind, and soul.

- Your mind is not solely in your head but is centered in your heart center. Your heart center is your true mind because the heart is the integrator of your mind, body, and soul.

- All of the *Power Point Centers* contain the intelligence of the higher mind. They each serve a particular function of integrating the body and the mind, thus creating the Bodymind.

- By connecting your mind into your solar plexus, you strengthen the portal in your body where spirit and the physical meet.

- By opening and expanding your energetic pathways, you open up energy centers in your brain, which enable you to perceive light to a greater degree and connect you into your divine higher intelligence.

- Awakening your senses helps you to BE One in Soul.

- The purpose of the divine feminine is to teach you how to embrace and love and BE who you are in your body, accept your sacred expression, reveal your spiritual gifts, and compassionately meet your deepest fears.

- Your divine masculine is your all-supportive embracing divine father that can help you trust the truth within yourself.

- Your heart is the portal into the love and power of infinite awareness.

BELIGHT MEDITATION

Igniting Your Body with Color:
An Open Eye or Closed Eye Practice

Part I

Begin by drawing pure white and golden light down from above your head as you inhale through your nose the golden white light into your *Second Power Point Center*—the center found by dropping your index (second finger) down on your belly as you place your pinky on your pubic bone and your thumb in your navel. As you inhale, send the breath into your sacrum and lower vertebrae's. Feel your lower belly gently expand and open. On the exhale, pull up white flames of fire from the core of the earth up through your genitals, lower vertebrae's and fill your *Second Power Point Center* with light.

On the next inhalation, gather the golden white light from the center of the earth and pull it up like taffy into your *Second Power Point Center*. Now, gently move it up inside of your spine into the area in between your shoulder blades. Just BE in the golden white light in between your shoulder blades and allow it to flow into your heart center. On the next inhalation, once again, pull up the golden white light into the space between your shoulder blades and the center of your heart center, your *Fifth Power Point Center*. Exhale the breath out of your mouth and allow the golden white light to flow down into your *Second Power Point*—your lower belly, your tantien. Create a circuit, a loop of pure white light that moves from your lower belly, sacrum and tailbone up the spine to the space between your shoulder blades, into your heart center and then down through your body to its starting point in the base centers of your body.

BE present with this circuit and feel the circular flow of golden white light flow from the center and back of your heart center—your *Fifth Power Point Center*—down into your *Second Power Point Center* and then up through your spine, back into your heart center. Maintain your focus in the flow of golden white light for 10 cycles.

Then, rest and BE still. Allow for total stillness.

Next, inwardly ask what color or colors your heart center would like to be filled with to feel nurtured and connected. Begin to bring the color or colors into your heart center and experience them flowing into you.

As you stay with your breath, inhale and expand the color or colors into your heart center. As you exhale, focus the colors in between your shoulder blades, the center of your "inner wings." Stay inhaling and exhaling with the colors, allowing them to fill your entire body.

With your next inhalation and exhalation, allow the swirling and flowing fields of color to move and expand into all of the cells in your whole body. Allow the colors to flow, take up space, and anchor their frequency in your body. Invite the colors to shift and change, watching the gorgeous hues of colors pour, ripple, stream, spiral, and pulsate.

Relax your muscles and your spine, and breathe. Just BE.

Allow the sensation from the colors that flowed and filled you to be imprinted into your body and soul.

Rest. BE still.

Part II

Direct your focus back into your breath. As you inhale, draw in one of the colors from the inside of your body that you discovered in the last meditation. Slow your breathing down as you feel the color in your body.

Now, give the color a tone, a sound, or a melody. Sense the color singing its tones, sounds, or feelings in your body. Allow your body to be imprinted with the color and the sound. Invite into the cells of your body the color and the sound. This will be the same process as receiving the imprint of a newly found soul aspect of yourself. By feeling your soul, and allowing it to imprint you with its essence, your body can begin to release its stresses, controls, and fears.

Rest. BE still.

PRACTICAL CONSIDERATIONS WHEN CONNECTING YOUR SOUL ENERGIES

Part III

Fill your body with golden white light. Allow your breath to be gentle and soft. Inhale through your nose and out through your nose. Bring your breath into the center of your heart, into the space between your shoulder blades. Wait until you feel your breath connected in to your consciousness, then shift your attention into your root center, your *First Power Point Center*, the space between your pubic bone and tailbone. Pull up golden white flames of fire from the core of the earth as you pull golden white light down from above your head. Allow them to both meet in each *Power Point Center*. BE aware of your breath, gently moving in and out of your body through your nostrils. Focus your attention into the golden white light in your root center. Become One with the light.

Invite the colors from the Part I exercise that rippled, streamed, spiraled, and pulsated in your body to be activated by your focus once again. Expand your breath on the inhalation and on the exhalation through your entire body. Ask your body what color it wants to invite in to open up the connection with your divine feminine. Allow the color to flow into your entire body and mind. Breathe into the back of your skull, your heart center, and your root center at the same time. Now, invite the presence of your divine feminine to begin to connect to you through the color and to touch you through your senses. Feel, hear, sense, and see her presence. Allow her to BE in you and to communicate to you. Breathe and fill yourself with her presence and the color or colors in which she is moving and BEing. Allow her to continue to fill your body. Listen and feel.

Now, invite the presence of your divine masculine to make itself known to you through a color and invite "him" to begin to connect with you through the color and to touch you through your senses. Feel, hear, sense, and see his presence. Allow him to

BE in you and to communicate to you. Breathe and fill yourself with his presence and the color or colors in which he is moving and BEing. Allow him to continue to fill your body. Listen and feel.

To complete, bring the colors of your divine feminine and divine masculine into a sphere of light in your heart center. Allow your body and soul to integrate. Rest.

CHAPTER FOURTEEN

Soul Reconnection: What to Expect

*"Dig deep to recover yourself.
Do not lose heart.
I will be by your side, in joy and in sorrow.
I will be by your side, in success and in failure.
Look within.
You are God."*
— Avatar Meher Baba

The Soul Path of BEing Human

The inescapable truth of human existence is that we all have soul truths, energies, light, love, and power to discover. We are all here on this planet to end our cycles of separation and pain and to discover BEing One in Infinite Source.

As we neglect, reject, or fear the light of our own soul, we withdraw into the safety net of our mind and encapsulate various parts of our soul power in the darkness within our body. We create suffering and pain through splitting our soul light into fragments that decrease its power, which reduces our connection to Infinite Source. We are given the opportunity to discover the pure light, wisdom, and knowledge of our soul as our True Self.

To re-enter BEing One as our Original Self, we have to unify the fragments of our soul into the light. When these fragments of our spiritual power retreat into the body, they hide in our survival and safety base centers. The darkness of unconsciousness within the lower planes of the universe are magnetized to the fragments of our soul in our body, which hide out in the base *Power Point Centers,* creating situations and relationships in our lives that cause us ongoing turmoil, pain or struggle. As we send a life stream of love, power and compassion to the aspects of our Self that went into hiding in our base *Power Point Centers*, we uncover the momentum and truth of our soul. Until we become unified and whole, life can feel unexplainably intense—we must learn how to surf a strong wave that once merged with can carry us through catastrophic or unexpected events, traumas, disappointments, illness, misfortune, or loss. Together, as a collective humanity, we experience both the joys and sorrows of life brought on by the unconscious separations within ourselves, our families, the masses, and within our political, business, health and educational systems. Yet, as we individually return to wholeness, we can globally create a renaissance of love, empowering one another, spiritual and divine intelligence and reconnection to the positive creativity of BEing One with the infinite.

As we walk through these challenging times on planet Earth, we each have the opportunity to awaken and step out of the separations we individually create and live within. It can be all too easy to ignore our internal separations and numb ourselves to what is really occurring within and around us. We can all too easily fall into resentment and fear as we witness the planet and many of its peoples ignore the invitation to consciousness and light that is presently being offered to all of humanity by higher universal beings. It can feel overwhelming at times to trust and create a new balance, authenticity, and expression that can and will take us out of the destruction and disconnection that we see and experience all around us.

As we choose to release our self-created walls and resistances and open to the voice of truth and fearlessness within us, we are able to emerge through the cycles of duality and discover Oneness.

The more whole that you become in your Bodymind and soul, the more grace, acceptance, and power can manifest in your life. What you may choose to tackle may appear challenging or feel painful, but if you stay in the presence of BEing who you truly are, and choose to BE ONE with your Self, others, and the world, then life will support you. How you choose to respond to even the most difficult life situations will create powerful openings within your Whole Self that will free your soul to BE.

All human beings on this planet at some moment in time must follow the calling and guidance of their inner most BEing. The more deeply you see, listen, feel, and connect into your soul, the more you can trust who you are. If you know yourself on a soul level, then when someone asks how you are doing, you will be able to respond with a truly authentic answer, empowering you and the person with whom you are speaking.

How often do you currently say one of the following?

"I am fantastic, filled with total joy and contentment."

"I am really beginning to figure out what I want and need in this life."

"I know how I want to serve others and the world and am ready to do it."

"I realize that I have been deeply unhappy for years because I have been judging everyone who doesn't think like me, and I didn't even know it. Now that I get it, I feel so much more in love with life."

"I have been fighting to hold my family together so I wouldn't have to go through the pain of divorce that I went through with my parents as a child, and I have decided to stop trying to control everything in my life and can finally exhale."

"I have been feeling really awful and realized that I have been listening to everyone else's views and opinions about what's really important in the world, and I realized that I do not even know how I really feel, so now I am going to find out."

"I have decided to end how I repress my anger and take it out on myself. I have had an addiction issue with sex, and I want to learn how to love myself."

"I have been in a relationship with a married man and I realize that I have been totally selfish and only thinking about my own needs. It's time for me to let go and face myself."

"I have been given six months to live, yes, I am in stage IV, and I am determined to live. I am going to do everything that I can to heal. Would you support me as I take my power back and move through this?

"I have been holding myself back from starting my own business. I feel afraid, but I am determined to give myself the chance to grow past my fears."

Imagine all of us choosing to break through one limiting belief a week. We could impact our lives and the world very quickly. We would discover the joy and exaltation of living fully as divinely lit human beings. Remember: open, trust, and listen to the truth within you.

> *The greater our return to wholeness,*
> *the greater can be our joy.*

Integrating & Healing Soul Fragments

As you anchor the awareness of your soul through your Whole Self you are able to move through the eye of the needle of your consciousness into a new paradigm operating system. As you become One in your soul, your relationship to universal consciousness increases, and the light of your God Self within your body expands and becomes the bridge to living your destiny path.

Once your soul aspects are reconnected, your emotional and physical body can fully heal, and your spiritual essence and power can be ignited and opened. When you reconnect to your spiritual source, your soul, body, and emotional centers begin to magnetically align—similar to the way the planets rotate around the sun. You become one with the sun (soul) of your being. Everything just begins to move as it is supposed to, in relationship to the greater whole.

Every aspect of your soul matters. Your natural state is to be whole, and it is important to get that despite what rationalizations may arise, no aspect of yourself can be left behind.

As you integrate and connect your soul aspects, the union of Infinite Source and your body awakens your spiritual essence and divine intelligence. Your soul aspects contain your spiritual light, exist as pure energy, and give you back your Whole Self. The direct connection that you feel with Infinite Source guides your life forward, enabling you to fully express the soul "beingness" you were born to bring forth. When you are One in soul, you are naturally One with Infinite Source. You just feel it. You realize that you are One and have always been One with the Infinite.

When you are living in union with the creative source and power that comes from your unified soul, an energetic and magnetic impulse is created that activates your life with impassioned action. You begin to feel as though you are living in the center of where both you and the universe meet simultaneously. Living in union with your creative source and power is a vertical alignment created through BEing One with the light through the core of your body—your sushumna. Moving your life forward with impassioned action is a horizontal alignment that expands who you are into the world. When brought together, like a "cross," you can live in the center of your spiritual energies and create in the outer world with awareness and light.

As you feel the presence and energies of a rediscovered soul aspect in your heart center, the more adept you can become in knowing and BEing yourself. As your rediscovered soul aspects expand into your entire body and ignite your *Power Point Centers*, you are able to create important boundaries to feel safe and anchored being in your body. Once you feel safe and grounded in your body, you are able to live in this world but not get pulled down or caught in the illusions (maya) that exist in duality.

> *The alignment and integration of your light, soul, and divine intelligence open the language of your soul.*

As you come into your body, and feel connected in your solar plexus—your *Fifth Power Point Center*, you can begin to experience the presence of your soul. There are sensations, feelings, and interactions within your body that are occurring in every moment, which connect you to what is really going on inside and outside of your Self. You will know when your body, mind, and soul are disconnected because you will experience tightness in the solar plexus, difficulty breathing, joint pains, heart constriction, digestive issues, anxiety attacks, fear-based thinking, or creative blocks. When your Bodymind and soul are connected, you will feel a lightness of BEing, heightened energy, enthusiasm, limitless joy, peace, and contentment. You might feel the light begin to open and move in your body. It might feel like you are coming to life and awakening from a long sleep or rising from being buried underneath a mound of earth, leaves, and rocks. As you begin to open to the deeper feelings, movement, rhythm, and energy flowing or not flowing inside of you, you unlock your capacity to live fully. You open the portal to what is real and can step into life and step out of the layers of fear that you thought were yours to live out.

Follow the Direction of Your Soul

The *One in Soul* experience creates the opportunity to think and BE directly connected to your spiritual wholeness and awakens your heart center. By shifting your point of focus from your head into your body through a new alignment with your energy matrix and Infinite Source, you are able to live in an expanded consciousness of love, energy, and spiritual integration. You naturally open, see, and feel from a perspective of body and soul Oneness for perhaps the first time. The direction that you have been walking may change, and you will be shifted in the correct direction for your soul's evolvement.

In most native cultures, ceremonies exist where a person faces the four directions—North, South, East, and West—as a way of honoring all of Creation. As part of this process, one calls in the powers, great beings, and gifts from each direction, along with the multi-dimensional realities of this world. If you close your eyes and inwardly turn towards each direction inside of yourself, and see the world through a broader lens, you can begin to feel a new relationship with the universe. When you do this, you will lose your short sightedness and limited state of knowing. You will feel connected to the joy, grace, empowerment, and creativity of your enlightening soul. You will begin to experience direct awakening into your True Self.

Finding the Light

Take a moment right now and close your eyes. Within your Inner Self, turn to the right and look for the light. Shift and slowly turn to the right again, each time gazing inwardly into each direction until you find and see the light. Face the light. Dwell in it. Stay facing it and receive its radiance. Feel the light in your body. As you see or sense the light, connect into your solar plexus. Now, ask Infinite Source to help you walk in the light following this new direction in your everyday activities.

The goal is to trust your connection to how the light from within you guides you. See and feel through your inner eyes. If you are struggling to move through feeling limited in your life by inner or outer circumstances, BE willing to ask the universe to show you a new direction to walk in.

> **BE willing to open and change direction in yourself.**

The reason for soul integration and for following this 21st century roadmap is not just about finding your Original and True Self and completing the circle of your life. It is also about tapping into your connection with the source of life itself. It is about BEING ONE with the greater circle of ALL life. You are not only completing your circle, you ARE THE CIRCLE where you and the Circle of life are ONE. When you are the circle, then you are living in the center of yourself and the light of the universe.

When this happens, you no longer feel and experience separation or feel like you must manipulate life and others to get what you want. Things will just start to flow and happen naturally. Everything becomes possible. You will begin to discover your place, fit, and connection in the larger universe. While you are learning to trust yourself and the trajectory of your life, you will also see your possible life directions and opportunities expand. The increased magnetism within you will draw to you the perfect experiences to support your soul prosperity and expansion.

The promise and possibilities through your own soul reconnection are unfathomable. And yet, you may continue to have a nagging question or uncertainty as to how you can actually accomplish the task before you. As a way to assist you in better understanding the soul integration process, here are several basic questions and answers to help clarify your next steps.

Practical Soul Integration Q & A:

How Do You Begin to See From Your Soul?

To know what runs you, you must pay attention to how you respond during the course of your day. How do you look in the mirror, speak to your colleagues, family, or dog? What are the thoughts in your head when you are alone or shopping at your favorite grocery store? Pay attention to what makes you anxious and whether you are trying to figure out your life from your connection to Infinite Source or through your fears—your ego. When you do these things, you are tapping into the buried sorrows within you that cover up living as the truth of your soul.

This will provide you the opportunity to see from your soul instead of from your ego.

When you begin your soul integration work open your heart to receive the essence of the soul aspect that you are meeting. Invite their spiritual presence into your heart and allow yourself to merge with them through love. Trust that being consistent with your practice of opening your heart to receive, feel and see the light of your soul aspect that in time you will become One. See through your heart—through the eyes of your soul—as you feel the connecting power of Infinite Source holding you and your newly found soul aspect together. Feel the embrace of love through your heart and soul reuniting.

In The Flow

BE willing to go into the light every day. Visualize and feel light enter your body everyday. You are naturally connected to the light at all times. The light flows into you from the top of your head through your body into the core of the earth. As you visualize and feel the light flow into you, be willing to open to it and feel your heart. How? When you sit with the light moving through your body, you have the opportunity to merge with the light and feel into it as a support for you.

Even if you have no time, take 5 minutes 2-3 times a day to simply focus and bring in light. Let it flow from the sky above your head and from the earth into your body. Feel into where the light wants to flow. It may be in your root center, your solar plexus or heart center or all three. Let the light flow and fill you.

Trust the light. It will guide you to open and feel within your body and heart center.

SOUL RECONNECTION: WHAT TO EXPECT

> *BE willing to go into the light every day.*

Part of integrating your soul aspects also involves allowing the pain within your emotional body to come up, and then being willing to track the pain back to the part of your soul that was denied, rejected, abandoned, or betrayed at some moment in your life or lifetimes. Be mindful not to engage with the emotion or "become the emotion". Feel it, observe it, be with it with love, and let it go. The emotion is not the real you. Emotions are created by the separations in your consciousness from BEing One with the divine. Emotions are portals into essence of your soul that exists beyond duality, pain, and separation. Your emotions are a gateway into the divine. Once you have identified the soul aspect linked with your emotion, you must then accept that this newly discovered soul part has something to give you. By opening and being willing to receive it, you are saying yes to the core power of your Self. You are guaranteed to feel connected to your self-worth, true expression, authentic power, and unlimited love. You will feel a deep connection as a divine and human being. Every emotion is an energy in motion: E=motion. Allow the energy beneath every emotion to open you to the power and truth of your heart. Allow the reactionary emotion to move, and to BE released, as you discover the creative impulse residing within it. Then, open to receive the feelings that exist from BEing reconnected to the source of your soul's inspiration.

The soul aspect that is your spiritual power will be seen and experienced as a version of yourself at the age when you last experienced feeling safe and whole BEing You, and created a "functioning personality Self that became who you presently are" to fulfill the expectations and demands of your life. You will probably experience the energy and presence of this soul aspect manifesting itself to you as an infant, toddler, child, or teenager. This soul aspect, when first discovered, may be angry, impatient, crying, happy, sad, withdrawn, hopeful, dynamic, lifeless, and yes, sometimes enlightened. BE willing to open. These hidden soul aspects of you hold the keys to your full power, life purpose, and potential as a human-spiritual being. The emotions are real, but they are not who you are. The parts of yourself that carry your spiritual power show themselves to you because your soul has a built-in goal to be whole, One with itself, and with God. The moment you unconditionally embrace your soul aspect while BEing One with the light of its essence, pain, and joy, you will ignite your relationship with your soul and Higher Self.

> *Your soul aspects hold the keys to your full power and potential as a human being.*

How Do Your Power Point Centers Support Your Soul Awakening Experience?

Many of you may have experienced maintaining your focus in your higher energetic centers while meditating. These higher centers—the heart, throat, back of the skull, third eye, and crown *Power Point Centers*—are gateways into the higher energies of your BEing. However, in order to live in union with them in the body, you need to fully become One with both the "higher and lower" *Power Point Centers*. Your "lower chakras," from your solar plexus down through your navel, creation point, lower belly, and pubic bone-tailbone are also gateways into God. As previously shared, it is in your lower centers where you will find many of your lost and hidden soul parts waiting to be rediscovered and reconnected.

You will find the most important aspects of your soul energies are tucked away in the *First Power Point Center*, your root center. Here is where your higher survival consciousness knew that the essence of your True Self could survive while your personality Self was adapting and changing to its environment. The aspects of your soul that are directly connected to the raw and creative power of Infinite Source find safe haven in your *First Power Point Center*. Your inner protector within your psyche will make use of the darkness within your base *Power Point Centers* to give shelter to your most powerful soul aspects. These soul aspects contain positive DNA energies of your universal Self, which have the potential to pull you out of negative past life and present life karmas. As your soul aspects are integrated, your DNA soul blueprint is revealed through feeling Whole and expansive through your heart center.

As an infant, young child, or teenager, we intuitively sense whether our soul powers are being welcomed, rejected, or denied existence. We will abandon, betray, or reject (ABR) the most profound and developed soul aspects of ourselves just to fit in, be loved, accepted, or to avoid anger, rejection, or judgment. When we ABR ourselves, we choose to protect the most light-filled parts of our Divine Self by separating emotionally, spiritually, and energetically. The vast potentiality of the root center of your body is so great that it can easily hold your disowned power.

The first and second *Power Point Centers* are incredibly powerful life force containers. They generate and receive the vital forces from Infinite Source necessary for your evolvement as a total human being. Remember, your essential and core creative energies of Infinite Source are brought down from the heavenly planes *and* up from the earth into your body. They clear the energies in your body that have been created from living in separation from Infinite Source. The divine feminine energies move into your body through the earth gateways, and the divine masculine energies move into your body through the heavenly gateways. Their union in the center of your heart is a powerful initiation on your soul awakening path and being *One in Soul*. Therefore, all of your *Power Point Centers*, and specifically your lower centers, must be engaged in your soul reconnection.

When you begin your *One in Soul* experience, you begin the evolutionary process of bringing back together the best of your divine and human nature. The *One in Soul* process gives you the tools to reconnect into the highest light and transform the deepest dark within you and in the universe. You learn to see, feel, and BE One with the greatest truth of your soul. In the more advanced levels of this work, you learn how to integrate the presence of your soul into your life and live fully aligned into Infinite Source to evolve your spiritual purpose. From this perspective of Oneness, you can find liberation, higher levels of business and relationship happiness, enhanced health, fulfillment of your soul mission, greater joy, compassion, and peace. Your life becomes an expression of being a co-creator with the universe.

> **The One in Soul experience integrates your divine and human consciousness.**

What Do You Do When You Access Your Soul?

When you connect with your soul, you are opening to the most spiritualized part of your Self. You are making use of all of your senses, both physical and spiritual: sight, hearing, touch, smell, intuition, feeling, expressing, observing, merging, and being. When you interact with your soul, you are going beyond normal and everyday perception. You are moving into the inner worlds and realms that can only be experienced when the mind, body, and soul come together in a higher form of communication. This communication becomes a new language, a heightened experience of BEing One in divine eternal order. This is ultimately a language of higher love.

It is essential when reconnecting to your forgotten soul aspects to accept whatever form love takes within you. You may find the energies of love within you flattened, defeated, lonely, and afraid. They may be exuberant, impassioned, and ready to jump into your arms. Every time your soul essence and soul power was knocked down or denied, a part of you had to "deal." You had to suck it up, find a different survival route, or push through with the strength of a warrior or warrioress, often at the expense of your emotional heart and your ability to love and be loved. You have to find and embrace the life force essential power of light within you that has the natural ability to break through the resistances built up through responding to yourself and life from fear.

A raging, crying, angry, lost, empty, or sad soul part of yourself is an aspect of you that has been in mourning from not being received, heard, seen, or being supported to exist. We make the decision to close the doors to the most light-empowered life force energies that live within us because our bodies have collected layers of fear over lifetimes. For many of us, our lives do not come together until we open the door to the energies of the light that are stored in our root, lower belly, creation point, and navel center—our *First, Second, Third and Fourth Power Point Centers.*

The feminine energy that ascends from the depths of the earth into our body reestablishes our alignment with the light. To reopen the doors to our True Self, we have to clear our base centers and pay attention to how our ego has taken control of our body in order to protect our most light-filled energies. Then, as we raise the light of our life force through the core channel and clear our energetic alignment, the ego has less ability to keep "who we are" down. Our feminine principle maintains the balance of our body and mind so we can walk the path of union with the divine. Our masculine principle builds and directs the potential and power of creative love and bliss to merge with life.

In the moment of leaving our Self as a child or young adult, we close the door to the spiritual gifts that hold and express the presence and voice of our True Self. Most of us are raised in families that do not know how to support our True Self. They have not developed their own spiritual eyes and ears to see, feel, and hear who we are. Most of the individuals who denied the truth of your full Self were filled with so much of their own pain and hurt that they were unable to be fully present with you from their hearts. The stresses of life, their own fears, past life karmas, self-judgment, familial or religious traditions that they were passing down to you, and their own inadequacies took them away from living from their most positive alignment. This is where ultimate forgiveness comes in. First, we must forgive ourselves for leaving the love that is our true identity, and second, we must forgive anyone who misused their role in our life. For those individuals graced with being born into a loving and spiritually integrated family, similar work must be done to clear past generational karma's and the personal sanskaras and beliefs surrounding our soul essence.

As we end our cycles of abandoning, betraying, and rejecting our selves, we are able to repurpose our life and find the meaning of our own existence. Most of us internalize the experience of feeling abandoned, betrayed, or rejected (ABR'd) from this lifetime and from past lifetimes. We then project our wound into life preventing our highest purpose from manifesting. The experience of feeling disconnected from the people and web of our life is extremely wounding and disempowering. Once reconnected to our soul essence, we can heal anything.

We are never taught how to recognize and support the deeper feelings of sorrow, hurt, or separation within us. It is often easier to split off from the light of our True Self and identify with the pain that manifests as resentment, anger, fear, despair, or sadness. We let our ego take over as the great protector and soother of our fragmented Self so we can survive. These feelings can live on for years until we recognize how we empower our ego to sedate the pain and fear of BEing who we really are. We each want to matter to those we love most, and to all of life. Yet, we must first learn how to love and embrace the hurt, separated parts of ourselves. To heal, we need to accept the light within each soul aspect and reconnect their gifts into our heart. Our purest power waits in our darkest and most hidden soul part. As we accept our newfound power, we must commit to using it in the highest ways possible. We have to commit to empowering our connection with our soul with the light and power of our True Self. It is very tempting to empower our ego Self with the pure light that resides within our deepest core wound. Even the most advanced spiritual seeker can ride the wave of their ego without even knowing it. Unless finely tuned, we can empower our ego Self with our spiritual energies. By breathing and BEing present in our body to what we are feeling, and to respond to our impulses with conscious love and awareness, we are able to step out of blame, shame and playing games with ourselves and others. Responsibility becomes a mindset, not by imposing control and domination, guilt and expectation, but through developing the "ability to respond" by listening and BEing with our heart and soul as One. Our ego Self will always work to create separation in some form. It takes being astute to how your mind takes charge and over rides the impulses and wisdom of your heart and soul to find your direct path home to your Whole Self.

> *As we collectively choose to remember, value, and cherish the love within ourselves and with one another, we will be able to step through the gateways to BEing a new divine human.*

All of the ways that our wounded ego and separate selves divert us from BEing One have one thing in common. They share a purpose to keep us separate from BEing the light—our true power. Undealt with anger, judgment, and fear keep us disconnected from seeing and recognizing what is truth, what is false, and of the dark. When we function from being split and give over our power to false authorities, false ideals, and false light, we are incapable of feeling worthy, wanted, lovable, valuable, powerful, insightful, loving, and courageous. We live our lives behind a veil that camouflages us from the pure light and power that we are.

Until each soul part is honored for the light that it is, your soul aspect that manifests as anger, fear, self-sabotage, etc. may shift and morph into many forms. It may be undetectable until you embrace it with so much love and trust, that the pain and anger within you can be rebirthed in your everyday life as true power.

When you see, receive, or hear the parts of yourself that were rejected, abandoned, or betrayed you become One with the full circle of yourself once again. You may have been living in separation for decades or lifetimes, but you will come back into wholeness once again.

SOUL RECONNECTION: WHAT TO EXPECT

The warrioress, warrior, mother, father, child, mystic, singer, painter, visionary, wise one, truth sayer, angelic, writer, dancer, poet, leader, healer, builder, director, inventor, medicine woman, medicine man, dreamer, inspirer, wonder man, wonder woman, initiator, problem solver, birther, awakener, and lover all live within you.

> *Our purest power waits to be found and transformed through our most hidden and forgotten soul aspects.*

What Specifically Happens When You Integrate Your Soul?

When you integrate your soul, your body opens to the life force energies that have always existed within you but may have been blocked, hidden, or minimized. All of your soul aspects want to reunite in your body, and to merge with your loving and open heart because their natural state is Oneness. For the integration process to "work," your thinking mind must be willing to allow energy and feeling to be opened in your body. This can challenge you, because even if you say "yes" and open to the expression within your soul, you may still resist the power of the life force energies that exist and move in your body.

Why? Well, at first your body doesn't know what to do with these new energies and their potential expressions. It has spent years being a completely different way. That way, if you recall, typically involves your egoic mind trying to be in control and squash all aspects of yourself that don't fit into the story, projections, and expectations of your life and how you are supposed to "be". Opening to your soul aspects may unleash a sense of empowerment and vitality, but it may also bring up feelings like anxiety, doubt, and insecurity if your ego Self is pushing to stay in control. The truth of who you are is revealed through becoming One with your emotions. Your emotions are the gateway to BEing. They have the power to open your heart to your soul.

When fear, resistance and control come up, you must remember that they are not "who you are," but are portals through what is unreal into what is most real within you. They can guide you onto the road of eternal wisdom and universal Oneness, and will inevitably be the underlying impetus to help you create the change that catapults your life forward on the pathway of your highest soul expressions and purpose. Yet ultimately, you need to release and let go of the emotions and beliefs that are being held by your fear, resistance and control, while you are simultaneously choosing to focus into the light. Once your light is awakened, it will crack you open to the real you. The old fear-based emotions slip away. When they do return, centering yourself into your *Power Point Centers* can instantaneously bring you into your true alignment and help you to let go of fear. As you integrate your soul, you will naturally want to let go of empowering your ego to abandon, reject, and betray, (ABR) your heart and soul.

For a long time, your unseen soul aspects have been waiting, sitting dormant, like a deactivated battery cell. Once you activate them into your life, they need a place to "live and flow." When you find the core aspects of your soul, you will need to know where to "house" them. You can ground your soul aspects in your body through connecting into your *Power Point Centers* and *Soul Integration Points*. The existence of your True Self is awakened as your soul aspects reunite in your body and open the doorways to who you truly are.

Your body is meant to be a temple and functional home for your soul to evolve. However, your body becomes cluttered with many different energies and blockages through the imbalances, perceptions, and projections that you create in your daily life.

When the *Power Point Centers* are opened and connected, they create a container in your body that house the love and power of your soul. Remember, your *Power Point Centers* are meeting points in your body where Infinite Source, light, and your soul connect. As energy portals they activate a higher dimension of love, connectedness, and integration. These points can help you move out of a slump, invigorate you energetically, emotionally move you into action, inspire fresh new ideas, heal long term issues, support you to let go, and trust in your connection with God—Infinite Source.

The *Power Point Centers* and *Soul Integration Points* reconnect the energy portals of light and Infinite Source in your body, giving you an anchor into Oneness. They feed your physical body with strength, nurture your mind and soul with life energy, and soothe your heart from the challenges of life. They balance the spiritual and physical frequencies in your mind and body to help you feel simultaneously aligned, balanced, peaceful, and highly charged. They receive and transmit the energies of "who you are" in every moment. Your *Power Point Centers* and *Soul Integration Points* are focus points to help you to train your mind to serve your soul. They connect your life force and God energies so you can become fully empowered as your Whole Self.

In the *One in Soul* Practice, your heart, soul, and your *Power Point Centers* meld and you can feel the light glowing in your spine and throughout your whole body. You can feel the center of where your mind, Spirit, and body meet. As you connect your heart and mind with your *Power Point Centers,* you will be able to feel, live, and BE in the loving and open space that you have created. You become connected to a force of light and power that feels bigger than yourself. It is infinite love. As you breathe into your body and open into your heart, you will experience an inner sanctuary that feels like home.

> *Your Power Point Centers activate a higher dimension of love, connectedness, and integration in your Bodymind and soul.*

What Can I Expect As I Begin Reconnecting Into My Soul?

Before you make the connection with your soul, you might feel anticipation, resistance, defensiveness, disbelief, fear, anxiety, physical or emotional pain, or generally like you are coming up against your own "baggage."

After you make the connection with your soul, you may feel buoyant, uplifted, peaceful, joyful, amazed, or renewed. Yet, as previously mentioned, there is also the possibility that you might feel sad, grief, despair, or anger because the longer that you have been away from your core Self, the more these feelings will rise up to be released. Many people feel grief for a few minutes to an hour or two when they reconnect back into their soul's love and power. In those moments, they are experiencing what it feels like to have been out of alignment and then moving into alignment. Your feelings rise up and then dissipate as the love that you are building and reconstructing within your Self grows. The love takes the place of the emptiness that previously caused your despair, depression, worry, fear, anxiety, or anger.

When you reconnect all of your soul fragments into the light within your body, your True Self can begin to BE revealed. Your OverSoul or Higher Self—the "you" that oversees and guides you in every lifetime—can fully integrate back into your body and soul. You get to come home. Yet, for this to happen, you must be willing to surrender your resistance to the divine through honoring the spiritual lessons and higher truths being given to you.

SOUL RECONNECTION: WHAT TO EXPECT

When you surrender, what you will receive in return is a pure love and power that is only possible from a direct connection with your Higher Self and Infinite Source. The awaiting power within you can be trusted to guide your life purpose, career, personal and business relationships, health, and greater dreams forward. Divine love is the highway home to Oneness.

> *When you reconnect all of your soul fragments into the light within your body, your True Self can begin to BE revealed.*

REMEMBER:

- The reason that it is so important for you to invite in your forgotten soul aspects is to remember who you really are. If you do not know your soul, it is not possible to fully BE yourself.

- When you reconnect the soul energies that have been locked away or dormant within yourself, you open to the "whole you" and clear the pathways that allow Infinite Source and your body to become unified.

- Your soul is what guides your connection to Infinite Source. The energetic light of your soul enables you to experience a direct connection to the divine intelligence of Infinite Source. It is also a catalyst for whatever you choose to do or be in this lifetime.

- The foundation for soul reconnection requires that you be willing to see and feel within your body, potentially for the first time, and BE willing to open and change direction in yourself, depending on what you find.

- The most life changing aspects of your soul consciousness are tucked away in the base *Power Point Centers*, particularly your root center.

- BE willing to go into the light every day through some type of meditation or focused prayer.

- Track back your emotional, physical or psychological pain to the part of your soul that was denied, rejected, abandoned, or betrayed.

- Find the light and consciousness of love underneath the pain. It is always there.

Accept the love within you, in whatever forms it takes. Your *Power Point Centers* and *Soul Integration Points* reconnect the light of Infinite Source in your body, giving you an anchor into Oneness.

CHAPTER FIFTEEN

The Whole Soul: One in Soul Reconnection

"Your soul is a fire of passion, clarity, determination, and peace that fuels the evolution of your BEing into its true destiny."
— *Mahama Iana*

Knowing Your Soul

You have heard this at the beginning of the book, but it bears repeating. You are unique, and there is no one like you. You have been developing your own soul gifts lifetime after lifetime. Now, in this life and at this moment in your history—herstory, your soul is seeking wholeness and what is right for its most expanded awakening. If you listen and take a risk outside of your comfort zone, you will find what your soul is seeking and desiring to give, discover, birth into life, express and become One with. To become *One in Soul* is your foundational step.

Daniel's Story

Daniel found himself in his 40s hitting a career wall and felt that no matter how hard he worked to advance past a certain point, he never could. After years of looking outside of himself for answers, he chose to discover what inner parts of himself he might need to reconnect with to help him break through living from his head and to feel more connected with his "greater Self." He was willing to explore what might be stopping him from creating greater success.

As he began the One in Soul Practice, he asked to reconnect with the part of himself who felt lost and unseen. As he opened to receive this soul aspect, he found a very young boy who felt unable to make his alcoholic mother happy.

After years of trying, but failing, to bring his mother joy, the little boy shut down. The little boy's love and presence could not be received by a mother who was so disconnected within herself. He chose to abandon a core part of his light and love to protect himself from further hurt and rejection.

After creating a bond of trust with the younger version of himself, he realized that who he really was, was an unstoppable dynamo of life-giving energy. He had closed the door to the possibility of ever being seen as worthy and of value from the outside. When he reconnected to this core aspect of himself, he found a fountain of love—a strength that had been hidden. Daniel gladly opened his heart to receive its love and life energy and committed to never abandoning his little boy again. Through learning how to align with Infinite Source within his Bodymind connection, he easily and naturally stepped into his "awaiting power," which catapulted his personal life and career upwards.

What will the result be from your leap of faith into your Divine Self? You will discover BEING FULLY YOU. What does it mean to be fully you? It really does depend upon what makes you, YOU, but there is a sense of anchored wholeness and inner connection to your deepest truths. Will that mean that you will be a "success" in this life? Inevitably it depends on your definition of success. All too often we define success in life by the amount of material things we have around us, or the amount of security that we attain through financial wealth. Is your life a success because you have learned to market your gifts and make tens, hundreds of thousands, or millions of dollars? Maybe. What do you do with your money? Are you a failure or less than whole because you do not have lots of money? No. Is it possible to have spiritual and material success at the same time? Yes. However, should you judge the value of your life based upon how much income you make or how many things you have acquired? No. Can you define your success by the level of alignment you live in as your whole Self? Yes. Can you define your success by how much love you give and how true you are to your Self? Yes. Can your external successes grow from BEing One in your Whole Self? Yes. Does this soul work make you any better than anyone else? No, but it does make you the best "you" that you can BE.

Consider the possibility that your life is a success when your human and divine will have become One, your soul consciousness has merged with Infinite Source, and you are BEing who you were born to BE. We each have different lessons and sanskaras (impressions, imprints and fixed patterns) to balance and master, so one person's success model will not be another person's success model. One person may need to step out and speak in front of an audience, and another person may need to teach and exude just as much wisdom and brilliance but from a position of quiet listening and solitude. Another person may need to do both and burn off their sanskara patterns through contrast and being diversified. One person may feel most productive supporting a vision that takes many people to fulfill, while another person may need to be the person leading the vision. One person may need to raise a family and shine the light on their children, while another person may need to start a non-profit organization and touch the lives of thousands of children—or to do both. One person may need to learn to manage and support other's to shine, and another person may need to be the star attraction.

> *Living in direct connection with your soul awakens your capacity to BE YOU.*

We are living in a time where we find and define who we are by the reflections and mirrors that we receive from the world around us. You are expected to define yourself by the definitions that the media, peers, family, teachers and others place upon you, rather than through the power, light, intuition, and wisdom of your own soul. Perhaps rather than illusory definitions of success, what we should all pray for is the wisdom to know what is truly right for us. It is important to realize that there may be a difference between what you think you want and what your soul actually needs to BE fully expressed. The only way to know what you need is to listen, be with, surrender, and respond to the truth within the joy, love, fear, anxiety, contentment, or pain within you. Listen to what it is telling you. Listen to its yearning and go through the emotion or feeling until you find your deepest truth and then surrender some more. The only way to trust what the universe is giving you is to live in a state of surrender to your divine heart and to let go of what your mind holds on to as its way to define itself. Watch how your mind drives you to "do" instead of BE. Question and observe how you are connected to any moment.

Your soul may need for you to heal, slow down, take a break, master a creative expression, manifest a dream into form, bring forth a huge mission or vision, focus upon the care of a child, create a successful marriage, heal others, practice honesty, build a profitable business, become a yogi, run for a political office, grow your own food, stop eating junk food, explore your past lives, become an activist, sit in silence, adopt a child, spend time in nature, take a pilgrimage or vacation, or just show up BEing completely real in your everyday day.

> ***Slow everything down inside of your Self and just BE.***

In each lifetime, you have chosen certain experiences to expand or contract your experiences with divine Source. There have been past lifetimes or cycles in your present life when you may have needed the experience of shining in the limelight, living on a remote vineyard in southern France, serving in the armed forces, feeding the homeless, living in a cave, becoming an inventor, architect, technician, singer, composer, painter, financial planner, pilot, doctor, healer, farmer, lawyer, parent, writer, film producer, engineer, teacher, designer, or just owning a small café that makes the best apple pie in town. Every possibility can mean "soul success." Your journey will unfold as you choose to BE.

As you uncover the truths of your Original Self, you will find a growing fluidity of freedom. You will move past fear and discover infinite love. Begin with the love that already exists within you. Then reconnect the parts of yourself that are not yet living in love into the already existing love within you. It does not matter what your soul aspects are like or how or why they were created. When you split off from your core spiritual power, it is always for a "good" reason. How you have given away your Self in past lifetimes or in this lifetime create your belief systems. Whether you believe that you needed to take care of everyone around you to get enough love to exist, or protect and hide your light so others would not hurt you, or disengage from your heart to close its door so you wouldn't have to feel the hurt from being ABR'd (abandoned, betrayed and rejected) by the ones who said they loved you, your ego set into motion your survival modus operandi. The human psyche will close the door to your most loving, brilliant, and spiritual energies if necessary, just to feel safe, be accepted and survive.

Life pushes us to reconnect our heart and soul through the challenges and suffering that we go through. Our society teaches us to ignore our spiritual existence by dancing around the hole that grows when our heart, body, mind, and soul are disconnected. We are encouraged to fill the hole, ignore the hole, and employ our ego to handle bypassing the pain created by living in separation. We leave our light and create an ego Self who plays the role of making everything right. We give our power to our ego Self, who survives through the power that we give it.

As you reconnect the power within your soul aspects, a momentum is created that builds an internal trust to grow into your greater Self and accomplish the mission and purpose of your soul.

It is vital to "get" that *only love can heal you*. Chances are that you may fear surrendering to love because deep down you do not trust that you are even worthy or deserving of love. You may also fear that your love is not big enough to change things around you. Instead of truly facing your "love issues," you may create a different version of yourself in every relationship or try on a new personal growth technique or a belief system as a way to get whole. These temporary fixes may sound like a good idea, but through loving yourself and BEing in the love that is You, you will create a shift within you that will change your life. The only way to change your life and help others make a change is by aligning and becoming One with the higher love that lives within you. BE guided by this love and fulfill what you came here for.

This is not about remaking or reinventing yourself to be a particular "kind" of person. It is about BEing who you are—the unique expression of love, empowerment, and consciousness that you are.

The enlightenment that you seek is already within you. The consciousness and wisdom within your soul is meant to be your guide. Many of you want to cover up your own fear, disempowerment, and helplessness so you take on a belief system and call it "the way" to enlightenment. You invest all of your time, energy, and resources in taking on the trappings of a system so you don't have to deal with your deeper Self. This is a bit like trying to wallpaper a room that has hidden black mold. It may look good on the surface for a while, but eventually what is beneath will come through. Moreover, it still has the potential to make you very sick if you don't deal with it.

The result is that you might find yourself uplifted one day, and down the next. Or whatever spiritual high or good feelings that you may have from taking on a new paradigm or approach will inevitably crash because you have not really dealt with your core. When it comes to soul work and your spiritual truth, YOU cannot be found through a belief system. You can only be discovered through an authentic connection with all of yourself—through direct awakening of your Original Self. You cannot fake it until you make it. To borrow from one of my favorite ad taglines, JUST DO IT. Reconnect with your soul and BE set free. JUST BE IT.

> *YOU cannot be found through a belief system.*
> *You can only be discovered through an*
> *authentic connection with all of yourself.*

In your next breath, just trust the love that you are in this moment and embrace the most wounded, dejected, rejected, lost, and confused part of yourself from your heart, and you will begin to find your soul. The secret to life exists in your heart. Your ego mind will always convince you that your soul is not as important as it is. Your ego will make you doubt your Self. Your ego mind will want everything to be perfect. It will search for a happy, sunny, well ordered, and controlled existence. Like a house with no dust, every book and thing in its place, a perfectly manicured yard, and state of the art technological gadgets inside its walls, you claim you are happy. But perhaps you might want to consider that you are just engaged in another mind game of life.

Integrating your soul reveals the roadmap of your life. It is not a belief system. It is a direct experience. You get to say, *"Wow, this thing called a soul really exists. I really do exist! I feel me! I know me! Yet, in reality there is no 'me!' Who am I really? I AM One with the eternal divine expansion of Source! I AM the light! I AM BEing the essence and the impulse of my heart! Everything that is covering up my Original Self must be recognized and released so I can BE me!"*

When you use a spiritual modality to just feel good and transcend your fears, you are just using a set of beliefs instead of drugs, alcohol, pot, sex, etc. to avoid your own spiritual path. There is a difference between walking your own spiritual path and using "spirituality" as a way to manipulate your mind and emotions to get what you want in life or to be recognized by others. When you follow your true spiritual path you may not get what you want, but you are given what you need to become Whole. As you trust yourself, you are able to trust the direction in which life takes you and face what has to be cracked open for you to evolve.

Tanya was longing for a new life. Her marriage of 24 years no longer brought her joy or happiness. She loved having a nucleus family and did everything that she could to keep her family together. Five years prior to ending the marriage, she had stopped having sex with her husband. She longed for a heart connection while making love and in their day-to-day life. The more she opened into her heart and expressed her Self, the more her partner would shut down and choose control. Her husband was stuck in the old paradigm of sexuality—in his First and Second Power Point Centers—in fantasy, control, and physical release. His needs for sex were never ending, yet he had no ability to share his feelings or open his heart or see Tanya for who she really was. He used sex as a way to avoid opening into himself and dealing with his emotional pain. He lived in his imagination of how he perceived his wife from the separations within his body and mind, instead of who she was becoming.

After years of spending hundreds of hours consciously trying to communicate with her husband and guide him to deal with the emotional issues that blocked his ability to be in relationship with her from unconditional love, Tanya felt stuck and afraid. She didn't have the courage to leave the marriage. The fear of being alone was so deep that she continued on in the marriage, secretly blaming herself for not being able to change their relationship or handle her husband's coldness, selfishness, and distance. He would shut down and cut off his emotions with himself and with her, as she worked hard to open the doors between them. Instead of opening the doors to her Self and letting go of trying to change him, she would eventually lose her Self.

The more she shared with her husband how she felt and what she needed, the more he withdrew. Their ten-year-old daughter was torn inside. She fluctuated between loving her dad to wanting to have nothing to do with his controls and bossiness.

Tanya did a soul reconnection with a part of herself that was a grief-stricken, desperate little girl who wanted positive attention and love from her parents but lived in a state of constant loneliness. She saw her inner self as a young child rolled up in a ball sleeping on the landing of the stairs in the house she grew up in. She craved to be seen, felt, embraced, and cared for. More than anything she did not want to feel so alone and ignored. She remembered family members just stepping over her while huddled in her sadness on the stairwell, as though she didn't exist.

Tanya split off from her self at this tender young age of four as a way to not have to feel her desperation and loneliness. She grew into a teenager and woman for the next 40 years who pretended that she was okay, covering over her sadness and acting like she had it all together. For years, Tanya avoided feeling her own inner hurt and pretended as though everything were okay. The day it hit her what she had been doing changed everything for her.

Reconnecting with this soul aspect who longed to love and be loved showed her how intensely she wanted to be seen as her True Self and acknowledged for the suffering and sadness that she had to endure. Her husband represented the family collective unconsciousness who couldn't love her and be there for her as a child. Tanya worked for many years trying to help him open his heart. The fear of being a failure for the marriage not working was more than she could bear. Her disconnected soul part believed that it was her fault that as a child she wasn't cherished, cared for, seen, and heard from her family of origin, and she projected this belief into her marriage. Inwardly, Tanya had been blaming herself for wanting to split up her family and go in the direction of divorce. Her little girl inner self was certain that it was her fault that she was ignored and seen as not good enough and not worthy enough to be loved. She believed that if her husband really loved her, that he would change. Her fear of upsetting her husband by sharing her deepest truths and feelings about their marriage kept her living in misery until the day she knew she had to choose loving herself over continuing her patterns of self abandonment, betrayal, and rejection (ABR). Tanya's childhood belief carried into her marriage with absolute certainty, that the love and light within her heart was not deserving enough to be received, that she was willing to live without love for decades.

As Tanya embraced and loved her wounded little girl soul aspect, she sobbed as she felt her own unconditional love for herself open. As Tanya held her little girl, she could feel that she was no longer afraid of dying and that she deeply wanted to be rebirthed as the essence and pure love of her Original Self.

She wanted to be comforted and seen as the loving and sensitive child that she truly was. She had grown used to not being seen and received for who she really is. She chose a husband who couldn't and wouldn't do his own inner work and be willing to learn how to receive her. Tanya realized that she had projected on to her husband from the beginning of their relationship that he was her protector. Without him, she felt unprotected and vulnerable. Yet, with him, she existed in an emotionally vacant relationship. When Tanya shifted out of living from her false projections and empowering her ego to make everything work, she could no longer relate to her husband and he could no longer understand anything that she was opening to within herself. The stronger she became, the easier it became to stand in her truth. Her husband began to understand that his wife wanted to set him free to find a compatible mate, and they could begin to talk about a conscious divorce without animosity.

Reconnecting with the essence of her Self that was trapped within her little girl soul aspect helped Tanya to have the courage needed to make a radical change in her life. As Tanya awakened and shifted, her daughter shifted and told her mom that she felt that she would be okay if her parents separated. It took Tanya another two years to let go of the external security of her marriage and to step through her fears of being a single parent. Trusting her desire to BE the love that she is, and to be seen, heard and received, she took the leap out of the dark into the light of beginning anew.

Excavate your innermost being for what is most arrogant, hidden, lost, disempowered, and shut down and beneath it you will find the opening to your radiant light. Face the part of you that is afraid to come out and love it into presence and that is where you will find the next step to take for your life to flourish. Your soul, once reintegrated, finds its true strength. You become truth. You know what is real and what is not. Your soul knows what it needs. You are able to choose what to take with you and what to let go of. One person may need XXQ meditation to move forward and another person may need ZYX practice. Embracing the essence of your spiritual power hidden within a soul aspect can catapult you forward and reveal your authentic spiritual path. Once you have begun to receive the wisdom, truth, light, creativity, power, focus, integrity, and nourishment from your soul aspects, you will move into your wholeness with lightning awareness.

> *Face the part of you that is afraid to come out. Love it into presence. This is how you will find the clarity and strength to take the next step in your life.*

Instead of *trying* to be all of the "wonderful" attributes of being spiritually awakened—embrace everything about you. Your humanness is your gateway. We live in very interesting times. We do not know how to be in touch with our humanness. We are afraid of letting go into our deepest vulnerabilities and fears.

We are afraid of being found out as a fake, and we project that onto others. We hold onto what makes us feel safe and avoid what feels uncomfortable. We fear our anger. We see it in others but do not know that we have anger. We stuff our anger and become passive aggressive or controlling. We fear the power that is beneath our anger. We fear the life force power within our body and deny how we misuse it against others and ourselves. Take responsibility for your fear. Feel it and see beneath its entanglements, and there you will find your True Self living in your soul and heart. Open to the reality that everything you need and seek lives within you. Embrace being vulnerable and honor your truth with that vulnerability.

Open to whatever God puts on your path with as much acceptance, love, and gratitude as you possibly can. Love yourself and let everything else be shown to you by grace itself.

> *To experience spiritual Oneness:*
> *BE open*
> *BE receptive*
> *Trust what you find*
> *Then, love and embrace it.*

The Spirit Gateways® BE System provides the opportunity to help you reestablish a new relationship with yourself, others, and all of life and creation. It anchors you to firmly stand on a new foundation that is created by BEing One in your Whole Self by awakening a new power within you. It moves you beyond fear and uncertainty and releases you from self-judgments and false expectations. You *can* live your everyday life from a zone of soul wholeness and connection to Infinite Source. You *can* know yourself and feel confident to take your next steps on your spiritual journey as a co-creator with Infinite Source, and as a divine being living a miraculous human existence from love. Your soul is a fire of passion, clarity, determination, and peace that fuels the evolution of your BEing into its true destiny. BEING *ONE IN SOUL* gives the gift of joy.

Sara's Story

Sara felt incomplete within herself, her life work, and her relationships with others, but she wasn't quite sure why. While she had done spiritual work before and experienced feelings of wholeness and joy, it never seemed to remain for very long. She always returned to feeling incomplete and unable to sustain her own vibration. When she did the One in Soul Practice, she asked to reconnect with the part of herself who felt unable to live. She initially connected into the experience of the death of her twin brother, who had died in utero 38 years prior. In the base of her Second Power Point Center, she found a part of herself that had energetically merged with her twin brother, who died. Her soul aspect wanted to live but had left its own light to be with her brother as he left his body.

Sarah also discovered how she had separated from her light during the death process in several past lifetimes. She had been reliving the same pattern lifetime after lifetime until such time that she was ready to connect and embrace her inner light. Once she shifted her pattern, she could step out of her deeply engrained despair and sorrow and step into the love within herself.

Sarah made the choice to stay in the light of her True Self and to create and live her life from the wholeness of her heart. This shift gave her the opportunity to recreate her life, step out of deep suffering, and find financial and soul-level happiness.

The One in Soul Experience™

When you open to the light within your body, mind, and soul, you increase the velocity of your spiritual power and open the gateways to experiencing and embodying the unique human expression of your Divine Self. Through the *One in Soul* experience you are giving highly developed spiritual aspects of yourself a loving space to live within that previously had "no place to go." You are moving into and expanding the space and light within you to contain the fullness that you truly are. When you integrate your light and dark, the unknown of your life becomes the known, and the known becomes the unknown. The invisible becomes the visible, and the visible becomes the invisible. The divine aspects of you become human, Spirit meets matter, and your human attributes are raised into the divine. It is the meeting point, the center point of your creation and all creation. Your entire understanding, perspective, and feeling of what life is expands.

Soul Integration Preparation Exercise

The first step in preparing for the soul integration process is to breathe into your body. Fill every cell and every organ with your breath. Continuing with your breath, gently allow your mind to descend down into your body into your solar plexus so your mind can relax and your body can open. Next, bring your attention into a wide and strong beam of light that exists 10–20 feet above your head. Allow the light to flow from above your head all the way down through your body into the earth. Next, bring your attention into a wide shaft of light around and inside of your spine and down into your root center. Know that this light is directly connected to Infinite Source, and once brought down into your body, it can begin to open you to living in Oneness. You will be reconnecting the highest light of your consciousness with your soul energies in your body. Stay with the above processes until you feel comfortable in your body and being connected to the light. Give yourself anywhere from 3–10 minutes to practice this preparation exercise.

The One in Soul Practice

STEP ONE:

BE willing to accept your Whole Self with love. Suspend disbelief. Your intention to BE ONE with the light is all that is needed.

STEP TWO:

Take the time that you need to BE with each step. Go at your own pace and savor each connection that you make.

From 5–10 feet above your head, create a waterfall of pastel-colored hues of dazzling and sparkling light. Send the waterfall of colors down through the top of your head, your chest, torso, your legs, feet, and deep into the earth. Feel the waterfall flow around and down through your body, clearing your energies.

STEP THREE:

From 10–20 feet above your head, create a beam of blue light and shine it down through the top of head, into your body—your chest, torso, pelvis, through your knees, ankles, feet, and deep down into the center of the earth, where there are flames of pure white fire.

STEP FOUR:

Begin to bring these flames of pure white fire up from the center of the earth, up through your feet, your legs—including your ankles, knees, and thighs—and into the space between your pubic bone and tailbone. Here, spiral the white flames of fire clockwise or counterclockwise. Your body will know what to do. Begin to bring the flames of pure white fire up through your *Second Power Point Center* into the space between your spine and the center of your lower belly. Next, bring the flames of pure white fire up into the space between your navel and your spine. Then, lift them up into your solar plexus, the space directly under your rib cage in the center of your body.

STEP FIVE:

Slide your focus from being in your head, down into your solar plexus, the *Fifth Power Point Center*, which is the space directly centered under your rib cage. Slide down a waterslide from your head into a warm pool of gold light within your solar plexus. Bring your full attention into the pool of gold light. Next, pull up the white flames of fire from your root center, so that they are directly below the pool of light in your solar plexus. Feel the white flames of fire warming up the pool of golden light to the perfect temperature for you to sit in as the flames become One with the water. Continue to bring your full focus from your mind down into your solar plexus and feel yourself sitting in the warm pool of golden light. As you sit in this pool, look up through the top of your head and watch a waterfall of pure white light pouring down onto you. Receive and take in the energy as you breathe and maintain your connection into your solar plexus.

STEP SIX:

Travel 10–20 feet above your head into pure, white light. Create a laser beam of light, a spotlight beam of love, and shine it down into a wide and open elevator shaft—a wide column of light—through the center of your body. Shine the light into the walls of the elevator shaft and all the way down into its bottom.

STEP SEVEN:

Look for a part of yourself that has never been allowed to exist and has been rejected by yourself or others. Send the light all the way into the bottom of the elevator shaft, and look to see where this part of you is sitting or standing. Look for the side of their head; see their ear and hair, as if you were behind a movie camera. Now come around from the side to the front view and look for their eyes.

Inwardly send them a message and ask this part of you if she/he knows who you are. If not, tell her/him that you are the "big" them.

STEP EIGHT:

Ask them what he/she needed his/her parents to know about him/her. Wait for the response. Ask them what he/she needs you to know about him/her. Ask how you can be there for him/her. Receive their response.

STEP NINE:

Ask him/her if he/she trusts you. If not, ask what you can do to help him/her trust you. Be with his/her energies. Feel their response in your heart center. Really listen. Then when complete, ask where in your body would she/he like to live.

STEP TEN:

Ask what color she/he would like you to bring into that part of your body. Fill that location in your body with the color that he/she requests and invite him/her to take up space in that part of your body.

STEP ELEVEN:

Deeply be with the connection and let this aspect of yourself fill you. Receive its energy. Dialogue and write in a journal with this aspect of yourself every day. Get to know him/her. Ask each of the following questions one at a time with your dominant hand, and then put your pen into your non-dominant hand to allow him/her to respond.

- What do you need from me to feel seen, heard, and received?

- How can I be here for you?

- What have you come into this life for?

- What kind of activities would you like for us to do together?

Give your acceptance and full, unconditional love to each aspect of yourself.

Pay close attention to how you feel about a soul aspect of yourself. If you have resistance, find out why. Once again, accept your feeling, but also choose to open beyond how you have shut out parts of yourself.

STEP TWELVE:

At your own pace, over the next several weeks, go back to the 2nd Step and while sitting comfortably, create the beam of light from 10–20 feet above your head and look for other soul aspects of yourself in any order that they show themselves to you or that you may choose. You may ask a friend to do the process with you. Feel free to do one or more soul aspects in a sitting.

Inquire and receive the following:

- An unseen and unheard aspect of yourself

- A resistant aspect of yourself

- An unexpressed and shut down aspect of yourself

- An angry aspect of yourself

- A helpless aspect of yourself

- A determined aspect

- A wounded and hurt aspect

- A sexually controlled, controlling, or fearful aspect

- A sad and lonely aspect

- A creative and powerful aspect

- A spiritually awakened and tuned in aspect

- A kind, gentle, and unconditionally loving aspect

Know that when all of these aspects of you are reintegrated, they ignite the core spiritual flame and consciousness of your True Self. Your soul aspects connect you into your eternal truth and infinite wisdom that transcend any particular age in your life. As you seek out your soul expressions, expect to see yourself at different biological ages. When you see yourself at a particular age, such as a young child or teenager, know that this form of you was the last time that this aspect of you felt received, seen, or heard.

You may find that a sad and lonely aspect may have developed when you rejected yourself as a teenager, or a brilliant but overlooked child may appear to you. When you discover your Inner Self, you will find that the significant spiritual aspects of yourself that became stuck at certain ages will come back to life once they are reintegrated within you. Know that as you reconnect all of yourself, you will feel strong, clear, and in-touch with "why you are here." You will also feel connected to your spiritual current, divine intelligence and soul expression. Know that this connection is a direct bridge into your True Self and has the power to open your heart to your soul.

Suggestions for how to BE with your soul aspects:

BE in conversation with your newly discovered soul aspect.
After you meet one of your soul aspects, send him/her a message that you want to contact him/her and that you are coming back for him/her. Tell him/her that you are really sorry

that he/she became wounded, felt hurt, neglected, judged, not seen, etc. Ask him/her what his/her parents needed to know about them. Ask him/her what he/she needs from you to trust you. They may say, "I want an ongoing relationship with you," or, "Please don't leave me again." How does his/her request make you feel?

You may find yourself feeling sad that you have been away for so long. You may express feelings such as, "I have felt irresponsible," "I am sorry that I have rejected and abandoned you," or, "I am the part of you that had to deal with all of the expectations and challenges of life, but I am back now for good." Speak to your newly found soul aspect with humility and humbleness from your heart.

Realize that we often role model our behaviors after our parents out of the need to be unified or aligned with the social or family structures we live within in order to be seen, loved, heard and to survive. Often times, we treat the soul aspect that we have abandoned, betrayed, or rejected the same way our parents did with theirs. We merge with the DNA of our ancestral patterns and behaviors, rather than lighting the lantern to loving our Self. Humans have a deep need to be accepted, and we will ABR ourselves just to get that acceptance and conditional love from those around us despite what it does to us. In an exasperated tone, your waiting soul aspect may say, *"Finally, I no longer have to be alone. I have been waiting for you."* You might find yourself saying to him/her, *"I am here. I am not leaving you again."* Whatever you say, say it with commitment and clear intention. Tell your newly discovered soul aspect that you love him/her. Then ask, *"What do I need to do for you to trust me?"*

You might receive an answer such as, *"Honor what I say to you." "Let's get our body healthy."* Or, *"Please don't leave me again. Stay connected to me."* You can ask yourself whether you are willing to let go of any negative attitudes or judgments that you have had towards him/her (yourself). These negative thoughts toward your soul selves create pain, sadness, health, weight challenges, money issues, relationship difficulties, self-sabotage, lack of self-esteem, etc. Ask him/her what he/she wants you to do to help you let go of the fear, grief, guilt, or sorrow that you hold. Ask him/her to share with you the original messages you gave him/her that pushed him/her away a long time ago. Take in his/her response and reshift your relationship to its core essence and heart. Ask your newly discovered soul aspect to share with you how it gave away its power to others and how you supported his/her ways of giving away its power. Ask your soul aspect how you can be there for him/her everyday. Really listen and commit to creating a relationship with this part of you. Remember you are the grown up "them", your ego structure was created to survive what they knew they could not handle. Their essence is what you want to "take in" and to receive in your heart and within your every cell of your body. Their essence is a vital part of your spiritual truth and light.

Invite the newly found soul aspect of yourself to consciously join with you and BE with you when you do any number of activities, including when you shop for food, cook, clean the house, fly a kite, work in the garden, go sailing, draw, sing, workout, take a shower, take a walk, swim, run, bike ride, or meditate. Your goal is to acknowledge and be aware of their presence and integrate their energies into yourself. Keep a journal and note what kind of emotional, mental, and physical changes you are going through. Notice what changes occur in your health, relationships, work, and life.

Invite each aspect of your soul to meet with the other soul aspects. See yourself on a beach, in the woods, or in a meadow. Then, build a circle of stones with your first soul aspect sitting with you. The circle of stones will surround a large fire that, once ignited, can be a focal point for you and your soul aspect to sit and watch the fire. Slowly begin to invite your other soul aspects to sit with you. Maintain your connection in your heart center as you become One with the flames of fire warming and illuminating you. Breathe into your body. Continue practicing BEing One with each soul aspect while you are doing yoga, making love, doing errands, doing laundry, cooking, communicating with others, etc.

> *You are beginning a new lifelong friendship with aspects of yourself that hold the answers to your awakening, self-realization, and freedom.*

As you build your relationship with your soul and your heart, you will find your body and mind relaxing. You will be able to let go of how you think things should be in your life. You will take steps to make new projects, dreams, and goals happen with greater confidence and ease. You will find new connections with your Self, friends, your partner, your work, and family. As you integrate your soul aspects that hold and carry a tremendous amount of your spiritual power, you will find yourself trusting life more. You will have greater focus and clarity to be with what is uncomfortable and not yet healed in yourself. You will experience the difference between living and feeling in separation from yourself and feeling whole and more empowered than you have ever been before.

The reconnection of your soul parts can happen in an instant. Trust the process and continue to feel, receive, and integrate the energies and truths that live within these precious parts of you. Know that humanity is evolving from a state of separation and suffering into a new paradigm of Oneness and wholeness. We must make the inner shifts first, so we can recognize and step into the purpose of our soul for this lifetime. Your soul's awakening will initiate you into the journey of living and BEing fully integrated, enlightening, and at peace.

REMEMBER:

- Unveiling the light of your soul awakens you to BEING ONE and BEING YOU.

- There may be a difference between what you think you want and what your soul actually needs to be complete.

- Only love can heal you.

- The enlightenment that you seek is already within you. The consciousness and wisdom within your soul is meant to be your guide.

- When it comes to soul work and your spiritual truth, YOU cannot be found through a belief system. You can only be discovered through an authentic connection with all of yourself.

- There is a difference between walking your own spiritual path and using "spirituality" as a way to manipulate your mind and emotions to get what you want in life. When you follow your true spiritual path, you may not get what you want, but you do get what you need to BE your Whole Self.

- Beneath what is most dejected, rejected, lost, wounded, and afraid within you is the beginning to finding your light.

- Your humanness is your gateway. BE kind and compassionate towards your self, accept your fears, and beneath them all, you will find your True Self living in your soul and heart.

- Open to whatever God puts on your path with as much acceptance, love, and gratitude as you possibly can. Love yourself and let everything else be shown to you by grace itself.

- *You do not have to believe in anything to find your soul.* It will speak to you and guide you because it is YOU.

- To experience spiritual Oneness: BE open. BE receptive. Trust what you find. Love and embrace what you find.

- Make a choice to BE with your soul every day, if only for a few minutes. When you choose to BE, you are choosing to meet, embrace, and love yourself. Remember, you deserve it. You *are* worth it.

BELIGHT MEDITATION

Practice the *One in Soul* Practice at least once a week for two months to create an ongoing relationship between your Bodymind and soul. Check in with the reconnected aspects of your Self, and integrate them daily until you feel completely connected with their essence, light, and power.

CHAPTER SIXTEEN

Soul Integration Actions

"The moment you change your perception is the moment you rewrite the chemistry in your body."
— Dr. Bruce Lipton

When you make the choice to discover, reconnect, and BE with your soul aspects, you are choosing to meet, embrace, and love all of you in a completely new and profound way. As you integrate your soul, you can BE the whole you. To successfully integrate your soul fragments, there are four key actions that you must embrace and practice.

The Four Soul Integration Actions:

ACTION 1: *See, Feel, and Hear*
ACTION 2: *Acknowledge and Honor with Love*
ACTION 3: *Receive and Accept*
ACTION 4: *Reconnect and Heal*

These four actions unite the body, mind, and Spirit through the heart, which allow the soul to be integrated into the unconditional and receptive nature of your True Self. Your heart center is a wellspring of unlimited energies and love, creating new expressions and breakthrough realizations to further you along your soul path. When your soul fragments reunite through your heart, you feel connected to the Infinite Source of life. You are able to access your truth and the energetic vitality of your feelings and soul essence at the same time.

When you reconnect all of the aspects of your soul, you experience stepping out of separation consciousness, and may experience for the first time the voice and truth of your Whole Self. In separation consciousness, the mind typically controls everything and tells the body to numb down, be quiet, and do what it is told. Your integrated soul aspects begin to have a greater impact on the trajectory of your life as the union of your Bodymind unites the desires and mission of your soul, so that they can be manifested in your everyday life. This creates the space for your divine masculine and feminine to unify, which further ends many of the battles in your mind.

As you practice and live the four soul integration actions, you will then continue to open to your soul through the reconnection and integration of your *Power Point Centers and Soul Integration Centers.* Remember that your *Power Point Centers* are the crossroads where your body, soul, and Spirit meet. They are portals into the Oneness of your soul and Spirit. As you join the soul integration actions with opening and connecting your *Soul Integration Centers*, you create a powerful energetic force that integrates your Bodymind with your soul.

SOUL INTEGRATION ACTIONS

FIRST SOUL INTEGRATION ACTION:
See, Feel, and Hear

Seeing

Seeing is a presence created by letting go of the limiting perceptions of your mind and BEing present to what exists within you. To be able to see, you must choose to let go of judging and looking at situations from your habitual mind chatter. You show up to life with a commitment to deeper clarity and with a capacity to experience events, actions, and words as they are. You see with the eyes of your heart. For example, if you are in a heated conversation with someone, and they feel differently than you about a subject, seeing would mean that you would not get caught up in the difference of opinion or find yourself reacting in self-defense. You would choose to come from a place without fear, listen to what is being said, and more deeply understand the context and content of whatever is happening. Deep seeing makes you feel steady, consistent, and powerful, regardless of what is said or whatever the outcome might be. You can be with whatever happens around you.

Deeper seeing integrates outer and inner sight. Outer sight is when your mind perceives what your physical eyesight can visualize. Inner sight allows you to begin to see the inner workings and energy of situations. Inner sight views the invisible energy that makes up individuals and relationships. Inner seeing allows you to see and BE with your Self. It allows you to embrace what is going on within you without fear. When you truly see what is "real," you are dual-seeing from the integration within your heart. When the two types of seeing are brought together through the heart, the truth of situations can be revealed. You will know that you are seeing clearly when your mind is no longer "butting in" to get things its own way. As you practice suspending your own need to control and manipulate a situation or judge what might be occurring, you can enjoy being comfortable and tuned into the invisible energies of any given circumstance.

Choose now to see from and through your heart. It will help you accept people and life situations for who and what they are, and give you clarity. Instead of responding to life from the stories in your head, connect to your heart first and then you will see life in its limitless possibilities. Life will become richer and more fulfilling. BE willing to release the attachment you hold to your stories and free yourself. Learn from them and then let them go.

Imagine within your heart a diamond of light so bright that its brilliance lights the way to become One with yourself and Infinite Source simultaneously. First you must see the sparkle and blaze of the light within your heart center. It is always there. As you see the light of love and vibrancy in your heart center, practice seeing outward through your eyes from the light of your heart. Imagine a vibrant life consciousness filling you from the inside out as the eyes of your soul view the world through the light of your own inner diamond. When you see through the light of your diamond, you are elevated into BEing One with your Self and with life. You will see the common thread of love between all people. You will also see when people are caught up in their own stories and by seeing through the light of your heart center you can help them by just BEing You. Your presence and willingness to BE real will help you and them. When you see through the light that is within your heart center, you will be able to see solutions and outcomes to problems in a more humane and all-encompassing way. It will also help to protect you from moving into potentially harmful situations. Importantly, it enables you to simultaneously see and open to how you feel and begin to fully receive the real you that lives beyond and beneath your feelings.

You can begin this new way of seeing by calling in a soul aspect waiting to be discovered within the darkness of your body. See through the darkness until you can sense the light hiding within this part of you. There is always light within darkness. Look for the light and see who is there and focus light from your heart into this aspect of you. Send an inner message that you are coming back for him/her. Look for the soul part of you that is needed in your life right now to move forward in your life. You will find enormous wisdom and an immediate release of trapped emotions. Meet the inner fear and darkness with your compassion and love. Show up completely. Embrace this soul aspect with your unconditional love. As you see your own fear and choose to embrace it with love, then the love for yourself and others will grow. This is how you love yourself. This is how you learn to see with new eyes.

As you integrate your left-behind soul aspects and exercise your expanded vision, know that you will also discover within the darkness of your body and psyche the core layers of your ego Self. Your ego Self will continue to hold on and work to control you as it has done for most of your life until you build a unified core Self of light. You must see how you give your power over to your ego as a way to reinforce your beliefs about yourself. Your ego is an expert on making sure that you are unable to see your True Self. It will shift and morph into different expressions of your core fear until you step through the veils of your fear. As you choose to live through and align to the higher truth within your heart, your soul is empowered to break through any obstacle.

Feeling

Feeling is a spiritual alignment in your body that is created by being fully present in a given moment or not. Feeling is a heightened state of presence. When you feel present in your body, you can sense, BE, and experience the infinite movement and eternal stillness that creates life through being energetically connected. You are not pulled down by one emotional response after another and are consciously feeling from a deeper place. You feel awake, ready, emptied, yet full to receive more life flow and exuberance.

For example, remember that person you were in conversation with who was upset at you? As previously mentioned, instead of rising up in self-defense or getting angry, you would be able to recognize and be with the bigger picture of the situation and not react personally to whatever is said. You can also acknowledge the other person's feelings and beliefs and directly ask them what they need you to understand about their situation. In other circumstances, by staying connected to your feelings you will know when you need to share your own truth or to be silent. Your intentions become centered in the thought-action of what is for the highest good of the individual I am speaking with.

When you feel in this way, you are in your body and clear about how you naturally need to respond to a situation. You truly care about the outcome of a situation. The key is that once you see and feel what's going on for you, then you must be willing to let go of your desired outcomes or expectations of how things should be. If you remain attached to the outcome, you will be unable to respond with total integrity. As soon as you become overly attached to something, you lose clarity and the ability to see and feel into the bigger picture. Instead, you remain stuck in your own expectations and projections.

How do you know if you are really feeling? You know that you are fully feeling when you are receiving, being, and giving simultaneously. You are One with the present moment, whatever it may be, and fully living in it. You *meet* the moment, the

SOUL INTEGRATION ACTIONS

situation, and even your own expectations or old beliefs, which no longer help you to expand into your authentic and Real Self. When the present moment is what it is, and not perceived or responded to based upon your past experiences, then you are feeling. You know you are feeling when the moment loses itself into the expansion of time. You are connected to the here and now. You know that you are feeling when you dissolve the past limitations that gauge your life. Whatever you haven't done, or you thought you couldn't do, loses its power over you. Possibility returns. The divine presence of the moment can move you into positive action. You begin to feel the divine presence of love.

Feeling through your body awakens a consciousness that makes you feel that you are no longer alone and realize that you have always been connected to the Creator. You might be doing something that brings you such joy that it makes you open up and cry with unexpected depth. You might think that everything is fine from your childhood and then all of a sudden you realize that your father emotionally and psychologically repressed you as a child, and it has colored and shaped your entire life, or that you shifted out of yourself to not upset your parents and shut down the doors to your heart. You might receive an inspiration or insight that gives you the next steps on your life journey to accomplish your dreams. You might feel a cellular memory emerge from a past life that you recognize as the key to a long lost inner door that is ready to open. You might have an awakening to being profoundly connected to your inner guides or God and realize you have always had the connection as far back as you can remember. However it happens, when you begin to fully feel through your body, you want to embrace life and experience all of its joys and opportunities for deeper connection with your Self and others.

To feel deeply, your emotional heart must feel safe. Placing your attention in your solar plexus and sitting in a golden and warm pool of light creates the foundation to opening into feeling. Your heart center can relax, and your solar plexus and your mind can merge, opening up pathways of light into your soul.

Once you feel relaxed in your solar plexus, focusing into your lower belly, your *Second Power Point Center,* and feeling from this point of power gets you in touch with feelings that, when honored, received, and acknowledged, become gateways into your wisdom and truth. Simply breathing into your lower belly, while your hands gently rest and connect with the energies in your *Second Power Point Center,* gifts you with instantaneous connection with universal, divine intelligence. Then, by connecting your *Second Power Point Center* awareness with your heart center, your *Sixth Power Point Center,* your every day chores and responsibilities become expressions of gratitude and Oneness, and are fueled with divine momentum. Through feeling what is real, you are able to bypass the procrastination and lethargy of your ego Self, who is never happy with the way things are. Once connected into your lower belly and heart center, you are able to feel and act upon the truth in the moment and follow your higher guidance with greater happiness and joy.

Hearing

You can develop your ability to spiritually hear through learning how to feel and be connected in your body. The truth of the matter is that you cannot hear anyone until you learn how to first hear yourself, and you cannot hear yourself until you can feel within your body. When you can hear yourself or another, your focus shifts from being in your head into your body. You can begin to hear your self and someone else by feeling the movement of energy and consciousness in your *Power Point Centers*, specifically your *Soul Integration Centers*. When you open your awareness into a *Soul Integration Center,* the

SOUL INTEGRATION ACTIONS

energies of your light grid are activated and your light bodies are awakened. Your soul communicates through your light grid, and when your light grid opens, your mind drops its guards and can begin to relax, receive and let go. As your mind surrenders its barriers, your soul can become One in your body. Subtle light energies can suddenly transport infinite wisdom, infinite intelligence, and unbounded love into your Bodymind "system." Your consciousness can now experience a heightened awareness of the union of light, spirit, and your soul in your body.

To help you bridge your mind into your body and to access your "soul hearing," connect into the following *Soul Integration Center*. (See illustration on page 103.) If you place the middle finger of your right hand on the tip of your rib cage, in the center, all the way at the bottom rim, you will feel a pointy protrusion. Slide your finger up over the "ledge," then slide into a valley, a second valley, and then into a third valley (they are very subtle and close to one another). You will then be in the *Sixth Soul Integration Center* to help you "hear" yourself. Be present and breathe into this *Center*. Take the time to dive deep with your breathe into its core. This *Soul Integration Center* helps to open the energetic gateway into your True Self. It helps you to take in the truth within you and to access your heart center. It serves as a protector and interpreter of your heart. Rest and relax into this center.

To hear the voice of your True Self, you must be able to feel from your heart center and be present to the silence within you. Instead of reacting or responding to the chatter of your mind, you become present to the truth, peace, and silence residing within you. Similar to receiving the tones of a tuning fork, you are in resonance to an inner state of peace. Your mind is harmonized with your soul, and you have released conflict. You become zoned into receiving and hearing the impulses, messages, and guidance from your inner Self. When you feel into that space, your soul can be heard. When listened to, your heart begins to open to the voice of your soul. Then, like a continuous circle, the voice and truth of your soul and heart continue to open, support, and nurture one another, opening you to life more fully. This is how you truly hear.

You will know that you are hearing when you suspend your need to snap to a conclusion about a situation. You will know that you are hearing when you are connected to your breath in your whole body and can feel your feelings through your heart and belly at the same time. You will know that you are hearing when you are surprised by the truths coming out of your mouth, and your life is rocked in the moment by the truth of Infinite Source speaking through you.

As your practice BEing One with your *Soul Integration Centers*, you will feel interconnected with the universal design of consciousness within your Bodymind. You will experience an increased expansion with your ability to maintain focused attention, inner confidence, strength, and clarity.

SECOND SOUL INTEGRATION ACTION: *Acknowledge and Honor with Love*

Acknowledge

When you acknowledge, you receive and give life, recognition, and energy to the existence of your own or someone else's soul. When you acknowledge the existence and reality of a moment, a feeling, or an experience, you are recognizing love and its potential power. The more you acknowledge the essence and truth within your soul, the more you will know your Self and your own existence. Reconnecting with the light of your soul aspects requires that you lovingly acknowledge the truth within you through seeing, feeling, and hearing. We all have a desire to be seen and heard as our unique and individual Self; our soul aspects are no different. Acknowledgment clearly demonstrates that all aspects of you matter and that all are worthy of recognition and love.

To acknowledge helps you let go of your desire to control the outcome of a situation. You must be with what is really happening, instead of what you would like to happen. Your mind tends to hold onto certain perceptions or ideas about what is "real" or how things are or should be as a way to maintain control. This keeps your mind in its loop of feeling important and valuable. Your mind always wants to be validated and will resist acknowledging truth that may be outside of its comfort zone. When you acknowledge what may be an uncomfortable truth or "reality," you are consciously going beyond your tendency to deny or remain blind to something that is bigger than your present perceptions.

Honor with Love

To honor with love is an act of devotion. It is an ability to be fully present with oneself or another. You are allowing for the full expression and unknown capacity that is within you or another to be seen, heard, and felt. When you honor with love, you allow for the unmanifested to become manifested. What is unrealized comes alive into the moment.

When you love and honor yourself in your everyday life, you choose to take care of yourself. You must first choose to love and honor yourself, to connect and be with yourself before you can effectively show up for others. This is possible through listening and receiving the messages from your body. Listen to how you want to show up, give and love, and what your truth tells you about who you are or who you want to be. Sit down and write about your desires. Exercise, meditate, create, rest, BE, or sleep as a way of listening and honoring the needs and desires in your body. To honor yourself, you must come from your heart and then choose to respond to what you are feeling.

An example of honoring one of your soul aspects might include honoring a part of yourself that wants to paint, create music, write, meditate, dance, or spend a Saturday taking a hike. Do something that gives special attention to the soul aspect with which you are reconnecting. You honor yourself by actually following through and fulfilling your desire. Choose to tend to the needs of your body, heart, and soul with attentiveness and reverence.

The best way to create a time of honoring is to make a safe space. Make a circle of stones to sit in the center of either inside or outdoors and pray, meditate, or just BE. Relax and take a hot bath. Focus your mind completely on connecting with your heart and BE. By walking on the beach, sitting on a rock in the woods, in a flower garden in your yard, or with a cup of tea on your porch, you are making time and space to respect and listen to the wisdom, pain, desires, reflections, insights, and love that reside within you. You allow them to BE and meet them with compassion and love. You might also write, draw, sit under a tree, cook yourself a pot of soup, or create a deluxe salad. Whatever you do, you are selflessly giving to yourself.

You also might find that you need to honor a part of yourself that is feeling an intense emotion, like anger. While you might be tempted to reject or stuff down the part of yourself that is angry, don't do it. This is really a part of you that needs to be seen, heard, or received. Your anger needs to be acknowledged and honored with love even more. You must look through the anger underlying the deeper truth of your soul aspect and see what denied needs and hurt are screaming out for attention. You will find a hidden part of you that just wants its existence acknowledged. Anger may also arise from a part of your power that has been denied expression by yourself or others. Most likely, your original pain comes from someone who abandoned, betrayed, or rejected "who you are" and the expression of your power and light early on in your life. You may end up projecting that pain onto someone else or through an action that physically and spiritually keeps you stuck, as a coping mechanism through your anger.

To begin to dissolve the anger, feel the part of your Self that you are reintegrating in your heart. Hold her or him close to your chest, take a walk, prepare a meal, and just love and acknowledge her or him in your daily activities. Open to the divine and invite it in to help bond with the pain secretly being held within you. Say yes to yourself. Hold yourself physically—literally give yourself a hug and surrender into your own love. It works.

Regardless of what the aspect is, you have to feel into the very essence of your being and fully receive and accept yourself. This can be done on a bus, in the shower, preparing for a business meeting, in a yoga class or while eating lunch. It is about being present with yourself in your body. Being present can be scary and frightening at first because you have to take responsibility for what you have been creating and denying in your life. You have to get clear about what you really feel and who you are. When you honor yourself with love, the love that you are then becomes the new foundation for how you want to be in the world.

By acknowledging and honoring yourself with love, it will also become easier to let go of attachments you thought you needed to be happy. You will learn to let go of things needing to look a certain way. You may have an image of how you want to be in this lifetime, but sometimes it is necessary to let go of that image to advance forward. What you really want to happen in your life can happen once you release your grip on how things need to be to make you feel valued and significant. As you allow yourself to merge with your heart, you realize that happiness comes from being in the heart of your soul.

As you open to life living through you as an intimate union with the divine, joy is released within you as an ecstatic expression of love. You realize that the more you honor your soul, the more you can give to the world what is whole, uplifting, and for the benefit of all beings. You become clear about the reasons why you want what you want. You experience a spiritual presence that allows you to be present with your Spiritual, Physical, and Emotional Self all at the same time. When this happens, you feel whole. The end result of honoring and loving yourself is that you create an inner world of love that magnetizes the outer universe to respond back to you with greater love and abundance. You exist within a zone of love where everything that comes to you feels like a heavenly gift.

When you choose to extend your honor and love to another, you also hold the space for miracles to happen in their lives at any given moment. You help create greater possibility for the other person to step into their Whole Self. When you honor another with love, you are choosing to be there for their highest good and what is ultimately best for them. You refrain from judging or projecting your own fears onto them. You go beyond how you want to change and control a person or a situation. You are BEing empowering and loving as you give yourself and others support, truth-recognition, and compassion. When you honor yourself or another with love, you are creating true freedom, expression, and the possibility for miracles to occur.

THIRD SOUL INTEGRATION ACTION:
Receive and Accept

When you reconnect with a part of your soul from which you have previously separated, you will first experience your fragmented part sitting or standing within you in your *First* or

SOUL INTEGRATION ACTIONS

Second Power Point Center. You may be seeing and receiving a part of yourself that looks like an infant, toddler, young child, a teenager, or even an elder because this is the age that the fragmentation happened. You may find yourself opening up to untapped fears, anger, profound clarity, or even unexpected joy. Whatever is present, you must become the receiver, the open vessel, and the conduit for this important and much needed aspect of your soul to be fully embraced into your heart.

The parts of you that hold the most spiritual power are the energies that your psyche will protect at all cost. Your psyche is the meeting point where your subconscious and conscious mind meet. Your psyche will hold the energies of your spiritual power and make sure that no harm comes to them. Your existence is all that matters to your psyche. It will love and protect you even if it means that the "real you" resides in isolation and separation.

Once your soul aspects are integrated into your energy matrix through your heart center, they have a need to express the spiritual essence that is at the core of their existence. In a supportive family environment, these energetic parts of you will choose to stay "above ground" in the playing field of your every day existence. In conflicting environments, these parts of you will absolutely go into hiding and "below the surface." When a forgotten soul aspect "gets" that who it is stirs the emotions of its parents, peer group, or authority figures, unless you are solidly anchored in your whole soul, it will run for cover, hide, separate, and alienate within you as its chosen way to self-protect until you come back for him/her and commit to giving it space to grow and expand in your body. The wounds of your past life time incarnations effect how you respond to being abandoned, betrayed, or rejected (ABR'd) or received by your family of origin. When we come into this lifetime, our emotional sanskaric imprints effect our ability to hold our own frequency of light. As you integrate all aspects of your soul you will trust the connection you have with the divine. It is not until our spiritual connection is strong enough, and we rely upon it over our ego Self, that we can BE One as our True Self.

Your soul aspects will live in your *First* and *Second Power Point Centers* because this is where they can feel connected to the security and rootedness of your being. Similar to a forest, there is stillness, containment, and safety in the roots of a tree.

Your spiritual power can easily hide and exist beneath your fear and go unnoticed for years. You may not even realize that you are closed to your true power until you reach a point in your life where you can no longer move forward on your life path. Unless you receive the ancient wisdom contained within your soul, and clear and integrate the power within your base *Power Point Centers,* your life will inevitably have a sense of restlessness and emptiness.

To receive your light, truth, and wisdom, you must move past your fears, and open beyond the parts of you that think they know what is best for you. Your separate Self is driven by the personal will that believes it can function on its own without the higher will of Infinite Source—God. When you receive and accept the light, truth, and wisdom within yourself that has never been seen, heard, or felt, you will open the gateway to the higher love within you. Solutions to life challenges or important decisions needing to be made spontaneously come to you. To receive, open your hands and heart to life, deepen your breath, and feel what life wants to give to you.

Each time you receive another aspect of yourself that you may not know, like, or understand, you move into self-acceptance. For instance, you may have developed a "rescuing personality" when you were a child, where your role in life was to save and protect your family. In order to become the "all together knowing or helping one," you had to sacrifice parts of yourself that longed for greater freedom and personal autonomy. As a reaction, these soul aspects "act out" in different ways, such as by not wanting to exercise or stay with a disciplined routine, communicate to you or others, stay in the shadows of your life, block you from succeeding, create dependence upon others for giving you needed answers or love, avoid confrontation, stay fixated on making money, misuse sex to fill your inner wounds, take care of others instead of yourself, spend too much time on social media, or keep you judging yourself through feeling superior or inferior to others. When you sacrifice the connection with your Self, there is no way to truly serve others.

When you choose to awaken, enliven, and help that part of yourself that shrinks back from opening and receiving energy, you are consciously choosing to "hold the space" for this aspect of yourself to feel accepted and unconditionally loved. Your acceptance helps this part of you come into life. It then allows you to move beyond the "things" that stop you from growing and changing with life.

When you receive and accept what is, you experience non-resistance. You feel flexible and at ease with the way that life moves you. When you actively receive, your body is open and relaxed.

You can begin to actively receive by taking a deep inhalation through both nostrils into your lower belly, fill your lower sacrum with the breath, and then as you exhale allow the breath to move through your navel, your solar plexus, your heart center, throat, and out your mouth. Now, with ease and depth, breathe into the space inside your spine between your tailbone and pubic bone first, then connect your breath into your navel, solar plexus, and through your heart center and into the back of your skull. Focus into these five points simultaneously and fill them with your breath. Hold and suspend the breath, then exhale through your mouth. This will help your body and mind ground and trust in the universal perfection of your life. As you surrender into the connection, you will be able to receive and accept everything that you need to heal, become stronger, and clearer.

Just by breathing and directing your attention into these five spaces at the same time will help you live in a state of acceptance of what is.

Remember, the most beneficial act of receiving begins with yourself and towards your Self. When you receive your own heart, your own feelings, and your own light, you begin to merge and become One with all that you are and born to BE.

Aaron's Story

Aaron was a transformational catalyst who had a passionate commitment to helping others. Aaron felt masterful in his work with his clients, believed that he came from his heart, yet was experiencing both professional and financial issues. He felt sincerely aligned to client breakthroughs and was completely unconscious of how his False Self and ego identity continued to run his life. He was devastated when he learned that people thought he was driven by his ego. He had no idea how aggressive or superior he came across to others.

When he reconnected to a hidden soul aspect using the One in Soul Practice, he discovered his feminine energy coiled up as a cobra within his First Power Point Center. This feminine aspect of him lived inside the cobra in the dark. He sent a powerful message to this part of himself that he had come back to reconnect with it.

When guided to use his connection with the light to see through the dark, he discovered a trap door beneath the cobra. Aaron realized that the cobra, his feminine energies, had been protecting the trap door. When further guided to open the trap door, he found a black panther protecting his Infant Self. As he sent love to his Infant Self, the panther embraced him around his shoulders. He was then asked to lovingly hold his Infant Self and send a message that he had returned. The unseen love and power within his soul that had been halted as an infant opened. Aaron's heart opened to receive his own soul.

After 58 years, he felt an immediate melting into himself. The aggression from his panther-self transformed, and his ego lost its grip as the controller and protector of his True Self. As Aaron integrated this newly found aspect of himself, he found a courageous, brilliant, clear, and enthusiastic presence. The gifts from his True Self, once integrated, were the keys to softening how he communicated with others. He was then able to trust being in his own heart, which then opened the hearts of potentially new clients, thus breaking through his self-made financial and professional barriers.

FOURTH SOUL INTEGRATION ACTION:
Reconnect and Heal

From the moment you are born, you make a moment-to-moment choice whether to stay connected to your original and authentic soul spark or to leave it. The reason you leave yourself is always dependent upon trying to get the love you instinctively believe that you need to survive, or because you felt unsafe being the light that you are in your body. You might have come into this lifetime with the engrained belief that dimming your light will prevent others from rejecting, hurting, or judging you. It is the way that fear consciousness seeks to survive. To become free, you must choose to stay with yourself and to no longer abandon yourself. Learning to discriminate what is your truth and what are the voices and beliefs of your False Self is crucial to staying connected to your Core Self. The strength of your connection with Infinite Source in your body will help you feel safe, unconditionally loved, and provide the clarity to heal.

As you move through your childhood, teenage, and adult years, each time that you leave yourself and split off from your connection to Infinite Source, you create self-suffering, shame, grief, sadness, pain, and anger. You come to doubt your own self-worth and question your own lovability. When you reconnect the energies of your soul that have split off to remain safe and to maintain their core spiritual power and essence, you will naturally align to Infinite Source. When you reconnect your soul aspects, you can feel a profound healing process occur in your body. This powerful gift to you restores the Oneness of your soul and gives you back your original truth and power. When divine and human polarities balance in your body and psyche, healing can occur. When you reconnect your soul aspects with Infinite Source in your heart center, you are able to reopen and say YES to the spiritual energies that comprise your True Self. Once whole and complete, you feel connected, tuned in, present, fully alive, integrated, and healed. Healing takes on a new meaning. The universe and you have the opportunity to BE One.

When you are One with yourself and life, it becomes easier to slow everything down in yourself. You find yourself needing to walk down the street a little slower, drive slower, eat slower, and find serenity through just BEing. Letting go in your body happens with greater ease. You feel less stress. It becomes easier to feel how and where in your body you hold on. As you allow your muscles to relax, feel your breath move into your lungs and then down into your lower belly. You are opening the gateways of your body to receive your greater light and wisdom. Allow your feelings to come up instead of pushing them down. Within your feelings are the gateways into and through the fears covering over your True Self. As you trust and listen to your feelings, they will help you to discriminate and choose how you wish to

SOUL INTEGRATION ACTIONS

relate to the world around you and to others. Your response will help you to create powerful boundaries that protect the essence of your soul.

Your mind will always want to perceive its own way and have an agenda. The one thing to remember is that following your soul instead of your mind will help you take the next best steps on your soul path. When your soul and your mind meet in your body through your *Soul Integration Centers*, you begin to feel life coming alive within you.

As shared in previous chapters, shift your focus into your *Fifth Power Point Center*, your Solar Plexus, by dropping your attention from your mind into your solar plexus. The shift from your mind into your Solar Plexus helps you to begin to realize that you are not the thoughts moving through your mind. You are actually the Oneness found in the stillness, in the presence, and in the life energy that is soaring through you, ready to be embraced, integrated, and ignited.

When you are reconnected in this Original Way, you will know yourself because all of you is present. You will feel One with life, nature, love, your body and sexuality, and your creative spirit, and seek to give and receive the most that you can from life. When you are One with a moment in life, with a person, or with yourself, you will feel connected into the center of your essence—the Infinite Source of life within you. You might feel infinitely grounded as though you are inside of a tree with roots firmly planted into the earth, or a blossoming rose fragrant in late spring, or as light as the heart of a hummingbird. You may feel completely in awe BEing amidst the silent nature of an animal, or you may feel as powerful as an eagle soaring with the wind and its currents. You will feel *One in Soul*.

REMEMBER:

- The soul reintegration process involves Four Key Soul Actions:
    - Action 1: See, Feel, and Hear
    - Action 2: Acknowledge and Honor with Love
    - Action 3: Receive and Accept
    - Action 4: Reconnect and Heal

These actions unite the body, mind, and Spirit through the heart, allowing the soul to BE integrated into a new Bodymind consciousness.

- Your essential soul reintegration steps:
    - Engage in dual-seeing from your heart to see what is "real."
    - Suspend your need to control, manipulate, or judge situations.
    - Tune into the invisible energy of given circumstances.
    - Fully feel every experience by being present in the moment.
    - Hear through BEing One in your *Soul Integration Centers*.
    - Acknowledge the existence and reality of a moment, feeling, or an experience.
    - Love and honor yourself in your everyday life through listening and receiving the messages from your body.
    - Receive what is within you without judgment.
    - Move through your fear. See the light that is within the aspects of your Self that live in fear.

SOUL INTEGRATION ACTIONS

- o Open your heart and expand your capacity to accept yourself.
- o BE open, kind, loving, gentle, and present with yourself.

- As you are healing your body, heart, and soul connection by listening and being with yourself, you will begin to access your connection to Infinite Source intelligence.

- When you get to the core of who you are, you must be able to be with even the most unlovable parts of yourself.

- When doing your soul integration work, keep in mind that if you really listen and pay attention to what your soul is saying, it may need something different from what you think. Be willing to follow what is says. It won't let you down.

- Only love can heal you and make you whole.

- The bottom line is that, until you know yourself on a soul level, you will always have nagging questions about yourself and your life purpose. You will always be asking the question, "Is this really it?"

- It does not matter what lifestyle, spiritual path, or belief system you adopt. Until you do your real soul work, nothing will be sustainable and you will inevitably be chasing your spiritual tail.

- Begin to see, feel, and know your Self. This takes three things:
    - BE Open
    - BE Receptive
    - Trust what you find

BELIGHT MEDITATION PRACTICES

Ignite Your Diamond of Light

Sit in a comfortable cross-legged position on the floor, on a pillow or mat, in your favorite chair, or on your bed before you go to sleep or first thing upon awakening. Inhale through your nose and fill your lungs with breath. Close your eyes except for a tiny slit of light shining in. Gaze down to the tip of your nose with your eyelids almost completely closed. Inhale to the inner count of 4, hold for the count of 4, exhale to the count of 4, suspend and "do nothing" for the count of 4. Repeat 4 times. Then, inhale to the inner count of 5, hold for the count of 5, exhale for the count of 5, suspend and "do nothing" for the count of 5. Repeat 5 times. Allow your mind to let go into the breath. BE with the breath. Then, inhale to the inner count of 6, hold 6, exhale 6, suspend for the count of 6, 6 times.

Allow your breathing to be slow and deep and fill your body with each inhalation and exhalation. Now, bring your inner focus into your heart and gaze into a large diamond of pure light. Continue to BE present to the light within your heart and expand your focus of awareness into the shimmering light. Drop your awareness into your heart center and merge with the diamond as you enter into its radiance. As you breathe, move your mind into the diamond. Gaze into the light in the diamond within your heart. See through your third eye the brilliance of the light. BE One with the light. Relax into the light. Stay with the practice until you feel immersed in the diamond's light radiance.

Listen, Hear, and Receive Yourself

To bridge your mind into your body and access your "soul hearing," connect into your heart center—the *Sixth Soul Integration Center*. If you place the middle finger of your right hand on the tip of your rib cage, in the center, all the way at the bottom rim, you will feel a pointy protrusion. Slide your finger up over the "ledge" into the first valley, then proceed upward through two more valley's (they are very subtle and close to one another). You will be in the *Sixth Soul Integration Center* to help you "hear" yourself. Be present and breathe into this *Center*. It will help to open the energetic gateway into your True Self and help you to feel the truth within your soul. It serves as a protector and interpreter of your heart. Continue to expand and BE. Rest and relax.

Acknowledge Your Anger, Learn from Your Anger

Get out a notebook or journal and, with your dominant writing hand, ask your anger what it has always needed. Ask it to share with you what has not been received, honored, heard, or seen about its existence. Close your eyes for a moment and receive its message with your non-dominant writing hand. Now using your dominant hand, ask your anger how you can be there for the feelings that have lived beneath it. Receive and write the response with your non-dominant hand. Close your eyes and look within the "energy of the anger" and look to see "how old" this expression of your Self is. BE aware of all of the images that come to you. Now, dialogue with each image, taking your time to BE with each expression of your Self. Know they are all parts of you, ready to be seen, heard, and received into wholeness. Feel, see and be with the essence of their presence. Feel where in your body you can locate the anger. Feel how the anger holds you back and creates distance from what it wants. Track the anger back to the original moment when you felt ABR'd (abandoned, betrayed or rejected). Now, feel what is beneath the anger—hopelessness, grief, loss, hurt, sadness or longing. Dive into your heart and invite the power, love, creativity, voice, and life force that has been hiding beneath the anger to merge into your heart center and Whole Self. When you end the battle of anger within yourself, between one part of your self with another part of your Self, you can begin to come home to You. It requires unconditional love, acceptance and surrender.

Receiving and Accepting What Is

Begin by breathing a long, deep inhalation in through your mouth into your lower belly. Draw your breath up into your solar plexus and then into the back of your skull. Then, exhale your breath slowly out of your mouth as you pucker your lips into an "O" shape. Repeat the breath again as you relax the back of your skull, and pull the breath up through the inside of your spine from your lower belly, your *Second Power Point Center*, through your solar plexus, into the back of your skull and out your mouth as you pucker your lips into an "O" shape.

Now, inhale through both nostrils and focus the breath into the space inside of your tailbone and pubic bone, your *First Power Point Center*—root center. Exhale, through your mouth as you gently pull up the muscles around your genitals and anus, as you pucker your lips into an "O" shape. Now, with ease and grace, inhale again through your nostrils, and lift the energies up through your navel, solar plexus, and heart center and into the back of your skull. Suspend the breath, by holding it to the count of three, and then gently exhale out your mouth. BE with the sensations and see the energies lifting up from the root center as pure white light. As the energies connect within you, feel the stability and steady strength this connection gives you. This will help you trust your relationship with your Self and with the universe. As you receive the energies, trust in their innate perfection and capacity to bring you everything that you need to heal, become stronger, and clearer.

Acceptance is a physical experience that comes from being connected into your heart, solar plexus, navel, lower belly, and root center at the same time. BE present in all five centers at the same time and allow your Self to let go, accept what is, and just BE.

Stillness and BEing

Begin to breathe slowly and deeply in through your nose and out through your mouth. With each inhalation, bring the breath into your lower belly and fill your lower sacrum and tailbone with your breath. With each exhalation, bring the breath up inside your spine, through a channel of light, and then exhale out of your mouth. As you go deeper into your breath, begin to focus into the space between your thoughts. Find the stillness and the emptiness in the space and allow the space to expand become larger with each breath. Just BE in this vast and infinite space as you find greater relaxation and presence with "all there is."

CHAPTER SEVENTEEN

Soul Challenges and Solutions

"Those who think they know falter and those who know they do not know are given the keys to the kingdom."
— Issa (Yeshua)

The soul reconnection and integration actions described in the last chapters may appear challenging, particularly when you are just beginning the process, but they actually possess a natural simplicity. As you open into your body, it will become easier to feel connected as you shift your focus out of separation consciousness into BEing in a new relationship with the creative life forces that live within you. As the energies of your Whole Self become integrated, you will find yourself trusting your intuition and taking the initiative to put into action your natural impulses and joy. You will experience a more relaxed, almost instinctual flow to how you respond to yourself. You will be able to navigate over the bumps, meandering curves, and occasional potholes with greater ease and grace. As you embrace and face your attachments, fear, and controls and make use of your determination and commitment to find the voice of your True Self, your courage grows. Your belief in yourself and your confidence to stand tall in your truth grows. Your willingness to discriminate and make new choices that bring you closer to BEing in a constant state of awareness and love grows.

Yes, there will be challenges and obstacles that come up as you step into your power, and to do so you must choose who you serve. Do you serve your ego or the light of your heart? How do you choose what to follow within yourself? How do you tell when your ego voice is dictating a belief system or reaction to support its survival over the freedom and empowerment of your soul? You must align into the light within your heart everyday. You must come into your solar plexus and create a warm golden pool of water to sit in with your inner child to create connection to the source of life within you. You must slow down how you interact with the world. Instead of rushing and dominating your life from your head, BE with your heart and the light within you. Fill every cell in your body with light. See from that light. Shine the light upon your path. Trust in that light.

Let's explore some of the common challenges you are likely to face and the solutions that can support you to move through them with greater ease and love.

Facing Your Separation

The purpose of becoming *One in Soul* is to heal the separations that block and prevent you from existing and living your life as your Whole Self. As you ignite a new power from BEing aligned with your True Self, you feel the support that you need to walk through your everyday challenges with a new confidence and clarity. You can feel and see that you are not being pulled into the chaos, confusion, pain, and suffering happening outside of your Self. As you surrender to the truth and wisdom of your evolving and expanding Whole Self, a deep level of inner trust takes the place of how you have previously dealt with your

SOUL CHALLENGES AND SOLUTIONS

inner battles created by how you have lived in separation from the light of your soul.

When your soul aspects are still living in isolation from one another, from your heart, and Higher Self, you will experience reliving certain situations that create pain and suffering. As the inner battles between your ego Self and your self-doubting Self continue, your inner battles are projected out into your life and into the world, creating a way of thinking that prevents your greater abundance, love, happiness, security, and health from being created. The root of every health, relationship, and money issue that you go through is caused by the internal warfare within you.

Your "war" is between your body, mind, and soul. The egoic structure of your body and mind fight to block out the truth of the higher wisdom of your soul so that its survival is ensured. Your mind will use the spiritual power of your soul to build the walls of control that separate your mind and body from feeling connected to Infinite Source—God. Your mind will continue to believe that "nothing" is wrong until your health, career, marriage, friendships, partnerships, finances, etc. are "hit hard" and even then your mind may stay in denial. The upset and trauma from something falling apart in your life exasperates the separations that you have been casually living in. When your own pain and suffering increase, the choice point between living in separation or coming closer to Infinite Source—God is magnified. The reason for awakening and connecting your body and mind with your *Power Point Centers* is to give you the opportunity to live in the center where peace, strength and clarity reside.

When the walls separating your body, mind and soul begin to dissolve, the activated energies within your *Power Point Centers* can illuminate your core shaft—your sushumna—your "truth channel." Imagine a wide grounding and polarizing rod of light power moving from the earth into your higher centers that vibrates to the consciousness of Infinite Source. This profound divine intelligence already exists within you, and can be accessed through the light of your heart and soul—and your sushumna.

Experiencing your true power, and choosing to trust it, is life changing. It really is. You begin to BE Self-sourcing and sense that you can trust who you really are. You are no longer trying to know your Self because you are BEing your Self.

As you walk your soul reconnection path and stay present in your heart, you will naturally come face to face with pain and sadness caused from the separation between your forgotten soul aspects and your heart center. From the first moment that you reconnect and integrate a lost or forgotten part of yourself, you will feel the release of sadness, grief, or sorrow that you have been carrying in your heart center sometimes unknowingly for lifetimes. When you heal the core issues of this lifetime you are automatically healing the separations between your mind and soul from your past lifetimes. You are given a family, a set of life circumstances and situations to master as a teaching roadmap to help you return to consciously being connected to your soul. As the gaping holes and spaces between your soul and heart, and forgotten ABR'd soul aspects dissolve, so do the painful emotions that your body and mind have suffered with.

The separations between your body, mind, and soul create physical, emotional, psychological, or spiritual pain.

Your physical, emotional, and physical bodies can heal when you reconnect your forgotten soul aspects into your heart center, your *Sixth Power Point Center,* and then invited to "take up space in your entire body." Once you experience the light of your soul becoming One with your emotional-physical energy matrix, your sadness, grief, and sorrow are transformed. Immediately after the moment of your reunion, they may come up for a few moments to be released. They will clear naturally because they are no longer needed. Once unified, your brain knows it, and feelings of joy and wholeness take the place of the old feelings that have been stored in the back of your skull in your reptilian brain.

Your old response patterns came from living in separation and weighing and balancing your thoughts with your ego Self. Even when whole, you may feel triggered by situations and people who lack the sensitivity to honor you, but your responses and actions will be very different from when you were surviving in separation consciousness.

As you step into BEing Whole, fear may come up as your mind begins to calculate the possibility of having to let go of control. In these moments, move the light of Infinite Source from the center of the earth into your body, up through a wide channel of light that expands through and around your spine, into the back of your skull, and through the top of your head into the heavenly dimensions beyond all thought. Once you've done this, then move the light back down into your body into your solar plexus. Rest and breathe into a wide space of love, and give yourself the opportunity to receive the love within you while BEing anchored in your solar plexus. Re-choose in the moment to release the cage of bondage that you have created for yourself. Choose instead to receive the deep power of love within your soul that yearns to come alive and BE expressed.

Each step on your path is a healing with your relationship with Infinite Source—God. Only your ego mind perpetuates the separation. Your ego mind can merge with your Whole Self, and confuse your perceptions. Remember your ego mind was created to protect you and to help you deal with situations that you felt unable to deal with as a child. If your wounded child Self is still too afraid to connect its heart to your heart and the heart of Infinite Source—God—you will project onto others and into the world, that it is not safe or loving to be here. Your core beliefs such as "I am not enough who I AM, I AM not worthy of being loved, I AM here to enjoy myself and I refuse to become too different in the eyes of other, so I will create an external personality that is glowing with super consciousness, yet, I AM still split inside, but no one will know. The only way through this gateway is to surrender your will into divine will. By finding and letting go of your anger towards Infinite Source—God and realizing how you blame an outside Source for how alone, abandoned or unloved you feel, has the power to set you on your highest destiny path.

Sit with yourself, and meditate into your heart. Inwardly chant, *I AM the infinite love of God*. Breathe into your heart. Place your focus into your third eye, the space in between your eyebrows and about one half to one inch up. Look into a blank screen, then shift the screen from blank to blue, then let go, and just BE. Maintain your connection in your heart and with the mantra.

As you reconnect the spiritual light and power of your soul into your solar plexus and into your heart center, you will experience what it feels like to be free of self-controls. A feeling of lightness will spread throughout your entire body. You will feel your mind letting go of its grip, and you will understand how and why your ego mind came into existence. Your ego was created by your psyche for one reason: to block and constrict the power of your light. Its purpose was to keep you safe and not judged for feeling inadequate, incapable, helpless, or unlovable. As you realize the beauty, pure wholeness, and intention of your True Self, you realize that you do not need to employ your ego to take care of you any longer. As you become One with the light within your heart, you have the opportunity to explore living as an unlimited human BEingness.

> *Re-choose in the moment to release the cage of bondage that you have created for yourself. Choose instead to receive the deep power of love within your soul that wants to BE expressed.*

As your soul light fills your body, you will feel your heart center ignite from the inside out. You will feel many emotions dissolve as you embrace what is true and real about you. As you bring in the love of your soul, you will begin to remember who you are. Receiving the love within you will strengthen and enlighten you. You will be able to access the aspects of yourself waiting to be resurrected from lifetimes of hiding out, withdrawing, isolating, feeling frozen, numb, or disempowered.

Remember, the aspects of your soul that have separated themselves the most from you hold the deepest and most spiritually developed parts of yourself. Through them you will find the truths of your soul that will not only give you joy and freedom but also the keys to connecting directly to God—Infinite Source.

Laurie's Story

Laurie's son, at the age of 16, had a serious alcohol and drug abuse issue. He was refusing rehab, and she felt up against the wall. She felt desperate and disempowered as a parent. As Laurie embarked upon the One in Soul work, she asked to discover the aspect of her soul that was afraid to be itself. She discovered the angry voice of her lonely and intimidated teenage self at the age of

17, who was forced by her mother to give up the baby that she had conceived with her boyfriend. Laurie had unwillingly given into her mother's demands, left her own power, and had repressed her own anger for 22 years. She realized that when she spoke to her son David about his issues, she came from the same controlling voice as her mother. Laurie's false persona was teaching David to do the same. She had repressed her own grief about giving up her baby and never marrying her high school sweetheart. Once honored, her heart opened through tears of self-forgiveness.

Without even saying a word about the inner work she had done, David came to her to ask her advice about what he could do to help him get through his addiction problems within a week of her doing this piece of work. By clearing her own pain and sorrow, Laurie began to clear the ancestral and karmic patterns that opened the door to help free both herself and her son. Within six months, David made a radical shift in himself, and he began to build a healthier relationship with his family, peers, and teachers.

Healing Sanskaras with Light

We carry in our energetic grid the seen or unseen, felt or unfelt imprints or impressions from past life and present life experiences that mold our thinking, responses, and behaviors. As you touch into your heart center through your soul's reconnection in your body and discover your Core Wound, layers of self-doubt, self-rejection, self-abandonment, and self-betrayal are released. As previously shared, the fear, grief, anger, sadness, or despair created by living in separation consciousness come up to be released. They are not who you are, but just expressions of having your body-mind-soul wiring short-circuited. When the despairs, beliefs, and impressions about your Self and others become stuck in the layers of your consciousness and subconscious, they become energetic blockages that create walls around your heart center.

The walls around our hearts are created whenever we feel unseen, unheard, or unreceived. Perhaps the walls around your heart were created over lifetimes from being condemned, rejected, or persecuted for being a light filled and embodied divine human being. Perhaps the walls were subconsciously built from lifetimes of betrayals or loss. Maybe one or both of your parents were unable emotionally or physically to bond with you at birth or in early childhood. Perhaps the love that you are was overlooked because of your parent's survival issues. Perhaps you left your Self so completely at some point in time that you doubted if you were worthy of love, of value, or even mattered. You created beliefs about yourself that created deep pain. These impressions became lodged in your heart center. They may be wounds, experiences, or beliefs that you've held onto for lifetimes. When healed, they give you the opportunity to BE living in alignment with your Whole Self. You will find yourself feeling present with a new ability to be with "what is." To clear a wound can be as simple as acknowledging its presence, directing light to the Core Wound, releasing the emotion as pure energy into the light, acknowledging who you really are and BEing who you are.

Sometimes we recreate a past wound in present-day time as a way to subconsciously heal wounds that we have carried forward from previous incarnations and early childhood. For example, you may have a Core Wound involving love and betrayal. Look at how you may have attracted people in this lifetime to help bring up your deepest and most unresolved pain by how they have treated you. You might stay in unhealthy relationships, work environments, or continue patterns of unhealthy living until you shift how you relate to your Self. Unhealthy living may include manipulating your environment to avoid your feelings; excessive eating, drinking, or use of drugs; over or under spending; avoiding and denying your feelings; procrastinating; building up debt; doubting your own gifts; playing small; choosing friends who can't support you; using sex to avoid true intimacy, etc. These are some ways of how you struggle with your Core Wound.

You may not be conscious of it, but you will continue to interact with people and situations that block you until you say, "I get it—I have to rise up." When you stay in your wound rather than taking responsibility to lift up into BEing whole in your life, it deprives you from living from soul. Avoidance can be like a warm, numbing blanket that keeps you stuck. You will continue to create ongoing suffering until you decide that you've had enough.

More often than not we dance around our wounds and become attached to the mystical, powerful, or addicted lifestyles that we live as a result of their presence. We live our lives in a veil of illusion where our wounds drive our thoughts and actions. Often one mind-set of society says, "You have no wound, move on." While another says, "Ignore your wound just live your life." By ignoring the shadow of our Core Wounds, we have created a world that acts out the most unhealed aspects of the collective wound and perpetuates judgment, violence, and hatred.

To heal our Core Wound requires suspending judgment and self-condemnation. Your wound can be healed when your heart can hold love for all of yourself, including your pain, grief, fear, resentment, or anger. It is so easy to get stuck and frozen in your emotions and to create your self-identity as your false Self. These emotions are not who you are, they are the feelings that are catalysts and portals of awakening into your True Self. As you find the light within your emotion, you open the gateway to the wisdom of your True Self. You are then given the choice by your higher Self whether to hold on to your Core Wound and live in the "story" of your pain, or let go and recreate your life from the light of who you are. When you take the time to unravel your emotions and to see and feel how the choices you made in your past, and how the circumstances of your life effected you, you are able to receive the truth being given by your soul.

Impressions, or *sanskaras,* the Sanskrit word for karmic imprints within your energy bodies and mind, carry the golden threads of your soul journey. Sanskaras can be embraced as blessings on your path to help you release the attitudes, habits, fears, projections, addictions, sorrows, and attachments that are the messengers of awakening for your life. Your sanskaras are the imprints of time and experience, chiseled into your energetic bodies that, once realized and released, open waves of potentiality in your life. These grooves, scars, wounds, holes, caverns, wellsprings, and oceans of impressions carry all past experiences, beliefs, and emotions. They color how you perceive, respond, think, and make choices and will hold tight until the light of your God Self penetrates them and begins to transform them.

Some of the most powerful impressions we experience manifest through our fears. Dormant in our minds and bodies, fear can encapsulate us. Fear can hide within us until enough pain is remembered, experienced, and allowed and we feel and follow our Soul guiding or pushing us to face our darkness. Each sanskara is a collection of circumstances and emotions that hold you hostage to old ways of seeing your self, life and others, and also have the ability to give you deep understanding, clarity and liberation. Each fear that you carry in your memory body comes from an emotional or psychological response, agreement, or reaction to an abuse, judgment, act of hatred, violence or control, or betrayal that created trauma. Fear is an energetic gateway that separates you from your Original Self. Your fear is a deadened space within you, where there is very little life energy. It disconnects you from feeling and BEing One. Your ego Self, as previously mentioned, is kept alive through your fear that who you are is not enough, unworthy of love, or that your existence does not matter. As you align your Bodymind and soul in the light, the power of your True Self is activated and increased, and your ego Self is gradually revealed. You are then given the choice by the light of consciousness within you to release the energetic cords that you have created to keep your ego Self in charge of your life. Your core sanskaras, the impressions that you have carried about yourself and life emerge from your subconscious to be released.

While fear and its companion control are the well-travelled part of the human experience, within our fears are the seeds of our original magnificence and self-recognition. The light of God moving through your body directly from Infinite Source helps you to move beyond your fears and sanskaras. It is the light and love within you that will heal and align you. The light will clear past memories, beliefs, or patterns that no longer serve your journey into your Whole Self. The *One in Soul* experience can begin to heal your sanskaras and recalibrate your Bodymind relationship with the source of God within you.

> *All transcendence happens through releasing fear and embracing love.*

When writing about how to free oneself from sanskaras, Avatar Meher Baba said, "To be free from sanskaras, the individual ego must be annihilated by service, or the limited self must merge in love."[3] The ego can only be transformed and then, in later steps, annihilated by increasing the amount of love within you. Each time you recognize and see the light within a

---

3 http://www.meherbabadnyana.net/life_eternal/Book_One/Sanskaras.htm

soul aspect of yourself, you are then able to absorb cosmic life energies that have been blocking your belief in yourself, your power, and your ability to love and BE yourself.

How you hold on, hold back, and hold in transform as you open your heart to the truth of your divine essence found through clearing your sanskaras.

The process of surrender that first begins when you discover, receive, and integrate a soul aspect sets into motion a consistent way to learn to surrender to the true you. You must choose love to reconnect your soul and to accept its power and presence. As you feel connected through your light-filled *Power Point Centers*, you will feel love beginning to grow and permeate your BEing. Each time that you allow the spiritual essence of your True Self to fill your spine, heart center, and soul, you are creating a new connection to God and a new structure to allow for the transcendence and release of your impressions, sanskaras, and ego mind.

Your true power is universal consciousness awakening as love. It is formed by reconnecting your Original and True Self with the consciousness of love and truth that you have known and experienced through thousands of lifetimes. Your true power is divine love that has awakened in your soul.

The integration of love in your Whole Self creates a new power. However, unlike a power that is created through attachment, vanity, self-centeredness, force, ego, and greed, your new power will feel expansive and in-sync with the universe. Your true power is not something used over anyone else to get what you want. Instead, it is the action of Spirit magnified to propel you through all of your life experiences with awareness, focus, love, and surrender.

"Spiritual advancement is emancipation from the bondage of sanskaras; it involves disentangling oneself from the false and, importantly, inviting the real into our BEing—opening to the truth within. This is in contrast to the psychological work of trying to get rid of our painful sanskaric patterns in order to create a pleasant existence in illusion—in other words, trying perhaps unwittingly to harmonize with our sanskaras."[4]

Healing Your Core Soul Wound

Each of us have experienced a level of emotional pain that originated from a past life, early childhood experience, or a moment of stress in utero or at birth, which we experienced through the ache of feeling separate from love and life, and which unconsciously became a belief system from that moment of separation on.

For each of us the story is different, but the outcome is the same. A decision that we made in a moment of intense emotional or mental pain gets carried in our cellular memory and restricts our life until it is cleared. Our cellular memory is a living energy residing in the energetic DNA of our causal (memory), emotional, and mental bodies and within our light grid. Our cellular memories are unique to each of us and have the power to create beliefs and judgments about ourselves and other's until we awaken the seeds of truth hiding within our consciousness. Embodying the seeds of your soul truth strengthen your conscious connection to Infinite Source. When you experience trauma your conscious connection to who you are can be distorted and you can disconnect from the light of your True Self. You may have been unwanted at conception or in utero in this lifetime. You may have been rejected by one or both parents. Your family of origin may have gone through a genocide. You may have experienced sexual abuse as a child. You may have been given up for adoption. In a previous incarnation you may have been burnt at

---
4 Effort and Grace, Darwin C. Shaw, 2005

SOUL CHALLENGES AND SOLUTIONS

the stake, beheaded, or exiled for being a holy woman or man teaching and standing in the light. You may have been wounded in battle as a warrior defending your people. You may have been a Native chief made to suffer as you watched your people being massacred. You may have been found guilty with or without a trial as a temptress, healer, and "evil doer" because you had direct connection with Infinite Source. You may have been a spy for the French Resistance in World War II who saved thousands of people's lives and captured and killed. You may have been abandoned, cast out, or exiled from all that you loved. You may have given away your power to a spiritual teacher who promised you love and more power only to have your life force stolen to empower him. You may have had to give up a child because you were a seer. You may have abused your power. You may have had to experience a pre-arranged marriage that turned into an abusive power struggle. You may have created a great work of art or music only to have it taken for someone else's fame. You may have experienced being of royalty and betraying your soul to fulfill the expectations placed upon you. You may have been falsely accused of a crime that you did not commit. You may have been hated for being a specific religion or race. You may have been forced to watch a family member being tortured. You may have lost a child. You may have mourned the loss of other's that you could not save. You may have betrayed your company, your nation, or your marriage. You may have chosen to become a false Master, a demi-God, and misused your power to run a country, a civilization, or religious order. You may have been left by a lover, which broke your heart. Such experiences have the power to create a Core Soul Wound.

Your greatest soul challenges are created in the moments that you split off from yourself in the most difficult of situations. In a moment of total despair, "you as soul" either chose to stay in the total light of who you are, remaining intact, or your mind chose to split off into an emotion and belief that spiraled you into the darkness of your dualistic nature and energetically have created your present dilemmas. A fearful part of you may have connected with the power found within a negative emotion, or you may have identified with an internal surge of energy from the darkness of your fear. Each time that you leave your light consciousness out of despair, fear, self-judgment, arrogance, or anger, you continue to create and embody pain and suffering.

Your human nature must go through its evolution of discovering both light and dark, separation and suffering, being asleep and awakening, until the moment that you move through the illusions of dualistic thinking. Over eons of time, you as an evolving soul and human being have explored both paths of light and dark. You've chosen to split off and live in separation and, at times, you've chosen healing and Oneness. You have judged, feared, and have doubted the light that you are, sometimes aligning your mind to the darkness of denial, and sometimes holding strong to the light within you. The remembrance of darkness and pain hold on within you alongside all of the moments that you chose to lift up into the radiance and God-lit consciousness of surrender and Oneness.

These remembrances have the power to catapult you forward into the holiness of the light within you. All aspects of you must be faced as you walk the path into your True Self. Becoming aware of *how* you have separated from your Original Self gives you the key to opening the door to your divine intelligence. The strength needed to open the door comes through clearing your sanskaras and choosing and following the love within you no matter how challenging. Love always takes you home. Always.

> *Your human nature must go through its evolution of discovering both light and dark, separation and suffering, being asleep and awakened, until the moment that you move through the illusions of dualistic thinking.*

As you choose to awaken and reconnect into the truth of who you really are, and forgive your self for living in a false, split or made-up reality, all is possible.

Here is a meditation to help you discover the interior story and original moment of your deepest split from your soul. Going through this soul opening experience will help you heal the cause of your biggest life challenges.

Whether you are struggling to reach your life goals, fulfill your heart's calling, create sustaining relationships, love unconditionally, step into financial abundance, let go of control, heal a serious health challenge, or just want to feel happy and whole, by doing this exercise at least twice a week over the course of two months, it will catapult your life forward. Repeat this exercise until you feel a new joy emanating from your heart. The light within your heart is the radiant healer that has the power to release your past hurts, guide you on your highest destiny path, align your Whole Self to BE who you really are, and reconnect you with God within your Self as your new "operational system" providing bliss, happiness, and abundance.

Healing Your Core Soul Wound Meditation

Sit on a cushion on the floor or in your favorite comfortable chair. Begin to breathe blue and gold light into your body. Taking your time, gaze into your heart center from a place of love. As you gaze into your heart center, look for radiant light. As you find it, continue to move your awareness deeper into the light within your heart. Gaze into the light within your heart center. Maintain your focus with your breath. Allow the light to grow as you enter into it with your full focus and attention.

When you are ready, ask your Higher Self or your spiritual inner master to come to assist the process. Ask for an image to be given to you of a situation in this lifetime or from a previous lifetime that you experienced an emotional reaction to. Look to see whether you cleared the emotion or not. Ask your Higher Self to show you the situation and what belief you concluded to, took on, and projected onto the situation, others and on to yourself. Feel in your heart where and how you split off from the light within yourself. Gaze with love through your reactions and look for the radiant and light-filled you beneath the emotionally charged or confused you.

With love, bring your focus deeper into the light within your heart. Release everything that is not "of love," and give yourself time to embrace any wounding within you. Stay in the frequency and dimension of this radiant love as you continue to open to any pain, anger, sadness, grief, etc. Choose the love to identify with and BE. Look directly through the emotions into the light within them. Give yourself the message to stay in your light. Practice not splitting off into the reactions. BE aware of staying centered in the radiant light within you.

Your focus helps you to connect to the light within your heart. Your desire to see, receive, and BE with the light in your heart opens up the portal within you to experience the grace and presence of your True Self.

Remember, the light within your heart is the radiant healer that has the power to release your past hurts, see who you really are, and trust the space of love that dwells as God within you.

Reconnect with the soul aspect that has been halted on its tracks within you. At first, you may not see him or her. It may feel stuck in time, glued to loss or sorrow, and possibly completely shut down from BEing in its conscious connection to Infinite Source. Hang in there until you make a connection with this soul aspect. Let this part of yourself know that you are there and gently, with patience, reach out through your love to its love. Know that the heart of your soul aspect is whole, and even though it has been buried in your subconscious, once liberated it has the ability to end the emotional, spiritual, and mental pain you have endured. It has hidden its light and power in the dark within itself until the moment you reached the point of understanding that in order to move forward, IT'S LIGHT and TRUTH HAD TO BE FOUND. Take your time in reconnecting with him or her. Know that he or she needs time and love to trust your connection. Keep returning to your soul aspect with an open heart and make it your first priority in your life. BE the flower and blossom. Attach yourself to the love within you. Trust it. Each day make a commitment to following the love.

When you feel complete with this exercise, bring your full attention into the *Sixth Soul Integration Center*. To find it, press your fingertip on the tip of your rib cage protrusion. Then slide your finger over the ridge and, as you ascend upwards towards your heart center, press into the four vertical hollows in between your ribs as you climb upwards to land in the hollow space in between the nipples in the center of your chest. Breathe and place your focus into this *Soul Integration Center*. Bring your shoulder blades together and extend your chest forward to feel it. Surrender your fear and resistance into the love within you and BE.

Practical Soul Challenges & Solutions

Every thought and every perception is intimately tied to the universal laws of creation. By trusting and letting go into the universal alignment of love and surrender within you, you can experience a direct connection and relationship with the eternal intelligence of the "everything and the nothing." When you slow everything down and invite your body and mind to let go and BE, you are able to sense, feel, and experience the stream of abundance that lives within you. Every path, every religion, has a different name for it. BEing in selfless service to the stream of Infinite Source light, power, and expression within you is all that is necessary. When your self-doubts, insecurities, and inner stories pull you away from the stream of awareness that flows through you, bring your focus back into the essence of your Self. Feel the peace, the prosperity of your soul, the love, passion, focus, determination, and promise to your Self to BE present to the whisperings of your heart.

As you expand into the ocean of Infinite Source within you and around you, create moments through your day to do nothing. Sit, close your eyes, focus into your heart, feel, and listen to your heartbeat. Feel the light within the earth move up through your feet into your lower belly. BE present with your breath. BE present to what you feel and just allow it all to BE. Then, ask your Self how you would like to show up in the moment. BE kind to your Self. BE gentle and listen. BE willing to make a new decision to support your Self to BE YOU.

Along the way, there are challenges that will emerge. Here are some helpful tips.

Challenges you may face along the way:

- **Challenge:** You may feel a bit disorientated at first while connecting to Spirit in your body. You may revert to being in your head and wonder if what you are attempting to do is "right."

Solution: BE for a moment and open your heart. Move light up from the center of the earth, through your feet, up your legs, and into your lower belly and solar plexus. Connect your focus into your solar plexus and then down into the space between your pubic bone and tailbone. Ground into your body, then trust the light flowing through you.

- **Challenge:** You may doubt that you have the courage, the tools, the patience, and the commitment to come back to your Self after leaving your Self.

   Solution: Ask from your heart for Infinite Source to bring you the courage, faith, and commitment needed to open when you may want to split off or close down. You can also access the strength, wisdom, and spiritual integrity of one of your newly discovered divine soul aspects and trust in its ability to guide you forward in your life.

- **Challenge:** You may come up against your patterns of how you accept or reject yourself.

   Solution: Choose to love yourself no matter what.

- **Challenge:** You may fight coming down into your body and want to stay in your head.

   Solution: Bring pure white light from above your head down into your heart center and breathe into your heart. Give a loving, brilliant, forgotten part of your soul a voice in the moment. Accept and honor its needs from your heart.

- **Challenge:** Your ego—the false protector within you, the one who keeps out all possibilities of having to give up its authority and position, may fight to stay in control.

  Solution: Thank it for its years of service to your life and give it a new job to do. Your protector may have placed itself in the position of being the relentless authority of control in your life. It may put you down and keep you feeling insecure about your capabilities to earn money, make your partner happy, and how you look. Perhaps it has protected you by keeping people at a distance to shield you from becoming hurt by others' insensitivities to who you are. Now you can tell your protector that you no longer empower it to block out life or keep you shut down and living in shame as a means to protect you. Instead, give it the new position of helping you to complete tasks or follow through in meeting deadlines in all aspects of your life. For example, it can ensure you get your oil changed in your car on time, go for your teeth cleaning, pay your car registration on time, remember your sister's birthday, prepare a document for a client, or remind you to renew your passport. Create the intention for your protector to protect you in practical and caring ways rather than blocking your evolutionary drive to be more self-expressed and joyful. It is up to you to end how you empower your ego Self to keep you disempowered and in self-doubt, or however you have created it to take the reins of your life. You can end how you keep it alive by no longer empowering its presence and existence in the same way.

- **Challenge:** You may have to face that at some level you treat yourself and others the same way that your parents and other authority figures in your early life treated you, whether positively or negatively.

Solution: Take responsibility for showing up for yourself with respect, honor, and loving kindness.

- **Challenge:** You may have to choose what aspect of yourself you want to identify with: the controller, the victim, the lover, the creator, the one in pain, the one who surrenders each thought and moment to Infinite Source, the one who wants to go beyond all fear, and heals and embraces their Whole Self.

  Solution: Identify only with what makes your heart open and gives you confidence, strength, and trust.

- **Challenge:** There may be times when you will feel that you cannot connect to yourself with love. There will be moments when you will wonder how to even find the love inside of you.

  Solution: Connect to the light flowing in from above your head into your body and allow it to flow into your *Solar Plexus—Fifth Power Point Center*. Then, reconnect into your *Lower Belly – Second Power Point Center* and *Solar Plexus—Fifth Power Point Centers* at the same time. This connection will always create a positive shift.

- **Challenge:** There may be times when you will feel emotional pain and not know what to do.

  Solution: If you accept and honor the most rejected part of yourself that is deep in your lower belly and in your heart center, you will come through the pain and into the light of your Self. Feel, express, and release the emotion with your breath and your intention to BE who you are.

- **Challenge:** There may be times when you will want to avoid your anger and deny its existence. Perhaps your anger was originally created because you separated from your core spiritual power, took on a false persona to please others, or experienced being rejected or betrayed for just BEing you. Beneath your anger lives a powerful life force energy that is directly connected to the Infinite Source of who you are. You find yourself identifying with your anger and rejecting the love within you.

   Solution: Feel the truth beneath your anger and accept and acknowledge it as a wayshower and teacher to the light within you. Acknowledge the anger and open to the power beneath the anger. Open to a new level of your soul's power.

- **Challenge:** You may find the thought of surrendering to a part of yourself that has appeared needy, weak, sad, angry, or resigned, almost unbearable. In truth, to surrender means that you are opening to allow this soul part to reconnect with your Whole Self and enter into a sacred relationship with you. When you truly surrender, you are receiving and empowering the part of your God Self that yearns to be seen, heard, received, and reconnected to.

   Solution: Accept yourself with zero judgment.

- **Challenge:** You will come to realize that you have not been living in your True Self, and you might feel sad.

  Solution: Shift into receiving and empowering the parts of your soul that yearn to be in your life, for they will give you back the joy you seek. Open to feeling, seeing and receiving their love within your heart.

More Solutions:

While it is easy to get caught up in daily living and BEing, focus on mastering a soul practice or meditation until you feel like you've "gotten it." Remember these helpful enlightening actions to support your swift progression along your life path:

- The personality Self cannot be perfect. Our alignment with Infinite Source is the only perfection. Just BE.

- If you find yourself comparing your self to others, stop. Breathe. BE.

- Stay with the aspect of your soul that has not been paid attention to or was not allowed to energetically exist in your family or early life. Acknowledge it and then allow it to exist.

- Choose to find the love in everything around and in you.

- BE willing to feel the energies in your *First and Second Power Point Centers*. Receive light from the center of the earth and draw it up into the space between your pubic bone and tailbone. Allow the light to build.

- BE willing to release and let go of how you have held on to control as the way you have managed your life.

- BE willing to be real with yourself. Say what you feel to yourself. Then, find the "truth voice" underneath the feeling. Empower this voice.

- Stop abandoning yourself. BE present with your Self.

- Stay in yourself with whatever age your soul part reveals itself to you to be and check in with it many times a day until the two of you remain reconnected.

- Introduce the parts of your Soul Self to one another during a meditation.

- Practice staying energetically connected to your solar plexus, inside your navel, your lower belly, and the space between your tailbone and pubic bone.

- Remain accepting and non-judgmental of yourself and others.

- As you open your heart and bring your focus into your heart, you will have greater access to all of you.

- Practice thinking from the union of two *Power Point Centers* at the same time: Third eye and lower belly; heart center and pubic bone/tailbone; back of the skull and pubic bone; and the navel and soles of your feet, throat center and creation point, solar plexus and root center. When you bring together two *Power Point Centers*, "BE" with both points at the same time. They will awaken and align your energy field, and integrate your body and soul.

- Practice being with yourself and be aware when you leave the connections in your body. Just decide to come back into your heart, solar plexus and root center when you leave.

- BE aware of how you control the environment around you to feel in control. Make a new choice to let go into yourself and to receive your feelings. BE with yourself.

- Allow yourself to "not know" and to BE willing to become friends with the unknown.

- Practice bringing light into your body and identify with the light and how it makes you feel. Send light into the places that feel stuck, frozen, and disconnected within your body. Allow the light to flow through you in streams of energetic aliveness.

- Keep your heart open to yourself and practice discernment when you are in a group situation. Practice being aware of losing yourself in other people's energies and situations. When you stay in your solar plexus, you will be less likely to take on or move into another person's energies.

- Spend quiet and alone time a few times a week. Begin to speak to the universe as a co-creator, someone who is here to serve and work in the highest good for everyone concerned.

- Bring in gold and white light into the center of your head and then pour it into your third eye. Think of your third eye as a portal of light. Invite the aspect of your soul that could not come into your body at birth to come in now. Feel its presence and invite it into your heart.

- Get creative. Write; create music, clothes, paintings, drawings, pies, cakes, raw food, a new soup, or take on a new community project. Volunteer to help others. Teach a teenager a new trade. Plant a tree. Collect seeds to start a garden. Learn about something new each week. Refuse to become bored. Find the beauty in life and embrace the small gifts and wonders that the universe presents every moment.

- Invite in all parts of your soul from past lives that have not yet been ready to come forth into the present moment. Fill yourself with the blue light of Infinite Source to assist these powerful and loving aspects of yourself to reconnect with your heart. Open to their wisdom, gifts, guidance and discernment.

REMEMBER:

- The purpose of becoming *One in Soul* is to heal the soul separations that block you from living in abundance, peace, greater connection, and joy.

SOUL CHALLENGES AND SOLUTIONS

- The inner warfare between your soul aspects that have not yet surrendered to higher love creates your pain and suffering.

- Connecting your soul aspects in your solar plexus and heart center through the light will free you from self-controls and open you to love.

- Each of us has a Core Soul Wound that is the gateway to our soul's karmic completion.

- To heal your wound requires suspending judgment and condemnation and releasing the pain, grief, fear, resentment, and anger within your heart. The light within your heart is the radiant healer.

- The sanskaras or impressions you hold from this lifetime and past lifetimes within your Bodymind matrix can begin to be cleared through accessing your inner light as you reconnect your soul aspects.

- Each time that you allow the spiritual essence of your True Self to fill your body and core container through your *Power Point Centers*, your spine, heart center, and soul, you are creating a new connection to God and a new structure to allow for the transcendence and release of your impressions and ego mind.

- Your true power is universal consciousness awakening as love. It is formed by reconnecting your Original and True Self with the consciousness of love and truth that you have known and experienced through hundreds or thousands of lifetimes.

- Practice the *Healing your Core Soul Wound Meditation* at least once a week for two months to feel a new joy coming from your heart.

- Review the challenges and solutions within this chapter whenever you feel stuck or unsure about what you are feeling or your direction. BE willing to stay aware, open, and receptive and embrace what is within you with love.

BELIGHT MEDITATION

Transforming Fears

STEP 1

Begin by sitting in a comfortable position, either in a chair or sitting in a cross-legged lotus position on a mat on the floor. Place your hands on your knees, palms facing up and through your nose slowly and steadily. Inhale for 8 counts, hold for 8 counts, exhale for 8 counts. Do this 8 times.

Now, inhale quickly, pulling the air into your nostrils and exhale quickly, pushing the air out of your nostrils. "Pant" in and out of your nostrils, lips slightly touching, increasing the rhythm. Do this 8 times. Repeat the whole sequence 4 times.

STEP 2

Call in the aspect of your soul that sees what others may not, that finds freedom through connecting to music, nature, yoga, sports, family, etc., and yearns for full expression. Allow this aspect of your Self to come up and be felt, acknowledged, and received. Give the reins of your life to this aspect of yourself and follow its lead. Put your faith and trust in its desire to break through the confines and limitations of your life. Feel its desire to love and open to becoming One with its love, life force energies, and passion. Open to the waves of love in your heart. Surrender into your breath. Practice each day until your connection happens spontaneously and naturally. Return to Step 1, and complete with a few rounds of the breathing sequence.

CHAPTER EIGHTEEN

Light Awakens Your Whole Self

*"My first memory is of light—
the brightness of light—light all around."*
— Georgia O'Keeffe

Light as the Awakener

Your soul has always been One with Infinite Source.
Your soul is a divine spark of God and
speaks the language of Love.
Your soul has the capacity to remember all of your past
adventures and journeys while being on planet Earth.
You have been taught to forget this.

By denying the existence of our soul, we as individuals and as a world collective have excommunicated from the part of ourselves that is God. For it is through the soul that the longing to know God and to open to the love that is beyond all suffering is found.

Your soul is the perfect aspect of God—Infinite Source that is given the opportunity to evolve and to remember it Self, just by existing. In a past lifetime, or at some point in this lifetime, in order to protect your heart and soul's light you separated from your Original Self. You came into this lifetime with plenty of hurts, wounds, and a laundry list of past sufferings that are easy to carry into your life without even knowing or wanting them. Our collective amnesia is not an unexpected experience. Over the past 2,500 years, the remembrance, experience, and existence of our soul as a fully integrated and direct expression of God Source has been removed from our world religions, history, and governing bureaucracies. Religions had good intentions by their "founders" but were often turned into belief systems by their followers that ended up separating people from their ability to connect with their inner True Self—their God Self directly. Those individuals who lived in direct connection with God—Infinite Source were often killed, exiled, and tortured. As a global culture, we have been expected and taught to live in separation and abandon our abilities to have a direct connection to God Divine.

Yet, existing within the essence of all world religions and spiritual paths is humanity's shared soul experience.

Together we are united in this sometimes challenging and earth quaking experience of opening up, letting go, and being birthed into a new level of light, infinite love, and authentic power. The teachings and belief systems that have brought us here have been perfect for the times they were created to serve. Religious beliefs of the past served the consciousness and needs of the masses of their time. The rituals and ceremonies from those times no longer have the power to lift humanity into the new frequencies needed to move forward. Our present global culture has new spiritual needs. As our consciousness is lifted up to evolve into higher expressions of our divine connection with Infinite Source, our present energetic matrix is shifting from being aligned to duality and reactionary models of conflict into a fractal matrix of Oneness. In the new fractal matrix, all dimensions of our awakening are experienced through pure consciousness—One light, love, and power—without separation—through our hearts. We become able to navigate our lives through maintaining a conscious connection to BEing One with our Whole Self. It is a feeling of BEing connected to the light within all of life in every moment. The brain, nervous system, energy bodies, physical, emotional, memory, etheric, and spiritual bodies are functioning as One unit. The egoic system that perpetuates the mind functioning in separations cannot survive in Oneness. The moments of giving away our power, denying our power, and living from our false Self can no longer work to solve the enormous challenges of these times. Love alone is the only power that can keep humanity on track. The power needed to uplift our world and one another is found only through illuminated love—authentic power.

> *In the new fractal matrix of Oneness, all dimensions of our awakening are experienced through pure consciousness—One light, love, and power—without separation.*

As humanity makes it through these times of separation and pain, we are embarking upon the new physics of BEing One with life. Creating life from Oneness puts into perspective a new way of integrating money, stability, creativity, health, family, education, politics, science, business, health, relationships, and happiness. As we expand into the awareness of being multi-faceted and multi-dimensional human beings, we can become quantum human beings—fully alive and activated as our Whole Self.

Within your consciousness and the DNA cellular memories of all that you have experienced throughout eternity lives the original spark and divine expression of You. The ability to be *One in Soul* will help you move through and release the old beliefs, habits, and judgments that you have created and lived by, and give you the courage and strength to step into the miracles of transformation that await you. BEing *One in Soul* helps your consciousness open to light and reconnect into the primal remembrance of your soul purpose. Whether you are a healer, leader, creative, visionary, entrepreneur, teacher, parent, director, guide, selfless servant, catalyst, friend, lover, dreamer, adventurer, team player, nurturer, coordinator, facilitator, mediator, innovator, inventor, researcher, bridge of light, financial or business wiz, brain stormer, social saint, loving partner, problem solver, systems change agent, manager, activist, public servant, builder, engineer, coach, initiator, implementer, integrator, or a combination of these, you will find the inner juice and vitality of your soul by unifying your mind and body in Oneness.

> *Creating life from Oneness puts into perspective a new way of integrating money, stability, creativity, health, family, education, politics, science, business, health, relationships, and happiness.*

When your soul is united in your body, your mind has a place to rest. Your body is the ultimate temple for the soul to discover, celebrate and express its existence. As your mind accepts the reality of your body and soul being unified, you have the opportunity to become synchronistic with time, space, and universal consciousness.

All of the lifetimes that make you who you are in this very moment have been experiences to help you grow closer to the infinite expression of Source that is within you. All of your lifetimes have been a dance with the polarities of light and dark—love and fear. This dance moves you in and out of the state of Oneness. Realize that your mind and body only split to the degree that you believe you are separate from Infinite Source. You choose your responses to every situation, and your responses are what create your karmas.

> *Realize that your mind and body only split to the degree that you believe you are separate from Infinite Source.*

Our soul is connected in every moment to Oneness, but our minds are sometimes the last to "get it." All of us have in common, whether consciously or unconsciously, the fragmentations of the world because we want to help the world evolve into its wholeness. We are intimately connected to the earth and are happiest when we are One with the creative essence and stillness that comes from BEing consciously connected to the divine feminine essence of her beauty and power. The earth is already whole and is the teacher for humanity to learn how to know and honor wisdom. When we become One and whole with our own hearts, only then can we hear and feel the earth and serve her by becoming an instrument of love and peace in our own lives, with others, and in the world. The peace that we create from within can be gifted to the world in our own unique and individualized ways. At times, it takes enormous faith and trust to want to do the work to awaken. We fear losing what we have, yet when we let go and surrender, we are given the treasures of the divine and initiated into true freedom and abundance.

> *All of us have in common, whether consciously or not, taken on the fragmentations of the world because we want to help the world evolve into wholeness.*

Imagine for a moment resolving your inner battles within your Self for the benefit of all beings. Imagine ending the wars within you, and creating peace within your Self. Can you embrace for a moment how powerful it would be to express peace in your life rather than your unresolved inner wars? We live in a world of duality, and all of us have the challenge of ending our attachments to how our mind controls through creating fear, and reacting to fear. As you become *One in Soul*, you have the opportunity and new momentum to discover, and implement new ways of leading, serving, and uplifting humanity. The sole purpose of the *One in Soul* work is to give people a direct way to end being the effect of their own inner war, which is always the cause for their own suffering, denial, and fear. When enough of us shift out of the frequency of separation and inner battle, we can create, and implement new approaches, systems, and models for business, finance, the arts, education, politics, social justice, leadership and global unity. Rather than leading through hate, separation, fear, and ego, humanity will be able to step through the veils of sorrow, injustice, pain and suffering into soul Oneness.

As your soul is ignited and awakened, you will remember the soul qualities of yourself that have been dormant for lifetimes. Integrating the truth of who you are helps you to BE present in the now, while giving you the opportunity to step out of separation and fear into Oneness and love.

The more that you let go of examining what is wrong with yourself and with your life and instead open to the light and power within yourself, the easier it becomes to move forward on your life path and soul destiny.

As the love within you begins to overflow, incredible joy and compassion for your life and for the world burst forth. As your heart opens, you may feel a surge of enormous emotion well up within your heart for the planet and for all of her inhabitants. Your truth will shine through your tears, blessing your life with healing, inspired action, and relationships that bring you endless joys. You will feel the love in your heart and soul overflow into your body to support and guide you to accomplish what you came here to BE and give in this lifetime.

God Unifying in the Body

Your Original Self is revealed through restoring and unifying the light of God in your Bodymind, heart, and soul. This reunion gives you the strength, courage, and clarity to move through your biggest life challenges and to live your dreams by BEing who you are. It is the catalyst and fuel for your expansion as a human and divine being. Light is the force of momentum that advances your evolutionary unfoldment into Oneness.

The essence of your soul exists as light and always knows love. The truth of who you are lives in the light that you are. The greater the light that you discover and integrate from your soul—the greater the clarity and vitality experienced in your Whole Self. Your light propels you through the hurdles and obstacles that present themselves on your life path. Light reconnects your body and mind into the love within your soul and reignites the full remembrance of that love. Light unifies the power of your creativity, spirituality, and physicality. Dropping your beliefs and stories that prevent you from believing that you are light reveals the truth of your essence and empowers you to embrace and live your soul's destiny path and purpose.

> **Light is the force of momentum that advances your evolutionary process into Oneness.**

When the light moves into the cellular level of the heart, mind, and soul, suffering on a human level can be transformed into universal understanding. You find yourself moving past your human limitations into divine connection and compassion. Remember that the purpose of this work is to liberate you into the full expression of your true essence. The truth of who you are is found by clearing the cellular memories within your body and choosing to see, feel, and be in the divine truth of who you really are. Through the darkness within you, the eternal blazing light that you are is found.

As you experience BEing your Whole Self, remember that your greatest weaknesses are not in your soul. Each moment that your mind reacts from being in separation from your God Mind, it creates a barrier or layer of disconnection within you. This separation to life creates a vault of emptiness, arrogance, greed, hatred, and self-preservation and inhibits the free flow of light and love within you.

> **The truth of who you are is found by clearing the cellular memories within your body and choosing to see, feel, and be in the divine truth of who you really are.**

Your mind will always create "a story" that helps it to deal with the separation it has created and wants to maintain. It grasps onto anything and everything to rationalize its existence, to be filled, and to feel safe and secure. Only when your mind has been guided by your higher Self to let go of its outer attachments and its perceptions can it begin to grasp the truth of your soul and feel the entryway into the God Body of breath and light that is within your physical and energetic light grid. As your body opens to receive the light of divine intelligence, it remembers how to trust its natural connection to Infinite Source. Your mind is then able to surrender, listen, receive, and BE.

If you sit in meditation or contemplation for moments or hours, or just take the time to BE with yourself and become aware of your beliefs, you will discover how the mind and body habitually create conflict with one another. Their struggle to stand alone and separate from conscious connection with Infinite Source creates your suffering. Your body and mind will align with the ego and all of its stories until you choose to identify with your God Self over your ego Self. As you choose to be directed by your soul and release the habitual thought patterns of how your mind directs you, long sought after solutions to your life problems are revealed as you trust your Self.

By engaging the channel of light from your solar plexus down into your root center, a veil is removed from your mind, and a gateway is opened into your deeper power. When you connect the light streaming from your solar plexus into your root center, a portal of well-being opens that increases the strength of your core Self.

Once you feel the connection from your solar plexus into your root center, include your lower belly into your energetic "trinity." Focus your attention into BEing in these three centers at the same time. You can ground, anchor, and integrate your higher energies in your body by BEing One in your root center

(*First Power Point Center*), your lower belly (*Second Power Point Center*), and your solar plexus (*Fifth Power Point Center*). When the mind is united with light, it thinks and perceives differently. You no longer feel separate from yourself or life. Your mind no longer has the ability to block your true calling and intuitive power. Each time that you allow greater light to come into your Whole Self, you create a momentum to evolve and move forward.

> **When your body remembers how to trust its natural connection to Infinite Source, your mind is able to listen, receive, and BE.**

When the Source of life is awakened within your consciousness, you understand that your body is a precious temple and home for your soul in this lifetime, while also being a temporary dwelling place of conscious evolution. Once you are connected to your soul's truth in your body, the next levels of realization, integration, and alignment in Infinite Source can occur. Your soul is always speaking the language of light and will guide you to awaken. As the light is ignited in all of your cells, a new DNA of joy, vision, and clarity can be birthed.

As you come into the light within your body, the presence of your Whole Self fills you with its radiant wisdom. You will feel love permeate your BEing that is a continual source of wisdom and nurturance. Your lower mind, through your own efforts, will surrender to your higher mind, which is the will of God. Your heart begins to live in a state of surrender to the greater plan of Infinite Source for you, while you are consciously co-creating with the path of your soul. Your greater purpose is rediscovered through aligning to the light within you. Its divine intelligence guides you through the battles of your egoic mind and its fears.

LIGHT AWAKENS YOUR WHOLE SELF

The light unifies your life force, energy bodies, and higher universal mind, while integrating the love and power of your soul. Your soul already knows why it came into this life. Your souls connection with Infinite Source created the life challenges, gifts, and successes needed to help you to become Self realized prior to your birth. Your soul will tell you why it is here. To strengthen your connection to finding and living in your soul purpose, take a moment to connect into your Creation Point. To review, your Creation Point is about 2.5 inches directly below your navel. Bring your awareness into your Creation Point and breathe 5 long and deep inhalations and exhalations in through your nose and out of your mouth into the lumbar vertebras (your lower spine vertebras, including your sacrum, directly across from your Creation Point). Drop your mind into your Creation Point and let go of your thinking mind. Feel your lower back growing wider as you breathe long and deep. BE with the energies of your Creation Point and meditate into your breath, allowing the flow of divine grace and wisdom to move into all of the cells in your body. BE still.

As you "think" from your Creation Point, you will align to the generator and storage tank of life force energy in your body that will strengthen your connection to your higher wisdom and power. By mentally connecting into your Creation Point, you will feel supported to BE the essence of who you are in every situation in your life.

> *Your purpose is always revealed as you integrate the spiritual power and love of your soul.*

Fulfilling your soul's calling may mean you have to shift how you think, where you live, who you work for, who you live with, how you engage sexually, how you treat other's or what you eat. Bodymind-soul reconnection does not necessarily require that you change everything about your life, but you may inevitably take the steps that come to you from your connection with Infinite Source and make some important changes. By honoring the voice of your soul, you honor your Higher Self and will make the right choices for yourself. Your soul will give you the ingredients to recreate your life no matter where you presently find yourself. The ultimate key to your breakthroughs originate from where you come from in yourself, when and how you ask yourself your inner questions, and how you show up to serve Infinite Source in your daily activities.

Whether you are planting a garden, sweeping the floor, creating a salad, fixing a roof, writing a new corporate or political policy, changing a diaper, sitting at your computer, helping your child with their homework, sharing a difficult feeling with your partner, being on Facebook, cooking dinner, or doing the laundry—BE One with the moment and with your heart. Enter into the light within yourself. Place your focus into the core shaft of light in your spine and breathe. Let it be the foundation of support from which you live your life. Anchor your awareness into the light within your heart. Choose the light over your thoughts and stories about yourself and others. Be aware of where and how you split off and leave your Self. Be aware of going into your head and obsessing over a thought.

When you split off into following a random thought in your mind, bring yourself back to the light within your heart center. See a diamond of light in your heart and move your mind into the diamond. Then, reconnect your focus from your heart center with the light within your solar plexus, Creation Point, and root center. You grow and expand where your attention goes. Where you focus your attention opens the gateway into your truth. BE present with your intention. What do you want to create? Joy, peace, love, true abundance on all levels, trust, courage, fulfillment, contribution, fearlessness, leadership, clarity, innovation, truth? What attribute vibrates your wholeness and full sense of Self? Commit to let go of anything that is a diversion to what you really want to create. As you align into the light, you can fully align into Oneness. Choose what you want to align with. You have the power to choose. The more you end how you deceive or deny yourself, the easier it will be to live fully connected in your Bodymind and soul. Lift up. Rise up into your highest frequency of BEing You.

To assist in the evolutionary process of reuniting your Bodymind and soul, these spirit gateways will support you in fully stepping into your light:

- Clear your false beliefs about your relationship with God—Infinite Source.

- Become aware of ancestral programming, attitudes, fixations, dogmas, and contracts that you have taken on and to which you have become attached. Make a choice to ground into a zone of neutrality and non-judgment in your mind. Let go and give over to Infinite Source your old ways of seeing, feeling, and believing.

- Clear divine feminine and masculine projections, beliefs, and "cover ups" that have prevented and stopped your process of liberation and reunion with Infinite Source.

- Release physical and emotional blockages into the light of Infinite Source, which will clear, renew, and energize you.

- Understand how you separate the dark and light in your body and psyche. Learn to embrace what is dark within yourself and find the light within the dark to transmute your energies into whole consciousness.

- Find and accept the love within you that resides under your protections, armor, and rigidities.

- Become willing to let go in the moment of anything blocking you from being the light that you really are.

- Actively choose to heal your heart.

As you step into your Whole Self presence, remember the following *Power Point Center* connections:

- Your open heart center—your *Sixth Power Point Center*—will become your built-in wayshower as you trust being in your body and feeling the wholeness of your Integrated Self guide you in new ways in your everyday life. As you bring your mind into your heart, you will go beyond your self-doubts, limitations, and fears. See from your heart.

- Your solar plexus—your *Fifth Power Point Center*—serves to maintain your connection between your body and soul. If you are trying to make a decision about something, or desire to hear your inner voice, drop your mind into your solar plexus. You will find balance and peace. BE centered.

- Your navel—your *Fourth Power Point Center*—will bring you into the moment. By dropping your mind into your navel, you will feel connected to who you are and the connectedness of life itself. Trust your connection to Infinite Source.

- Your Creation Point—your *Third Power Point Center*—will align your mind into the Source of Oneness in your body. When you let go of trying to get your needs met and instead BE centered in your Creation Point, life brings to you what you need. Ground into BEingness.

- Your lower belly—your *Second Power Point Center*—when unified, will ground you to BE One with your personal power, fearlessness, creativity, and life force energies. When your mind and your lower belly connect, you can embrace change, heal your body, and release the blockages that cause self-doubt and indecision.

- Your root center—*First Power Point Center* (located in between your pubic bone and tailbone)—when unified with your mind, awakens and clears your sexual energies, facilitates health and longevity, dissipates fear, heals your emotional body, grounds your life purpose, and reveals the spiritual realization of your hidden gifts. Know your Self.

Fueling Your Inner Connection

All of life is made up of light. For many of us, our cells have become accustomed to being denied the vibrational power of light. When you send light into your body, you may also want to bring in sound. Sound resonates to light. So, when a sound vibration is chanted into the cellular "heart" of Spirit in your body, its frequencies will open what is in the dark and transmute the matter into light. Sing or chant a vibrational sound such as "ah," "eee," "ong," "hum," "hung," or "hu" into the cells of your body and into the space in between your cells. Stay connected to the light within your core shaft—your sushumna—as you chant. BE ONE with Infinite Source through all of your *Power Point Centers*. BE present to staying present in your Original Self as you open with sound. Stay connected to the light within you.

When you begin to resonate sound in your body, you will feel it transform fear and negativity immediately. Feeding your body with healthy nutrients, sounds, tones, and the power of light will fuel your inner connection and expansion. If you prefer to solely focus on the light alone, know that your total union with the light will heal everything. The light will go deep and open old emotion or belief systems that hold you back. The light will give you back yourself, and the light will open up the ancient memories within you that remind you who you are and what you are here for in this life. The light will expose your darkness and also BE the One that is able to heal the split between your dark and light. The light assists you in remembering who you are and in BEing who you are.

Igniting True Power through Light

The recognition and awakening of your soul essence found within your sushumna—your core shaft of light—invites your Higher Self, the eternally loving and guiding you, to integrate energetically on a cellular level in your body.

As the light of love increases within you, your ego is unable to maintain its grip, your mind becomes unable to live from fear, and your heart becomes unable to stay closed. Living in union bridges light and dark and cracks through your veils of illusion. While in your past, you may have embraced theories and concepts about understanding or believing in God, this profound pathway creates a direct highway into feeling and BEing One with God—Infinite Source.

Always trust that your soul ultimately knows what it wants and will guide you as you allow it to. As you connect into the light and unite your mind and body, you will be able to move through dualism—the split between what you think and what to believe is real and what actually is. Your lens of perception shifts from identifying with illusion and fear into BEing One with your higher and multi-dimensional energies in your body. BEing deeply anchored in your energetic light grid gives you a new support from which to live life. You are able to live through your heart and experience the full vibrational resonance of your unique essence and soul design.

The light awakening in your body cracks open the truth of who you are. When you follow the light within, it supports you to end how you energetically repress your spiritual power and helps give birth to a new power within you. As the light ignites the infinite love within you, natural resistance may arise. The old power matrix within you will hold on to thinking and doing things to keep you in a comfort zone and in control. It will work hard to have you stay subservient to its arrogance and seductions. Realize that your old power lives as fear within your body. It was originally created by your ego as a way for your unrealized soul aspects to survive. Your soul aspects and ego have only known how to function through reactivity and control. Your soul reconnection with the light changes that dynamic.

> *Light is the magnificence of love magnified*
> *beyond what is imaginable.*

Give over to the light everything that you hold onto or cannot change. Letting go is essential to live in self-forgiveness. By letting go, you give to Infinite Source your thoughts about yourself without judgment. You accept yourself for who you are in your body. As you release what holds you back and offer it over to Infinite Source—the Infinite gives you back a 360-degree perspective that empowers you to awaken. Ironically, it is through facing your life challenges with love and self-forgiveness that a deeper relationship with Infinite Source is created. When you forgive you are giving to Infinite Source what you no longer need to carry by your Self. When you forgive you allow the Infinite to fill the spaces within you that were filled with your hurts, angers, and resentments. To forgive is a state of BEing. By forgiving you honor your own truth and existence. Through forgiveness you discover who you are because you are freeing your Self to BE. Forgiveness is the action of freeing your Self to BE love. The love of your True Self is given and received for your Whole Self. Forgiveness is a state of BEing that only happens when we align to our highest state of love. By forgiving you receive the grace, truth and unconditional love that is the voice of your soul. Forgiveness opens the gateways to love.

By inviting into your body, and especially into your solar plexus and heart centers, the penetrating white and gold light of Infinite Source, you will clear the old power that fuels your fear and blockages, and keeps you "walled in and small." By asking the universe for guidance from your heart center—you will always be shown.

The difficulties and challenges that come up in your life are meant to be teachers; things you learn from and then let go of. As you welcome, accept, and surrender to the infinite love that is the divine expression of you and Infinite Source in union, the unique qualities of your light can manifest in every area of your life.

As your ego mind lets go and surrenders to "running the show of your life" and instead follows how the love within your soul leads you, you will come through the battles between your mind and soul. It is important to know what part of yourself is leading you. Whoever leads, whether the controls and fears of your ego, or the love of your heart and soul, the outcomes in your life are your choice. The battles between your ego mind and heart are resolved by trusting the voice of the universal infinite love within you. The part of you that wants to block you from BEing the light that you are—your ego Self—begins to lose its grip.

As you identify your ego Self, give it a new job to do and choose to stop giving it the energy and the attention to exist. Depending upon your own unique evolution, your ego may habitually jump in and exert its control, but by restructuring your relationship to your ego, and not feeding it, you can begin to build the strength and core of your enlightening Self through taking responsibility for following the path of love and service. When you stop enabling your ego's role of being the know-it-all, the martyr, the judge, the victim, the bully, the humiliator, the controller, the doubter, the manipulator, the fake, etc, your True Self is able to emerge and lead your life with success.

The key to your happiness is choosing what part of your Self you will follow. When you follow the voice of your truth, your ego Self cannot hold on. When you are ready, through God's graces, your ego will dissolve, deflate, and fall away like a scab on your body, leaving you with the fresh new skin of Oneness that, at first, is tender to the touch. Then, as the new layers of your confidence emerge by BEing the voice of your soul's truth, you will be ready to create your life from being a conscious Creator with Infinite Source to manifest your life purpose with joy in your life and in the world.

Facing Your Mind's Fear

Fear lives in the gap between your mind and body and is created by the level of separation in your perception and infinite consciousness.

Fear takes up space in the solar plexus, heart, and lower belly. When these three centers are blocked in fear, the throat center is also blocked. Once the light is liberated within your energetic matrix, you will feel and speak your truth.

To unblock the light in your throat center, we are going to open the channels of your higher *Power Point Centers*.

Begin to chant AUM by pronouncing the Ah and resonate the sound into your throat center, your *Seventh Power Point Center*. Bring your focus into your heart center, your *Sixth Power Point Center* and resonate the sound U as OOO. Then, bring your focus into the upper palate of your mouth and resonate the sound MMM. Energetically release all thoughts and consciously merge with the resonance of each sound. Pay close attention to the final MMM sound in your upper palate, allowing the sound to travel up through the top of your skull. AH-OOO-MMM.

The most important focus when working with sound is to keep your internal attention on Infinite Source, the ALL, the ONE, the Source of all Life. Practice staying with and in your Original Self through your heart center. BE in the love. If you find your mind separating from your life force energies in your body, bring your focus back to them. Feel the connection. BE in the connection. True meditation brings you closer to your Self, not further away. Rest.

Next, we are going to open a highway of pure golden light from Infinite Source into your third eye, your *Ninth Power Point Center*. Begin by connecting with the light in your solar plexus, lower belly, and heart centers. In your mind's eye, your third eye, create a window that is located directly diagonal of your forehead, by approximately 45 degrees. Allow the window to open and focus upon a steady stream of sunshine flowing into your third eye, melting away all resistance. As the light flows into your third eye, just relax and breathe, exhaling away all tensions. After you feel filled and opened, allow the light to move into your heart and solar plexus and be in its radiant glow.

As you reconnect into the light and love within you, your body, feelings, and mind are awakened, giving you a permanent initiation with Infinite Source. As you practice staying connected into Infinite Source, you are filled with a wellspring of true power. The Infinite Source within you starts out as a distant and unknown power, but over time becomes the center from which you reside. It eventually becomes your home.

Remember, your true power is divine love experienced as pure creation energy; it is the source of all life, connected into your body through the divine union of divine masculine and feminine energies. Its pure wellspring of consciousness will touch you from within. However, it is up to you how you will ultimately choose to receive this power, where you will direct its energies, and how willing you will be to go deep into its currents and become One with its transforming presence. Just as a river carves the rock layers of a canyon, so does the power of Infinite Source sculpt through the layers of your mind, heart, and soul to reveal your Original Self.

> *Fear is just a thought, a perception created from the mind believing it is the center of its own existence.*

As the light of your soul increases in your consciousness, you will be able to move through many of the fears that have blocked your abilities to BE One with life. Each time that you experience the feeling of being connected to your soul aspects, remember the feeling. Memorize it in your mind and body. Each time your heart bursts open in joy, remember the feeling and hold the space to open a little bit more into Infinite Source. Enjoy the feelings and experience what thoughts or attitudes need to be released to be able to bring this new opening and awakening into each moment. It is similar to practicing an instrument, learning a song, practicing a martial art, or learning to paint or to dance. Stay consistent with your practice of BEing in the light.

You will want to care for your body and treat it as a sacred temple. You will want to understand with enormous compassion the expanded role that your body plays for your spiritual evolution. By aligning with Infinite Source, you will need to face the ways that you turn against your Self by turning against your body. Instead of disconnecting to your body, you will establish a new connection to your whole Self and to the consciousness, thoughts, feelings, and healing light that are constantly evolving through your relationship with Infinite Source. When you are *One in Soul* and in conscious connection with Infinite Source, you may feel a surge of gold light filling your body and a direct knowingness that you no longer need to empower your mind to control you. As you open to and receive the light within your *Power Point Centers*, you will feel the barriers to yourself and to life dissolve. You will no longer need to protect yourself by blocking out love, life, or guidance from the greater divine intelligence within you. When the ego is diminished, realization happens by it Self.

Building an Inner Container of Light

When you create an energetic container of light you are able to discern your needs, stay connected to your True Self, live through your own connection with Infinite Source, maintain healthy boundaries with others, build and sustain your life force energies in your body, strengthen your magnetic field, maintain a healthy polarity between your masculine and feminine energies, and balance the forces of resistance and surrender within you.

As the essence of your soul begins to reunite within the heart-mind of your body, you need a container of light to be able to access your True Self. When the life force energies and spiritual power of your soul aspects are reconnected in your body, you need a way to hold their frequencies.

When your container is strong you can ignite, realize and implement your life purpose with greater ease, grace, and momentum. You can create sustainable higher love by having a container of light within your body.

An inner container is an expanded space within your body that stabilizes the frequency of the light of your soul. It resonates in your body as a vibration of life force energy. You will see it as a translucent vessel, oval, goblet, sphere, cave, well, or bowl. It can be built by directing the light from within your *Power Point Centers* into a "living energetic container of love. The *One in Soul* experience naturally creates your heart center to become a container. Your heart center opens to receive the aspects of your soul that have awakened to love through the BE practices and meditations. By expanding your container into your solar plexus, navel, lower belly, and into the pubic bone-tailbone space, you will feel grounded, creative, and present. Past attachments to others, and from them to you, can be cleared.

Within you is an energetic body that is seen as an oval of light. It extends from the space in between your pubic bone and tailbone, moves up through your lower belly, your creation point, navel, solar plexus, heart center, throat center, and third eye and fills the space around and through the length of your spine. By creating a container, you are allowing your spiritual energies to become One with the light energies in your body. The energies of your *Power Point Centers* are safely protected in this cocoon. Creating a container serves the very important function of rooting the power and light of higher frequencies and your Higher Self in your body. It provides the space for you to be integrated and balanced. Creating an inner container of light helps you to grow and develop your personal connection with the divine, hold the frequency of your True Self, feel energetically protected, and feel confident, connected and happy. Creating an inner container restores the circuitry damaged through trauma, abuse, neglect, judgment, fear and emotional pain. It provides a matrix for Infinite Source to meet in your body and lift you up into the bliss of your soul.

Oval of Love

Close your eyes and visualize a translucent oval that fills the space between your third eye, throat center, heart center, solar plexus, navel, creation point, lower belly, and the space between your pubic bone and tailbone. Invite in a color to fill it, and bring your focus inside the oval. Fill the oval with your love.

Invite a soul aspect of your Self to step into the oval. Some examples could include an angelic soul aspect, an infant aspect who felt abandoned and alone, an awakened, angry, confused or happy pre-teen or teen soul aspect, an ignored or unseen five-year-old, a seven-year-old puppet or "doll" for needy relatives, a determined to succeed nine-year-old aspect, a ten-year-old aspect shut down by parents who violated and ignored personal space and needs (a home life without stable boundaries), a twelve-year old soul aspect who was inappropriately touched by an alcoholic relative, or a vivacious and expressive fourteen-year-old, who doubts herself. Allow the essence of one of your soul aspects to come into the oval. Breathe and BE with this part of your Self. Permit the oval to energetically hold its essence and energies.

In your heart, be present with the essence of a soul aspect who has been waiting for you to return. Feel, hear, or see who he or she really is beneath the emotion. Do not abandon him or her. Stay truly present. You will experience living in your solar plexus, lower belly, navel, or inner space between the pubic bone and tailbone in a whole new way. Allow your heart center to expand by taking in the true presence, power, and light of your soul aspect. The container bridges your spiritual and soul nature with your body.

Focus into the colors of your inner oval. As you fill the oval with love, be aware of the colors that come into view. Now, expand the colors of your inner oval into an oval surrounding your entire body. Increase your outer oval until you can breathe fully into its width and depth. Breathe into both ovals at the same time until they become one circle of light and color.

We need an inner container to expansively hold our feelings, soul energies, and our light. Without an energetic container, we are unable to support the feelings that arise from our childhood, teen years, and adult experiences and transform them into love. We are unable to build the light frequencies within our body and create a new matrix of higher consciousness to reside in. We need a container to integrate our soul aspects with our Higher Self in our heart center.

As you reconnect and reunite your ABR'd (abandoned, betrayed, and rejected) soul aspects within your heart, you are freeing old energies by letting go of their old belief structures and creating a connection with the new power of your soul truth. You are recreating your relationship with your essence—the You that has the power and potential to live in Oneness with all of life. For instance, you may have soul aspects that bonded in a negative way to a parental figure. As human beings, we carry on the energetic grid of our family of ancestry to the point of having our energetic constructs within our consciousness patterned exactly like our ancestry. We often hold our attachments to familial energies in our root center or navel center, which intensifies the feelings of our separation with Infinite Source. Your root center holds the traumas and fears that go back in your body seven generations. When cleared and connected to

Infinite Source in your body, you are able to hold your energetic frequency and fulfill your soul purpose. The Infinite Source of light when allowed to move through your body will awaken you to the truth of who you are beyond the entanglements of your family karma. When the root center is disengaged from the heart center, sexual, creative and financial stability and security are difficult. When the root center is anchored in the light of your divine feminine and masculine, you experience joy, innovative action, and trust in your Self.

The clarity in your navel center determines your ability to survive on your own, BE self-actualizing, source life force energies directly, know your truth, feel your soul identity, and navigate through spiritual emptiness into enlightened states of BEing. Until we release and clear the shadows of our family ancestry, we end up carrying on the same psychological attitudes and judgments as our family of origin, even if we "do not want to." Through clearing your navel energies, the power of your newly found soul aspects can manifest into your life and into the world the presence and power of your Original Self.

> *Creating a container serves the very important function of rooting the power and light of higher frequencies and your Higher Self in your body.*

If you are hold anger or anger easily, talk too much, deny dealing with intense feelings, avoid communication in relationships, need outside distractions to function, live in your head and close your heart, shift your personality to fit in with others, use sex to avoid emotional pain and stress, or hold secrets or lies and cannot handle the unknown, you lack a container in your energetic and emotional body. If you were bombarded by family dysfunctions such as non-communication, alcoholism or drug problems, control issues, rigidity, unrealistic expectations, obsessive-compulsive behaviors, sexual abuse, religious dogmatism, mental illness, poverty, or conditional love, then chances are you were never allowed to truly be your own person. The art of creating a container in the emotional body in childhood happens if you are fortunate enough to have a parent or teacher who encourages you to be with your feelings and not abandon your Self, and are given the opportunity to be creative without judgment.

Until your divine and human selves are reconnected and merged within your body, you may feel ungrounded and unsure of yourself. To unite the divine and human selves, you need to create a sanctuary—a chalice large enough to contain the universe within you. By diving deep into the space within your solar plexus and descending downward, you will find a portal directly above your navel area and deep within your lower belly that opens into a safe sanctuary. A universe of softness, strength, security, and earthy depth, your chalice is a sacred and mystical chamber of regeneration and self-sustaining peace. After you create your chalice, reach into the universe within your heart, plant a seed, and watch a tree grow with deep roots. Your roots nurture and grow YOU into wholeness.

By having a container, you can deepen your spiritual practices of opening your higher centers. Your container stabilizes the energies and power within your etheric, energetic, emotional, and physical bodies, supporting you to BE interconnected with all of the dimensions of your awakening Self. Your container anchors your pure creative, sexual and personal power helping you to stay rooted in your base *Power Point Centers*.

> *After you create your chalice, reach into the universe within your heart, plant a seed, and watch a tree grow with deep roots. Your roots nurture and grow YOU into wholeness.*

    The light within you can be sensed, felt, and intuited. To intuit something, you must "move into it." You want to merge your awareness into your heart. To see the light within your heart and within your soul aspects, focus into your third eye while maintaining a conscious connection into your root center and lower belly—your *First* and *Second Power Point Centers*. To awaken and develop your third eye, sit quietly and gently gaze into blue light or a blue star in the space in between your eyebrows and then raise your inner gaze slightly higher within your forehead, just above your eyebrows. Allow your eyelids to almost close, keeping a slight space open so you see just a small amount of light filtering through. Follow your breath and let go into an open inner space of peace and expansion, as you receive the light shining within your third eye. Begin to inwardly chant the word "HU" as you open your gaze into your third eye and heart.

    Next, connect your third eye into the gateway of your chalice sanctuary in your navel center and enter into its portal into the infinite. Breathe slowly and deeply in through your nose, filling your solar plexus and lower belly with breath, and exhale the breath out of your mouth. Now, move your focus in through the gateway at your navel point and follow a highway of stillness. Imagine it as a passageway, an eternal highway into creation. Still your breath and focus into the silence of the void—a vast expansion of eternal possibility.

    BE still and breathe.

    As you follow along the winding highway of stillness, track your pathway back through existence into your Original Self, your spark of life—the light of your BEing. Move through stillness and into inner silence. Just BE.

Now, feel, see, and hear the inner currents, rhythms, and messages of the earth, inner dimensions, your heart, and the hearts of others. Utilize as much space as you can within your inner sanctuary to support your Whole Self and then show up with others from this divine presence and BEingness in your work and everyday life.

Bring the peace of your sanctuary—the clarity and presence of BEing in your chalice to your Whole Self and to others—especially to the children in your life that you know and meet. Your presence will have an impact that creates a conscious connection to Infinite Source. When you teach and help children to BE and feel safe in this open space within themselves, they feel valued, honored, and creatively limitless. Help them remain open to their power; guide them to self-nourish. Teach them to water the inner gardens of their heart. Help them keep the light radiating in their sanctuary.

BE in your chalice and hold space for your co-workers, clients, students, family, and friends. BE in the expansion that your chalice creates for yourself and others while practicing being in the purity and power of your presence. Trust your Self.

When building your inner chalice, know that it will be a container for your life force and the light of the universe. The more light that you can contain, the greater your physical, spiritual, creative, and soul energies will become. True abundance is born by receiving and giving the reservoir of wealth created by an overflowing chalice.

> *The beauty of BEing One is possible when the indescribable joys of life are sourced from within you.*

Your Inner Container

Opening Your Inner Container

Connect With the Earth

Your container is created by first connecting to the light within the center of the earth. As you pull the light up from the earth's core, you will be activating the magnetic core of your body that serves as a container for life force energies.

1. Receive the light of the deep earth through your feet.

2. Pull up flames of pure white fire up from the earth through your feet.

3. Bring the light up into your body, raising it through your legs, the space between your pubic bone and tailbone (your root center), your creation point, navel, solar plexus, and heart center. Breathe and BE in the light.

Connect Your Solar Plexus

Your solar plexus stabilizes the divine and earth energies in your body. Your awareness, when connected inside of your solar plexus, allows your Whole Self to become a container for Spirit—the essence of life. Connection with your solar plexus anchors your energy and mind in your body and builds a container for your life force, love, and light to exist within.

1. Breathe into your solar plexus and fill it with pure gold light—sunshine.

2. Lift the gold light into your heart.

3. Send this gold light to every part of your body, down to your feet, and into your palms. Allow your entire body to be filled with gold light. Sit and radiate from within for the amount of time needed to feel full.

Connect Your Bones

Your bones are conduits for light energies to move into the structure of your Bodymind and soul matrix. They hold the best of your soul ancestry and spiritual power, and when "fed" with light and good nutrition, you can succeed with your divine and human aspirations.

1. Inhale light into your bones as you breathe in through your mouth and exhale through your mouth, expelling any stale energy inside of your bones.

2. Inhale energy and light through your skin, then into your bones and exhale.

3. Inhale and exhale again, and as you exhale, allow the energy to fill up the space inside of your bones. Breathe deep into your bones until you feel open and expansive.

4. Direct this energy deeper and deeper into your bones as you inhale through your nose for 10 counts. Hold the breath for 10 counts. Exhale out 10 counts through your mouth keeping the energy in the bones.

5. Repeat ten times.

Awakening to Light

Deepening Your Inner Container Connection

As your container expands to hold greater light and soul Oneness, you can integrate how you identify with "who you have been" with the new expansive you.

Your *First Power Point Center*—your root center—plays the important role of stabilizing and building your inner container. It does this by supporting two functions. First, your root center receives and stabilizes the divine feminine currents of your soul. Your root center does this by channeling the earth and universal energies to flow up from the center of the earth into your body. Secondly, your root center is a magnet of energy that draws the universal divine masculine energies to flow down from above your head and awaken the spiritual pathways in your body.

Your container helps you to feel your spiritual and physical energies, and holds the space for your sacred and divine masculine and feminine energies to meet and merge. Your body and mind are supported to become One in your container, creating a neutral zone within you that is naturally non-reactive. Here, you can BE and feel connected into Infinite Source. It is a zone where there are no thoughts, and the spaciousness of the universe can be accessed.

As you bring flames of pure white fire up from the center of the earth, drop your mind down into your root center to meet the flames. These divine feminine flames of pure white fire are the transformational powers of divine consciousness. They have the ability to dissolve the cords of attachment between your thoughts, beliefs, and heart. When thoughts come up that you know you want to let go of, send them into flames of pure white, or violet flames of fire in your *First and Second Power Point Centers*, the root center and lower belly, and then through your intention release the energies into Infinite Source.

Now, from above your head, send the white or blue light of your divine masculine energy through the core shaft of light in your body and guide the light down to meet your divine feminine in your root center. As they unite in your root center, allow the light to move up and ignite the inside of your spine and the space surrounding your spine, touching into and through each *Power Point Center* connection. As the light ignites your root center, you will feel your container grow stronger and make it easier to ascend upwards through the center of your core shaft of light with love.

As you feel lighter and freer inside, practice staying connected into your container. Feel the new spaces of freedom that you are creating within yourself. They will make possible new ways of being in your life with authenticity and greater strength to release how you hold on to your ego and fears.

The activation of your divine feminine and masculine energies heal and revitalize your Whole Self. Their union creates the spiritual space of love in your body and mind that will transform you. The union and integration of your divine feminine and masculine energies will balance your brain functions and all of the systems in your body—including your circulatory, nervous, endocrine and respiratory systems—by reconnecting the cellular DNA information within your cells. This is possible because they ignite and strengthen the connection between your physical and spiritual bodies.

As you focus the divine light of the flames of pure white fire into your root center, simultaneously bring light into your solar plexus and heart center. Practice holding the consciousness of a rediscovered soul aspect with the light of love into these three centers at once and you will experience profound shifts in every area of your life from the inside out.

You will begin to notice how your mind may habitually jump in and take over, or block the authentic voice of your soul. By remaining grounded in the light within your root center, solar plexus, and heart center, you will be able to let go and release the pain that in the past would steer your mind to be in control.

As an expanded step, simultaneously ground into the divine feminine of your root center and heart center with the focus of your mind. You will continue to feel inwardly supported in new ways. You will feel more confident, experience a new level of courage and strength, find clear determination and willingness to hold your own, and be supported to BE YOU now instead of who you were yesterday, last week, or two decades ago. You will feel and see the universe support your core truth, light, and love.

> *Uncovering the layers surrounding your True Self will set you free into the illuminating gold light of liberation—pure and infinite love.*

As you focus into the Oneness of your heart and soul, you will feel the limitless possibilities of living in Infinite Source. Remember to fill yourself with the light of love and allow it to take up full space in your energy and physical bodies. Remember to acknowledge that your body is a temple for the light of the divine to shine through.

Don't be surprised if people start responding to you in new ways. As you embody more and more light, your presence will create shifts around you whether you can see them or not. As light becomes your teacher, you will have to surrender your own stuff and your own will. In their place, the light will connect you into divine will. As divine will merges with your heart and soul, your attachments to your identity and what you think is important in your life will begin to melt down and shift. The raw and core truth of who you are and what you are supposed to be doing will reveal itself. You will discover that the essence of who you are has always been love.

> ## *Unifying Your Inner Family with Light*
>
> We are living in times where many of us are awakening to a deep knowingness that we are all connected. As we move out of a separation paradigm that has been based upon individuals, cultures, families, societies, nations, and religions holding values of separation and perpetuating core wounds of the heart and soul, we realize that to sustain Oneness as a world model we need to be in a new relationship with *our inner family*.
>
> You have an inner family made up of your soul parts and psyche that bring your emotional, psychological, spiritual, creative, and physical love and power together. All of the forms that your soul has manifested throughout eons of time exist in your psyche, and as they are purified and healed through the light, they are able to unite with your Whole Self.
>
> Find your inner mother, inner father, and inner child and bring them to the light. Invite their essence, their unique ray of love, to penetrate your being. As you become One with your inner family, your soul will expand and become stronger and you will feel more confident BEing You. As you feel supported by your inner family—your divine feminine and divine masculine, you can finally say YES without fear to deeper levels of change in your life and NO to the situations and energies that hold you back from living the life that you desire.
>
> Embrace your soul. Increase the space in your Bodymind and Spirit to join the planet in her evolutionary movement into BEing and living as One Family united to create a new humanity.

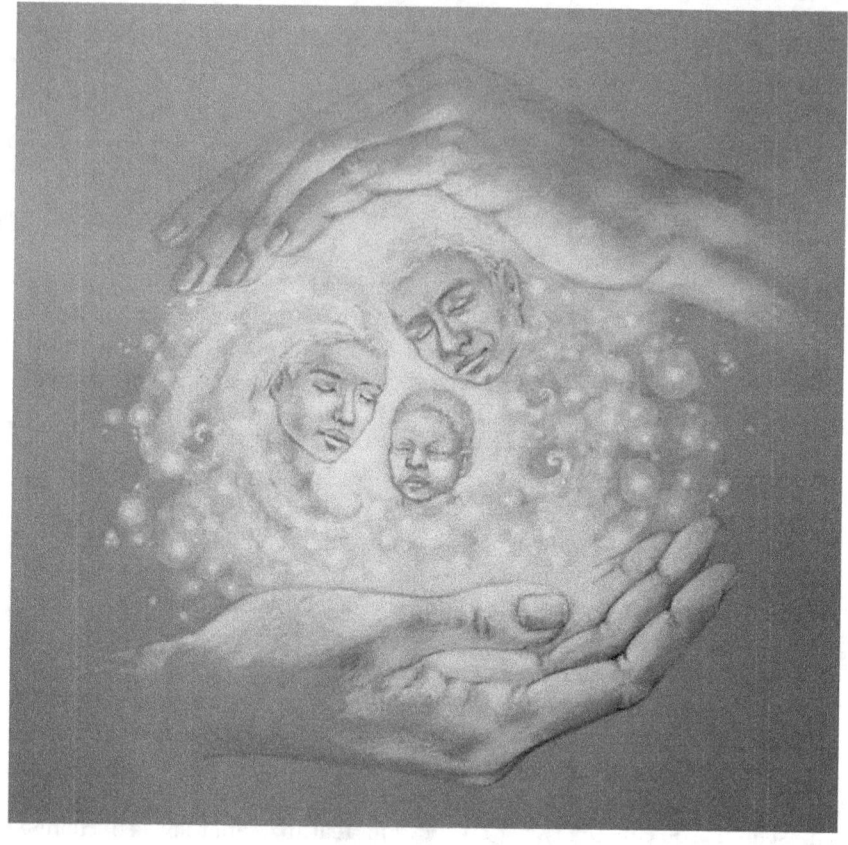

Loving your Inner Family

Love all of yourself and become the unique expression and spark of your divinity. Every aspect of your spirituality, sexuality, creativity, light, and emotional and mental bodies align through your physical body to directly help you become a direct expression of God—Infinite Source. Surrender into the love that you are. It is time to step into the pulse of life that inspires you to the greatness of your BEing. Become the initiator for higher insights, solutions, and brilliance in your life, with others and in the world, by BEing you.

REMEMBER:

- Your soul has always been One with Infinite Source. You have been taught to forget this. Your soul longs to know God—Infinite Source and to open to the love that is beyond all suffering.

- Your mind and body only split to the degree that you are separate from Infinite Source.

- Your soul helps you to remember your Self as a divine partner with Infinite Source. It helps your mind to stop choosing falling in and out of the love within you and abandoning the real you.

- The more that you let go of examining what is wrong with yourself and with your life and instead open to the light and love within yourself, the easier it will become to move forward on your life path and soul destiny.

- Your body is the container holding the love of your True Self. It bridges your soul and God, and integrates Spirit and your mind.

- The greater the light that you uncover in each soul part, the greater the light can reconfigure your body and mind into your Bodymind.

- The truth of who you are lives in the cellular memory within your body.

- Your mind holds on to your greatest weaknesses when it is separate from Infinite Source. Each moment that your mind reacts from being separate from its God Mind, which is pure love, it creates a barrier or layer of fear and disconnection within you.

- Your mind will continue to jump in and try to lead your life until the moment that you step up, stand up, and actively say yes to your soul guiding your life.

- Your purpose is always revealed as you integrate the spiritual power and love of your soul.

- Where you focus in yourself, and how you show up to serve Infinite Source in your daily activities determine your soul breakthroughs.

- The union of light within your mind, body, soul, and Higher Self ground and create your life. As you spiritually evolve, your ego will let go, your mind will move beyond fear, and your heart will open.

- Fear exists only in separation. Fear is created when you separate from your authentic Self. Love and embody your Self completely.

- Invite the white and gold light of Infinite Source into your body, and especially into your solar plexus and heart centers, and BE.

- Remember, your true power is *not* a power that is dominating, overbearing, ego driven, or insecure. Your true power is pure creation energy; it is the source of all life.

- The *One in Soul* experience naturally creates your heart center to become a container. By expanding your container into your solar plexus, you will clear past attachments to others, and from them to you.

- The more light that you open to, the more you will connect into divine will and be able to release your attachments to your identity.

- As you become present in your body to who you are, you will discover that the essence of who you are is and always has been love.

BELIGHT MEDITATION

Please take the time to practice the exercises in this chapter at your own flow and timing. Each time that you show up for yourself and practice BEing with your Self, the more you will experience freedom and joy opening up for you in every facet of your life.

CHAPTER NINETEEN

Living in the Love and Power of Your Whole Self

> "Body, heart and soul obscured the path,
> Until body melted into heart,
> Heart into soul,
> And soul in love itself."
> — Rumi

Infinite Source as Love and Power

The truth of your soul vibrates at the same frequency as God—Infinite Source, and when you focus the passion of your soul into living life from your heart's desires, you can move mountains.

Infinite Source is experienced as Oneness. Infinite Source lives as love and power uniquely expressed as you. All of your soul aspects are comprised of the two ingredients of love and power—divine masculine and feminine energies. These two qualities are discovered each time that you reconnect your soul aspects and bring forth the truths within you that are waiting to be revealed. Yet, to live within the integrity of your True Self, the forces of love and power must be balanced and unified within your body, mind, heart, and soul.

Love and power are our birthright as human beings. Yet we have been trained to separate love and power for centuries. By separating these two vital energies, we have created the dynamics of pain and suffering in our lives and in the systems of the world. This reality manifests as worldwide personal and global disconnection and division from Infinite Source. We all separate the love and power of our true nature until we recognize how they exist within us.

Most governments, institutions, businesses, and corporations are built upon separation thinking. They create false power and influence through being attached to their disconnections in their body, mind, and soul. Decision's made from separation thinking creates suffering. All war, poverty, and issues of violence are created from battling the two polar forces of love and power, our divine masculine and feminine, up against one another within the individual and within the collective. However, by creating inner union with the polarities of love and power on the inside first, we can then learn how to create peace and unity on the outside as well. Unifying the essences of love and power heals the personal and collective wounds created by the separation of consciousness from Infinite Source.

When we bring together the energies of soul love and power, we can solve any problem in the world. Each and every one of us is vitally important to the evolution of our planet. Each time that one more person becomes whole inside, and innovates their wholeness into their daily life, our collective ability to transform our world increases.

LIVING IN THE LOVE AND POWER OF YOUR WHOLE SELF

> *All war, poverty, and issues of violence are created from battling the two polar forces of love and power, our divine masculine and feminine, up against one another.*

Love and power originally separated in the soul when the masculine and feminine powers separated many millennia ago. When that soul break occurred, the mind and body split, creating a separation from Infinite Source. It is through our separation from God—Infinite Source that we then created religions in all of their various forms as a means to re-find our lost Source connection. Within every religion and spiritual path exists the possibility for the union of love and power, but in most cases, access to this spiritual intelligence has been lost. When religions struggle with the separation of love and power within their own belief and organizational structures, it becomes impossible to find, let alone teach the union of love and power to the people.

To re-find the Oneness of love and power that we have been searching for, sometimes it takes going back to the original spark, or the liberator who brought forth a religion and its teachings, and letting go of any dogma associated with it. It is not a belief system that takes us to the liberation of our soul; it is the devotion of love we bring to the ceremony, ritual, prayer, or meditation. It is time to take down the walls of separation we maintain between religions. The state of Oneness with Infinite Source is a natural state that is within each and every one of us, no matter what religious training we are born into. Learning how to live in the union of love and power has been denied to the masses for thousands of years. The authentic power of BEing One with Infinite Source naturally creates love. How we abuse or correctly use the power within ourselves, whether through union with the ego mind or with Infinite Source is the main issue for humanity to face at this time.

As we move into the next phase of our spiritual evolution, we have the opportunity to take the direct path back into union. To find the path, we must choose to walk through the doorway of involution, and follow the movement inward towards the source within ourselves—into divine truth and infinite love. A magnetic attraction between your soul and the heart of the universe will pull you home. Always remember that within your BEing exist the portals and pathway back to divine union. Here is where your bliss, joy and true happiness reside. You can ask the divine to reveal the portals of truth on your path, but you must be the one to walk through them. It is always your choice. The fastest way to reunite the pure soul components of love and power within you is to practice paying attention to how you inwardly control and block the emergence of your divine feminine and divine masculine energies. You must be the One who asks how am I using my power? Who am I serving, ego or God—Infinite Source? Whether through sex, money, self-expression, food, the friends you keep, how you spend your time, who and when you give your power away to, are all gateways of awakening into reigniting and reconnecting your divine power— your divine feminine and masculine soul aspects and energies. Their reunion, bridge your body, mind, soul, and Spirit with Infinite Source—God, and are revealed in greater depth in *BE: The Humanity Blueprint-Divine Masculine and Feminine Integration-Volume III*.

> ***Always remember that within your BEing exist the portals and pathway back to divine union.***

Freeing Your Spiritual Power

You were born with a built in treasure chest of spiritual power in your soul. The breath of God—Infinite Source is experienced as spiritual power in your body and soul and within the energetic matrix of nature. Just as a molecule of water has a distinctive, faceted geometric design, you came into this life with a spiritual design all your own. The lifetime-to-lifetime expansion and contraction of your soul and all of your previous experiences still exist in your spiritual and physical DNA. They make up the molecules of your spiritual power. As a social collective over the last 3,500 years, we chose to leave the full light and wholeness of our True and Original Selves. The result of leaving our connection with the divine led us on a journey into exploring imbalanced power and manifesting a world culture from this imbalance. We have turned gender, race, culture, nation, and religions against one another because we have collectively been turning against our True Selves.

Spiritual power exists within us all, and how we use it is our greatest individual challenge. Over centuries, it became more and more difficult to BE the light and full radiance of our joyous and illuminated selves. Individuals who lived in direct connection with Infinite Source and were One with their spiritual power were often persecuted, killed, exiled, or betrayed for BEing a power that was perceived as a threat to the masses and to the patriarchy.

As integrated love and power became practically extinct in our global culture, societies turned spiritual law into civil law and obedience based upon fear, repression, and hatred.

Today, the split between love and power within our own souls and within the collective has become an epidemic causing the loss of health and vitality, marriages, focus, mental and emotional stability, basic human values, honor between the sexes, and global security and business integrity. A new embodiment of wholeness and union in soul is needed to step into living love. We must become whole thinkers and be able to see from a 360-degree perspective to initiate positive change and differentiate true power from false power.

In a past lifetime, or at some point in this lifetime, in order to protect your heart and soul, you separated from your Original Self and, without knowing, divided the love and power of your soul. You left parts of your soul behind because you didn't know how to bring them along or there wasn't enough room in your psyche to bring them along. Your awakened consciousness may have felt too big or overwhelming to bring into this lifetime. You may have felt that you were too much for others. Sometimes, your disconnection with Infinite Source caused from past emotional or soul traumas in your past incarnations would block your ability to fully come in at birth and experience conscious connection and alignment to your soul path. Sometimes, your True Self chooses to stay hidden and on the side lines of your life by creating wounded ego selves that battle amongst themselves to stay in control. Sometimes the wounds of your mother and father, which you energetically take on, combine with your cellular memories from past lifetimes and your own self-judgments inhibit how you bring in your own spiritual power.

Whatever beliefs you have about your own existence based upon the judgments and actions of others towards you must be realized and released. Your perception of the world is either through the eyes of your belief that you are alone and in pain, or that you are One and living in the light that you are. How you perceive your entire life is either seen through the system of your wounded ego or through the eyes of joy and expansion.

Living life through your wounded ego involves two distinct parts. One part, the negative wounded ego, stores the pain, shame, and your hurt from feeling unlovable, undeserving, unworthy, and unvalued. The other part, the positive wounded ego, holds the role as protector, savior, and controller who micro-manages your wounds to remain undercover. You begin the cycle of living from ego the moment that you choose, for whatever reason, leaving your original state of Oneness—BEing One. BEing You.

> *In a past lifetime or at some point in this lifetime, in order to protect your heart and soul, you separated from your Original Self and divided the love and power of your soul.*

As the wounded ego creates layers of beliefs about it self and others, DNA cellular memories collect in our cells and hold the imprints of traumas, judgments, fear, and pain. When we split off from our spiritual power, we align with the emptiness within our being, which is experienced as darkness. This remains until we reopen the gateway to the light. In the moment we separate from Infinite Source and our Original Self, we experience deep despair and loneliness. Our positive wounded ego is catapulted into action to step up and "manage" the emotional pain created by the separation of our heart center, higher mind, and Infinite Source. We embody the pain and unconsciously define who we are from this wounded perspective and hold onto past traumas and imbalances as if they are real and happening in the present moment.

The Ego Self, with all of its parts and layers, thrives upon internal struggle as it increases your self-doubt, self-blame, self-judgment, and feelings and belief that you are unworthy to BE who you are. It takes the role of director and steps in to sublimate the essence of who you are. The ego lives off of the energies of opposition and disempowerment and works hard to push the real you into a lock-down position. The ego wants to protect you but will also attempt to block and control your Original Self—the essence of your BEing—from emerging. For instance, in a past incarnation, if you were shamed, judged, or persecuted for your spiritual power, you may find yourself living out the pain of those memories in your present life and relationships. The past and the present remain energetically entangled within you, creating pain and reinforcing your separation from your true spiritual power and Infinite Source.

You may choose external relationships and situations that represent your own soul repression and separation, or you may find yourself connecting with egos of individuals who are energetic duplicates of individuals from your childhood or past lifetimes that have previously repressed you. When you hit the ceiling of your life and feel blocked to move through the eye of the needle of your consciousness, your self-doubt shows as fear. You must move through the portal of fear and separation and step into the light to end your cycles of pain and suffering. To live fearlessly requires only one thing: complete trust in the light that you are.

> *The ego wants to protect you but will also block and control your Original Self—the essence of your BEing—from emerging.*

Healing Your Pain

Women and men feel pain in their bodies differently. Each month when a woman begins her menstrual cycle, she experiences the flow of life force—emotions, psychic energies, and blood. Her womb expands into a cosmically tuned vessel of spiritual energy. The *First, Second, Third, and Fourth Power Point Centers* (root, lower belly, creation point, and navel centers) in women are gateways into divine power. A woman's womb is a vessel of infinitely powerful cosmic forces. Even 2,000 years ago, girls were trained in the ancient traditions of accessing their spiritual power through BEing One with universal forces. A woman's womb holds the same consciousness and energies as mother earth. Rich, deep, tender, powerful, life-giving, awakened, nourishing, gentle, creative, empowering, determined, succulent, and ripe, a woman's womb feels the joys and pain of all life because she carries the seed of life within her. The sperm ignites the egg into life. The two are needed to create new life.

A woman not only feels her own connection to Infinite Source but also the feelings of others and the entire universe. Her psyche, her subconscious, conscious mind, and soul are in tune with the subtle forces of universal energies through her body because her hormones ignite brain patterns and perceptions that are constantly in relationship to the whole. When a girl or a woman is not allowed, not taught, not supported, and is discouraged from speaking and BEing her Self, she holds the pain of withholding her own life force expressions in her womb.

When the first 4 *Power Point Centers* are closed out of fear, it becomes almost impossible to access spiritual power. A woman's karmic, ancestral, and familial patterns influence how she is going to respond to the world around her, to her own emotions, and to her power. The expression of her BEingness is crucial to her ability to take responsibility—to be able to respond to her deepest inner yearning and callings. When girls and women are supported to follow the rhythm and divine intelligence from within their wombs, they grow up with self-dignity and vision to heal and lead the world to live in divine order with natural law, not man "made up" law. Harmony and fearless power are the natural state for a woman.

Once a woman clears old patterns of self-hatred that she took on from her ancestry, past lives, from her own self-judgments, and from others, she can access her true power by energetically connecting her heart, solar plexus, creation point, womb, and root energies. As these energies unite, she is able to access her heart and discover the essence of her soul.

During childbirth, when a woman opens completely to the incoming soul of her baby, she is able to bring in all of its soul-God energies into its physical body. This is a woman's most precious gift to give to her newborn child. A child brought into the world this way grows up having access to its True Self, which helps it experience joy and its own spiritual power to help her or him face their daily life and soul challenges. The essence of a woman's soul can be felt through the expansion of her sexuality, whether through childbirth or higher octave lovemaking. A woman's soul is profoundly connected through her sexuality, and as she opens to the light moving through her body, she can experience her divine essence. The reconnection to the divine feminine as flames of pure white fire from the earth's core has the power to ignite a woman's remembrance of her soul essence.

Men also go through hormonal changes, but they go through the full cycle of their hormonal peaks and valleys all within a 24-hour window. When a man chooses to be attentive and present with each moment, he can live through his essence and attunement to his higher purpose. This supports his process of BEing One with himself and the world. A man who is awakening learns to work with his own energy field. When a man ignores or denies his emotions and energetic cycles and works to control the impulses in his body, or allows them to dominate him, he creates a controlled and disconnected reality to live within. This produces fear, and his fear produces resistance in his body, mind, and psyche. Resistance creates pain. When a man realizes how he controls the impulses and energy flows in his mind and body, and confronts his own patterns instead of engaging with his ego to lead him through his life maze, he can engage his deep heart, and begin his path of awakening. It is through feeling life through his heart that a man awakens to his destiny path. His mind must release into his heart to accept being a warrior servant to life and others.

A man discovers his soul essence through fully coming into his body on a feeling level and clearing all of the cords that block his connection to Infinite Source, from his heart center down into his root center. A man must clear the energies that he takes on from his mother in utero and in early childhood and give her back all of the energetic patterns that he takes on and lives out for her. A man must be clear that he is walking his soul blueprint and not his mothers. Most women energetically transfer their emotional needs, which are not being met by their partner, on to their son. A boy grows into a man forging through his guilt, resentment, denial, despair, or anger at his mother for emotionally bleeding him of his journey of becoming an expression of his True Self and taking back his power, rather than fulfilling the expectations she holds for him to be there for her. A mother's greatest gift to a boy is not to mother him to smother him, or impose her fears and unmet needs upon her son. When a woman gives a boy or a man space to BE himself, she provides for him the opportunity to come through his dilemmas, fears and spiritual pain created by his own past choices, behaviors and past life karmas. Boys are deeply sensitive and must first embrace their sensitivity and then transform their feeling nature into intuition and then into being the heart of their warrior Self, fully ignited and contained within the light of their soul.

A man's spiritual pain evolves through the process of leaving himself, ignoring his feelings and energetic cycles, becoming someone else's image of who he should be, and by rejecting how the love within himself naturally wants to be expressed.

A man's inner pain and suffering is created by building walls of denial to his Original Self while he proves to others that he is a capable man worth trusting. Boys are rarely taught how to love themselves and are instead taught to get love and approval through things, sex, false power, money, success, and people. For a man to move through his spiritual pain, he must first open his solar plexus and clear his root centers—feel the essence of his existence—and then find the womb of his life energies in his heart center. This will help him to discover infinite love, the source of his strength and power.

The life force powers of the earth and heavens meet in a man's heart and open the gateways to living in the transformative power of Spirit. His sexuality must reunite with his heart so that he can find his own connection to his divine feminine. His sexuality is one with his primal force of survival and unless he is supported to physically integrate his masculine drive for life, understand his yearning to merge, touch and feel, and know how to constructively challenge himself to go beyond the limits of his own mind, imagination and expression, he holds himself back, represses his life force instincts and hides his soul, emotions, and subverts his sexuality into anger, addiction, control, and fear.

Most boys and men are taught to reject their own divine feminine essence and the heart of their divine masculine. Their divine masculine will instantly transform as the essence of their divine feminine power is received and integrated.

As a man unites his head, body, and heart, he is able to permanently transform his relationship to his ego by entering into his eternal presence, his Original Self. A man must create a relationship of trust with his body and mind from a heart level. As he discovers, receives and trusts the love within his heart, he can release his grip on control as a way to endure his emotional, psychological and physical pain. He awakens to the ways that he has perpetuated inner pain and self-hatred, and as he embodies the light of his soul, he can forgive himself and others in a profound way that brings peace to him Self, others, and the world.

Remember, whether you are a man or a woman, your most important inner work to do at this time is to awaken and integrate your soul energies and re-unite their essence into your new light energy matrix in your body. As you experience the fragmentations of your soul consciousness reunite in your body, your mind can let go of how it controls and represses your true spiritual power. By clearing and strengthening your lower base *Power Point Centers,* the fear entangling your energy matrix and mind begin to lessen. Your lower base *Power Point Centers* hold your sexuality, creativity, spiritual endurance, integrity, power, light, and ability to transform illusion and fear into strength of purpose. When your subconscious foresees control and manipulation, or experiences the fear of being able to fully exist in its surroundings, it will give containment to the spiritual power within your soul, so it can survive in your base *Power Point Centers*. These centers are the *Feminine Power Centers* that are naturally rooted in the earth. They have a built in, innate system of providing you with security, nourishment, containment, and all the powers of the divine feminine. As you call in, draw up from the earth its light and power into your base *Power Point Centers*, you can transform any energy and shift it into light.

The wounded ego can fully heal when the lower base *Power Point Centers* are cleared, healed, and integrated with your higher centers, and the light of your Original Self. As you release your dependence upon your ego to hold things together, the clarity of the light aligns you into a new frequency that has the power to change your life. The *One in Soul* experience will help to restore any fragmentation that you might have gone through and clear and integrate your base *Power Point Centers* with your heart center. Once you invite in and make space for these vitally important energetic soul aspects of yourself into your *Power Point Centers*, you will be able to BE fully in your body. Being fully in your body gives you the ability to experience and create your life fully and to receive the consciousness and presence of your higher Self.

The more aligned you are in Infinite Source, the greater the flow of spiritual power in your Bodymind and soul. The greater the obstructions and walls you have to BEing and living in your Source power and alignment, the greater will be your need to create a false front, personality, and ego structure. The more you practice BEing in the love of your heart and soul, the easier it becomes for your God Self to emerge. The more you are open to BEing touched by Infinite Source, the easier it becomes to realize what is true and what is false about your nature. Your soul rejoining in love within your body ignites your spiritual power and creates the foundation of truth for you to ground your mind and heart. When your body and soul are aligned in Source power, your radiant light can shine forth, emanating power, joy, and love. Your Original True Self is always present and ready to align the rest of you into its wholeness.

> **The more you are open to be touched by Infinite Source, the easier it becomes to realize what is true and what is false about your nature.**

Ten Soul Sourcing Tools to Build and Purify Divine Power

The following are Ten Soul Sourcing Tools to help you clear the way to build and purify yourself as a temple for divine power.

1. BE conscious to not live through another.
2. Do not allow another to live through you.
3. Pay attention to external forces working to control and distract you from being self-sourcing.
4. The more your attention is brought outside of you and the less that is focused within you, the greater the chance for political, social, personal and moral corruption. The power is meant to BE within you.
5. Learn to open and connect your *Power Point Centers* which source your physical and spiritual energies: crown, third eye, back of the skull, throat, heart, solar plexus, navel, creation point, lower belly, sacrum, sexual organs, pubic bone-tailbone, hands, and soles of the feet.
6. Bring light to the dark places of your psyche in your body to awaken your true power.
7. Dissolve fear by reconnecting to your spiritual power.
8. Choose connection to your heart, love, and the expression of your power to experience the freedom of liberation in the mind and body.
9. Align your *Power Point Centers* in your sushumna, the core shaft of light that connects Spirit into your body.
10. Reconnect the spiritual aspects of your soul that have been abandoned, betrayed, rejected, and left behind by you into the light of your love.

Facing Spiritual Power Bumps

It is easy to forget why we are here and who we are. All of us, no matter "where we are at" on our path of spiritual evolution can have an unexpected diversion or fall. We compare ourselves to others and leave living in love. We lose connection to our body and go up into our head. We build up our wounded ego without even knowing it by over identifying with our spiritual power, roles we play, emotions, and lose connection with our Original Self. We empower our ego through our spiritual intellectual knowledge and can fall off of our true path, and not even know it. We can act out our deepest fear by manipulating another or shutting down the wellspring of emotion and wisdom within our Self. We can get caught up in surviving rather than thriving. We can enter into a sexual relationship with an individual who has the same level of undealt with core inner wounds and begin to lose our self in the relationship. We can promise our self that we won't base our self worth upon the money that we make, but once successful unless we have healed our fear issues of love and survival, we become attached to our lifestyle of comfort and security. We can draw to us people who hide behind a false mask, sometimes undetectable because we deny and abandon some part of our self that is in pain. Their presence can trigger deep pain ready to be transformed into light and clarity. We are given so many opportunities to BE free.

We have spent lifetimes rejecting, accepting, fighting, judging, leaving, wanting, being, succeeding, and learning how to be in relationship with Infinite Source, the All That Is. The moment that you feel an aspect of your soul take root into your heart center and fill you with its essence, your life begins to align with your destiny. Each time that you say YES to the bigger you, the one who loves no matter what and is willing to see through illusion, you discover the truth that catapults you into joy.

The sorrow and suffering that we all encounter at some point in our lives are gateways into the next level of our enlightening. The situations and people that have served the purpose to crack open our hearts, stir us to break free of how we limit our selves, and push us to confront what we do not want to see—help us to discover the courage to step up and change, and when viewed in gratitude have the power to humble and shift us. Never forget that our greatest challenges given from the divine are to help us get to the point where we desire, beyond anything else, to become One and whole with the source of love, once again.

When you do business with someone who rubs you the wrong way, when someone you care about misperceives or projects on to you, a sudden illness confronts you with a backlog of old issues to face, a friend turns against you, or a financial loss spins your head around, dig deep and find your connection to Infinite Source amidst any upset and seek the lessons being given. All of these situations offer the gift and common thread to help you discover the real you. Each awakening gives you back the immediate realization of your higher truth. You realize who you are and who you are not. It is not about what you do, but *the IS that is you.*

How you accept the IS that is you and what you do with it *is* what makes your life whole. The love that you open into for yourself and for others, begins to remove the separations that you have created over time. As you hear, feel, see, and know your True Self, the anger, hurt, sorrows, and pain that were created by living in separation can dissolve, and the love that you are can emerge.

Anytime that you have had your power taken from you or you have given it away, you have the choice to practice compassion for yourself and hold a big space of acceptance, self forgiveness, and receiving the lesson given by the experience. If you go into self-judgment and separate from loving your self, you step into shame and begin to spiral down. When you step into shame, anger and hurt follow. Whether you stuff it or express it, your anger and grief can be healed by embracing the original core wound and shift what you believe about yourself. Each moment is a choice point to BE or not to BE.

Anger is created through life experiences when your power was taken from you or you gave your power away. The lesson given through power struggles and feeling dishonored is to stay anchored and connected to the truths of your True Self and acknowledge the presence and clarity of your love. Fear that who you are should not exist or does not matter creates anger. Beneath anger lives the hurt and sorrow created by not being seen, heard, or received. As you see, hear, and receive yourself you are then able to end the cycles of fear, hurt, and anger and the blocking of your own creative, intuitive, and integrated Self. Once you can feel the anger, and re-find the creative and heart energies of your True Self beneath the anger, then you can grow into the union of human and divine power. This is why it is necessary to become aware of your emotions and move through them from a space of unconditional love to find your true power and to be willing to let go of the people and situations in your life that have agenda's about who and what you are supposed to be for them.

> *As you hear, feel, see, and know your True Self, the anger, hurt, and fear that were created by living in separation can dissolve, and the love that you are can emerge.*

You must accept the truth that exists beneath your emotional or psychological pain to find the power of your soul. Individuals who become identified or addicted to unprocessed pain are unable to find their authentic power—their awakened love. Once you embrace and let go of what creates the pain, you are freed to begin feeling a surge of passion for life. Once you choose Oneness over all of the ways that you remain separate from the ultimate truth of who you really are, you can shift your life. You are able to see, feel, and know when you are blocking

Infinite Source from guiding you in the right direction and begin to trust its infinite wisdom over your wounded ego.

Connecting with Your Wounded Ego

Your Wounded Self will always hold you back from creating a life filled in joy. Take a moment to remember a time when you felt total joy, and allow this memory to fill your Whole Self. As you become One, you are able to BE your joy. The moment that you leave the light that you are, is the moment that you create your ego. It only takes a moment to create a full time ego to take charge of your life.

Take the time to identify the emotions of your negative wounded ego when it shuts down your heart, and place it on a cushion to your side. Then, identify the voice of your positive wounded ego, who needs to have everything together and perfect, and place it on a cushion on your other side. Your negative wounded ego is the part of you in reaction. Your negative wounded ego feels like it is not enough—"Do I even matter?"—and lives in doubt and self-rejection. Your positive wounded ego controls and manipulates to maintain its position and to get its own way. Your positive ego thinks it knows what to do and how to do it, and re-enforces your negative wounded ego to stay small, helpless, dependent upon others and insecure.

You want to ask them what they were trying to accomplish by blocking out the light of your Original Self—your God Self. Understand their intention, and make the decision to take back the reigns of your life. Who and what you align to within your Self is the key to stepping through your fears of BEing You.

Feel the energetic cords that attach you and your positive and negative ego personalities. Take out the cords that you have had into them, and take out the cords "they" have had into you. Your cords into them have been a hopeful attempt at trying to control their impact on you. Their cords into you have been to keep you feeling small and insignificant. Focus into the light within your heart center and BE One with the light of your Original Self. Take your power back from the wounded ego and come back into the light of your soul. By choosing to stop abandoning, betraying, and rejecting the light that you are, you can begin to live as the *Whole You*. You can close your eyes and move ten feet above your head and gaze down into your body. Look to see the energetic cords that have bound you to feeling restricted. Begin to send white light into their enmeshment and see them dissolve.

The light within your heart holds the space for the power within your soul aspects to be received and transformed. Always remember that the fragmented soul aspects that hide in the dark of your lower *Power Point Centers* contain your spiritual power and light. Your power is ignited and opened as you love and accept the soul qualities that have been contracted in your *Base Power Point Centers*. Many of your soul aspects have been hiding out for so long that you may not even know they are there. The parts of your soul that have been asleep in the dark want to awaken in the light and bring new sources of divine creativity and brilliance into your everyday life. Their integration into your body make possible living and BEing fully awakened in the light. Take the time to call into your Self an aspect of your soul that will open your heart and expand your light. Breathe into your lower belly with the intention of making space for your wholeness to be embodied.

From your soul, be direct with your mind and send it a message with tender and firm love that it is time for IT to serve you. Feel in your body an expansion by creating the space within you to surrender to the divine light and Oneness of your soul.

Waiting in the subconscious of your body is a soul aspect bursting to love, a soul aspect ready to bring joy, a soul aspect waiting to explode your creativity wide open, and one that will connect you to your Higher Self. When unified, these aspects exude the essence of your Original Self. Trust the power of light that is ignited as your awakened soul merges with the pure BEingness of Infinite Source.

> *Take the time to call into your Self an aspect of your soul that will allow your heart and soul to expand into light.*

Embracing Love

When life brings you challenging situations to deal with, call up the love from the depths of your *First, Second*, and *Third Power Point Centers*—your root center, lower belly, and creation point—and draw the love up into your heart center, pulling its essence into your conscious awareness. It is in those moments that feel difficult that you want to receive the love you have worked so hard to initiate. Each time that you practice being in the essence of your truth and True Self, fill your inner spiritual fuel tank. When life's difficulties strike, the reservoir of your awakened energies will get you through your life challenge. Even in the most difficult moments, embrace the love that you are and become the love. This helps you to move through isolation, fear, control, pain, and separation into embodying love and connection. Choose the love with determined ferocity and an unbreakable focus.

When you step out of how you align to suffering and pain and observe how your thinking patterns create your suffering, you will find the doorway of love that will empower you to fulfill your vision, goals, dreams, and higher needs.

Each time that you meet sorrow or suffering with love and melt down your resistances, an emergence through the separations of your mind and heart can occur. You must allow your mind to surrender to the love within your heart. Your thinking mind may think that it is fine functioning without a consistent connection to your heart center. But your heart will grow weary adapting to the projections and illusions of your over-thinking head. Remember to slide down a waterslide from your head into your solar plexus to deepen your presence with your Self. Here, sit in the warm pool of golden water and feel safe, nurtured and strengthened. Then, open your heart center to receive the energetic nourishment from your solar plexus and breathe. Align your Self into the light of your heart, the light in the core of the earth, and the light above your head simultaneously and just BE.

As the divine currents of life flow up from your root center, through the inside of your spine, and into your heart center, while simultaneously flowing down from the higher centers above your head, through your crown, and down into your heart center, the divine masculine and feminine energies of your soul can meet within the chambers of your heart. Here, your soul finds refuge and becomes the way station of your mind as it practices new skills of focus and conscious connection. As you activate the energies and intelligence of your soul aspects through your heart center, you will discover the emergence of divine love. Your soul knows love because it is love. It is the only divine force of life that can free you.

I kept myself small. The more I realized the potency of my light and the love that flowed through me, the more insignificant I would make myself. I created plenty of emotional suffering and pain until it felt like I was on an endless wheel of consistent hard-

ship and disappointments. I was carrying a long-term wound of feeling that the light that I AM was not enough. I had many past life memories of being blamed and condemned for holding and being the power of light. I held myself accountable for the accusations that were thrust upon me. I unconsciously took them on, consequently having to process not only my own pain but also the pain of others. I carried great guilt and shame about not being enough. Deep inside, I felt insecure and afraid. I wanted to be rescued and not have to deal with how I ran from my fear and power.

If we substitute the word power for God, I was actually running from the power of God within myself. I did not want anyone to see it. I carried an unconscious inner story that someone could take my power, or that I would give it to get love, which I did many times, or that I would lose it somehow by making a mistake. One day I realized that I AM the expression of God completely, always have been and always will be, and that only I can block myself. There was no way to have it taken away because I AM a living light of God, just as everyone is, whether recognized or not. When we give over everything to God, we find love. We find that love—God—has always been there. It is who we are.

Love is your root. Love is your true power. It is the foundation of all life. It can dissolve all fear. Fear keeps the door shut to feeling, knowing, and being in your real power. The power of the love within you is so strong that the universe will do anything it can to have you surrender to its ultimate truth. Through your heart center you must call in the higher light of God and plant your focus into its radiance. The light has the power to dissolve how you maintain ego and fear in your life. The light of your Original Self, the YOU that existed before you entered into your present body, wants to be aligned in this power.

Your love is a flame. Your love is a warm, tender, and roaring fire of light communion with sacred truth. Who are you within the borders of your heart? Can you feel its essence burning, surging, touching, holding, pushing away, sometimes fragile, listless, aching, wanting? Can you know its flame? You are that. All that you are is the golden embodied flame of Oneness that exists within you. BE within the earth of yourself, the water of your deep well, the air of your breath, the fire of your passion, and the etheric expansion of your infinite nature. May these elements give you serenity and comfort and peace.

When you surrender to love, you become One with life because you are living from the original essence that you truly are. As you practice filling yourself in love, you are fulfilling what you came here for. How to love yourself is the ultimate lesson and enables you to love the world and BE in service to the world.

By becoming *One in Soul,* you will experience the beauty and truth of your full heart. You will become flooded with love that will fill you and take you over until all that you are is love.

BE
Walk the path without a name,
Sing the song that's yours to claim.
BE the dance that's in your heart
Allow yourself to make a new start.

Find the love that waits to BE,
Through the gateways that set you free,
Feel the strength
Here is the key.

Awaken the power that honors You.
Here is your chance,

Now is the moment,
Meld into Oneness
Love beyond limit.

Sometimes it takes lifetimes to get it right.
Choose this moment,
Trust the wholeness that you are
Embody the light within your heart.

You are the answer.
Create your life through BEing One,
Allow the truth to set you Free.
To BE.

Shine through the darkest night.
Joyfully illuminate,
Your eye of the divine,
Leap to embrace the light,
Each moment becoming the gift of delight.

Break through the silence
Break through the pain
Let go of wondering what there's to gain,
The final frontier is in the receiving
The release of the me,
Into thee.

In the last moments of life, people don't think about the money they have or don't have. They think about love, the beautiful moments sharing love, and who has touched their lives. In the beginning all there is love. In the end, love is all there is. In between the two, you are given the opportunity to know the true wealth of love and the source codes into eternal happiness.

When you choose the love in your Self, you can finally heal and BE free. *When you are One in Soul—love is who you are.*

> ***The power of the love within you is so strong that the universe will do anything it can to have you surrender to its ultimate truth.***

The Call to Love

Come to love. Find what you are looking for.
As you love yourself you will be One with yourself and everything will be possible.
As you love yourself,
Your life will bring greater joy.
As you love yourself,
Loving others becomes effortless.
As you love yourself,
God is able to speak to you,
Through the silence within your heart,
As you love yourself,
The doors to freedom open from within.
As you love the holiness within you,
You will be able to forgive yourself,
Have compassion for yourself and others,
Trust yourself and God.
As you love yourself,
You will find,
The light of God BEing
Itself as You.

As you embrace your path of becoming One in Soul, Remember:

You are not your thoughts.
You are the spark of soul that lives within you.
God lives as Itself as your soul.
Seek God and love completely.
BE the heart of love.

Divine Union's Promise

As you are present in your body to the love and power of your soul, the greatest potential of your own being is revealed. Each day becomes a practice to live in authenticity and to feel the limitless possibilities of BEing One with Infinite Source.

Practice BEing One with the source of love and power within your heart and BE in Union with the presence of your soul. Do nothing each day for at least 15–30 minutes except to BE One with the silence and grace of Infinite Source within your heart. Empty yourself and feel into the space within your heart where there is stillness. BE One with the nothingness and allow your Self to expand through your heart into infinite love.

The pure spiritual light within you and the essence of universal love merge and become One within you as you let go and trust.

BE in the silence, the stillness, the movement, the song, and the joy within your heart.

As you walk forward on your life path from BEing aligned with your soul, you will generate love to channel into every area of your life. Once you embrace living in your heart and BEing present to the love within you, the power of Infinite Source will flow into your cells and rewire you into a new frequency. This gift from God brings happiness and requires BEing patient with yourself, life, and how your needs are fulfilled. As you receive the light of love, you will feel a stirring in your body that is the beginning of understanding the greater purpose of BEing here. As your soul aspects reunite within you, you may ask the question, *"What is my sacred passion? What ignites my heart and soul?"* Feeling and listening to that response is what sets you on fire to be the greater you. Just by becoming quiet and present with yourself gives you the opportunity to BE in your heart and with your deepest truths.

> *As you receive the light of love, you will feel a stirring in your body that is the beginning of understanding the greater purpose of BEing here.*

As you bring the light of your heart into every aspect of your life, you will authenticate how you live your life. Trust the lessons life brings to you, and strive to surrender to the higher truths being awakened within you. God is divine love, and your choice to find union with love no matter how difficult your life circumstances, guides your way home through the veils and obstacles of illusion itself.

BEing *One in Soul* requires the willingness to:

- Live in the presence of Spirit, the divine intelligence of life that fuels and sustains you, instead of living in your head alone. An awakened mind is a mind that is One with Spirit.

- Feel connected in your heart, and see the light in your heart as a golden globe, a sphere, and glowing ball of light in your upper chest.

- Accept that fear can no longer manipulate or control you, and you no longer choose to push love away.

- Own your feelings and move through them. Your feelings do not define you. They are not who you are. They are gateways into your greater truth and True Self.

- Let go of the belief that the challenges or dramas of life will leave you alone and miserable. They can be shifted into breakthrough experiences that set you free to BE you.

- Unify your heart and soul.

- Feel connected to the power of truth, light, responsibility, and accountability.

- Perceive life from a 360-degree perspective. Your mind is One with Infinite Source and is a servant to your divine Self—your Whole and True Self.

- Live in the center point of existence. You and the universe become One.

- Take responsibility for your own issues and baggage, learning through your own choices, and practicing BEing in alignment with your Whole Self.

- Identify "what is your stuff" and what is another person's energies, projections, and responsibility. You can then make better choices to not engage with energies that will take you out of your Self, divert your path, or take on energies that are not yours.

- Practice your ability to discriminate people, situations, and opportunities so you can make better choices for your Self. You will feel whether a situation is beneficial for your spiritual growth or not with greater ease and grace.

- Embrace everything that has happened in your life and respect the situations as awakeners to help you BE who and what you are, let go of fear, and trust who you are becoming.

- Release your attachments to what you believe others did to you so you can forgive your self and others with greater spiritual understanding and move on.

- Find unlimited compassion for everyone and to feel love for all peoples.

- Create and define your boundaries more clearly regarding who and how you give your personal love.

- Discern which energy exchanges with others support your life purpose and which ones do not.

- Open into the light within your soul, and the eternal beauty, grace, truth, wisdom, creative genius, and the power of integrity of your Whole Self.

- Trust the insights coming through you.

- Trust that you are BEing guided to shift your outer reality and relationships to support the integration of your Whole Self.

- Build your relationship to your soul.

- Align your life with the freedom that you find through your soul.

- Live in constant connection to Infinite Source.

- Say, "I am ready to expand, evolve, and enlighten my life."

Divine Union's Expression

As you become One with the family of humanity inside of your soul, you can then touch and feel all souls—their pain, suffering, joy, happiness, and sorrows. For inside of you exists every culture, creed, nationality, and gender. People who reject, betray, or hate others, are violent in their thoughts and actions—hate parts of themselves that they do not understand, have separated from, judged, and have turned against. To express their self-hatred, they hate others.

Beyond the dualistic polarities of love and hate, and fear and separation, exists the universal quality of Oneness. It is a place of union and connection that, once felt, is never forgotten. We are all One, united by love. When we are one with our whole soul, we are One with God.

There will be times when you will feel emotions that are not only yours but are shared by all of humanity. When you open the door to your heart, you will discover not only your own grief, sadness, longing, and despair, but all of humanity's.

Choose love as your "come to place" and uplift someone else next time you feel upset or down about the state of the world. Each time that you choose courage, fearlessness, determination, love, and compassion, know that someone else is benefitting by your choice. You can be sure that someone will feel it. We are all linked together by a golden light grid of love. The more of us that do this, the more we can help to shift the vibrations around the globe.

As you become *One in Soul,* you will find the freedom to embrace your life passion, bring forth the gifts from within your heart, and discover that your spiritual path is already the path that you are walking. You will create authenticity in your career, feel actualized in your life purpose, and work; create and maintain loving partnerships and relationships, including excelling as a parent; and become a master of your craft and soul's expression. You will function logically and intuitively at the same time. You will feel in your body what it means to surrender to Infinite Source and find your True Self in the process.

Walk your BE path with honor. Bless and release the hurts and disappointments of your life. Hold the space of unconditional love and support from your whole heart for your journey. Release the sorrows from your past. Forgive yourself for your actions and words that hurt others and your Self. Give to your Self the love that you yearn for. Let go of what no longer supports your soul and you will draw to you what you need to BE happy. Stay connected to your inner divine family made up of all of the expressions of your soul, and you will draw to you a new divine family of like-hearted souls who are already walking this path of BEing One with their truth and light. They will magnetically be drawn to You.

May you trust BEing your divine expression of wholeness, love, serving and enlightening the world.

REMEMBER:

- God—Infinite Source lives as love, power, and light uniquely expressed as you. All of your soul aspects are comprised of the two ingredients of love and power.

- As your heart center is activated by divine love you will find the gateway into full awakening and remembrance of who you are and why you are here.

- Love and power are our birthright as human beings. We have been trained to separate love and power for centuries. By separating these two vital energies, we have created the dynamics of pain and suffering in our lives and in the systems of the world.

- The fastest way to reunite the pure soul components of love and power within you is to reignite and reconnect your divine masculine and feminine soul aspects and energies.

- A consequence of our separation is that we unconsciously define who we are and hold onto the traumas and spiritual power imbalances from past lifetimes as if they are real and happening in our present life.

- The sorrow and suffering that we all encounter at some point in our lives are gateways into our next level of enlightening. Never forget that they are given from the divine to help us become One and whole.

- How you accept the IS that is you and what you do with it *is* what makes your life whole.

- You must accept the truth that is always beneath any emotional or psychological pain as a gateway to help you to find your power.

- Your fragmented soul aspects, which hide in your lower *Power Point Centers,* contain your spiritual power and light.

- In the most difficult moments, embrace the love that you are and become the love. This helps you to move through isolation, fear, control, pain, and separation into love and connection. How to love and BE your Whole Self is the ultimate lesson.

- As you activate the energies and intelligence of your soul aspects through your heart, you will discover the emergence of divine love. The heart of your soul knows love because it is love. It is the only activation of life that can free you.

- Love is the root. Love is the true power. It is the foundation of all things.

- Continually choose to build the stability created within your relationship to your soul. This anchor will give you the courage to enter through the higher energies and more advanced gateways of Spirit.

- No one can ever take away the freedom that you find through your soul. Whatever is needed to uplift and awaken your soul to make the connections into self-love and surrender and live in the simple truth of your heart will happen once you say, "I am ready."

- Your Whole Soul is the reunion of all aspects of your psyche that create an inner family based upon divine love in full expression.

BELIGHT MEDITATION

Integrating Your Power #1

The power of your soul is either supported to expand and evolve to exist at an early age or discouraged to BE who it is. The messages that you were given as a young child from your parents, elders, religious leaders, and schoolteachers have the ability to build your soul essence into full expression or to diminish its light. Nothing can destroy your spiritual essence and light. It is always within you, waiting to be ignited, grown, expanded, and implemented into your life.

Call to mind an individual from your life who you gave your power away to get something: love, attention, acknowledgement, care, recognition or support. See him or her standing in front of you. Tell them that you are now going to take back the power that you gave to them out of the fear of BEing You. Thank them for playing the role of making you doubt that who you are is worthy of love, you who are matters, and that who you are is enough to be abundantly supported and loved by the universe.

Close your eyes and look to see where in their body they are holding your energies. Tell them inwardly that you are taking back your power now. Unhook the energies of your power out of their body by using blue light. As you gently unhook your energies, bring them back into your body *(into your solar plexus—your Fifth Power Point Center)* as you move them through a field of white light to clear the energies before they come back into you. Send blue, white and gold light into the area's of their body where your energies were being held. This will uplift and heal them.

Now, feel where in your body you are holding their energies. You can do this by shifting your focus 10–20 feet above your head into pure white light and looking down into your body. Notice all of the spots where you can see their energies lodged. Making use of blue light, unhook their energies and send them back into their body, down through their legs, feet, and into the earth. Then, connect them into pure white light above their head. Release them with love. Send blue light into the areas of your body that were holding their energies.

Thank them for the lessons that they were instrumental in providing you.

Feel the new space in your body. Fill the space up with blue light, and the power of your light, love, compassion, insight, wisdom, and clarity. Practice this as many times as you feel called to with the people in your life with whom you feel inclined to do this exercise with. Take the time to observe the differences in your energies and perceptions.

Integrating Your Power #2

Create the time to sit and BE. Begin to breath in through your nose and fill your lower belly and lower back simultaneously with light. Repeat for at least 2 minutes. Now, begin to breathe into your heart center and move your focus into a spark of light within your heart. Connect your heart center, your lower belly and lower back through one deep inhalation in through your nose, hold and suspend the breath, while you place your focus in between your eyebrows—in your third eye. Exhale out your nose.

Now, travel in your consciousness into a point of awareness before you closed the door to the light that you are. As you focus into your third eye, call in the pure light of your inner child under the age of 5, infant, or pre-birth self. Ask her/him to just BE with you, as you open through your heart to see the light that they "are." Hold your inner focus with their light through feeling and BEing in your core column of light in the center of your body. Receive their light as a frequency, as a radiance, vibration and consciousness into your heart. Repeat this practice daily for as long as you receive benefits from it.

CHAPTER TWENTY

The Song of Your Soul

*"The great sea frees me, moves me, as a strong
river carries a weed.
Earth and her strong winds move me,
take me away, and my soul is swept up in joy."*
— Uvavnuk (Iglulik Eskimo, 19th century)

In between your ears, in the center of your head, is a portal where your soul connects with the infinite. Listen, BE, and let go into its silence and feeling of infinite space; open into the opportunity to commune with Infinite Source and the Master Beings of Light who work with you. You are being called home. Through the *One in Soul* and entire *BE* journey, you will discover how to trust and let go into BEing guided by your God Self, the eternal part of you that is One with all creation and beyond creation.

Your soul is here for a spiritual, creative, and karmic purpose. As you discover the wonder and brilliance within you and allow it to emerge, you and Infinite Source can meet in the union of your heart. Your happiness comes from BEing in the natural expression of who you are and serving all people with the gifts and song of your soul.

As your soul opens, you will hear its song. The song of your soul is a melody, a rhythm, a silence, a joyful feeling, a creative urge or impulse that melts the resistances that you have believed you need to survive in this world. Within its melody, rhythm, and vibration dwells its true expression. It will guide and feed you with its essence of love. It is your personal connection to life. As your soul is received, the music of your heart is ignited, and the song of your soul sings to you the secret messages of your BEing.

As you reintegrate your soul aspects into your heart, your soul song will come forth. It may be felt, heard, or sensed. You may feel it as you take in a blossoming rose in early summer, walk on a beach, prepare a special meal, smell the wet grass after a morning rain, watch birds in flight, commune with the stars on a clear night, listen to the wind, witness the sunrise, watch leaves fall off a tree in autumn, or feel embraced in your lover's arms. God will speak through your heart, and you will be able to hear its message as your heart, soul, and body reunite. This is the promise and joy being offered you so your life can be an expression of your light and love.

The light that you are may at first be seen in your heart as a small flame, but trust that it will turn into a blazing fire. With your intentional focus to BE reconnected to the peace, power and potential of your Whole Self, the gateways within your heart will open. All around you is a sphere of infinite light that feeds the essence of your BEing. It is your yearning for union that pulls the light to you. Your soul is larger than you have any concept of. Invite the light of truth and Infinite Source to pour through your body and fill you with strength and renewal.

Every moment has the potential to be an ignition of love that moves you deeper into your heart, awakening and returning you to your true home. Your soul rejoices as you remember and reconnect to your home of light in your heart. Your soul is you, the eternal child, wise elder, angel, creator, healer, innovator, peacemaker, awakener, lover, and giver. Your soul dances, sings, and lives in awe as it expands and merges with God—Infinite Source lifetime to lifetime. If you have any doubt that your creative and expanding soul can coexist and transform the linear and structured part of your brain, trust that your body, mind, and heart will reconnect and co-create in Oneness together.

> *Your soul is you, the eternal child, wise elder, angel, creator, healer, innovator, peacemaker, awakener, lover, and giver.*

Trust that your cells are being activated and ignited into the highest light. Know that your soul's ignition is your first step in helping you to release the ancestral, karmic, and genetic programs that have run your life and have kept you separate from the life stream of dynamic light. Pulsating through your body, currents of unexplainable bliss and divine love await you as you take the steps forward through the gateways of your heart. Keep letting go of your past beliefs and conclusions about your life and others, allowing the walls of your resistance and ego to crumble—expanding your heart, and soaring with new wings. Hear the song of your purpose and the messages being given to you. All awaits you.

The blessings being bestowed upon you come from your decision to love and to serve from your heart. Love opens and begins to flow as you say yes to the wisdom, brilliance, and light that live within you. As your soul ignites the light within your body, a new matrix is created, allowing higher frequencies of love and divine intelligence to enter into your energetic field and awareness. Your divine truth—your soul essence—is the nectar of healing and rejuvenation in every cell of your body.

The universe and you become One as the molecules of thoughts, feelings, and energies emerge and blossom from the seeds of your soul. There is no going back once you walk through the doorway of your heart. What awaits you is a torrential ongoing wave of divine guidance, support, and love that vaporizes your past, clears your wounds, unlocks the gates to heaven, and reminds you in every moment that you are an incarnated holy and whole precious spark of God—Infinite Source.

Love opens the doors to pure abundance. As the circuits of divine intelligence are reconnected and opened within you, it becomes a reality to directly access Infinite Source. Having direct connection to Infinite Source awakens the magnetic qualities of love that have the power to ignite your soul matrix design. Within your soul matrix is the blueprint of your life purpose, service, lessons, and challenges. As your emotional, physical, mental, etheric, higher Spirit, and soul energies become One, the pieces of the puzzle of your destiny path come together. You will feel unified with the bliss of Infinite Source and the blessings given through serving the One.

Relax into feeling your soul singing through your body. Keep your body open through how you think, feel, love, and communicate. Give yourself the space inwardly and outwardly to BE with what is emerging. Trust what bubbles up in you. Give yourself permission to BE creative with each moment. BE willing to go beyond what your mind is saying and to love the essence of who you are, rather than what you think you are and what you have or do not have on the external. Find the bliss of BEING the essence of *who you are*.

As you drop the resistance and the veils that block you from seeing, feeling, knowing, and BEing the radiance that you are, the essence of who you are is revealed in your heart and your life begins to bear fruit like never before. True prosperity is born through recognizing and knowing what and who you really are, and it can take the place of lack, emptiness, remorse, self-judgment, burnout, fear, and pain. As you embody the pure light of truth to radiate and fill your Whole Self, you become a magnet for prosperity. The gates of the inner kingdom open within you, revealing God's love and eternal freedom. The truth will set you free to BE.

> *BE willing to go beyond what your mind is saying and to love the essence of who you are, rather than what you think you are, and what you have or do not have on the external.*

Trust that you can step through every portal and every gateway that presents itself. Trust that you will succeed with your dreams, vision, and goals. As you live BEing the love that you are, miracles happen. All it takes is BEing willing to trust that you are never alone, and that you are always BEing guided by your higher power—God—Infinite Source. If you ask to BE guided by the divine, you will BE.

Your old ways will no longer work to give you what you want, and it will take a willingness to walk through the unknown and trust your soul over your fear. Sometimes you will wonder how you will make it across the bridge of the unknown, but you will. How do I know this? Because the bridges that I have had to cross were vast and sometimes seemed endless, and once I let go into trusting love, everything that needed to happen to release fear and expand into Oneness did happen and was filled in the miraculous. Everything that you need to become whole, and to fulfill your soul's promise and song, will be provided, I promise.

"There have been many times in my life where I had to let go of my need to know what was ahead of me and learn to let go into the

unknown. For many years, I would feel anxious when I was being called to open my heart to the unknown and let go of my pictures of how I wanted my life to unfold. I would feel fearful to walk forward until I knew what was ahead of me and what I would need to let go of. I had a lot of lessons to learn about truly letting go and letting go of control. As I began to inquire deeper into my True Self, I became aware of what I was attached to. Whether a specific outcome, the need to feel loved, validated, seen, received, valued, etc, or being attached to having what I thought I needed, had to be released. When attuned to the universe and God, then choosing to live in a state of receptivity, I was always given what I needed. When I gave God the reins of my life completely, I began going through a massive transformation.

During the six years of having progressed Lyme Disease, I lost my ability to help others and make a living, sustain my energies, use certain functions in my brain, and my physical body and nervous system fell apart. I had to let everything go including a home to live in. I had to let go of my attachment of ever doing healing work, spiritual mentoring or teaching ever again. I went from practicing yoga and hiking every day to a woman who had broken her foot tripping on a broken step due to her Lyme and co-infection brain imbalances and sudden co-ordination problems, which left me barely able to walk or function. Not being able to think, move, or serve brought me many tears, but it also became the vehicle to learn greater trust, surrender and humility. Even on crutches, I began my journey to find treatment in both in the USA and Europe. My endurance and faith were tested. I learned that God is everywhere and in every cell of my body and consciousness—in my entire BEing. My heart went from feeling despair into trust and faith unlike anything I had felt for lifetimes. 'Yea, though I walk through the valley of the shadow of death, I will fear no evil: for thou art with me; thy rod and thy staff they *comfort me,' became my mantra. Through walking through the unknown, I found God within me.*

I lived in many places for those years as a guest in other people's homes and was given what was needed to give me the time and space to recover and heal. It took those six years of being homeless to feel comfortable living in the unknown. I went from homeless to heart full, realizing that home is in my heart, and that God and I really were One. I noticed after a few years that my heart felt fuller and constantly overflowing. The secret was to live and trust BEing in my heart 24/7 no matter what. It was during this time that I was blessed by Beloved Meher Baba's direct guidance, which I followed with unswerving obedience and love. His constant presence in my life became the greatest gift of my life."

As you trust and let go into the unknowns of your life, feel the real you emerging and the false you dissolving. The voice of your True Self communicates directly with Infinite Source. As your soul receives the outpouring from Infinite Source into your Bodymind, you will feel yourself expand. As you listen to the song of your soul, you will want to let go and to surrender into the voice of your True Self. You will want to recognize the power and the love streaming into every cell of your body.

The song of your soul is more powerful than the negative messages stuck in your body and mind. When you listen and open to the surge of creative energy and guidance from the light of the divine, you will know what to trust. The divine will speak through your heart and soul's expansion. Even at times when your heart begins to shut down, nurture it with tenderness, and open to the light in your heart beyond what your mind can perceive. Listen to the song of your soul. As you feel the expansion of yourself, call in the energies of the earth, sky, water, breath, and fire. Envision them igniting your soul. Feel them penetrating your skin, cells, blood, and bones. Feel yourself becoming One with Spirit. BE in your body. BE the Enlightening.

A Message for You

No longer can you wait to fulfill your soul destiny.

Remember the magnificence of BEing One with Infinite Source.

You are a unique expression of the divine with a special purpose that serves the greater whole of humanity.

The divine will speak through your heart and soul's expansion, bringing you fulfillment and right action.

Listen and open to the expansive energy and guidance from the light of the divine.

The original spark of God is BEing birthed through you.

Love will awaken your heart and reveal the jewels of your soul shining and penetrating into all corners of your life.

Live BEing the love that you are and experience the miracle of your existence.

The pulse and rhythm, the ebb and flow, the expansion and contraction of your soul create a symphonic celestial roar of ecstatic union with the divine in your body.

Life wants to give you the keys to the great mystery within you.

Whether you have awakened years ago or in this very moment, trust the process of your life that directs you forward.

Step into your truth.

Trust that you are never alone.

You are a divine gift waiting to BE born.

Fulfill your soul's greatest yearnings to BE love.

Within your heart is the voice of freedom, calling you home from the eternal depths of Infinite Love.

BE in the power and love streaming into every cell of your body. Call in the energies of the earth, sky, water, breath, and fire. Feel them penetrating your skin, cells, blood, and bones. Feel yourself becoming
ONE
in
Infinite Source.

Feel into the light and open to its sanctuary of love within your entire body.

Trust that you can step through every portal and gateway that presents itself.

You are always BEing guided.

BE blessed in radiant light and align your Whole Self into Oneness.

Continue onwards now, my friend

Through the portals of light, wonder, freedom, and love within you.

BE ONE. BE YOU.™

REMEMBER:

- Listen, BE, and let go into the silence, the feeling of infinite space, and open into the opportunity to commune with Infinite Source and the Master Beings of Light who work with you.

- As your soul opens, you will hear its song. It will guide and feed you with its essence of love and sing to you the secret messages of your BEing.

- Your soul is you, the eternal child, wise elder, angel, creator, healer, innovator, peacemaker, awakener, lover, and giver.

- Keep letting go of your past, crumbling the walls of your ego, stepping into the expansiveness of your heart, and soaring with new wings.

- Trust that you can step through every portal and every gateway that presents itself. Ask to be guided and you will BE.

CHAPTER TWENTY-ONE

The End is Just the Beginning

"There are only two mistakes that one can ever make on the path to truth. Not starting and not going all the way."
— Buddha

As you welcome the ultimate expression of your soul and Source in union, the divine love and expression of your Whole and True Self provide the foundation to integrate your human and divine energies into every area of your life. Within the union of your soul exists your True Self. The light of your True Self will awaken you into life and remove the veils that have prevented you from answering the age-old questions of "Who am I?" and "Why am I here?"

By choosing to embark upon the journey to BE *One in Soul*, you are choosing to walk through the gateways into full self-actualization.

When you feel One with the light, love, and power of Infinite Source, you receive the strength, courage, clarity, and grounding to go through the eye of the needle of your own consciousness.

The greater the integration of your soul aspects, the easier it is for your Higher Self to merge into the light grid within your body. Your Higher Self holds the vibrational essence of who you have always been and will always BE. Your Higher Self or "Over Soul" protects and guides you as a steady flame of illumination. Your Higher Self is awakened in your consciousness through your devotion and surrender to God—Infinite Source. When you ask to BE guided on your soul journey by the masters of the light and by God, your Higher Self is reunited through your humble and heart-felt invitation.

The experience of having your Higher Self energetically connect with your mind and subtle bodies can be life changing. Later, in the work, you will learn how to bring your Higher Self into your body and live in Oneness with its guiding light.

> *The reunion of your soul gives you the strength, courage, clarity, and grounding to go through the eye of the needle of your own consciousness.*

As you allow the light that you are to shine forth, the diamond consciousness of your whole soul emerges. You resemble a fully faceted diamond, both absorbing and reflecting the light of the universe. Your heart center becomes your barometer for truth. How you choose to respond to yourself and each situation becomes the gateway for your evolution.

As you become *One in Soul*, you discover that how you respond to everyday life situations changes. It becomes more difficult to distance yourself from the spark of love within you. The magnitude of your love *is* Infinite Source fully expressing itself through you. It awakens within you the desire to love deeply, BE loved, and bring forth your gifts to the world. In your authenticity, you will create genuine connection everywhere you go. You experience BEing a role model through your grounded, expanded, and integrated presence. Here you will feel free and spontaneous, daring and bold, gentle and kind simultaneously. The duality and conflict found within the opposing parts of your false Self melt away, revealing a steady alignment with Infinite Source. This alignment brings integrity, joy, freedom, and trust.

Humanity must shed the skins that sustain illusion and give birth to living, thinking, and BEing from whole body-mind and soul integrated Oneness. The new paradigm of BEing *One in Soul* in ourselves and with one another births us on a universal level of living light with absolute love and authentic power. As we learn how to re-enter into the energies of our whole soul, we are then able to hold the door open for others in our lives to find their gateway into infinite love.

"I was sitting quietly and letting go of living in the past. I was choosing to BE present to everything in the now. I shifted all of my focus into my heart and allowed it to expand. All of a sudden, I experienced a veil being lifted from above my head. I slipped through a portal of light, similar to a sliding glass door opening, and stepped into pure light. I had shifted into Oneness. I slid through the eye of the needle. Beyond duality and into the light. Effortless, conflict, and pain free. Zero resistance, yet joyful. My only thought was how simple it was to move through the gateway; yet, it took years of commitment to my own journey to get to that moment. I felt free. But, I also knew there was more to learn, surrender to, and BE honest about in my Self."

Your Humanity Blueprint Journey: Next Steps

One in Soul is a loving invitation to embrace the power and presence of your soul, for it is the journey of your life. Through the progressive gateways given through this volume and the entire *Humanity Blueprint* series, the answer to the question,

"What is the *meaning of my life?*" is found. You receive your higher purpose through BEing One with the clarity of who you are. The *One in Soul* process guides you to rediscover the original light of peace, radiance, power, love, joy, and playfulness within you.

As previously shared, *One in Soul* gives you the foundation needed to experience the matrix of your own creation with love, and to heal the causes blocking you from BEing One and whole as your true empowered, passionate, magnetic, and successful Self. Up until now you may have come in and out of being in your heart. You may have unknowingly spent time each day stepping back into old behaviors and multi-lifetime patterns of controlling and repressing your soul energies, emotional joy and happiness, and life force vitality in your body.

While your soul is the foundation for who you are, becoming *One in Soul* is really the first step to being fully embodied as your Divine Self. The integration that you experience through BEing *One in Soul* activates the channels in your Bodymind connection. You will experience further initiations of your soul and divine awakenings with your light and energy field to ignite your full potential. The ascending steps in this body of work will support you to learn how to directly connect to Infinite Source and confidently access these spiritual dimensions that are aligned to your soul.

In Volume II of *BE: The Humanity Blueprint: Whole Body Enlightening*, you have the opportunity to step through the world of the psyche, the wound and the ego. You will experience being guided to unravel how you are in relationship to your psyche, emotional body, mind, and ego Self with the intention of freeing all of you to BE the whole You. You will continue to open your light body, deepen into your heart center, and heal the energetic connections between your physical, spiritual, and energy bodies. The points of power in your body that can help you break through your ancestral and karmic patterns will be further activated and enlightened. This supports the ignition of your full potential and gives you back the Source Codes of your own life. Each step that you take in the BE work returns the keys to your freedom, happiness, joy, fulfillment, and the power to BE who you were born to BE.

When you experience the *Spirit Gateways® BE System* through the *BE: Humanity Blueprint* book series and *Spirit Gateways® Institute courses, trainings and intensives* you will be empowered to:

- Clear and heal on a cellular level your ancestral lineage and karmic patterns

- Integrate your inner divine masculine and feminine energies

- Discover joy and love from within yourself

- Know yourself so you can BE all that you can BE

- Create a relationship with your light body and energy system that sustains and develops your abilities to live in the divine power that is your birthright

- Clear, deepen, and bridge your sexual energies to help develop your alignment in Infinite Source

- Move through the trenches of your psyche and soul that were created by leaving the light through fear, being judged, persecuted, abandoned, betrayed, and rejected

- Integrate your body, mind, and soul with Infinite Source

- Open the circuits of God light in your body that help you to shed layers of old mental body and emotional body energies

- Leave the path of pain and step on to the path of love

- Ignite and activate the leadership powers of compassion, fearlessness, and brilliance to awaken, shine and be expressed

- Discover Your Soul Imprint

- Experience living in the center of God in your Body

- End living out your old stories that block you from being truly happy

- Become One with life

- Integrate love and power

- Release your ties to your ego

- Trust in the divine

- Embody your spiritual nature into a new consciousness matrix of light

- Reunite your Higher Self, also known as your I AM presence, into your body

- Become the *Real and Authentic You*

- Open to the language of love that is distinctive to you

- Express the essence of your Original Self into your life

- Unite with God

- Live from love; BE the light that you are

- Create your life to be a natural expression of who you are

- Go beyond fear, resistance, arrogance, pride, and willfulness

- Heal the wounds of your heart

- Know truth

- BE healed

- Shift your perceptions to know greater peace and acceptance of everything that occurs in your life

- Create evolutionary change in the world

- Transform your experiences with money and sexuality through your heart

- End the battles between your mind and soul

- Fully understand the meaning of your life

- BE your True Self

- Open to your highest destiny path

We are all created equal in God's holy light and love. It is inevitable that, as a global culture, the soul within every individual—regardless of the outer classification of nationality, race, sex, religion, creed, or culture—will be honored and supported to BE all that they are meant to BE. We are all destined to hear the call of our soul and to be given the opportunity to awaken to the deep presence and truth of our True Self during these times of light and dark struggle. It is time to dissolve the ways that we create separation within our Selves and with one another.

The infinite intelligence of the universe expresses the powers of the divine that awaken and birth your soul into action. They will crack you open with tenderness, magnitude, compassion, and grace. They will get your attention by bringing you into situations that will confront the fears, beliefs, addictions and disconnections separating you from your True Self and offer you the choice to end the cycles of your suffering and how you effect others and the world. The universal powers within your soul want you to listen, go beyond your comfort zones, and take the call from the divine. Are you listening? Are you taking the call?

Take my hand and step forward into your enlightening Whole Self and divine connection with Infinite Source. Remember who you are. May light and blazing love pour through you, and may the preciousness of your heart fill the cells of your body and mind with infinite love. May living your divine purpose magnetize and restore the Original Way of Oneness. May all hearts BE ONE.

BE ONE. BE YOU.™

REMEMBER:

- Read and re-read—practice and re-practice what moves you in this book. Use the following *One in Soul* Practice Roadmap as your guide.

- *The Spirit Gateways® BE System Experience,* our signature training, will give you a transformational experience that teaches you how to step into BEing your Whole Self in every area of your life.

Become the light of love.
BE One in Soul.

For more information about

The Spirit Gateways® BE System Experience

plus

Spirit Gateways® Institute
Intensives, Retreats, Courses, and Facilitator trainings

and

Spirit Gateways® Foundation

visit:

www.ianalahi.com

CHAPTER TWENTY-TWO

The One in Soul Practice Roadmap

"And behold I have found that which is greater than wisdom. It is a flame spirit in you ever gathering more of itself."
— Kahlil Gibran

Dear Reader,
Contained within this chapter are all of the *BELIGHT MEDITATIONS*™ from *One in Soul*—Volume I.

Explore, enjoy, and practice them at your own pace.
May their benefits bring you peace, joy, bliss, and happiness.

BELIGHT MEDITATION — *Chapter 1* — *Page 12*

Relaxing

Create a space and a time to open and read this book when you have few distractions. Take a deep, full breath from your diaphragm, through your nose, and when you exhale, let go of all of the stresses and dramas of your day and the mental backlog that remains stuck in your head out of your mouth. Breathe long and deep four times.

Now, as you inhale through your nose, send the breath into your lower belly; and as you exhale, pull the breath up through your spine and out of your mouth. Repeat four times.

Place your hands with palms facing up on your thighs or above your knees while either sitting in a chair or cross-legged in an easy, relaxed position sitting on a pillow or mat on the ground. Take a few moments to follow your breath and to allow your mind to rest into the rhythm of your breathing. Sit for as long as you can. Just BE.

BELIGHT MEDITATION — Chapter 2 — Page 27

STEP 1: TAKE THE CALL

To prepare to take the call of your soul, you must shift how you LISTEN. Instead of engaging in the limited listening through your head that most of us do, practice listening from your whole body, focusing into the space beneath your rib cage, into your solar plexus. This is the central switchboard in your body where Spirit, emotions, and your mind meet. The goal is to LISTEN, FEEL, and FOCUS your attention in a new way. This will allow you to connect with the deeper truth within yourself and to hear the truths that others are giving you. Listening creates an opening and a space for you to realize and begin to embrace the true force and power of your soul.

Inhale through your nose and exhale out of your mouth. Become aware of being in your head. Then, slide down a waterslide from the inside of your head into a pool of warm, golden water in your solar plexus. Immerse yourself into the pool and sit in your solar plexus in the golden white light.

THE ONE IN SOUL PRACTICE ROADMAP

STEP 2: LISTEN IN A NEW WAY TO WHAT IS INSIDE YOU

Have a journal or notebook and pen by your side.

Instead of ignoring the thoughts, feelings, and emotions inside of yourself that may be giving you a sense of discomfort with your life, open to them. Find a few minutes (10 minutes) in your day, possibly first thing in the morning or at the end of the day, to focus on yourself. Tune out all of the mindless noise around yourself, and **turn up** the volume on the feelings inside your entire body. Be present with whatever is inside of you. Breathe deeply from your gut. Don't try to stop it, clear it, or ignore it. What is it saying? How does it make your body feel? What is it telling you that you want or need? Acknowledge what you are feeling.

Pick up your journal and pen and, with your writing hand, direct a question to the feeling. Ask one question, then switch your pen into your non-dominant hand and allow this aspect of you to respond. Begin by writing with your dominant hand: "I am here for you. What do you need me to know about you?" Switch your pen into your non-dominant hand, close your eyes for a moment, and allow this soul aspect of yourself to respond as you open your eyes and write. Next ask, "How can I be here for you?" Receive and BE with the energetic feelings from within you.

STEP 3: OPENING THE INNER CIRCUITS

While lying down, place your left hand approximately 2 inches below your collarbone, in the center of your upper chest. Here you will find your heart center. Breathe into your upper chest, into your heart center. Listen, Focus, and Feel. Now, place your right hand on your lower belly, in between your navel and your pubic bone, and breathe, allowing the breath to fill your belly and move into your lower spine. Focus your attention into your lower belly and heart center at the same time, and bring your breath into both locations. Allow the sensation of energy to move from one hand to the other hand and through your body. Listen, focus, and feel what is inside you.

BELIGHT MEDITATION — Chapter 3 — Page 38

Your Right to Exist

Take a moment and contemplate an experience in your life where you felt or perceived that you "did not exist." This could be a time when you felt who you really are was not seen or honored. Call up from within yourself what decision you made in that moment of feeling that you did not and "could not" exist. With your intention, dive into the truth and hear the voice within your heart that exists and just sense it. Whether it has a mighty roar, a song to sing, a tearful plea, a peaceful presence, or an impatient request, invite the "you" that wants to emerge to step up and be with you in this moment.

BELIGHT MEDITATION — Chapter 4 — Page 47

Opening

Find one moment in the past 24 hours that you chose to judge something about yourself or someone else.

Choose unconditional love and forgiveness for yourself for falling into judgment. Breathe into your heart center.

THE ONE IN SOUL PRACTICE ROADMAP

BELIGHT MEDITATION — Chapter 6 — Page 74

Here are *Twelve Practices* to help you clear and release sanskaras to evolve your soul:

- Practice forgiveness
- Chant and vibrate these sounds of God long and deep into your heart center or third eye—or both. Allow the tongue to touch the roof of the mouth when natural. Place your hands on your thighs, palms up, with your thumb and second finger (index finger) touching. Experience which of the following vibratory sounds of God work the best for you:
  AH HUM (ah-hoom)
  OM HUM (oh-mm-huu-mm)
  ELOHIM (ee-lo-heem)
  EE-AH-OO-AY
  OM-AY-AH
  OM (AUM)
  SAT NAM
  HU (huuuu)
  ONG SO HUNG (ang so hung)
  EEE (eeee)
  EEE VAH (eeee-vah)
  ELAH-HA (eeee-la-ha)
  AH (ahhh)
  SO HUNG (so-hunngggg)
  ONG SAU (ong sa)
  OM KAUR
  HAM SA (ha-mmm-sa)
  SO HUM (sew-hummm)
  AESHAMAY (ay-ee-sha-may)
  EASHOA (ee-ay-show-ah)
  LA ILAHA ILLALLAH (la-ee-la-ha-il-lal-lah)

- End cyclical patterns of giving away your power, repressing your creativity, loving the wrong people, empowering your ego, separating from your divine feminine or divine masculine, or both, living in your head, etc.
- Refuse to act out of greed, ignorance, attachment, anger, vanity, and pride. Avoiding these can prevent the creation of new sanskaras
- Practice non-attachment to outcomes
- Realize the beliefs you created during a past experience, trauma, or situation and let them go
- Do your *One in Soul* reconnection work to initiate the truth of your soul
- Live fearlessly, and find the light in your heart
- Be self-less and giving to others
- Meditate, develop breath awareness
- Live in your Whole Self by connecting your mind, body, and soul as One in the light and wisdom of Infinite Source within you
- Pay attention to what the universe is trying to teach you

BELIGHT MEDITATION — Chapter 7 — Page 96

Accessing Your Power Point Centers

Think of your mind as a strong and gentle beam of light that has the power to merge with any *Power Point Center* inside of your body. To access a *Power Point Center*, begin by placing your attention into the chosen *Power Point*. Similar to how you would gaze into the flame of a candle, place your focus into your root center, your *First Power Point Center*. As you focus into the *Power Point Center*, look for the light within it. Then, breathe into the *Power Point Center* to expand your connection with it.

Begin your practice time at 11 minutes and work up to 22 minutes.

Each day, begin with your *First Power Point Center* and then add the next *Power Point Center* into your practice. When you connect to the spheres of light above your head, invite the light to show itself to you. Allow yourself to open and connect to the light around you while you are holding a connection to your solar plexus, navel, and *Second Power Point Center.*

BELIGHT MEDITATION — Chapter 8 — Page 104

How to Find and Connect with Your Soul Integration Centers:

Lie comfortably flat on a blanket, mat, or towel on the floor. You can be naked or wearing a long shirt, tunic, or dress that is light weight to assist you in easily finding your *Soul Integration Centers.*

Practice this simple 1-time-a-day exercise for one month to open access to your feeling body and soul.

Preparation:

Place the middle finger of your right hand into your navel. Place the middle finger of your left hand into the soft indentation below your rib cage, into the soft hollow of your solar plexus. Breathe into these two points at the same time, inhaling and exhaling deeply with focus into the present moment.

First Soul Integration Center

To find your *First Soul Integration Center*, place your pinky, the little finger of your right hand, into your navel and your right thumb into your solar plexus. Drop your middle finger down into your torso and press into your body. This first *Soul Integration Center* is the clearing & self-empowerment point. It may feel tender. This point can hold a lot of past unprocessed or un-dealt with emotion. Tenderly breathe into it, for it contains the spiritual power to help shift willfulness into alignment with Infinite Source. Your first *Soul Integration Center* is a portal into the vast silence of the universe and the inner expansion of your soul and its power.

Allow your mind to drop down into your first Soul Point. Breathe until you can maintain the connection. Give yourself the message to breathe, let go, release, and relax into this *Soul Integration Center*. Release your mind and let go into the point. Trust your connection into your body.

Second Soul Integration Center

To find your *Second Soul Integration Center*, place your middle finger into the deep hollow space at the base of your rib cage. This is your solar plexus. Your *Second Soul Integration Center* is the center where your emotional, soul, etheric, and physical body meet. Ignite your *Second Soul Integration Center* by pressing it gently in a clockwise circular motion with your third finger. Relax, breathe, and focus your attention into your solar plexus. Open to the unlimited light dwelling within this inner sun. When your solar plexus *Soul Integration Center* is balanced, you feel energetically and emotionally secure within yourself. You know what are your energies and what are other people's energies. You can be who you are.

Third Soul Integration Center

To find your *Third Soul Integration Center*, gently slide your third finger up from your solar plexus until it touches where the bones of your ribcage meet. It will feel like a pointy ridge.

This is your *Third Soul Integration Center* the self-acceptance point. Press your finger into the point and move it in a clockwise circular motion while continuing to breathe into your *Third Soul Integration Center*. Continue breathing and deepening your focus into the tip of your ribcage for at least two minutes, until you feel a mental and energetic connection into the point.

Fourth Soul Integration Center

To find your *Fourth Soul Integration Center*, slightly inch up your finger, approximately 1/8 of an inch. Feel for a slight indentation, a valley, a concave slight softness. This is your *Fourth Soul Integration Center* the grounding point for body and soul integration. You are in the "first indentation." Bring your mental focus fully into this point through shifting your attention down into the solar plexus. Breathe and be in yourself. You will feel a sense of being centered and coming into your body. The *Fourth Soul Integration Center* helps you to let go, feel connected, and trust yourself.

Fifth Soul Integration Center

To find your *Fifth Soul Integration Center*, inch up another 1/8-inch and press into the next hollow indentation. Sense an opening and widening of your soul as you enter into the center of your breastplate. You are now in the "second indentation." Continue the process of gently moving your *Fifth Soul Integration Center* in a circular motion. Breathe into your breastplate and focus into what you feel. This *Fifth Soul Integration Center* helps you release fear and transform it into positive self-expression.

Sixth Soul Integration Center

To find your *Sixth Soul Integration Center*, slide your middle finger up another 1/8 of an inch into the next hollow indentation. Gently press your finger into this spot and just feel the energy within the point. Breathe, keep your mind focused into the indentation. You are now in the "third indentation." Feel your breath expand deeper and allow your body to connect into your breath and become "larger." The *Sixth Soul Integration Center* connects you into your truth. It brings you into the reality of being one with what is true for you in that moment.

Seventh Soul Integration Center

To find your *Seventh Soul Integration Center*, slide your finger up into the next and final *Soul Integration Center*. This final point is located in the center point between your nipples if you were to draw an imaginary line. You are now "in the fourth indentation." Allow your breath to expand into the space in the center of the valley of your upper chest and simultaneously into your upper back. The *Seventh Soul Integration Center* opens you into love and takes you through the blocks to receiving, giving, and being in love. It prepares you to move into your heart center, which is directly above the *Seventh Soul Integration Center*. Your heart center is the meeting point where your soul and spirit meet. It is the gateway into the light and joy of Infinite Source.

The *Soul Integration Centers* help to clear your core wounds and help you to live "present" and in the moment of your life. These soul-related *Integration Centers* ground, calm you, and bring an inner peace. They help you to find and BE who you are. When they are blocked, you will feel disoriented and separated from your truth. When they are clear and open, your energies will flow, your mind will be clear, and you will feel One with your Self and life.

Recap of *The Soul Integration Centers*

Soul Integration Center #1: Clears and supports self-empowerment. Contains the spiritual power to help shift willfulness into alignment with Infinite Source.

Soul Integration Center #2: Creates stabilization in the physical and emotional bodies. It is the meeting point of your soul, etheric, emotional, and physical bodies.
Soul Integration Center #3: Promotes self-acceptance.
Soul Integration Center #4: Grounds you.
Soul Integration Center #5: Releases fear and transforms it into positive self-expression.
Soul Integration Center # 6: Connects you to your truth.
Soul Integration Center #7: Opens you to infinite love and prepares you to enter into your heart center.

Your *Soul Integration Centers* are focus points for you to place your attention while you integrate your soul with your heart center. If you are feeling anxious or overwhelmed, you can focus light just by your intention into the *Soul Integration Centers* two **"notches"** above the tip of bone that protrudes at the base of your rib cage. When breathed into, this *Soul Integration Center* will immediately recalibrate your emotional, soul, and energy field. Whether you focus and meditate into one *Soul Integration Center,* or two, or more at a time, you will experience the multi-dimensional awareness and presence of your whole soul in your body. Similar to enjoying a long and sensual dinner with many tastes and nuances that bring relaxation and fulfillment, when letting go and deeply surrendering into your *Soul Integration Centers*, you will experience greater balance and increased clarity and happiness.

BELIGHT MEDITATION — Chapter 8 — Page 110

Uniting With Your Soul Integration Centers

Practice locating and connecting with your *Soul Integration Centers* once a day for at least one month to open access to the love and power of your soul. Focus and meditate into these *Soul Integration Centers* to directly align and integrate your soul energies in your body and further open your inner connections to the light of Infinite Source.

BELIGHT MEDITATION — Chapter 9 — Page 114

Power Point Center Clearing Meditation

Sit comfortably in either a chair or on a comfortable cushion on the floor. Create a stream of pure white light to pour down from above your head, through the center of your head, and down through a wide column of light that extends through your torso, legs, and feet into the earth. Bring the light from above your head down into your heart center, your *Sixth Power Point Center*. Gaze into your heart center and look for its light. Look for a glimmer or a blaze of light in the center of your heart center, which is in the center of your chest. As you gaze into your heart center, focus with a steady connection into seeing a wide-open space of light, then look for a flicker of light, then a blaze of light. Gently draw the light up into your third eye, your *Ninth Power Point Center*. Feel your third eye by entering into it through the center of your head and fully immerse yourself into it. Stay in your third eye until you sense its light. BE in your third eye until you feel yourself enter its "expansive zone," then once again shift your focus into your heart center and, when fully in its light, reconnect into your third eye and be in both centers at the same time—unite your heart and third eye.

Each time that you do this meditation, go into your heart center a little more. Feel the vibrational quality of your authentic Self and open into the presence of light.

THE ONE IN SOUL PRACTICE ROADMAP

BELIGHT MEDITATION — Chapter 9 — Page 132

The Power of Being You – A Daily Practice

Place your right hand on your lower belly and begin to breathe in long and deep breaths filled with light and love into your entire body. When relaxed, bring your breath into your chest. Now, bring the middle finger of your right hand into the hollow space in between the nipples on your chest. Breathe in light into this portal of light. It is your *Seventh Soul Integration Center*. Bring your middle finger down a notch, into a hollow space directly below your *Seventh Soul Integration Center* into the *Sixth Soul Integration Center*. Press your finger into the hollow space a little deeper and bring light and your breath into this *Soul Integration Center*. Bring your shoulder blades together just a bit. Allow yourself to BE and experience what you feel. Your *Sixth Soul Integration Center* strengthens you to BE YOU and activates the confidence within your Bodymind to express who you are.

BELIGHT MEDITATION — Chapter 9 — Page 136

How To Find Your Creation Point

Your Creation Point is located approximately 2.5 inches below your navel. An easy way to locate it is to place your thumb in your navel, your pinky on the top of your pubic bone, and then drop your index finger down on to your lower belly with your right hand. This point is your second *Power Point Center*, also known as your tantien. Now, bring your index finger from your left hand down on to your belly in between your index finger and your thumb. This is your Creation Point.

BELIGHT MEDITATION — Chapter 9 — Page 139

How to Create a Sphere of Protection Using Your Creation Point

Your Creation Point is a powerful meeting place of highly attuned energies that, when activated, can supercharge your energy field and amp up your focus to fulfill your life tasks and goals. The Creation Point, being a generator of pure energy, has the ability to be a source of energetic protection for you. We all need to know how to create a sphere of light protection to protect our energy field. One effective tool to put into practice is to create a sphere of light from your Creation Point.

To begin, bring your focus into your Creation Point and look for sparks of light that are moving and shooting upwards from deep within its center. Bring your awareness into the core of light within you and merge with them. As you keep your eyes closed, send the sparks of light out around your body and create a strong crystalline sphere that completely encompasses you. Your Creation Point Sphere is a full 360-degree circle that can help you hold the frequencies of your light and support being in full awareness. As you create your Creation Point Sphere, step into the center of your Self and breathe into your Self with a long inhalation and exhalation. Keep your focus in your heart center and then create a layer of gold light around your sphere to add to its strength. Feel free to add a layer of platinum, bronze, or silver for added protection. Your Creation Point Sphere will be sufficient to protect you from negativity, low vibrations, and other people's projections.

BELIGHT MEDITATION — Chapter 9 — Page 140

3 Steps to Awakening Your Creation Point

As you begin the following three-step process, bring your awareness into your heart and into the present moment.

Step 1

Sit in easy pose, a simple cross-legged position, spine upright. If sitting on a chair is more comfortable for you, please do. Reach your chest forward, reach your shoulder blades together, and extend your tailbone towards the earth.

Raise your chest upwards a bit, slightly bring chin down towards the chest.

Begin to breathe into the Creation Point.

Allow your breath to fill the space within your Creation Point.

See the light within your Creation Point.

Feel the light.

Bring your focus into the Creation Point.

Merge your focus into your Creation Point.

BE One in the Creation Point. See flames of pure white fire in the Creation Point.

Feel them begin to move.

See, Feel, BE. Allow them to expand into the spine and to take up more space.

Very slowly, very, very slowly, like a butterfly emerging out of a cocoon, begin to allow the breath and prana (life force energies) to move up through the spine. Focus into each vertebrae, filling them with light.

Feel warmth rise up the spine. Visualize the energy moving through the spine into the center of your skull. Expand your attention and energy into the back of your skull. Allow the energy to expand into the center of the head and then into the third eye, which is the pituitary gland, about two inches inside of the forehead.

Once again, move the energy slowly up the spine, through each vertebrae, into the back of the skull, and then into the third eye. Relax. Remember, it is subtle.

Allow the energy and light to move down inside of the central core channel of the body as you allow your breath to gently inhale and exhale into your Creation Point.

Step 2

Sit in easy pose, a simple cross-legged position, spine upright. Raise the chest upwards a bit, slightly bring chin down towards the chest.

Inhale through your nose and fill the lower belly as you gently pull the Creation Point into the lower spine. With as little effort as you can, exhale your breath through your nose in a continual rhythmical breath. Gently pump the Creation Point through the action of your breath. Focus on the exhalation through your nostrils, and the inhalation will happen naturally. This is the breath of fire. See the light in your Creation Point as flames of pure white fire. Feel the energy gently massaging your spine. BE One with the breath.

Let it BE.

Subtle.

Gentle.

Relaxed.

As you gently pull the Creation Point into the spine, expand the breath into your sacrum and tailbone area. Fill your lower back with breath. As you gently draw the light energies up your spine, let them kiss your third eye with butterfly wings.

Stay with the Breath of Fire for as long as you want and is comfortable. Feel the prana gently move up the spine, touching the third eye. Rest and BE in the stillness within your third eye. Rest and BE in stillness in your heart. Rest and BE in stillness in your third eye and in your heart at the same time.

Step 3

Place your right palm on your lower belly and your left palm on your forehead.

Feel the connection of the energy as you gently inhale and exhale.

Begin a very gentle Breath of Fire. Make sure that you focus on the exhalation of the breath through your nostrils, pulling the Creation Point into the spine.

Now, shift the positioning of your palms on your lower belly and forehead to placing your left thumb on your third eye and your right thumb on your Creation Point. Feel the connection of energies between the two points. Continue Breath of Fire until you feel a deep connection. Take a deep inhalation in through your nose. Hold the breath. Suspend the breath. To suspend your breath, you will pull up your spine out of your navel, pull up the muscles around your genitals, pull up your diaphragm, and lower your chin a bit. Maintain your thumb positions. Exhale. Rest. Relax.

BELIGHT MEDITATION — Chapter 9 — Page 142

Activating Your Power Point Centers

Spend 5-15 minutes each day activating your *Power Point Centers* with the following practice:

Begin by bringing light into your heart center from above your head. Fill your heart with light. Then, bring your focus into the light within your heart by dropping your focus into the larger space between your heart center and solar plexus. Allow the energetic pull into your solar plexus to center you. BE in your heart.

Next, bring light down from above your head into your root center, your *First Power Point Center*. Fill your root center with light. Then, bring your focus into the light within your root center.

Continue the exact same process, bringing and focusing light into each *Center*:

- *Second Power Point Center*, your lower belly
- *Third Power Point Center*, your creation point center

- *Fourth Power Point Center,* your navel
- *Fifth Power Point Center,* your solar plexus
- *Sixth Power Point Center,* your heart center
- *Seventh Power Point Center,* your throat center
- *Eighth Power Point Center,* back of the skull
- *Ninth Power Point Center,* your third eye
- *Tenth Power Point Center,* your crown center

Remember to:
- Focus light into each *Power Point Center* for as long as you can.
- Keep your focus into each center of light up against the inside of your spine.
- Accept however the experience happens for you. All that is important is practicing shifting into the light and BEing in the light.
- Just stay with the intention and focus to increase being in the light in each *Power Point Center.* By doing this exercise every day you will experience rapid results.

BELIGHT MEDITATION — Chapter 9 — Page 146

Integrating Your Power Point Centers

You can step into mastery levels of integration by working daily with your *Power Point Centers.* First, practice holding your focused attention into one *Power Point Center,* then two or more *Power Point Centers* simultaneously. Each time that you hold the light in one of your *Power Point Centers,* you establish an anchor into your core strength. A profound synergy that resembles the interconnection within a molecule opens in your body as you reconnect the energy grid of light that is found within your *Power Point* network.

Outcomes when you focus and unify two or more *Power Point Centers* at the same time:

Power Point Center Integration Chart

Integrating Your Power Points	Outcome
6th, 3rd, 1st *Power Points* Heart Center, Creation Point, Root	Energy Field Protection & Whole Self Empowerment
9th, 5th and 1st *Power Points* Third Eye, Solar Plexus, Root	Integrated Thinking
9th, 5th, 2nd *Power Points* Third Eye, Solar Plexus, Tantien	Integrated Emotions
6th and 2nd *Power Points* Heart Center and Tantien	Aligned Intuition
6th, 3rd and 2nd *Power Points* Heart Center, Creation Point, Tantien	Personal Power Integration
8th, 6th and 1st *Power Points* Back of Skull, Heart Center, Root	Grounding of the Heart
10th, 5th, 2nd and 1st *Power Points* Crown, Solar Plexus, Tantien, Root	Clear Decision Making
22nd, 21st, 11-14th, 6th *Power Points* Center of both feet, center of earth, 4-dimensional levels of soul above the head, Heart Center	Energetic Healing and Awakening
9th, 6th, 3rd, 2nd *Power Points* Third eye, Heart, Creation Point, Tantien	Being Present

Integrating Your Power Points	Outcome
21st, 20th, 8th, 6th, 5th, 1st Power Points Center of earth, God dimension above head, Back of Skull, Heart, Solar Plexus, Root	Sexually Connected
10th, 9th and 6th Power Points Crown, Third Eye, Heart	God Focused
7th, 6th, 3rd, 2nd, 1st Power Points Throat, Heart Center, Creation Point, Tantien, and Root	Standing in and Speaking Your Truth

Spirit Gateways®/Iana Lahi All Rights Reserved ©

BELIGHT MEDITATION — Chapter 10 — Page 180

Opening To Your Soul Theme

Take some time to sit quietly and gently begin to look for the light within you. Prepare to practice a meditation to open your senses. Bring an image of a rose into your mind and inhale its scent. Receive the feeling that it arouses into your body. Open all of your cells to the bliss of the rose. Fill your body with this feeling. Receive the light from within the feeling. See the light glow within you. Now, listen for a sound emanating from the light inside of your body and in between your ears. Focus upon the rose opening within you.

Allow yourself to:

Smell what you are seeing. Hear what you are seeing. Feel what you are hearing. Invite your inner knowing to emerge and be present with yourself.

Be open to align your senses to one of four soul themes: joy, truth, love, or union. Which one of the following four soul themes do you relate to the most? Are you most aware of joy, truth, love, or with union in the present moment? Be with what is real for you. Breathe in the feeling and presence of one of these soul themes into your body. Next, be with a present life challenge from the perspective of one of the soul themes. Align a challenge in your life to this soul theme. Each day, consciously align your thoughts and perceptions to your chosen soul theme. Allow it to help you make decisions and to shift your priorities. Make use of being in your soul theme as a grounding exercise to help you stay true to yourself and to not abandon, betray, or reject your Self.

BELIGHT MEDITATION — Chapter 11 — Page 211

Reconnecting Your Soul Fragments with Light

Breathe into your heart center. Feel into your heart and allow any feeling of hurt, the realization of something important not coming to fruition, sadness, emptiness, aloneness, longing, grief, or sorrow, etc. to BE present.

Focus so deeply into your heart that you can feel the feeling, *yet do not become the feeling.* Have compassion for the feeling. BE with the feeling as a friend and partner.

Go so deeply into your heart that you find light. Keep going inside as you enter into a wide space, or cave of safe space. Now, bring light into your heart using just your intention. Focus light from about 10–20 feet above your head directly into your heart. Fill your heart with light. The light that you send into your heart is going to loosen up the feelings that have been blocking you, holding you back, or creating angst. Invite the light to clear the feelings that have been holding on. Then, fix your attention into the space of love underneath the old feeling. BE in the love, in the light, in your heart center.

Remember the soul is accessed through the heart. So, anytime that you move light into the heart, you will awaken, open, clear, transform, and have the opportunity to heal a soul fragment into the light of acceptance, grace, and love. Your soul fragments can be directly accessed through your heart. The light can and will bring you into a state of aligned focus, healing, and renewed vitality.

Each time that your mind plays out an old tape loop from fear, come back into your heart. Each time that your ego Self works to separate you from the love that is your True Self, and divides you from life through being judgmental, resistant, defensive, manipulating or controlling, align your heart, love, and power to the light.

BELIGHT MEDITATION — Chapter 12 — Pages 237-246

Everyday Ways to Build Trust

As part of your healing process, trust must be established before healing can occur. Your feminine needs to feel safe to express and evolve as you create an inner and outer container.

Everyday ways to build trust with your feminine:
- Place money in all of its forms—paychecks, business and personal checks, and cash that you receive—on a sacred alter that is filled with meaningful pictures and objects of beauty, and give thanks for the abundance given to you. Watch monies and opportunities increase in your life. (You are giving thanks to divine mother.)

- Notice when you have a pain in your body, then track the pain to a feeling that needs to be expressed and received by you. Practice an active mode of opening and receiving with full intention and full presence.
- Feel the earth element through your skin. Skin brush, apply balancing oils to your body, and drink medicinal herb teas daily. The earth element creates prosperity, longevity, health, grounding, and nurturing for the self and others, and the ability to complete projects.
- Allow yourself to live within the space within your heart as you speak, and envision your life and work. Expand yourself in your heart to connect with God—Infinite Source. Bring the focus from your mind into your heart and open to gold light in your heart as you think about the fulfillment and completion of your intended project, goal, or dream.
- Remain open to all of your feelings without judgment. If you do not know what you feel, find a way that helps you find your feelings. Some of these ways include gardening, jogging, writing, cooking, pranic breathing, yoga, dance, journaling, painting, pottery, laughing, singing, sailing, hiking, BEing, etc. Each time you do a chosen activity, feel your way into the space of clarity and neutrality with the full range of feelings within you.
- Be spontaneous. Do things in your day in a new way. Practice seeing the world around you in a new way.
- Listen to your heart and BE in it. Practice shifting your attention from your heart, through your feet, and into the center of the earth. To find the core light in the center of the earth, look for a large, clear white crystal or flames of pure white fire. Then, breathe into your heart from your connection with the earth.

- Pay attention to being in and with your Self first before you try to make something better for someone else.
- Learn to give yourself "space" in the moment. Before you speak, or do "anything," give yourself space to feel where you are and how you feel. Receive your own energies first, then speak or "do."

Similar to your feminine, you must take the time to reinforce your sacred space and build trust with your masculine in your everyday life.

Everyday ways to build trust with your Masculine:
- Journal with your wounded Masculine Self and look through his pain and see his light with compassion and acceptance.
- Spend a day doing nothing but being with him in your heart.
- Throw yourself into a project that you haven't done in a long time, and do it without judgment.
- Observe how you go into your head during the course of your day and create logical denial. Choose to let go of the stories that you make up to confirm your thoughts and perceptions.
- Do a word cluster on paper. Write down one feeling that you are having and circle it. Then draw a line connecting to the next level of feeling and circle it. Go down 20 levels into your Self, each time finding another word that describes the feeling, all the way into your core.
- Find an object that interests you and observe it, such as a piece of fruit, a sculpture, a piece of pie, a plant, an animal, etc. Study it first from your head, then your heart, then through your senses: feel, smell, hear, see, taste, and experience its movement. Write your observations.

- Choose to have compassion for a total stranger every day for a week.
- Breathe into your heart center once a day and envision a part of your inner masculine joining with you. Surround him in gold and light white with love.
- Move from one side of a room to another walking backward, breathing into your spine and allowing your spine to guide you.

BELIGHT MEDITATION — Chapter 12 — Page 261

Clearing Your DNA Strands in Your Emotional, Etheric and Physical Bodies

Begin by breathing blue light into your lower belly. Fill your lower belly with blue light as you inhale and exhale. As you inhale, in your own timing, carry the blue light up to your upper chest and fill your collarbone area in this light. Repeat 4 times.

Drop your focus into the center of the earth where there are flames of pure white fire. Draw these flames of pure white fire up through your feet, legs, and into the space between your pubic bone and tailbone. Just BE with these flames of pure white fire and sense them or feel them.

Now, allow the flames of pure white fire to become two strands of white light that reach up from the space between your pubic bone and tailbone, your root center—your *First Power Point Center*. As you inhale, begin to *arc* the strands to either side. On your exhale, crisscross the light strands so that you are creating a double helix of light, like a DNA strand, through each *Power Point Center*, slowly and deliberately. Focus your attention into the space between your spine and the inside of a column of light. Go through each *Power Point Center* from the root center up through the second *Power Point Center*, and through your creation point, navel, solar plexus, heart, throat, back of the skull, third eye, and crown. Allow the energy to flow up through your crown chakra and flow down the sides of your body. Repeat 12 times.

Now, create three strands of color on either side of your starting point in your root center, inside the space of your tailbone and pubic bone. Repeat the crisscrossing pattern with the three strands of color this time through the central core shaft of each *Power Point Center*. As you arrive in the third eye, crisscross the strands several times through the third eye before moving into your crown center. To complete, sit and bathe in the light overflowing through your crown center.

For those of you who want to take the practice further:

Create 6 strands of gold light on either side of your root center, crisscrossing them and looping them through each *Power Point Center*. When you arrive at the third eye, loop the golden energy through the third eye, then bring the light upwards through the crown center, allowing it to spill over and back down to the tailbone-pubic bone area. Repeat the circuit until it is flowing like a swift river of light.

BELIGHT MEDITATION — Chapter 13 — Page 278

Igniting Your Body with Color: An Open Eye or Closed Eye Practice

Part I

Begin by drawing pure white and golden light down from above your head as you inhale through your nose the golden white light into your *Second Power Point Center*—the center found by dropping your index (second finger) down on your belly as you place your pinky on your pubic bone and your thumb in your navel. As you inhale, send the breath into your sacrum and lower vertebrae's. Feel your lower belly gently expand and open. On the exhale, pull up white flames of fire from the core of the earth up through your genitals, lower vertebrae's and fill your *Second Power Point Center* with light.

On the next inhalation, gather the golden white light from the center of the earth and pull it up like taffy into your *Second Power Point Center*. Now, gently move it up inside of your spine into the area in between your shoulder blades. Just BE in the golden white light in between your shoulder blades and allow it to flow into your heart center. On the next inhalation, once again, pull up the golden white light into the space between your shoulder blades and the center of your heart center, your *Fifth Power Point Center*. Exhale the breath out of your mouth and allow the golden white light to flow down into your *Second Power Point*—your lower belly, your tantien. Create a circuit, a loop of pure white light that moves from your lower belly, sacrum and tailbone up the spine to the space between your shoulder blades, into your heart center and then down through your body to its starting point in the base centers of your body.

BE present with this circuit and feel the circular flow of golden white light flow from the center and back of your heart center—your *Fifth Power Point Center*—down into your *Second Power Point Center* and then up through your spine, back into your heart center. Maintain your focus in the flow of golden white light for 10 cycles.

Then, rest and BE still. Allow for total stillness.

Next, inwardly ask what color or colors your heart center would like to be filled with to feel nurtured and connected.

Begin to bring the color or colors into your heart center and experience them flowing into you.

As you stay with your breath, inhale and expand the color or colors into your heart center. As you exhale, focus the colors in between your shoulder blades, the center of your "inner wings." Stay inhaling and exhaling with the colors, allowing them to fill your entire body.

With your next inhalation and exhalation, allow the swirling and flowing fields of color to move and expand into all of the cells in your whole body. Allow the colors to flow, take up space, and anchor their frequency in your body. Invite the colors to shift and change, watching the gorgeous hues of colors pour, ripple, stream, spiral, and pulsate.

Relax your muscles and your spine, and breathe. Just BE.

Allow the sensation from the colors that flowed and filled you to be imprinted into your body and soul.

Rest. BE still.

Part II

Direct your focus back into your breath. As you inhale, draw in one of the colors from the inside of your body that you discovered in the last meditation. Slow your breathing down as you feel the color in your body.

Now, give the color a tone, a sound, or a melody. Sense the color singing its tones, sounds, or feelings in your body. Allow your body to be imprinted with the color and the sound. Invite into the cells of your body the color and the sound. This will be the same process as receiving the imprint of a newly found soul aspect of yourself. By feeling your soul, and allowing it to imprint you with its essence, your body can begin to release its stresses, controls, and fears.

Rest. BE still.

Part III

Fill your body with golden white light. Allow your breath to be gentle and soft. Inhale through your nose and out through your nose. Bring your breath into the center of your heart, into the space between your shoulder blades. Wait until you feel your breath connected in to your consciousness, then shift your attention into your root center, your *First Power Point Center*, the space between your pubic bone and tailbone. Pull up golden white flames of fire from the core of the earth as you pull golden white light down from above your head. Allow them to both meet in each *Power Point Center*. BE aware of your breath, gently moving in and out of your body through your nostrils. Focus your attention into the golden white light in your root center. Become One with the light.

Invite the colors from the Part I exercise that rippled, streamed, spiraled, and pulsated in your body to be activated by your focus once again. Expand your breath on the inhalation and on the exhalation through your entire body. Ask your body what color it wants to invite in to open up the connection with your divine feminine. Allow the color to flow into your entire body and mind. Breathe into the back of your skull, your heart center, and your root center at the same time. Now, invite the presence of your divine feminine to begin to connect to you through the color and to touch you through your senses. Feel, hear, sense, and see her presence. Allow her to BE in you and to communicate to you. Breathe and fill yourself with her presence and the color or colors in which she is moving and BEing. Allow her to continue to fill your body. Listen and feel.

Now, invite the presence of your divine masculine to make itself known to you through a color and invite "him" to begin to connect with you through the color and to touch you through your senses. Feel, hear, sense, and see his presence. Allow him to BE in you and to communicate to you. Breathe and fill yourself with his presence and the color or colors in which he is moving and BEing. Allow him to continue to fill your body. Listen and feel.

To complete, bring the colors of your divine feminine and divine masculine into a sphere of light in your heart center. Allow your body and soul to integrate. Rest.

BELIGHT MEDITATION — Chapter 14 — Page 290

Finding the Light

In most native cultures, ceremonies exist where a person faces the four directions—North, South, East, and West—as a way of honoring all of Creation. As part of this process, one calls in the powers, great beings, and gifts from each direction, along with the multi-dimensional realities of this world. If you close your eyes and inwardly turn towards each direction inside of yourself, and see the world through a broader lens, you can begin to feel a new relationship with the universe. When you do this, you will lose your short sightedness and limited state of knowing. You will feel connected to the joy, grace, empowerment, and creativity of your enlightening soul. You will begin to experience direct awakening into your True Self.

Take a moment right now and close your eyes. Within your Inner Self, turn to the right and look for the light. Shift and slowly turn to the right again, each time gazing inwardly into each direction until you find and see the light. Face the light. Open to the light. Dwell in it. Stay facing it and receive its radiance. Feel the light in your body. As you see or sense the light, connect into your solar plexus. Now, ask Infinite Source to help you walk in the light following this new direction in your everyday activities.

The goal is to become whole, to be a complete person, and to see and feel from all perspectives. If you are struggling to move through how you feel limited in your life by inner or outer circumstances, BE willing to ask the universe to show you a new direction to walk in.

BELIGHT MEDITATION — Chapter 14 — Page 292

In the Flow

BE willing to go into the light every day. Visualize and feel light enter your body everyday. You are naturally connected to the light at all times. The light flows into you from the top of your head through your body into the core of the earth. As you visualize and feel the light flow into you, be willing to open to it and feel your heart. How? When you sit with the light moving through your body, you have the opportunity to merge with the light and feel into it as a support for you.

Even if you have no time, take 5 minutes 2-3 times a day to simply focus and bring in light. Let it flow from the sky above your head and from the earth into your body. Feel into where the light wants to flow. It may be in your root center, your solar plexus or heart center or all three. Let the light flow and fill you.

Trust the light. It will guide you to open and feel within your body and heart center.

BELIGHT MEDITATION — Chapter 15 — Page 333

The One in Soul Experience™

When you open to the light within your body and soul, you increase the velocity of your spiritual power and open the gateways to experiencing and embodying the unique human expression of your Divine Self. You are giving aspects of yourself an expanded space to live within that previously had "no place to go." You are moving into and expanding the space and light within you to contain the fullness that you truly are. When you integrate your light and dark, the unknown of your life becomes the known, and the known becomes the unknown. The invisible becomes the visible, and the visible becomes the invisible. The divine aspects of you become human, Spirit meets matter, and your human attributes are raised into the divine. It is the meeting point, the center point of your creation and all creation. Your entire understanding, perspective, and feeling of what life is expands.

Soul Integration Preparation Exercise:

The first step in preparing for the soul integration process is to breathe into your body. Fill every cell and every organ with your breath. Continuing with your breath, gently allow your mind to descend down into your body into your solar plexus so your mind can relax and your body can open. Next, bring your attention into a wide and strong beam of light that exists 10–20 feet above your head. Allow the light to flow from above your head all the way down through your body into the earth. Next, bring your attention into a wide shaft of light around and inside of your spine and down into your root center. Know that this light is directly connected to Infinite Source, and once brought down into your body, it can begin to open you to living in Oneness. You will be reconnecting the highest light of your consciousness with your soul energies in your body. Stay with the above processes until you feel comfortable in your body and being connected to the light. Give yourself anywhere from 3–10 minutes to practice this preparation exercise.

The One in Soul Practice

STEP ONE:

BE willing to accept your Whole Self with love. Suspend disbelief. Your intention to BE ONE with the light is all that is needed.

STEP TWO:

Take the time that you need to BE with each step. Go at your own pace and savor each connection that you make.

From 5–10 feet above your head, create a waterfall of pastel-colored hues of dazzling and sparkling light. Send the waterfall of colors down through the top of your head, your chest, torso, your legs, feet, and deep into the earth. Feel the waterfall flow around and down through your body, clearing your energies.

STEP THREE:

From 10–20 feet above your head, create a beam of blue light and shine it down through the top of head, into your body—your chest, torso, pelvis, through your knees, ankles, feet, and deep down into the center of the earth, where there are flames of pure white fire.

STEP FOUR:

Begin to bring these flames of pure white fire up from the center of the earth, up through your feet, your legs—including your ankles, knees, and thighs—and into the space between your pubic bone and tailbone. Here, spiral the white flames of fire clockwise or counterclockwise. Your body will know what to do. Begin to bring the flames of pure white fire up through your *Second Power Point Center* into the space between your spine and the center of your lower belly. Next, bring the flames of pure white fire up into the space between your navel and your spine. Then, lift them up into your solar plexus, the space directly under your rib cage in the center of your body.

STEP FIVE:

Slide your focus from being in your head, down into your solar plexus, the *Fifth Power Point Center*, which is the space directly centered under your rib cage. Slide down a waterslide from your head into a warm pool of gold light within your solar plexus. Bring your full attention into the pool of gold light. Next, pull up the white flames of fire from your root center, so that they are directly below the pool of light in your solar plexus. Feel the white flames of fire warming up the pool of golden light to the perfect temperature for you to sit in as the flames become One with the water. Continue to bring your full focus from your mind down into your solar plexus and feel yourself sitting in the warm pool of golden light. As you sit in this pool, look up through the top of your head and watch a waterfall of pure white light pouring down onto you. Receive and take in the energy as you breathe and maintain your connection into your solar plexus.

STEP SIX:

Travel 10–20 feet above your head into pure, white light. Create a laser beam of light, a spotlight beam of love, and shine it down into a wide and open elevator shaft—a wide column of light—through the center of your body. Shine the light into the walls of the elevator shaft and all the way down into its bottom.

STEP SEVEN:

Look for a part of yourself that has never been allowed to exist and has been rejected by yourself or others. Send the light all the way into the bottom of the elevator shaft, and look to see where this part of you is sitting or standing. Look for the side of their head; see their ear and hair, as if you were behind a movie camera. Now come around from the side to the front view and look for their eyes.

Inwardly send them a message and ask this part of you if she/he knows who you are. If not, tell her/him that you are the "big" them.

STEP EIGHT:

Ask them what he/she needed his/her parents to know about him/her. Wait for the response. Ask them what he/she needs you to know about him/her. Ask how you can be there for him/her. Receive their response.

STEP NINE:

Ask him/her if he/she trusts you. If not, ask what you can do to help him/her trust you. Be with his/her energies. Feel their response in your heart center. Really listen. Then when complete, ask where in your body would she/he like to live.

STEP TEN:

Ask what color she/he would like you to bring into that part of your body. Fill that location in your body with the color that he/she requests and invite him/her to take up space in that part of your body.

STEP ELEVEN:
Deeply be with the connection and let this aspect of yourself fill you. Receive its energy. Dialogue and write in a journal with this aspect of yourself every day. Get to know him/her. Ask each of the following questions one at a time with your dominant hand, and then put your pen into your non-dominant hand to allow him/her to respond.

- What do you need from me to feel seen, heard, and received?
- How can I be here for you?
- What have you come into this life for?
- What kind of activities would you like for us to do together?

Give your acceptance and full, unconditional love to each aspect of yourself.

Pay close attention to how you feel about a soul aspect of yourself. If you have resistance, find out why. Once again, accept your feeling, but also choose to open beyond how you have shut out parts of yourself.

STEP TWELVE:
At your own pace, over the next several weeks, go back to the 2nd Step and while sitting comfortably, create the beam of light from 10–20 feet above your head and look for other soul aspects of yourself in any order that they show themselves to you or that you may choose. You may ask a friend to do the process with you. Feel free to do one or more soul aspects in a sitting.

Inquire and receive the following:
- An unseen and unheard aspect of yourself
- A resistant aspect of yourself

- An unexpressed and shut down aspect of yourself
- An angry aspect of yourself
- A helpless aspect of yourself
- A determined aspect
- A wounded and hurt aspect
- A sexually controlled, controlling, or fearful aspect
- A sad and lonely aspect
- A creative and powerful aspect
- A spiritually awakened and tuned in aspect
- A kind, gentle, and unconditionally loving aspect

Know that when all of these aspects of you are reintegrated, they ignite the core spiritual flame and consciousness of your True Self. Your soul aspects connect you into your eternal truth and infinite wisdom that transcend any particular age in your life. As you seek out your soul expressions, expect to see yourself at different biological ages. When you see yourself at a particular age, such as a young child or teenager, know that this form of you was the last time that this aspect of you felt received, seen, or heard.

You may find that a sad and lonely aspect may have developed when you rejected yourself as a teenager, or a brilliant but overlooked child may appear to you. When you discover your Inner Self, you will find that the significant spiritual aspects of yourself that became stuck at certain ages will come back to life once they are reintegrated within you. Know that as you reconnect all of yourself, you will feel strong, clear, and in-touch with "why you are here." You will also feel connected to your spiritual current, divine intelligence and soul expression. Know that this connection is a direct bridge into your True Self and has the power to open your heart to your deepest Self.

Suggestions for how to BE with your soul aspects:

Be in conversation with your newly discovered soul aspect.

After you meet one of your soul aspects, send him/her a message that you want to contact him/her and that you are coming back for him/her. Tell him/her that you are really sorry that he/she became wounded, felt hurt, neglected, judged, not seen, etc. Ask him/her what his/her parents needed to know about them. Ask him/her what he/she needs from you to trust you. They may say, "I want an ongoing relationship with you," or, "Please don't leave me again." How does his/her request make you feel?

You may find yourself feeling sad that you have been away for so long. You may express feelings such as, "I have felt irresponsible," "I am sorry that I have rejected and abandoned you," or, "I am the part of you that had to deal with all of the expectations and challenges of life, but I am back now for good." Speak to your newly found soul aspect with humility and humbleness from your heart.

Realize that we often role model our behaviors after our parents out of the need to be unified or aligned with the social or family structures we live within. Often times, we treat the soul aspect that we have abandoned, betrayed, or rejected the same way our parents did with theirs. Humans have a deep need to be accepted, and we will ABR ourselves just to get that acceptance and conditional love from those around us despite what it does to us. In an exasperated tone, your waiting soul aspect may say, *"Finally, I no longer have to be alone. I have been waiting for you."* You might find yourself saying to him/her, *"I am here. I am not leaving you again."* Whatever you say, say it with commitment and clear intention. Tell your newly discovered soul aspect that you love him/her. Then ask, *"What do I need to do for you to trust me?"*

You might receive an answer such as, *"Honor what I say to you." "Let's get our body healthy."* Or, *"Please don't leave me again. Stay connected to me."* You can ask yourself whether you are willing to let go of any negative attitudes or judgments that you have had towards him/her (yourself). These negative thoughts toward your soul selves create pain, sadness, health, weight challenges, money issues, relationship difficulties, self-sabotage, lack of self-esteem, etc. Ask him/her what he/she wants you to do to help you let go of the fear, grief, guilt, or sorrow that you hold. Ask him/her to share with you the original messages you gave him/her that pushed him/her away a long time ago. Take in his/her response and reshift your relationship to their core essence and heart. Ask your newly discovered soul aspect to share with you how it gave away its power to others and how you supported his/her ways of giving away its power.

1. Invite a newly found soul aspect of yourself to consciously join with you and participate with you when you do any number of activities, including when you shop for food, cook, clean the house, fly a kite, work in the garden, go sailing, draw, sing, workout, take a shower, take a walk, swim, run, or bike ride. Your goal is to acknowledge and be aware of their presence and integrate these energies into yourself. Keep a journal and note what kind of emotional, mental, and physical changes you are going through. Notice what changes occur in your health, relationships, work, and life.

2. Invite each aspect of your soul to meet with the other aspects of your soul. See yourself on a beach, in the woods, or in a meadow. Then, build a circle of stones with your first soul aspect sitting with you. The circle of stones will surround a fire that, once ignited, can be a focal point for you and your soul aspect to sit and watch the fire. Slowly begin to invite your other soul aspects to sit with you. Maintain your connection in your heart center as you

become One with the flames of fire warming and illuminating you. Breathe into your body. Continue practicing being One with each soul aspect while you are doing yoga, making love, commuting to work, doing laundry, cooking, etc.

BELIGHT MEDITATION — Chapter 16 — Page 335

The Soul Actions

The soul reintegration process involves Four Key Soul Actions:
- o Action 1: See, Feel, and Hear
- o Action 2: Acknowledge and Honor with Love
- o Action 3: Receive and Accept
- o Action 4: Reconnect and Heal

These actions unite the body, mind, and Spirit through the heart, allowing the soul to be integrated into a new Bodymind consciousness.

- Your essential soul reintegration steps:
  - o Engage in dual-seeing from your heart to see what is "real."
  - o Suspend your need to control, manipulate, or judge situations.
  - o Tune into the invisible energy of given circumstances.
  - o Fully feel every experience by being present in the moment.
  - o Hear through BEing One in your *Soul Power Points*.

- Acknowledge the existence and reality of a moment, feeling, or an experience.
- Love and honor yourself in your everyday life through listening and receiving the messages from your body.
- Receive what is within you without judgment.
- Move through your fear. See the light that is within the parts of your Self that live in fear.
- Open your heart and expand your capacity to accept yourself.
- Be open, kind, loving, gentle, and present with yourself.

- As you are healing your body, heart, and soul connection by listening and being with yourself, you will begin to access your connection to Infinite Source intelligence.
- When you get to the core of who you are, you must be able to be with even the most unlovable parts of yourself.
- When doing your soul integration work, keep in mind that if you really listen and pay attention to what your soul is saying, it may need something different from what you think. Be willing to follow what is says. It won't let you down.
- Only love can heal you and make you whole.
- The bottom line is that, until you know yourself on a soul level, you will always have nagging questions about yourself and your life purpose. You will always be asking the question, "Is this really it?"
- It does not matter what lifestyle, spiritual path, or belief system you adopt. Until you do your real soul work, nothing will be sustainable and you will inevitably be chasing your spiritual tail.

- Begin to see, feel, and know your Self. This takes three things:
  - BE Open
  - BE Receptive
  - Trust what you find

BELIGHT MEDITATION — Chapter 16 — Pages 358-361

BELIGHT MEDITATION PRACTICES:

Ignite Your Diamond of Light

Sit in a comfortable cross-legged position on the floor, on a pillow or mat, in your favorite chair, or on your bed before you go to sleep or first thing upon awakening. Inhale through your nose and fill your lungs with breath. Close your eyes except for a tiny slit of light shining in. Gaze down to the tip of your nose with your eyelids almost completely closed. Inhale to the inner count of 4, hold for the count of 4, exhale to the count of 4, suspend and "do nothing" for the count of 4. Repeat 4 times. Then, inhale to the inner count of 5, hold for the count of 5, exhale for the count of 5, suspend and "do nothing" for the count of 5. Repeat 5 times. Allow your mind to let go into the breath. BE with the breath. Then, inhale to the inner count of 6, hold 6, exhale 6, suspend for the count of 6, 6 times.

Allow your breathing to be slow and deep and fill your body with each inhalation and exhalation. Now, bring your inner focus into your heart and gaze into a large diamond of pure light. Continue to BE present to the light within your heart and expand your focus of awareness into the shimmering light. Drop your awareness into your heart center and merge with the diamond as you enter into its radiance. As you breathe, move your mind into the diamond. Gaze into the light in the diamond within your heart. See through your third eye the brilliance of the light. BE One with the light. Relax into the light. Stay with the practice until you feel immersed in the diamond's light radiance.

Listen, Hear, and Receive Yourself

To bridge your mind into your body and access your "soul hearing," connect into the following *Soul Integration Center*. If you place the middle finger of your right hand on the tip of your rib cage, in the center, all the way at the bottom rim, you will feel a pointy protrusion. Slide your finger up over the "ledge," then slide into a valley, a second valley, and then into a third valley (they are very subtle and close to one another). You will be in the *Sixth Soul Integration Center* to help you "hear" yourself. Be present and breathe into this *Soul Integration Center*. This *Soul Integration Center* helps to open the energetic gateway into your True Self. It helps you to open to the truth within your heart center. It serves as a protector and interpreter of your heart. Continue to expand and BE in your heart center—your *Sixth Power Point Center*. Rest and relax.

Acknowledge Your Anger, Learn from Your Anger

Get out a notebook or journal and, with your dominant writing hand, ask your anger what it has always needed. Ask it to share with you what has not been received, honored, heard, or seen about its existence. Close your eyes for a moment and receive its message with your non-dominant writing hand. Now using your dominant hand, ask your anger how you can be there for the feelings that have lived beneath it. Receive and write the response with your non-dominant hand. Close your eyes and look within the "energy of the anger" and look to see "how old" this expression of your Self is. Be aware of all of the images that come to you. Now, dialogue with each image, taking your time to

BE with each expression of your Self. Know they are all parts of you, ready to be seen, heard, and received into wholeness. Dive into your heart and invite their power, creativity, voice, and life force to merge with the energies of your Whole Self.

Receiving and Accepting What Is
Begin by breathing a long, deep inhalation in through your nose into your lower belly. Draw it up into your solar plexus and then into the back of your skull. Then, exhale your breath slowly out of your mouth as you pucker your lips into an "O" shape. Repeat the breath again while relaxing the back of your skull, as you pull the breath up through the inside of your spine from your lower belly, your *Second Power Point Center*.

Now, inhale through your nostrils once again and breathe into the space inside of your tailbone and pubic bone, your *First Power Point Center*—root center. Inhale and expand the breath into your root center, gently pulling up the muscles around your genitals. Now, with ease and grace, lift the energies up through your navel, solar plexus, and heart center and into the back of your skull. BE with the sensations and see the energies lifting up as pure white light. As the energies connect within you, feel the stability and steady strength this connection gives you. This will help you trust your relationship with your Self and with the universe. As you receive the energies, trust in their innate perfection and capacity to bring you everything that you need to heal, become stronger, and clearer.

Acceptance is a physical experience that comes from being connected into your heart, solar plexus, navel, lower belly, and root center at the same time. BE present in all five centers at the same time and allow your Self to let go, accept what is, and just BE.

Stillness and BEing

Begin to breathe slowly and deeply in through your nose and out through your mouth. With each inhalation, bring the breath into your lower belly, and fill your lower sacrum and tailbone with your breath. With each exhalation, bring the breath up inside your spine, through a channel of light, and then exhale out of your mouth. As you go deeper into your breath, begin to focus into the space between your thoughts. Find the stillness and the emptiness in the space, and allow the space to expand become larger with each breath. Just BE in this vast and infinite space as you find greater relaxation and presence with "all there is."

BELIGHT MEDITATION — Chapter 17 — Page 379

Healing Your Core Soul Wound Meditation

Sit on a cushion on the floor or in your favorite comfortable chair. Begin to breathe blue and gold light into your body. Taking your time, gaze into your heart center from a place of love. As you gaze into your heart center, look for radiant light. As you find it, continue to move your awareness deeper into the light within your heart. Maintain your focus with your breath. Allow the light to grow bigger as you enter into it with your full focus and attention.

When you are ready, ask your Higher Self or a spiritual inner master to come to assist the process. Ask for an image to be given to you of a situation in this lifetime or from a previous lifetime that you experienced a reaction to with intense emotion. Look to see whether you expressed that emotion outwardly or not. Ask your Higher Self to show you the situation and what belief you concluded to, took on, and projected onto the situation, others and on to yourself. Feel in your heart where and how you split off from the light within yourself. Gaze with love through your negative reactions and look for the radiant and light-filled you inside or beneath the emotionally charged you.

With love, bring your focus deeper into the light within your heart. Release everything that is not "of love," and give yourself time to embrace any wounding within you. Stay in the frequency and dimension of this radiant love as you continue to open to any pain, anger, sadness, grief, etc. Continue to look through these emotions directly into the light within them. Give yourself the message to stay in your light. Practice being aware of not splitting off into the reactions but staying centered in the radiant light within you.

Your focus helps you to connect to the light within your heart. Your desire to see, receive, and BE with the light in your heart opens up the portal within you to experience the grace and presence of your True Self.

Remember, the light within your heart is the radiant healer that has the power to release your past hurts, see who you really are, and trust the space of love that dwells as God within you.

Reconnect with the soul aspect that has been halted on its tracks within you. At first, you may not see him or her. It may feel stuck in time, glued to loss or sorrow, and possibly completely shut down from BEing in its conscious connection to Infinite Source. Hang in there until you make a connection with this soul aspect. Let this part of yourself know that you are there and gently, with patience, reach out through your love to its love. Know that the heart of your soul aspect is whole, and even though it has been buried in your subconscious, once liberated it has the ability to end the emotional, spiritual, and mental pain you have endured. It has hidden its light and power in the dark within itself until the moment you reached the point of understanding that in order to move forward, IT'S LIGHT and TRUTH HAD TO BE FOUND. Take your time in reconnecting with him or her. Know that he or she needs time and love to trust your connection. Keep returning to your aspect with an open heart and make it your first priority in your life. BE the flower and blossom. Attach yourself to the love within you. Trust it. Each day make a commitment to following the love.

When you feel complete with this exercise, bring your full attention into the *Sixth Soul Integration Center*, your heart center, in the center of your chest. To find it, press your fingertip on the tip of your rib cage protrusion. Then slide your finger over the ridge and, as you ascend upwards towards your heart center, press into the four vertical hollows in between your ribs as you climb upwards to land in the hollow space in between the nipples in the center of your chest. Breathe and place your focus into this *Soul Integration Center*. Surrender your fear and resistance into the love within you and BE.

BELIGHT MEDITATION — Chapter 17 — Page 381

Practical Soul Challenges & Solutions

Every thought and every perception is intimately tied to the universal laws of creation. By trusting and letting go into the universal alignment of love and surrender within you, you can experience a direct connection and relationship with the eternal intelligence of the "everything and the nothing." When you slow everything down and invite your body and mind to let go and BE, you are able to sense, feel, and experience the stream of abundance that lives within you. Every path, every religion, has a different name for it. BEing in selfless service to the stream of Infinite Source light, power, and expression within you is all that is necessary. When your self-doubts, insecurities, and inner stories pull you away from the stream of awareness that flows through you, bring your focus back into the essence of your Self. Feel the peace, the prosperity of your soul, the love, passion, focus, determination, and promise to your Self to BE present to the whisperings of your heart.

As you expand into the ocean of Infinite Source within you and around you, create moments through your day to do nothing. Sit, close your eyes, focus into your heart, feel, and listen to your heartbeat. Feel the light within the earth move up through your feet into your lower belly. BE present to your breath. BE present to what you feel and just allow it all to BE. Then, ask your Self how you would like to show up in the moment. BE kind to your Self. BE gentle and listen. BE willing to make a new decision to support your Self to BE YOU.

Along the way, there are challenges that will emerge. Here are some helpful tips.

Challenges you may face along the way:
- **Challenge:** You may feel a bit disorientated at first while connecting to Spirit in your body. You may revert to being in your head and wonder if what you are attempting to do is "right."
  Solution: BE for a moment and open your heart. Move light up from the center of the earth, through your feet, up your legs, and into your lower belly and solar plexus. Connect your focus into your solar plexus and then down into the space between your pubic bone and tailbone. Ground into your body, then trust the light flowing through you.

- **Challenge:** You may doubt that you have the courage, the tools, the patience, and the commitment to come back to your Self after leaving your Self.

THE ONE IN SOUL PRACTICE ROADMAP

  Solution: Ask from your heart for Infinite Source to bring you the courage, faith, and commitment needed to open when you may want to split off or close down. You can also access the strength, wisdom, and spiritual integrity of one of your newly discovered divine soul aspects and trust in its ability to guide you forward in your life.

- **Challenge:** You may come up against your patterns of how you accept or reject yourself.
  Solution: Choose to love yourself no matter what.

- **Challenge:** You may fight coming down into your body and want to stay in your head.
  Solution: Bring pure white light from above your head down into your heart center and breathe into your heart. Give a loving, brilliant, forgotten part of your soul a voice in the moment. Accept and honor its needs from your heart.

- **Challenge:** Your ego—the false protector within you, the one who keeps out all possibilities of having to give up its authority and position, may fight to stay in control.
  Solution: Thank it for its years of service to your life and give it a new job to do. Your protector may have placed itself in the position of being the relentless authority of control in your life. It may put you down and keep you feeling insecure about your capabilities to earn money, make your partner happy, and how you look. Perhaps it has protected you by keeping people at a distance to shield you from becoming hurt by others' insensitivities to who you are. Now you can tell your protector that you no longer empower it to block out life or keep you shut down and living in shame as a means to protect you.

Instead, give it the new position of helping you to complete tasks or follow through in meeting deadlines in all aspects of your life. For example, it can ensure you get your oil changed in your car on time, go for your teeth cleaning, pay your car registration on time, remember your sister's birthday, or remind you to renew your passport. Create the intention for your protector to protect you in practical and caring ways rather than blocking your evolutionary drive to be more self-expressed and joyful. It is up to you to end how you empower your ego Self to keep you disempowered and in self-doubt, or however you have created it to take the reins of your life. You can end how you keep it alive by no longer empowering its presence and existence in the same way.

- **Challenge:** You may have to face that at some level you treat yourself and others the same way that your parents and other authority figures in your early life treated you, whether positively or negatively.
  Solution: Take responsibility for showing up for yourself with respect, honor, and loving kindness.

- **Challenge:** You may have to choose what aspect of yourself you want to identify with: the controller, the victim, the lover, the creator, the one in pain, the one who surrenders each thought and moment to Infinite Source, the one who wants to go beyond all fear, and heals and embraces their Whole Self.
  Solution: Identify only with what makes your heart open and gives you confidence, strength, and trust.

- **Challenge:** There may be times when you will feel that you cannot connect to yourself with love. There will be moments when you will wonder how to even find the love inside of you.

Solution: Connect to the light flowing in from above your head into your body and allow it to flow into your *Solar Plexus—Fifth Power Point Center*. Then, reconnect into your *Lower Belly—Second Power Point Center* and *Solar Plexus—Fifth Power Point Centers* at the same time. This connection will always create a positive shift.

- **Challenge:** There may be times when you will feel emotional pain and not know what to do.

  Solution: If you accept and honor the most rejected part of yourself that is deep in your lower belly and in your heart center, you will come through the pain and into the light of your Self. Feel, express, and release the emotion.

- **Challenge:** There may be times when you will want to avoid your anger and deny its existence. Perhaps your anger was originally created because you separated from your core spiritual power, took on a false persona to please others, or experienced being rejected or betrayed for just being you. Beneath your anger lives a powerful life force energy that is directly connected to the Infinite Source of who you are.

  Solution: Feel the truth beneath your anger and accept and acknowledge it as a wayshower and teacher to the light within you. Acknowledge the anger and release it to find your heart. Open to a new level of your soul's power.

- **Challenge:** You may find the thought of surrendering to a part of yourself that has appeared needy, weak, sad, angry, or resigned, almost unbearable. In truth, to surrender means that you are opening to allow this soul

part to reconnect with your Whole Self and enter into a sacred relationship with you. When you truly surrender, you are receiving and empowering the part of your God Self that yearns to be seen, heard, received, and reconnected to.
Solution: Accept yourself with zero judgment.

- **Challenge:** You will come to realize that you have not been living in your True Self, and you might feel sad.
  Solution: Shift into receiving and empowering the parts of your soul that yearn to be in your life, for they will give you back the joy you seek.

More Solutions:

While it is easy to get caught up in daily living and BEing, find yourself focused on perfecting a certain soul practice or meditation until you feel like you've "gotten it." Remember these helpful enlightening actions to support your swift progression along your road:

- The personality Self cannot be perfect. Our alignment with Infinite Source is the only perfection. Just BE.
- If you find yourself comparing your Self to others, stop. Breathe. BE.
- Stay with the aspect of your soul that has not been paid attention to or was not allowed energetically to exist in your family or early life. Acknowledge it and then allow it to exist.
- Choose to find the love in everything around and in you.
- BE willing to feel the energies in your *First and Second Power Point Centers*. Receive light from the center of the earth and draw it up into the space between your pubic bone and tailbone. Allow the light to build into a spiral.

THE ONE IN SOUL PRACTICE ROADMAP

- BE willing to release and let go of how you have held on to control as the way you have managed your life.
- BE willing to be real with yourself. Say what you feel to yourself. Then, find the "truth voice" underneath the feeling. Empower this voice.
- Stop abandoning yourself.
- Stay in yourself with whatever age your soul part reveals itself to you to be and check in with it many times a day until the two of you remain reconnected.
- Introduce the parts of your Soul Self to one another during a meditation.
- Practice staying energetically connected to your solar plexus, inside your navel, your lower belly, and the space between your tailbone and pubic bone.
- Remain accepting and non-judgmental of yourself and others.
- As you open your heart and come into your heart, you will have greater access to all of you.
- Practice thinking from the union of two *Power Point Centers* at the same time: Third eye and lower belly; heart center and pubic bone/tailbone; back of the skull and pubic bone; and the navel and soles of your feet. When you bring together two *Power Point Centers,* "BE" with both points at the same time. They will integrate your body and soul.
- Practice being with yourself and be aware when you leave the connections in your body. Just decide to come back in when you leave.
- BE aware of how you control the environment around you to feel in control. Make a new choice to let go into yourself. BE with yourself.
- Allow yourself to "not know" and to be willing to become friends with the unknown.

- Practice bringing light into your body and identify with the light and how it makes you feel. Send light into the places that feel stuck, frozen, and disconnected within your body. Allow the light to flow through you in streams of energetic aliveness.
- Keep your heart open to yourself and practice discernment when you are in group situations. Practice being aware of losing yourself in other people's energies and situations. When you stay in your solar plexus, you will be less likely to take on or move into another person's energies.
- Spend quiet and alone time a few times a week. Begin to speak to the universe as a co-creator, someone who is here to serve and work in the highest good for everyone concerned.
- Bring in gold and white light into the center of your head and then pour it into your third eye. Think of your third eye as a portal of light. Invite the aspect of your soul that could not come into your body at birth to come in now. Feel its presence and invite it into your heart.
- Get creative. Write; create music, clothes, paintings, drawings, pies, cakes, raw food, a new soup, or take on a new community project. Volunteer to help others. Teach a teenager a new trade. Plant a tree. Collect seeds to start a garden. Learn about something new each week. Refuse to become bored. Find the beauty in life and embrace the small gifts and wonders that the universe presents every moment.
- Invite in all parts of your soul from past lives that have not yet been ready to come forth into the present moment. Fill yourself with the blue light of Infinite Source to assist these powerful and loving aspects of yourself to reconnect with your heart.

THE ONE IN SOUL PRACTICE ROADMAP

BELIGHT MEDITATION — Chapter 17 — Page 392

Transforming Fear

STEP 1

Begin by sitting in a comfortable position, either in a chair or sitting in a cross-legged lotus position on a mat on the floor. Place your hands on your knees, palms facing up and lightly touch the pads of your second finger and thumb together. Inhale and exhale out through your nose slowly and steadily. Inhale for 8 counts, hold for 8 counts, exhale for 8 counts. Do this 8 times.

Now, inhale quickly, pulling the air into your nostrils and exhale quickly, pushing the air out of your nostrils. "Pant" in and out of your nostrils, lips slightly touching, increasing the rhythm. Do this 8 times. Repeat the whole sequence 4 times.

STEP 2

Call in the aspect of your soul that sees what others may not, that finds freedom through connecting to music, nature, yoga, sports, family, etc., and yearns for full expression. Allow this aspect of your Self to come up and be felt, acknowledged, and received. Give the reins of your life to this aspect of yourself and follow its lead. Put your faith and trust in its desire to break through the confines and limitations of your life. Feel its desire to love and open to becoming One with its love, life force energies, and passion. Open to the waves of love in your heart. Surrender into your breath. Practice each day until your connection happens spontaneously and naturally. Return to Step 1, and complete with a few rounds of the breathing sequence.

BELIGHT MEDITATION — Chapter 18 — Page 416

Building an Inner Container of Light

As your soul aspects reunite within the mind-heart of your body, you will need to create a container of light. When the life force energies of your soul aspects are released in your body, you need a way to hold their frequencies.

An inner container is an expanded space within your body that stabilizes the frequency of your light. It resonates in your body as a vibration of life force energy. You will see it as a translucent vessel, oval, goblet, sphere, cave, well, or bowl. The *One in Soul* experience naturally creates your heart center to become a container. Your heart center opens to receive the aspects of your soul that have awakened to love through the BE practices and meditations. By expanding your container into your solar plexus, navel, lower belly, and into the pubic bone-tailbone space, you will feel grounded, more creative, in tune, and clear. Past attachments to others, and from them to you, can be cleared.

Within your energetic body is an oval of light. It extends from the space in between your pubic bone and tailbone, moves up through your lower belly, your creation point, navel, solar plexus, heart center, throat center, and third eye and fills the space around and through the length of your spine. By creating a container, you are allowing your spiritual energies to become One with the light energies in your body. The energies of your *Power Point Centers* are safely protected in this cocoon. Creating a container serves the very important function of rooting the power and light of higher frequencies and your Higher Self in your body. It provides the space for you to be integrated and balanced.

Oval of Love

Close your eyes and visualize a translucent oval that fills the space between your third eye, throat center, heart center, solar plexus, navel, creation point, lower belly, and the space between your pubic bone and tailbone. Invite in a color to fill it, and bring your focus inside the oval. Fill the oval with your love.

Invite a soul aspect of your Self to step into the oval. Some examples could include an angelic soul aspect, an infant aspect who felt abandoned and alone, an awakened, angry, confused or happy pre-teen or teen soul aspect, an ignored or unseen five-year-old, a seven-year-old puppet or "doll" for needy relatives, a determined to succeed nine-year-old aspect, a ten-year-old aspect shut down by parents who violated and ignored personal space and needs (a home life without stable boundaries), a twelve-year old soul aspect who was inappropriately touched by an alcoholic relative, or a vivacious and expressive fourteen-year-old, who doubts herself. Allow the essence of one of your soul aspects to come into the oval. Breathe and BE with this part of your Self. Permit the oval to energetically hold its essence and energies.

In your heart, be present with the essence of a soul aspect who has been waiting for you to return. Feel, hear, or see who he or she really is beneath the emotion. Do not abandon him or her. Stay truly present. You will experience living in your solar plexus, lower belly, navel, or inner space between the pubic bone and tailbone in a whole new way. Allow your heart center to expand by taking in the true presence, power, and light of your soul aspect. The container bridges your spiritual and soul nature with your body.

Focus into the colors of your inner oval. As you fill the oval with love, be aware of the colors that come into view. Now, expand the colors of your inner oval into an oval surrounding your entire body. Increase your outer oval until you can breathe fully into its width and depth. Breathe into both ovals at the same time until they become one circle of light and color.

We need an inner container to expansively hold our feelings, soul energies, and our light. Without an energetic container, we are unable to support the feelings that arise from our childhood, teen years, and adult experiences and transform them into love. We are unable to build the light frequencies within our body and create a new matrix of higher consciousness to reside in. We need a container to integrate our soul aspects with our Higher Self in our heart center.

As you reconnect and reunite the feelings of your abandoned, betrayed, and rejected soul aspects, you are freeing old energies by letting go of old belief structures. You are recreating your relationship with your essence—the You that has the power and potential to live in Oneness with all of life. For instance, you may have soul aspects that bonded in a negative way to a parental figure. As human beings, we carry on the energetic grid of our family of ancestry to the point of having our energetic constructs within our consciousness patterned exactly like our ancestry. We often hold family energies in our root center or navel center, fueling our separation with Infinite Source. Your root center holds the traumas and fears that go back in your body seven generations. When cleared and connected to Infinite Source in your body, you are able to hold your energetic frequency and fulfill your soul purpose.

Your navel center determines your ability to survive on your own, BE self-actualizing, source life force energies directly, know truth, and navigate through the void of spiritual emptiness into enlightened states of being. Until we release and clear the shadows of our family ancestry, we end up carrying on the same psychological attitudes and judgments as our family of origin, even if we "do not want to." Through clearing your navel energies, the power of your newly found soul aspects can manifest into your life and into the world the presence and power of your Original Self.

If you anger easily, talk too much, don't know how to deal with intense feelings, avoid communication in relationships, need outside distractions to function, stay in your head and close your heart, shift your personality to fit in with others, or hold secrets or lies and cannot handle the unknown, you lack a container in your energetic and emotional body. If you were bombarded by family dysfunctions such as non-communication, alcoholism or drug problems, control issues, rigidity, unrealistic expectations, obsessive-compulsive behaviors, sexual abuse, religious dogmatism, mental illness, poverty, or conditional love, then chances are you were never allowed to truly be your own person. The art of creating a container in the emotional body in childhood happens if you are fortunate enough to have a parent or teacher who encourages you to be with your feelings and not abandon your Self, and are given the opportunity to be creative without judgment.

Until your divine and human selves are reconnected and merged within your body, you may feel ungrounded and unsure of yourself. To unite the divine and human selves, you need to create a sanctuary—a chalice large enough to contain the universe within you. By diving deep into the space within your solar plexus and descending downward, you will find a portal directly above your navel area and deep within your lower belly that opens into a safe sanctuary. A universe of softness, strength, security, and earthy depth, your chalice is a sacred and mystical chamber of regeneration and self-sustaining peace. After you create your chalice, reach into the universe within your heart, plant a seed, and watch a tree grow with deep roots. Your roots nurture and grow YOU into wholeness.

By having a container, you can deepen your spiritual practices of opening your higher centers. Your container stabilizes the energies and power within your etheric, energetic, emotional, and physical bodies, supporting you to BE interconnected with all of the dimensions of your awakening Self.

Each day, give yourself a few moments to awaken your third eye. To develop your third eye, sit quietly and gently gaze into blue light or a blue star in the space in between your eyebrows and then raise your inner gaze just slightly higher in your forehead. Allow your eyelids to be almost closed, but keep a slight space open so you see just a small amount of light filtering through. Follow your breath and let go into an open inner space of peace.

Connect your third eye into the gateway of your chalice sanctuary in your navel center and enter into its portal into the infinite. Feel, see, and hear the inner currents, rhythms, and voices of this planet, other dimensions, your heart, and the hearts of others. Bring this gift into your life and apply it to your relationships with everyone. Utilize as much space as you can within your inner sanctuary to support your Whole Self and then show up with others from this divine presence and BEingness in your work and everyday life.

Bring the peace of your sanctuary—the clarity and presence of BEing in your chalice—to others, especially to the children in your life. When you teach and help children to hold open this space within themselves, they feel valued, honored, and creatively limitless. Help them remain open to their power; guide them to self-nourish. Teach them to water their inner gardens and forests. Help them keep the light radiating in their sanctuary.

BE in your chalice and hold space for your co-workers, clients, students, family, and friends. BE in the expansion that your chalice creates for yourself and allow others to expand in your presence.

The clearer and stronger you become inside the inner core column in your body—your sushumna—the more your container, your chalice —can be filled. When building your inner chalice, trust that it will be a container for your life force. The more light you can contain, the greater your physical, spiritual, creative, and soul energies will become. True abundance is born by receiving and giving the reservoir of wealth created by an overflowing chalice.

BELIGHT MEDITATION — Chapter 18 — Page 425

Opening Your Inner Container

Connect With the Earth

Your container is created by first connecting to the light within the center of the earth. As you pull the light up from the earth's core, you will be activating the magnetic core of your body that serves as a container for life force energies.

1. Receive the light of the deep earth through your feet.
2. Pull up flames of pure white fire up from the earth through your feet.
3. Bring the light up into your body, raising it through your legs, the space between your pubic bone and tailbone (your root center), your creation point, navel, solar plexus, and heart center. Breathe and BE in the light.

Connect Your Solar Plexus

Your solar plexus stabilizes the divine and earth energies in your body. Your awareness, when connected inside of your solar plexus, allows your Whole Self to become a container for Spirit—the essence of life. Connection with your solar plexus anchors your energy and mind in your body and builds a container for your life force, love, and light to exist within.

1. Breathe into your solar plexus and fill it with pure gold light—sunshine.
2. Lift the gold light into your heart.
3. Send this gold light to every part of your body, down to your feet, and into your palms. Allow your entire body to be filled with gold light. Sit and radiate from within for the amount of time needed to feel full.

Connect Your Bones

Your bones are conduits for light energies to move into the structure of your Bodymind and soul matrix. They hold the best of your soul ancestry and spiritual power, and when "fed" with light and good nutrition, you can succeed with your divine and human aspirations.

1. Inhale light into your bones as you breathe in through your mouth and exhale through your mouth, expelling any stale energy inside of your bones.
2. Inhale energy and light through your skin, then into your bones and exhale.
3. Inhale and exhale again, and as you exhale, allow the energy to fill up the space inside of your bones. Breathe deep into your bones until you feel open and expansive.
4. Direct this energy deeper and deeper into your bones as you inhale through your nose for 10 counts. Hold the breath for 10 counts. Exhale out 10 counts through your mouth keeping the energy in the bones.
5. Repeat ten times.

BELIGHT MEDITATION — Chapter 18 — Page 428

Deepening Your Inner Container Connection

Your *First Power Point Center*—your root center—plays the important role of stabilizing and building your inner container. It does this by supporting two functions. First, your root center receives and stabilizes the divine feminine currents of your soul. Your root center does this by channeling the earth and universal energies to flow up from the center of the earth into your body. Secondly, your root center is a magnet of energy that draws the universal divine masculine energies to flow down from above your head and awaken the spiritual pathways in your body.

Your container helps you to feel your energies and holds the space for your sacred and divine masculine and feminine energies to meet. Your body and mind are supported to merge in your container, creating a neutral zone within you that is naturally non-reactive. Here, you can BE and feel connected into Infinite Source. It is a zone where there are no thoughts, and the spaciousness of the universe can be accessed.

As you bring flames of pure white fire up from the center of the earth, drop your mind to meet the flames in your root center. Your divine feminine flames of fire are the transformational powers of divine consciousness. They have the ability to dissolve the cords of attachment between your thoughts, beliefs, and heart. When thoughts come up that you know you want to let go of, send them into flames of pure white, or violet flames of fire in your *First and Second Power Point Centers*, the root center and lower belly, and then through your intention release the energies into Infinite Source.

Now, from above your head, send the white or blue light of your divine masculine energy through the core shaft of light in your body and guide the light down to meet your divine feminine in your root center. As they unite in your root center, allow the light to move up and ignite the inside of your spine and the space surrounding your spine, touching into and through each *Power Point Center* connection. As the light ignites your root center, you will feel your container grow stronger and make it easier to ascend upwards through the center of your core shaft of light with love.

As you feel lighter and freer inside, practice staying connected into your container. Feel the new spaces of freedom that you are creating within yourself. They will make possible new ways of being in your life with authenticity and greater strength to release how you hold on to your ego and fears.

The activation of your divine feminine and masculine energies heal and revitalize your Whole Self. Their union creates the spiritual space of love in your body and mind that will transform you. The union and integration of your divine feminine and masculine energies will balance your brain functions and all of the systems in your body—including your circulatory, nervous, endocrine and respiratory systems—by reconnecting the cellular DNA information within your cells. This is possible because they ignite and strengthen the connection between your physical and spiritual bodies.

As you focus the divine light of the flames of pure white fire into your root center, simultaneously bring light into your solar plexus and heart center. Practice holding the consciousness of a rediscovered soul aspect with the light of love into these three centers at once and you will experience profound shifts in every area of your life from the inside out.

You will begin to notice how your mind may habitually jump in and take over, or block the authentic voice of your soul. By remaining grounded in the light within your root center, solar plexus, and heart center, you will be able to let go and release the pain that in the past would steer your mind to be in control.

THE ONE IN SOUL PRACTICE ROADMAP

As an expanded step, simultaneously ground into the divine feminine of your root center and heart center with the focus of your mind. You will continue to feel inwardly supported in new ways. You will feel more confident, experience a new level of courage and strength, find clear determination and willingness to hold your own, and be supported to BE YOU now instead of who you were yesterday, last week, or two decades ago. You will feel and see the universe support your core truth, light, and love.

> *Uncovering the layers surrounding your True Self will set you free into the illuminating gold light of liberation—pure and infinite love.*

As you focus into the Oneness of your heart and soul, you will feel the limitless possibilities of living in Infinite Source. Remember to fill yourself with the light of love and allow it to take up full space in your energy and physical bodies. Remember to acknowledge that your body is a temple for the light of the divine to shine through.

Don't be surprised if people start responding to you in new ways. As you embody more and more light, your presence will create shifts around you whether you can see them or not. As light becomes your teacher, you will have to surrender your own stuff and your own will. In their place, the light will connect you into divine will. As divine will merges with your heart and soul, your attachments to your identity and what you think is important in your life will begin to melt down and shift. The raw and core truth of who you are and what you are supposed to be doing will reveal itself. As you become present in your body to who you are, you will discover that the essence of who you are is and always has been love.

BELIGHT MEDITATION — Chapter 19 — Page 451

Ten Soul Sourcing Tools to Build and Purify Divine Power

The following are Ten Soul Sourcing Tools to help you clear the way to build and purify yourself as a temple for divine power.

1. BE conscious to not live through another.
2. Do not allow another to live through you.
3. Pay attention to external forces working to control and distract you from being self-sourcing.
4. The more your attention is brought outside of you and the less that is focused within you, the greater the chance for political, social, and moral corruption. The power is meant to BE within you.
5. Learn to open and connect your *Power Point Centers* which source your physical and spiritual energies: crown, third eye, back of the skull, behind the eyes, throat, heart, solar plexus, navel, creation point, lower belly, sacrum, sexual organs, pubic bone-tailbone, hands, and soles of the feet.
6. Bring light to the dark places of your psyche in your body to awaken your true power.
7. Dissolve fear by reconnecting to your spiritual power.
8. Choose connection to your heart, love, and the expression of your power to experience the freedom of liberation in the mind and body.
9. Align your *Power Point Centers* in your sushumna, the core shaft of light that connects Spirit into your body.
10. Reconnect the parts of your soul that have been abandoned, betrayed, rejected, and left behind by you into the light of your love.

THE ONE IN SOUL PRACTICE ROADMAP

BELIGHT MEDITATION — *Chapter 19 — Page 455*

Connecting with Your Wounded Ego

Your Wounded Self will always hold you back from living life with full joy. Take a moment to remember a time when you felt total joy, and allow this memory to fill your Whole Self. As you become One, you are able to hold your joy. The moment that you leave BEing One in God—Infinite Source, the light that you are, is the moment that you create your ego. It only takes a moment to decide to create a full time ego to take charge of your life.

Take the time to identify the emotions of your negative wounded ego when it shuts down your heart, and place it on a cushion to your side. Then, identify the voice of your positive wounded ego, who needs to have everything together, and place it on a cushion on your other side. Your negative wounded ego is the part of you in reaction. Your negative wounded ego feels like it is not enough —"Do I even matter?"— and lives in doubt and self-rejection. Your positive wounded ego controls and manipulates to maintain its position. Your positive ego thinks it knows what to do and how to do it, and re-enforces your negative wounded ego to stay small, helpless, and insecure.

You want to ask them what they were trying to accomplish by blocking out the light of your Original Self—your God Self. Ask them if they are ready to let go and allow you, your True Self, to take the reigns of your life and be in charge of your destiny.

Feel the energetic cords that attach you and your positive and negative ego personalities. Take out the cords that you have had into them, and take out the cords "they" have had into you. Your cords into them have been a hopeful attempt at trying to control their impact on you. Their cords into you have been to keep you feeling small and insignificant. Focus into the light within your heart center and BE One with the light of your

Original Self. Take your power back from the wounded ego and come back into the light of your soul. By choosing to stop abandoning, betraying, and rejecting the light that you are, you can begin to live as the *Whole You*.

BELIGHT MEDITATION — Chapter 19 — Pages 471-473

Integrating Your Power #1

The power of your soul is either supported to expand and evolve to exist at an early age or discouraged to BE who it is. The messages that you were given as a young child from your parents, elders, religious leaders, and schoolteachers have the ability to build your soul essence into full expression or to diminish its light. Nothing can destroy your spiritual essence and light. It is always within you, waiting to be ignited, grown, expanded, and implemented into your life.

Call to mind an individual from your life who you gave your power away to get something: love, attention, acknowledgement, care, recognition or support. See him or her standing in front of you. Tell them that you are now going to take back the power that you gave to them out of the fear of BEing You. Thank them for playing the role of making you doubt that who you are is worthy of love, you who are matters, and that who you are is enough to be abundantly supported and loved by the universe.

Close your eyes and look to see where in their body they are holding your energies. Tell them inwardly that you are taking back your power now. Unhook the energies of your power out of their body by using blue light. As you gently unhook your energies, bring them back into your body *(into your solar plexus—your Fifth Power Point Center)* as you move them through a field of white light to clear the energies before they come back into you. Send blue, white and gold light into the area's of their body where your energies were being held. This will uplift and heal them.

Now, feel where in your body you are holding their energies. You can do this by shifting your focus 10–20 feet above your head into pure white light and looking down into your body. Notice all of the spots where you can see their energies lodged. Making use of blue light, unhook their energies and send them back into their body, down through their legs, feet, and into the earth. Then, connect them into pure white light above their head. Release them with love. Send blue light into the areas of your body that were holding their energies.

Thank them for the lessons that they were instrumental in providing you.

Feel the new space in your body. Fill the space up with blue light, and the power of your light, love, compassion, insight, wisdom, and clarity. Practice this as many times as you feel called to with the people in your life with whom you feel inclined to do this exercise with. Take the time to observe the differences in your energies and perceptions.

Integrating Your Power #2

Create the time to sit and BE. Begin to breath in through your nose and fill your lower belly and lower back simultaneously with light. Repeat for at least 2 minutes. Now, begin to breathe into your heart center and move your focus into a spark of light within your heart. Connect your heart center, your lower belly and lower back through one deep inhalation in through your nose, hold and suspend the breath, while you place your focus in between your eyebrows—in your third eye. Exhale out your nose.

Now, travel in your consciousness into a point of awareness before you closed the door to the light that you are. As you focus into your third eye, call in the pure light of your inner child under the age of 5, infant, or pre-birth self. Ask her/him to just

BE with you, as you open through your heart to see the light that they "are." Hold your inner focus with their light through feeling and BEing in your core column of light in the center of your body. Receive their light as a frequency, as a radiance, vibration and consciousness into your heart. Repeat this practice daily for as long as you receive benefits from it.

Enjoy your ENLIGHTENING.

For more information about

Our signature training

The Spirit Gateways® BE System Experience

plus

Intensives, Retreats, Courses, and Facilitator trainings

and

Spirit Gateways® Foundation

visit:

www.ianalahi.com

CHAPTER TWENTY-THREE

Expanded BELIGHT Practices

For those adventurers and intrepid spiritual seekers who are moved to soul reconnection and expansion in deeper ways, you are invited to explore the following additional soul exercises in this chapter. Choose the ones that move you or that you naturally gravitate towards. Your soul knows what it needs. Pay attention and then practice.

Living a Reconnected Life Practice

Each morning, begin your day by focusing on a stream of white light, which you can bring down from above your head and pour into your throat center, heart center, your pelvis, tailbone, thighs, knees, and feet, and allow it to move into the center of the earth. Then, pull light up from the center of the earth, up through your feet, legs, *First, Second, Third, Fourth, and Fifth Power Point Centers,* and then up into your heart center. Begin your day with a declaration of intention statement, such as the following:

- I receive loving kindness from the universe today.

- I open to giving and receiving the light of Source.

- I create a day that is life giving and empowering.

- I enjoy good health, long life, prosperity, happiness, wisdom, and peace.

- I open to the highest light in the universe to work through me today. I am here to serve the light.

- I choose to stay with myself and to BE One with myself.

- I call in God—Infinite Source to BE with me today and to guide my actions.

- Connect to your body in one of these ways:

- First thing in the morning jump on a trampoline to open up your circulation and come into the present moment.

- Greet the sun, the rain, the birds, the sky, and your heart.

- Rub warm sesame oil over your body and let it sit for at least 10 minutes. Then wash it off in a hot shower. At the end of the hot shower, turn cold water on at the base of your spine. Then allow it to hit your whole spine. (This strengthens your immune system.)

- Sit in prayer for 10 minutes and give thanks for your life and everything that you have, all the people in your

EXPANDED BELIGHT PRACTICES

life, and the guidance you receive directly from Infinite Source. BE in complete gratitude.

- Send a silent or written message to at least 5 people each day thanking them for how they show up for you in your life. Appreciate them, send them love, and BE in gratitude.

- Ask Infinite Source to help you to love more and more, and take a moment to offer your words, thoughts, and actions for the highest benefit of all BEings.

- Practice compassion and loving kindness towards yourself and others.

- Connect to the earth and feel her love, and walk into your day with acceptance for your short comings, successes, and yearnings with connection to the light within you.

After your morning self-care, BE with a quality of your True Self such as absolute love, infinite wisdom, expansion, humility, power, clarity, or receptivity. From a place of unconditional love, BE with these energies in your heart and take them along into your day. Continue to feel your connection with your essence throughout the day. Meet yourself exactly where you are. Remain connected to the light as you stay connected to your heart.

Before you go to sleep at night, focus in to your heart center. Shift from being in your head into your heart, and BE ONE with your Self.

Try to check in with your soul aspect a few times a day. You want to emotionally show up and give voice to the soul part of you that has been abandoned, betrayed, or rejected through being unreceived, unseen, or unheard for too long. Allow her/him to exist, to just BE.

Before you go to sleep at night, focus in to your heart center. See and feel the light of your divine Self. Look for its spark, the diamond of its light. Shift from being in your head into your heart, and BE ONE with the soul aspect of yourself with which you made an agreement to connect with. Receive the essence of your awaiting Self. As you gaze into the diamond of light in your heart, lose your self, let go of your mind and enter into the full radiance of its light. Expand your energy field as you merge into its vivacity. BE with yourself fully in your heart. Become comfortable being in the known and the unknown.

Activating Your Power Point Centers- A Daily Practice

Spend 5 minutes each day activating your *Power Point Centers* with the following exercise:

Begin by bringing light into your heart center from above your head. Send the light down into your root center, your *First Power Point Center*, and chant the sound AH HUM, either inwardly or outwardly, to begin. Keep your focus in your third eye and heart centers.

Go slowly through the following light circuit for *Power Point Centers one through ten*, from the root center, up through the lower belly, creation point, navel, solar plexus, heart center, throat, back of the skull, third eye, and into the crown center, vibrating the sound AH HUM into each *Power Point Center*.

Focus light into each *Power Point Center* for as long as you can. Keep your focus into each center up against the inside of your spine. There is a doorway there that will open just through a gentle focus. You may begin with just a small amount of connection to the light, but that is fine; it will become stronger. Just stay with the intention and focus to increase being in the light in each *Power Point Center*. The light will open as you let go, relax, and release your worries and fears.

BEing In Your Center—A Daily Practice

Sit quietly and bring your focus into your solar plexus. You will be dropping your mind down into your solar plexus—your *Fifth Power Point Center*. Feel your mind descend and take up all of the space in your solar plexus. Enter into a warm golden pool of water. Breathe. BE. Draw the light energies up from the earth, and down from above your head into your *Fifth Power Point Center* filling a *merkaba*—two overlaying pyramids or triangles in your solar plexus, also known as a Star of David. BE in the center of the merkaba. Sit inside of the merkaba. Receive the light of the merkaba within your solar plexus and breathe your light into the merkaba. Now, begin to expand the merkaba and allow it to grow larger. Mentally align your energy field with its power from the center point of your focus in your heart center. Begin to spin the merkaba around you remaining stationary in the center of its hub as you build the momentum of its orbit. Breathe. BE. Relax.

When you have more time to immerse yourself into the light, enjoy the following BELIGHT MEDITATION™:

Opening into the Light within You

Gently breathe into your whole body. Breathe light into your heart center, then exhale. Stay with your body while you feel the light touching you.

As you feel touched by the light, feel into where there may be a wall or some kind of resistance. BE with it. Do not push anything. Allow yourself to open like a flower to the light of the sun. Tell yourself that it is safe to receive. Relax your body as completely as you can. Receive and embody the light.

Begin to go deeper into your heart until your heart opens and a portal, or open door, makes itself visible to you. Gaze into the opening, enter, and meld into the light. Feel the embracing quality of pink and gold light cocoon you in love. BE in the light. Walk through the open door when you are ready.

Draw light up from the center of the earth, into your base centers, and up into your heart. Breathe into the light, into your heart, and allow it to move up through the inside of your neck, into the back of your skull, and into your *Crown Power Point Center*. Open your focus into a sphere of light 5 feet above your head. Allow the light to expand into the sphere of light above your head. Send the light back down into your heart center, receiving its cleansing and rejuvenating strength. Continue with the circuit, sending the light from your heart to the sphere of light above your head and then back into your heart center. Repeat 12x.

Take some time every day to practice the following at least two times a day. Expand your inner eye to see and open to the light from the cosmos—the planets, stars, and the entire universe by focusing into a blue star of light in your third eye. Draw light down from above your head through your *Crown Power Point Center*, filling your body. Send the light through your body, through the center of the earth, and through the earth, returning into the cosmos. Begin the circuit again, drawing in the cosmic light into your *Crown Power Point Center*, through your body, the center of the earth, and through the earth. Send the light back into the universe. Open your awareness into the void of this open space. Then, allow the light to come into you naturally, without doing anything but BEing open to receive. Sit in conscious receptivity, receiving the light into your whole BEing, into every cell of your body.

Remember to:

- Receive the light through your crown center.

- Receive the light through your heart.

- Receive the light behind the walls you have created.

- Receive the light and feel it as love as the walls dissolve.

- Receive light as pink and gold radiance awakening you into your eternal self.

- BE the love.

A Diamond of Light

Bring in gold light from above your head, down through your crown center, through the core shaft of light in your body. Send the light down through your feet and into a large crystal in the center of the earth. Pull light up from the crystal in the center core of the earth through your feet into your root center, your *First Power Point Center*.

Allow the light in your root center to move up through a wide channel of light—your sushumna—into a large diamond that fills your heart center and solar plexus. Feel yourself expand into the diamond. BE in the diamond.

From 10 feet above your head, bring light down through your *Crown Power Point Center* through the core shaft of your spine into the diamond in your *Heart Center—your Sixth Power Point Center*. Allow yourself, once again, to expand into the light of the diamond.

Relax and gaze into the light of the diamond and receive its magnificence through your heart.

Now, as you inhale, expand and send the light out from the diamond into a sphere of iridescent light that surrounds your entire body. On the exhalation, pull in and receive the light back into the diamond. Allow the light to fill the interior core of your body.

Now, focus into the diamond light in your heart center as you chant Ahhhh-hummmm. With your next breath, see and feel the wings of your heart open as they expand and open from in between your shoulder blades on your back. Feel your heart open. Gaze into a bright ball of sunshine in the center of your heart on your next breath and open to its radiance.

Remember to:

- Feel your root center become activated.

- Take your time to experience the crystal in the center of the earth.

- Feel the width of your core shaft of light.

- See and feel the light twinkle in your diamond.

- Allow your heart to open.

- Feel the cosmic sound vibrate your heart.

The Light Bulb

Bring white light down through your *Crown Power Point Center*, through the core shaft of light in your body—your sushumna. Feel the light come down through all of your *Power Point Centers* and into the core of the earth.

Lift the light up from the center of the earth and up through the core shaft of light into your lower belly, creation point center, navel, solar plexus, and heart. Now, send the light back down into the earth and find your personal energy spot in the center of the earth. Receive the light in the earth's core etheric center and pull it up into your root center, your *First Power Point Center*. Ignite a light bulb in your *First Power Point*. Now, continue to move your awareness into each *Power Point Center*, igniting a light bulb in each center.

Travel up through your core shaft of light from your root center, igniting a light bulb in each center—your lower belly, creation point, navel, solar plexus, heart center, throat, back of the skull, third eye, and crown center. Then, continue to slowly move your awareness up through the crown center into 5 spheres of light above your head. Feel yourself expanding and growing lighter as you travel into a zone of no thought, and only light. Feel all of the light bulbs lit up as you receive greater amounts of light into your body.

Remember to:

- Receive and feel the light in the earth.

- Sense a magnetic force of energy as you move the energies down and pull them back up.

- See and sense the light in each *Power Point Center*.

- Feel the connection of light in your core shaft of light.

- Feel the expansion in your core shaft of light.

- Each time that you do the exercise, feel the light bulb grow stronger and bigger inside your core shaft of light.

Developing your Spiritual Circuitry

The following two exercises work well being practiced separately, at different times, or as one continuous meditation.

Part I: Creating the Container

Begin by deeply breathing, inhaling and exhaling from your lower belly (*Second Power Point Center*). Inhale light and loving kindness. Release any stresses, anxieties, or discomforts through the exhale.

Allow a flowing waterfall of white and gold light from above your head to flow down through your crown chakra, your *Tenth Power Point Center*. Allow the light to fill your whole body.

Next, allow the light to fill a large crystal that fills the interior of the center of your body and runs the length of your *Throat Power Point Center* (*Seventh Power Point*) into your root center (*First Power Point*).

As you inhale on your next breath, fill the crystal with gold or white light. As you exhale, let go of all stress, negative thoughts, and worries.

Open to take in the clarity and love emanating from the crystal core of your Self. Receive and absorb the radiance and light from your crystalline Self.

On your next inhalation, continue to receive the light and focus on filling your heart center and lower belly with light. Then, on your next breath, expand your heart center with greater overflowing light from your crystal. As you continue to breathe, expand and fill your entire body with the light flowing from your crystal.

Once the light fills your body, on your next inhalation expand the light from the center of your body to create a sphere of light encircling you. As you exhale, pull the light back into your body. With each inhalation, enlarge the sphere around you as you expand into greater light. With each exhalation, feel nurtured as you continue to receive the light sourced from your crystal core.

Rest in the light and stay with the fullness until you feel ready to move onto the next practice.

PART II: Light Circuits

Light Circuit 1

From above your head, receive a waterfall of light pouring down into your *Crown Power Point Center*. Bring the light into your solar plexus, creating a warm golden pool of light that reaches from the front of your solar plexus into your spine. Sit in the warm pool and focus your attention into your solar plexus. As you sit in the warm pool of water, look up through the top of your head and watch a waterfall of beautiful, sparkling lights flowing down in to you.

Now create a circuit of light from your solar plexus into your heart center and back down into your solar plexus. Feel the light flowing in the circuit effortlessly. Move the current of light from your solar plexus up through the center of your spine and into your heart center. Then, send the light back into the solar plexus, creating a flowing circuit of continuous light. Repeat the circuit 6 times.

Light Circuit 2

From above your head, pull in and breathe pure white light down through your crown center into your navel, filling the space from the front of your navel to the back of your spine. Bring your attention and focus into your light-filled navel. Then, create a circuit of light that flows from the front of your navel, through your middle back and into your spine, and then up through the center of your spine into your heart center. Once your heart center receives the light, send the light back into your navel, creating a flowing circuit. Repeat the circuit 6 times.

Light Circuit 3

From above your head, pull in and breathe pure white light down through your crown center into your creation point center, filling the space from the front of your creation point to the back of your sacrum. Bring your attention and focus into your light-filled creation point. Then, create a circuit of light that flows from the front of your creation point, through your middle back and into your spine, and then up through the center of your spine into your heart center. Once your heart center receives the light, send the light back into your creation point, creating a flowing circuit. Repeat the circuit 6 times.

Light Circuit 4

From above your head, pull in and breathe pure white light down through your crown center into your *Second Power Point Center*, your lower belly. (To find this point, place your thumb in your navel and your pinky finger on your pubic bone. Let your index finger drop down onto your belly.) Fill your *Second Power Point Center* with white light that reaches all the way back toward your spine. Bring your attention and focus into this *Power Point Center*. Next, create a circuit of light beginning from your *Second Power Point Center* that flows up through the inside of your spine and into your heart center. Once in the heart center, send the light back into your *Second Power Point Center,* creating a continuous flow. Repeat the circuit 6 times.

Light Circuit 5

From above your head, pull in and breathe pure white light down through your crown center into your *First Power Point Center*, the space between your pubic and tailbone. Bring your attention and focus into your root, your *First Power Point Center*. Create a circuit of light from your root center, up through the inside of your spine and into your throat center. Then, send the light back into your *First Power Point Center*. Repeat the circuit 6 times.

Light Circuit 6

Pull in light from above your head, and breathe pure white light down through your crown center into your *First Power Point Center,* the space between your pubic and tailbone. Bring your attention and focus into your root center as you draw up white light from the center of the earth, so that light flows from above and below into your root center. Create a circuit of light that flows from your root center up through the inside of your spine, into your third eye center. Then, let the light seamlessly flow back into your *First Power Point Center*. Repeat the circuit 6 times.

Light Circuit 7

From above your head, receive white light through your crown center, down through your body, and into a sphere of light below your feet. Then breathe up pure white light from the core of the earth into the sphere of light directly beneath your feet. Create a circuit of light from the sphere up through your spine into your crown center, then back through your spine into the sphere of light beneath your feet. Repeat the circuit 6 times.

Light Circuit 8

Bring your attention and focus into the center of the earth into flames of pure white fire. Pull these flames of fire up from the center of the earth and absorb the light from the flames of fire into a beautiful crystal in the interior length of your body. Bring the light all the way up inside your body, completely filling your inner crystal and spine, while simultaneously touching and expanding each *Power Point Center,* reaching up to your crown chakra and into the next 3 *Power Points* above your head. When you reach the *Thirteenth Power Point Center* (the third point beyond your crown), connect your focused attention in the light from your *Thirteenth Power Point Center* into the light in the center of the earth. BE One with both energy centers at the same. Gently feel the circuit of light move. Feel and be with yourself. Rest and relax.

In Conclusion:

May the Light reveal to you the love that you are.
May you embrace the power to BE all
that you came here to BE.
May you discover the truths within your heart and soul.
May the light shine upon you always.
And fill you with love.

For more information about

The Spirit Gateways® BE System Experience

plus

Spirit Gateways® Institute
Intensives, Retreats, Courses, and Facilitator trainings

and

Spirit Gateways® Foundation

visit:

www.ianalahi.com

www.ingramcontent.com/pod-product-compliance
Lightning Source LLC
Chambersburg PA
CBHW060906300426
44112CB00011B/1367